THE GUIDE TO NATIONAL PROFESSIONAL CERTIFICATION PROGRAMS

SECOND EDITION

by Phillip A. Barnhart

HRD Press/CRC Press

Published by:

HRD Press, Inc.
22 Amherst Road
Amherst, MA 01002
800-822-2801 (U.S. and Canada)
413-253-3488
413-253-3490 (Fax)
http://www.hrdpress.com

CRC Press
2000 Corporate Boulevard NW
Boca Raton, FL 33431
407-994-0555

ISBN 0-8493-9960-2

Typesetting by Michele Anctil
Cover design by Eileen Klockars
Editorial work by Mary George

TABLE OF CONTENTS

PREFACE xv

INTRODUCTION 1

NATIONAL SKILLS STANDARDS 13

HOW TO USE THIS BOOK 17

BUSINESS AND MANAGEMENT
Professional
Certified *Archivist* (C.A.) 19
Certified, *Auctioneer's Institute* (CAI®) 19
Child Development Associate (CDA) 20
Certified *Customer Service* Specialist (CSS) 20
Certified *Disaster Recovery* Planner (CDRP)
   Associate <u>Disaster Recovery</u> Planner (ADRP)
   Certified Master <u>Disaster Recovery</u> Planner (CMDRP) 21
Certified *Economic Developer*® (CED®) 21
Certified *Electronic Imager* (CEI) 22
Certified Professional *Estimator* (CPE) 23
Certified Cost *Estimator/Analyst* (CCEA) 23
Certified *Form Systems* Professional (CFSP) 24
Certified *Forms Consultant* (CFC) 24
Certified *Home Economist* (CHE) 25
Certified *Interior Designer* (NCIDQ Certified) 25
Certified Professional *Manufacturers Representative* (CPMR)
   Certified Professional *Food Broker* (CPFB) 26
Certified Professional *Photographer* (CPP) 27
Certified *Planner* (CP) 27
Certified *Quality Auditor* (CQA) 28
Certified Professional *Secretary*® (CPS®) 28
Certified *Speaking* Professional (CSP) 29
Accredited *Translator* (ATA Accreditation) 30
Certified *Value* Specialist (CVS)
   Associate *Value* Specialist (AVS)
   Value Methodology Practitioner (VMP) 30

Accounting and Finance
Accredited in *Accountancy*/Accredited Business Accountant^{SM} 33
Certified *Cash Manager* (CCM) 33
Chartered Accountant (C.A.) 34
Certified International *Financier* (CIF) 34
Certified *Fraud Examiner* (CFE) 35
Certified *Hospitality Accountant Executive* (CHAE) 35
Certified *Insolvency and Reorganization Accountant* (CIRA) 36
Associate in *Insurance Accounting* and Finance (AIAF) 36
Certified *Internal Auditor* (CIA) 37
Certified *Investment Management* Analyst (CIMA) 38
Certified *Management Accountant* (CMA) 39
Certified *Municipal Finance* Administrator (CMFA) 39

Accounting and Finance (continued)

Fellow, Society of *Pension Actuaries* (FSPA)
  Member, Society of *Pension Actuaries* (MSPA) 40
Associate Professional Member {*Pension Actuary*} (APM) 41
Qualified *Pension Administrator* (QPA) 41
Associate in *Premium Auditing* (APA®) 42
Certified *Public Accountant* (CPA) 42

Financial Institutions

Chartered *Bank Auditor* (CBA™) 43
Certified *Bank Compliance* Officer (CBCO) 43
Certified *Collection Agency* Executive (CCAE) 44
Certified *Collection Sales* Professional 44
Certified *Collector* 45
Certified *Consumer Credit* Executive (CCCE) 45
Certified *Corporate Trust* Specialist™ (CCTS™) 46
Credit Associate (CA) 47
Certified *Credit Bureau* Executive (CCBE) 47
Associate *Credit Executive* (ACE) 47
Certified *Credit Union* Executive (CCUE) 48
Certified *Financial Counseling* Executive (CFCE) 49
Accredited *Financial Examiner* (AFE®) 49
Certified *Financial Examiner* (CFE®) 50
Certified *Financial Services Security* Professional™ (CFSSP™) 50
Certified *Mortgage Banker* (CMB) 51
Certified *Regulatory Compliance* Manager™ (CRCM™) 51
Accredited *Residential Underwriter* (ARU) 52

Human Resource Management

Certified Employee *Benefit* Specialist (CEBS) 53
Registered Employee *Benefits* Consultant (REBC) 53
Certified *Benefits* Professional (CBP) 54
Certified *Compensation* Professional (CCP) 54
Certified *Employee Assistance* Professional (CEAP®) 55
Employment and Training Generalist (ETG)
  Employment and Training Master (ETM) 56
Professional in *Human Resources* (PHR)
  Senior Professional in *Human Resources* (SPHR) 56
Certified *Human Resources* Executive (CHRE®) 57
Member, *Outplacement* Institute
  Fellow (Practitioner), *Outplacement* Institute
  Fellow (Manager), *Outplacement* Institute 58
Registered *Organization Development* Professional (RODP)
  Registered *Organization Development* Consultant (RODC) 58
Certified *Payroll* Professional (CPP) 59
Certified *Pension* Consultant (CPC) 59
Certified *Personnel* Consultant (CPC) 60
Certified *Professional Employer* Specialist (CPES) 60
Certified *Quality Manager* (CQM) 61
Certified *Relocation* Professional (CRP™)
  Senior Certified *Relocation* Professional (SCRP™) 61
Certified Professional *Résumé Writer* (CPRW) 62
Certified Administrator of *Suggestion Systems* (CASS)
  Certified Manager of *Suggestion Systems* (CMSS) 62

Human Resource Management (continued)
Certified *Technical Trainer* (CTT) 63
Certified *Temporary-Staffing* Specialist (CTS) 63
Vocational Expert (Diplomate, Fellow) 64

Legal
National *Court Reporters* Association Certification Programs 65
Certified *Legal Assistant* (CLA)
    Certified *Legal Assistant Specialist* 66
Certified *Legal Investigator*® (CLI) 66
Accredited *Legal Secretary* (ALS) 67
Certified Professional *Legal Secretary* (PLS) 67

Logistics, Packaging, and Purchasing
Certified Associate *Contracts Manager* (CACM) 69
Certified Professional *Contracts Manager* (CPCM) 69
Certified Professional *Fleet Manager* (CPFM) 70
Certified Professional *Logistician* (C.P.L.) 71
Professional Certified in *Materials Handling* (PCMH)
    Professional Certified in *Materials Management* (PCMM) 71
Military Packaging Professional (MPP) 72
Certified *Packaging* Professional (CPP)
    Certified Professional in Training {*Packaging*} (CPIT) 73
Certified in *Production and Inventory Management* (CPIM®)
    Certified Fellow in *Production and Inventory Management* (CFPIM™) 73
Certified *Purchasing* Professional (CPP)
    Certified *Purchasing* Executive (CPE) 74
Certified Professional *Public Buyer* (CPPB) 75
Certified *Public Purchasing* Officer (CPPO) 76
Certified *Purchasing* Manager (C.P.M.) 76
Accredited *Purchasing* Practitioner (A.P.P.) 77
Certified in *Transportation and Logistics* (CTL) 78

Management
Certified *Architectural Administrator* (CAA) 79
Certified *Association* Executive (CAE) 79
Certified *Automotive Fleet* Manager (CAFM) 80
Certified *Emergency* Manager (CEM) 80
Certified *Energy* Manager (CEM) 81
Certified *Franchise* Executive (CFE™) 82
Certified *Fund Raising* Executive (CFRE)
    Advance Certified *Fund Raising* Executive (ACFRE) 82
Certified *Graphics Arts* Executive (CGAE) 83
Certified *Graphics Communications* Manager (CGCM) 83
Certified in *Integrated Resource Management* (CIRC™) 84
Certified *Laundry/Linen* Manager (CLLM) 84
Registered *Laundry/Linen* Director (R.L.L.D.) 85
Certified *Mail and Distribution Systems* Manager (CMDSM) 85
Certified *Mail Manager* (CMM) 86
Certified *Management Consultant* (CMC) 86
Certified *Manager* (CM)
    Certified Administrative *Manager* (C.A.M.)
    Associate Certified *Manager* (ACM) 87
Certified *Professional Consultant* (CPC) 87
Certified *Professional Services* Manager (CPM) 88

Management (continued)
Project Management Professional (PMP) 88
Center for International *Project and Program Management* (CIPPM®) 89
Certified Administrator of *Public Parking* (CAPP) 89
Certified *Records* Manager (CRM) 90
Certified *Service* Executive (CSE)
   Associate *Service* Executive (ASE)
   Lifetime Certified *Service* Executive (LCSE) 91
Certified *Shopping Center* Manager (CSM) 91

Marketing and Public Relations
Accredited Business *Communicator* (ABC) 93
Certified Business *Communicator* (CBC) 93
Certified Rural Electric *Communicator* (CREC) 94
Certified Manager of *Exhibits* (CME) 94
Certified *Marketing* Director (CMD) 95
Certified *Marketing* Executive (CME) 95
Marketing Professional (MP)
   Senior *Marketing* Professional (SMP)
   Fellow *Marketing* Professional (FMP) 96
Accredited in *Public Relations* (APR) 96
Certified *Sales* Executive (CSE) 97

Security
Certified *Confidentiality* Officer (CCO) 99
Certified *Protection* Officer (CPO) 99
Certified *Protection* Professional (CPP) 100
Personal *Protection* Specialist (PPS) 101
Certified *Security* Supervisor (CSS) 101
Certified *Security* Trainer (C.S.T.) 102

INSURANCE AND PERSONAL FINANCE
Insurance
Associate, Insurance Agency *Administration* (AIAA™) 103
Accredited *Adviser* in Insurance (AAI®) 103
Associate in *Claims* (AIC) 104
Associate, Life and Health *Claims* (ALHC) 104
Certified *Claims* Assistance Professional (CCAP) 105
Certified Electronic *Claims* Professional (CECP) 106
Associate, *Customer Service* (ACS®) 106
Accredited *Customer Service* Representative (ACSR) 107
Associate in *Fidelity and Surety* Bonding (AFSB) 108
Health Insurance Associate (HIA) 108
Registered *Health Underwriter* (RHU) 109
Certified *Insurance Counselor* (CIC) 109
Certified *Insurance Examiner* (CIE)
   Accredited *Insurance Examiner* (AIE) 110
Certified *Insurance Rehabilitation* Specialist (CIRS) 111
Associate in *Insurance Services* (AIS) 112
Certified *Insurance Service* Representative (CISR) 112
LIMRA® *Leadership* Institute Fellow (LLIF) 113
Fellow, *Life Management* Institute (FLMI®)
   Master Fellow, *Life Management* Institute (FLMI/M®) 113
Life Underwriter Training Council Fellow (LUTCF) 114
Chartered *Life Underwriter* (CLU) 114

Insurance (continued)

Associate in *Loss Control Management* (ALCM®) 115
Managed Healthcare Professional (MHP) 116
Associate in *Management* (AIM) 116
Associate in *Marine Insurance* Management (AMIM®) 117
Chartered *Property Casualty Underwriter* (CPCU®) 118
Associate in *Reinsurance* (ARe) 118
Associate in *Research and Planning* (ARP) 119
Associate in *Risk Management* (ARM) 120
Associate in *Underwriting* (AU) 120

Financial Advising

Enrolled *Agent* (EA) 121
Certified Trust and *Financial* Advisor™ (CTFA™) 121
Personal *Financial* Specialist (CPA/PFS) 122
Chartered *Financial Analyst* (CFA®) 122
Chartered *Financial Consultant* (ChFC) 123
Accredited *Financial Counselor* (AFC) 124
Certified *Financial Planner*® (CFP®) 124
Registered *Financial Planner* (RFC) 125
Certified *Fund Specialist* (CFS) 125
Certified *Housing Counselor* (CHC)
    Accredited *Housing Counselor* (AHC) 126
Registered *Investment Adviser* (RIA) 126
Chartered *Market Technician* (CMT) 127
Accredited *Tax Advisor*ˢᴹ 127
Accredited *Tax Preparer*ˢᴹ 128
Certified *Tax Preparer* (CTP)
    Certified *Tax Preparer* Specialist (CTPS)
    Certified *Tax Preparer* Master (CTPM) 128

REAL ESTATE AND APPRAISAL
Appraisal

Certified *Business* Appraiser (CBA) 131
Certified *Commercial Real Estate* Appraiser (CCRA) 131
General Appraiser, Appraisal Institute (MAI) 131
General Accredited Appraiser (GAA)
    Residential Accredited Appraiser (RAA) 132
Accredited *Machinery and Equipment* Appraiser (AMEA)
    Certified *Machinery and Equipment* Appraiser (CMEA) 132
Registered *Mortgage Underwriter* (RMU) 133
Graduate *Personal Property* Appraiser (GPPA) 133
Registered *Professional* Member (RPM) 134
Certified *Real Estate* Appraiser (CREA) 134
Real Property Review Appraiser (RPRA) 135
Residential Appraisal, Appraisal Institute (SRA) 136
Certified *Review* Appraiser (CRA) 136
Accredited *Rural* Appraiser (ARA) 136

Facilities Management

Certified *Building Service* Executive (CBSE) 139
Registered *Building Service Manager* (RBSM) 139
Certified *Demand-Side Management* Professional (CDSM) 140
Facilities Management Administrator (FMA) 140
Certified *Facilities Manager* (CFM) 141

Facilities Management (continued)

Certified *Housekeeper* (C.E.H.)

    Registered Executive *Housekeeper* (R.E.H.) 142

Certified *Indoor Air Quality* Professional (CIAQP) 142

Certified *Inspector* (ICBO) 143

Certified *Parking Facility* Manager (CPFM) 144

Certified *Plans Examiner* 144

Certified *Plant Engineer* (CPE) 145

Real *Property Administrator* (RPA) 145

Systems Maintenance Technician (SMT)

    Systems Maintenance Administrator (SMA) 146

Certified *Uniform Fire Code* Inspector 147

Property Management

Certified *Apartment* Manager (CAM) 149

Certified *Apartment Property Supervisor* (CAPS) 149

Professional *Community Association* Manager (PCAM®)

    Association Management Specialist (AMS®) 150

Certified in Professional *Downtown Management* 150

Accredited *Farm* Manager (AFM) 151

Certified Professional *Property* Specialist (CPPS)

    Certified Professional *Property* Administrator (CPPA)

    Certified Professional *Property* Manager (CPPM)

    Consulting Fellow {*Property*} (CF) 151

Certified *Public Housing* Manager (PHM) 152

Accredited *Residential* Manager (ARM®) 152

Real Estate

REALTOR® *Association Certified Executive* (RCE) 155

Accredited *Auctioneer Real Estate* (AARE) 155

Master of *Corporate Real Estate* (MCR)

    Associate of *Corporate Real Estate* (ACR) 156

Counselor of Real Estate (CRE®) 156

Registered *Environmental Property Assessor* (REPA)

    Associate *Environmental Property Assessor* (AEPA) 157

Graduate, REALTOR® Institute (GRI) 158

Certified *International Property* Specialist (CIPS) 158

Society of *Industrial and Office* REALTORS® (SIOR®) 159

Leadership Training Graduate (LTG) 160

Certified *Real Estate Brokerage* Manager (CRB) 160

Distinguished *Real Estate Instructor* (DREI) 161

HOSPITALITY AND TRAVEL

Certified *Catering* Executive (CCE) 163

Certified *Club Manager* (CCM)

    Master *Club Manager* (MCM) 163

Certified *Corporate Travel* Executive (CCTE) 164

American *Culinary* Federation Certification Program 165

Certified *Destination Management* Executive (CDME) 165

Certified *Engineering Operations* Executive (CEOE®) 166

Certified *Festival* Executive (CFE) 166

Certified *Food and Beverage* Executive (CFBE®) 167

Foodservice Management Professional (FMP) 168

Certified *Food Executive* (CFE)

    Certified *Food Manager* (CFM) 168

HOSPITALITY AND TRAVEL (continued)

Certified *Hospitality Educator* (CHE®) 169
Certified *Hospitality Housekeeping* Executive (CHHE®) 169
Certified *Hospitality Sales* Professional (CHSP®) 170
Hospitality Skills Certification 171
Certified *Hospitality Supervisor* (CHS®) 171
Certified *Hospitality Technology* Professional (CHTP®) 172
Certified *Hotel Administrator* (CHA®) 173
Certified *Hotel Sales* Executive (CHSE) 173
Master *Hotel Supplier* (MHS®) 174
Certified *Leisure* Professional (CLP)
    Certified *Leisure* Associate (CLA) 174
Certified *Meeting* Professional® (CMP®) 175
Registered *Meeting* Planner (RMP)
    Certified *Event* Planner (CEP)
    Certified *Destination* Specialist (CDS) 176
Certified *Park Operator* (CPO) 176
Certified *Rooms Division* Executive (CRDE®) 176
Certified *Travel Counselor* (CTC) 177

SCIENCE AND ENGINEERING

Speciality

Certified Specialist in *Analytical Technology* (CSAT) 179
Registered *Biological Photographer* (RBP) 179
Broadband Communications Engineer (BCE)
    Broadband Communications Technician (BCT) 180
Certified *Broadcast* Engineer
    Certified *Broadcast* Technologist 180
Certified Professional *Chemical Engineer* (CChE)
    Certified Professional *Chemist* (CPC) 181
Certified *Cogeneration* Professional (CCP) 181
Corrosion Specialist, Technologist, Technician 182
Certified *Cost Consultant* (CCC)
    Certified *Cost Engineer* (CCE) 183
Professional *Engineer* (P.E.) 183
Certified *Engineering Technologist* (CT) 184
Board Certified *Entomologist* (BCE) 184
Certified Professional *Ergonomist*® (CPE®)
    Certified *Human Factors* Professional® (CHFP®) 185
Certified *Fluid Power* Professional 186
Certified *Hydrographer* 186
Certified *Lighting Efficiency* Professional (CLEP) 187
Certified *Lighting Management* Consultant (CLMC) 187
Certified *Manufacturing* Engineer (CMfgE)
    Certified *Manufacturing* Technologist (CMfgT) 188
Certified *Mapping Scientist*, Remote Sensing and GIS/LIS 188
Certified Consulting *Meteorologist* (CCM) 189
Registered *Microbiologist* (RM[ASM])
    Specialist *Microbiologist* (SM[ASM]) 190
NARTE Certified Engineer (NCE)
    NARTE Certified Technician (NCT) 190
Certified *Photogrammetrist* 191
Certified in *Plumbing Engineering*® (CIPE®) 191
Certified *Quality Engineer* (CQE) 192
Certified *Reliability Engineer* (CRE) 192

Speciality (continued)

Certified *Safety* Executive (WSO-CSE)
  Certified *Safety* and Security Director (WSO-CSSD)
  Certified *Safety* Manager (WSO-CSM)
  Certified *Safety* Specialist (WSO-CSS)
  Certified *Safety* Technician (WSO-CST) 193
Certified *Safety* Professional® (CSP®)
  Associate *Safety* Professional (ASP) 194
Certified *Welding Inspector* (CWI)
  Certified Associate *Welding* Inspector (CAWI) 195

Computers/Information Systems

Adobe Certified Instructor 197
Apple Certified Server Engineer (Apple CSE) 197
Automated Examination Specialist (AES℠) 197
Associate in *Automation Management* (AAM®) 198
Cisco Certified Internetwork Expert (CCIE) 198
Compaq Accredited Systems Engineer (ASE) 199
Certified *Computing* Professional (CCP®)
  Associate *Computing* Professional (ACP®) 199
Certified *Computer Applications* Trainer (CCAT) 200
Electronic Document and Printing Professional (EDPP) 200
IBM Certification Program 201
Certified Document *Imaging* Architect (CDIA) 201
Certified *Imaging* Consultant (CIC)
  Certified *Imaging* Market Specialist (CIMS)
  Certified *Imaging* Systems Developer (CISD)
  Certified *Imaging* Systems Manager (CISM) 202
Certified *Information Systems Auditor* (CISA®) 203
Internet/Intranet Certified Engineer (I²CE) 203
Learning Tree Professional Certification Programs 204
Certified *Lotus* Professional (CLP) 204
Microsoft Certified Professional 205
Netscape Certified Instructor 205
Certified *Network* Expert™ (CNX™) 205
Certified *Network* Professional™ (CNP) 206
Novell Certification Programs 206
Certified *Oracle7* Database Administrator (DBA) 207
Certified *PowerBuilder* Developer (CPD) 207
A+ *Service* Technician Certification (A+) 208
Certified *Software Manager* (CSM) 209
Certified *Solaris* Administrator (CSA) 209
Solomon Professional Skills Certification 209
Certified *Sybase* Professional® 210

Environment

Certified Professional *Agronomist* (CPAg)
  Certified Professional *Crop Scientist*/Specialist (CPCS)
  Certified Professional *Horticulturalist* (CPH)
  Certified Professional *Plant Pathologist* (CPPP)
  Certified Professional *Soil Classifier* (CPSC)
  Certified Professional *Soil Scientist*/Specialist (CPSS)
  Certified Professional in *Weed Science* (CPWS) 211
Certified *Crop Advisor* (CCA) 211

Environment (continued)

Certified *Ecologist*

Certified Senior *Ecologist*

Certified Associate *Ecologist* 212

Diplomate *Environmental Engineer* (DEE) 212

Certified *Environmental Health* Technician (CEHT) 213

Registered *Environmental Health* Specialist (REHS)

Registered *Sanitarian* (RS) 214

Certified *Environmental Inspector* (CEI) 215

Registered *Environmental Manager* (REM) 215

Associate *Environmental Professional* (AEP) 216

Certified *Environmental Professional* (CEP) 217

Qualified *Environmental Professional* (QEP) 217

Registered *Environmental Professional* (REP) 218

Registered *Environmental Scientist* (RES) 219

Certified *Environmental Trainer*® (CET)

Associate *Environmental Trainer* (AET) 220

Certified *Hazardous Materials* Executive (WSO-CHME)

Certified *Hazardous Materials* Supervisor (WSO-CHMS)

Certified *Hazardous Materials* Technician (WSO-CHMT I/II) 221

Registered *Hazardous Substance* Professional (RHSP) 222

Registered *Hazardous Substance* Specialist (RHSS) 223

Certified Professional *Hydrologist*

Certified Professional *Hydrogeologist* 223

Certified *Industrial Hygienist* (CIH)

Industrial Hygienist in Training (IHIT) 224

Certified *Irrigation* Contractor (CIC)

Certified *Irrigation* Designer (CID)

Certified *Irrigation* Manager (CIM)

Certified *Landscape Irrigation* Auditor (CLIA) 224

Certified *Landfill* Manager

Certified *Landfill* Inspector

Certified *Collection* Manager

Certified *Municipal Solid Waste* (MSW) Manager I

Certified *Recycling* Manager

Certified *Transfer Station* Manager 225

Certified Professional in *Soil Erosion* and Sediment Control (CPESC) 226

Technician/Technology

Broadband Installer Certification 229

Certified *Construction Health and Safety* Technician (CHST) 229

Certified *Control Systems* Technician (CCST) 230

Certified *Electron Microscopy* Technologist (CEMT) 230

Certified *Electroplater-Finisher* (CEF)

Electronics Specialist, Certified (ESC) 231

Certified *Electronics Technician* (CET) 231

Certified *Engineering Technician* (CET) 232

Registered *Environmental Laboratory* Technologist (RELT) 233

Certified *Mechanical Inspector* (CMI) 234

NABER Certified Technician 235

Certified *Occupational Health and Safety* Technologist (COHST) 235

Certified *Quality Technician* (CQT) 236

Certified *Safety Trained Supervisor*—Construction (STS-Construction) 236

Certified *Satellite Installer* (CSI) 237

Technician/Technology (continued)
Certified *Survey Technician* (CST) 237
Certified *Technology Specialist* (CTS) 238
Certified *Water Treatment* Professional (CWTP) 238

MEDICAL
Management
Certified *Case Manager* (CCM) 241
Certified *Dietary Manager* (CDM) 241
{*Healthcare*} Fellow (FHFMA) 242
Certified *Healthcare Executive* (CHE)
  Fellow of the American College of *Healthcare Executives* (FACHE) 242
Certified Professional in *Healthcare Quality* (CPHQ) 243
ACSM *Health/Fitness Director*^{SM} 243
Certified *Managed Care* Executive (CMCE) 244
Certified *Managed Care* Professional (CMPC) 245
Diplomate, American Board of *Medical Laboratory Immunology* (ABMLI) 245
Diplomate, American Board of *Medical Microbiology* (ABMM) 246
Certified *Medical Staff Coordinator* (CMSC) 246
Registered Nurse, Certified in *Nursing Administration* (RN, CNA)
  Registered Nurse, Certified in *Nursing Administration*, Advanced (RN, CNAA) 247
Certified *Nursing Home* Administrator (CNHA) 247
Certified Manager of *Patient Accounts* (CMPA) 248
Program Director Specialist (PDS) 248
Regulatory Affairs Professional Certification 249
Retirement Housing Professional (RHP)
  Retirement Housing Professional Fellow (RHP Fellow) 249
Certified *Sterile Processing and Distribution* Manager (CSPDM) 250
Certified *Sterile Processing and Distribution* Supervisor (CSPDS) 251

Practitioners
Activity Consultant Certified (ACC)
  Activity Director Certified (ADC)
  Activity Assistant Certified (AAC) 253
Nationally Certified *Counselor* (NCC) 254
Registered *Dietetic Technician* (RDT)
  Registered *Dietitian* (RD) 254
Disability Analyst and Fellow
  Senior *Disability Analyst* and Diplomate 255
Certified *Disability Specialist*
  {*Disability Specialist*} Diplomate, ABPDC 255
Certified *Family Life* Educator (CFLE) 256
Certified Registered Nurse *Intravenous* (CRNI) 256
Nationally Certified in Therapeutic *Massage* and Bodywork (NCTMB) 257
Internationally Certified *Massage Therapist* (ICMT®)
  Internationally Certified *Bodywork Therapist* (ICBT®)
  Internationally Certified *Somatic Therapist* (ICST®) 258
Certified *Medical Assistant* (CMA) 258
Registered *Nurse Certified* (RNC) 259
Registered *Nurse, Certified* (RN, C)
  Registered *Nurse, Certified* Specialist (RN, CS) 259
Certified *Nurse-Midwife* (CNM)
  Certified *Midwife* (CM) 260
Occupational Therapist, Registered (OTR) 260
American Board of *Opticianry* Certified (ABOC) 261

Practitioners (continued)
Orthopaedic Nurse Certified (ONC) 262
Certified *Pediatric Nurse* (CPN)
   Certified *Pediatric Nurse* Practitioner (CPNP) 262
Board Certified Nutrition Support *Pharmacist* (BCNSP)
   Board Certified Nuclear *Pharmacist* (BCNP)
   Board Certified Pharmacotherapy *Specialist* (BCPS) 263
Physician Assistant-Certified (PA-C) 264
Physical Therapist Specialist Certification 264
Certified *Rehabilitation Counselor* (CRC) 265

Medical Technology/Allied Health
Certified *Anesthesiologist Assistant* 267
Assistive Technology Practitioner (ATP)
   Assistive Technology Supplier (ATS) 267
Certified *Biomedical Equipment* Technician (CBET) 268
Registered Diagnostic *Cardiac Sonographer* (RDCS) 268
Registered *Central Service* Technician (RCST)
   Certified Registered *Central Service* Technician (CRCST) 269
Registered *Dental Assistant* (RDA[AMT]) 270
Certified *Dental Technician* (CDT) 270
Registered *Electroencephalographic Technologist* (R. EEG T. ®) 271
Registered *Evoked Potential* Technologist (R. EP T.) 272
ACSM *Exercise Leader* ℠ 272
ACSM *Exercise Specialist* ℠ 273
ACSM *Exercise Test Technologist* ℠ 273
ACSM *Health/Fitness Instructor* ℠ 274
Board Certified in *Hearing Instrument Sciences* (BC-HIS) 274
Certified *Laboratory Equipment* Specialist (CLES) 275
Registered *Laboratory Technician* (RLT) 275
Registered *Medical Assistant* (RMA[AMT]) 276
Medical Laboratory Technician (MLT®[AMT]) 276
Registered Diagnostic *Medical Sonographer* (RDMS) 277
Medical Technologist (MT®(AMT)) 278
Registered Medical Technologist (RMT) 278
Certified *Nuclear Medicine* Technologist (CNMT) 279
Certified *Occupational Hearing* Conservationist 279
Certified *Occupational Therapy* Assistant (COTA) 280
Physician *Office Laboratory* Technician (POLT) 280
Board Certification in *Pedorthics* (C.Ped.) 280
Nationally Certified *Pharmacy Technician* (NCPT) 281
Registered *Phlebotomy* Technician (RPT[AMT]) 282
Nationally Certified *Psychiatric Technician* (NCPT) 282
Certified *Pulmonary Function* Technologist (CPFT℠) 283
Registered *Pulmonary Function* Technologist (RPFT℠) 283
Certified *Radiology Equipment* Specialist (CRES) 284
Certified *Respiratory Therapy* Technician (CRTT℠) 284
Registered *Respiratory Therapist* (RRT℠) 285
Certified *Sterile Processing and Distribution* Technician (CSPDT) 286
Certified *Surgical Technologist* (CST®)
   CST® Certified *First Assistant* (CST®/CFA®) 286
Registered *Technologist* (R.T.[ARRT]) 287
Certified *Therapeutic Recreation* Specialist® (CTRS®) 288
Certified Medical *Transcriptionist* (CMT) 289
Registered *Vascular Technologist*® (RVT)® 289

TRADE/TECHNICAL

Certified *Apartment Maintenance* Technician (CAMT) 291
ASE Certification Program 291
Auto Glass Technician
   Senior *Auto Glass* Technician
   Master *Auto Glass* Technician 292
Certified *Bathroom* Designer (CBD) 292
ACI {*Concrete*} Certification 293
Certified *Drafter* 294
Glazier
   Commercial Interior/Residential *Glazier*
   Storefront/Curtainwall *Glazier*
   Master *Glazier* 294
Certified *Kitchen* Designer (CKD) 295
Certified *Photographic Consultant*™ (CPC) 295
Certified *Picture Framer* (CPF) 296
Certified Graduate *Remodeler*™ (CGR) 296
Certified *Remodeler* (CR)
   Certified *Remodeler* Associate (CRA) 297
Certified Inspection, Cleaning, and *Restoration* Technician 298
Certified *Restorer* (CR) 299
ADS® *TechCert* Certified Technician
 ADS® *TechCert* Certified Master Technician 299
Certified *Turfgrass* Professional (CTP) 300
Certified in *Underground Storage Tank* Installation/Decommissioning (UST) 300
AWS Certified *Welder* 301
Certified *Welding Educator* (CWE) 301
Certified *Well Driller* (CWD)
   Certified *Pump Installer* (CPI)
   Master *Ground Water* Contractor (MGWC) 302

APPENDIX A:
Certification by Designation Index A-1

APPENDIX B:
Keyword Index B-1

PREFACE

The Second Edition of *The Guide to National Professional Certification Programs* has been updated to include both new programs and new ways we communicate. Many of the new certifications reflect the increasing number of information systems specialties. Also included in this edition are Web-page URL's and E-mail addresses for most program sponsors. All certification descriptions have been updated from the 1994 edition, and reflect new program data, testing, qualification, and recertification information.

The author thanks the 300 certification sponsors who completed questionnaires on their programs and sent testing, qualification, and curriculum materials. Without the cooperation of these organizations, this book would not have been possible.

INTRODUCTION

Work and organizational changes in the past several years have forced organizations to reinvent themselves and individuals to reeducate themselves. No company or employee can escape today's workplace challenges: the shifts in traditional hiring and promotion practices; the increasingly specialized workplace and mobile workforce; the rise of new job positions essential for success and the decline or revision of once-secure positions. To adapt, companies must find innovative ways of recruiting, assessing, training, and developing human resources; to stay employable, individuals must find new ways to grow, depending on more than traditional educational resources.

One tool that organizations and individuals need in order to adapt and grow is already available, developed by the very professionals that organizations seek. It is voluntary professional certification—a third-party endorsement of an individual's expertise. More and more companies are joining the certification movement and benefiting from this tool's high measure of success.

To understand the effectiveness of the certification process, you need to know what certification programs are available in your area of interest and what requirements are set by those programs. This guidebook lists hundreds of certifications and describes their basic requirements. It is your indispensable start to understanding the importance that certification can have on your career, your organization, and your industry.

Why Professional Certification?

Three trends act together to make professional certification important to both the organization and the individual. First, university degrees no longer represent, if they ever did, the ultimate measure of professional knowledge and capability. A certification, by measuring job-related expertise, more closely reflects an individual's capacity to perform. Second, the downsizing of corporations, coupled with teaming, outsourcing, and temping, has forced professionals to take control of their own careers independent of their employers. A certification, awarded by a third party, endorses skills beyond the requirements of a specific position or role. Third, the business environment requires almost constant training, development, and professional involvement beyond one's particular job title. Certification programs, especially through their recertification requirements, provide guidance to individuals working to stay current in their profession.

Voluntary certification programs are not licenses to work in a particular profession. Licensure is performed by a government agency, often at the state level, and acts to restrict the profession to individuals meeting certain minimum requirements. Voluntary certification endorses skilled expertise; licensure protects the public from incompetent practice. Many certification programs exist in areas where no regulatory requirements exist. Others, such as those in real estate, appraisal, and nursing, recognize competence in advanced or specialized areas not covered by state licensure.

Taking Control of the Profession

Voluntary professional certification now reaches into more areas of professional development than any other trend in human resources. This movement is shaping the way that people in many professions educate, promote, and develop themselves.

Associations, industry groups, and corporations see professional certification as a natural outgrowth of the quality and empowerment movements. Many professional organizations also view certification as a continuation of their mission to promote their profession.

From technicians and tradespeople to senior managers and skilled engineers, certified professionals set new standards in expertise and organizational contributions. This movement is changing the way companies train and promote employees. Certification changes the criteria used to select consultants and temporary professionals. Organizations are recognizing the power of this revolution, and now, by using this book, they can understand how to evaluate these programs.

Certification allows its participants to define their profession, to establish its standards of performance and knowledge, and to create an objective standard of quality to which others within the profession can aspire. Rather than continue to allow companies to narrowly define "positions," voluntary professional certification programs allow those within the profession to take control.

Defining a Profession

Powerful forces—the professionals themselves—work to keep certification substantial and worthwhile. Most certification programs are created, sponsored, or affiliated with professional associations and trade organizations interested in raising standards. Even those programs completely independent from membership organizations enjoy association support and endorsement.

Most certifications are not membership benefits or fund-raising ventures. These programs are serious attempts to create standards for a specific profession *and to evaluate* whether individuals have the education, experience, and professional knowledge to meet these standards. By creating a standard for a particular profession, complete with performance standards, ethics, and career paths, professions seek to define themselves independent of company job descriptions and academic degree programs.

The growth of certification programs is also a reaction to the changing employment market. Certifications are portable, since they do not depend on one company's definition of a certain job. Certification stands above the résumé and the professional reference by being an impartial, third-party endorsement of an individual's professional knowledge and experience. Certification allows individuals to participate in their own professional destiny.

How Certification Helps Organizations

Using Certification in Assessment

No assessment tool, whether it is certification, personality testing, or job interview, can guarantee that the person selected for a job can actually perform the job. There are simply too many components, many of them difficult to define, for any one tool to analyze effectively. How good a crystal ball is professional certification? The fact that an individual is certified may be the best indicator of the quality of a current or potential employee.

Companies now use many forms of professional assessment. College degrees, references, and résumés are all used to evaluate an individual's capabilities. What distinguishes professional certification is what it says about the individual. The basic requirements for many programs require extensive personal commitment. Individuals who show the motivation, time, and expense necessary to pursue and maintain certification have made a serious commitment to their profession.

What Does Certification Demonstrate?

Job Knowledge. A person must have the right knowledge to do a job. College degrees and job training programs used to fill this role, but are now considered little more than basic, entry-level prerequisites. Universities may teach, but they may not teach the "right stuff." College courses rarely fit neatly into job elements. Knowledge requirements are based on academic opinion, not the current reality of the workplace.

Interviews are the worst place to assess someone's professional knowledge. Interviewers, especially in technical situations, may come from an entirely different field than the candidate. Interviews rarely assess the depth of a candidate's job knowledge.

Most certification programs have a knowledge requirement based on real-world requirements and situations. Many certifications are based on a profession's common body of knowledge derived from the workplace. A certification examination based on professional requirements may be the only tool available to measure a candidate's knowledge. In fact, a certifying body may be the only group capable of defining the knowledge required for a specific field.

Experience. How much experience does someone need to do a job independently and competently? How relevant is that experience to the requirements of a certain job? Experience alone rarely marks competence. After all, someone may have 10 years of progressive experience, or one year of entry-level experience 10 times. Is experience in performing at one job enough to provide the skills needed for another job?

Many certification programs not only require a certain amount of experience, but also define what is truly relevant experience. Since the members of a profession help define what a certain field involves, they are the best qualified to understand what constitutes experience within the field. This doesn't guarantee that a certified individual comes to a job with experience in all constituent skills. But it does demonstrate that the person has experience in performing the *important* skills.

Background. Many certification programs do what few employers do today: verify professional and educational backgrounds. Few employers review college degrees, continuing education, and professional involvement. Many certification programs go over this material very carefully. Many programs require professional recommendations and proof of employment. Some even conduct background checks. Certification provides the documented professional "track record" many employers want.

Motivation and Commitment

Time and again, a person's motivation to succeed in a position is the deciding factor in whether he or she does succeed. An unmotivated person with the required knowledge and experience may act as incompetent as someone highly motivated but completely lacking in skills. Certification shows that an individual believes in his or her career and acts on that belief.

Personality tests claim to predict motivation, honesty, and success, but motivation is at best a fuzzy concept, easily preached but difficult to quantify. Commitment to a profession simply cannot be measured based on an interview or a résumé. The proof is in the doing. The most motivated individuals are the ones committed to their profession and who see themselves as professionals. A job is more than just a paycheck to them. This willingness to invest in their own professions makes certified professionals valuable both today and tomorrow.

Most certifications require individuals to demonstrate an ongoing commitment to their profession. This may include continuing education, involvement in professional organizations, and attending conferences and symposia. Certified individuals are more likely to be aware of their profession's constantly changing environment. They have the tools to anticipate and respond to change.

Certification as Incentive

Certified professionals believe both in themselves and in what they do. An employer recognizing this aspect of certification can find ways to reward and motivate in this era of reduced promotions and incentive budgets.

Many companies pay at least part of their employees' college costs. This made sense when a company had something to offer employees when they finished a degree: a higher position, more responsibility, increased compensation. Now, the only way many employees can benefit from additional academic work is to leave their organizations. How smart is it to pay out thousands of dollars to force employees to go to a competitor when they finish?

Professional certification promotes growth and professionalism *within* the job, rather than preparing for growth beyond the job, and recognizes achievement without internal competition. Certification also usually costs less than college courses, and more directly builds competence within a position.

3

Alternative Training Resource

No matter what the profession, staying on top of changes can be difficult. The function of corporate training must be more than simply preparing an employee for a new job or position. Training must focus on changes to current jobs. It must continuously provide new skills and update and expand old ones for employees to remain productive.

Professional certification can provide an alternative, low-cost source of training for new skills and revising old ones. The certification process often requires candidates to study aspects of the profession to which they may not be exposed in their day-to-day work environment. Many programs require candidates to stay involved in professional issues, current trends, and innovations. Through their recertification process, currently certified individuals continue to learn about changing technology and business environments.

Certification-preparation materials represent the richest sources available for training and professional study. These resources often incorporate the latest legal, ethical, technological, and professional topics. Many programs have materials already produced for classroom use, facilitated instruction, and self-learning.

Elements of Certification

While most certification programs offer quality resources, a few fail to reflect job competence. Each program must be evaluated on its own merits. Each program should provide organizations hiring and promoting their certificants some affirmation of utility.

First, we'll look at the different parts of a certification program; then we'll take a look at organizations approving certification programs.

Title/Designation

The certification's name is the program's official title or designation. To show certification, many programs allow individuals to use a designation symbol; for example, John Doe, CPM. Some titles and symbols are trademarks or service marks; the certification includes a license to use the mark.

Sponsor

The sponsor of a certification program is the organization responsible for setting certification criteria, assessing candidates, and awarding the certification. Sponsors may be associations, independent boards, a consortium of organizations, or for-profit corporations. Within many associations, independent boards manage the certification program.

Ethics and Conduct

Certification programs lead in recognizing, defining, and promoting professional ethics. Many certifications define and require adherence to a set of professional ethics. Certifications may be revoked for ethics violations. The ethics portion of certification programs provides participants with the foundation to act appropriately when faced with difficult professional choices. Many programs require professional letters of recommendation as part of their ethics assessment. Several investigate ethics complaints.

Eligibility for Certification

Most certifications require that candidates meet certain prerequisites before entering the program. Some programs require minimum levels of education and years of experience. Other programs use a point system to assess varying levels of education, experience, and professional involvement. A few programs require association membership.

Experience
Since certifications have the goal of recognizing competent individuals, many programs require professional experience. Programs review and confirm an applicant's job positions, require employer verification, and validate other work records. Experiential components may use a point system, time in position, or range of responsibilities to determine an applicant's experience.

Academic Education
Academic education rarely provides enough training to consider graduates completely competent within a certain skill set. However, college coursework provides a solid base for professionals to build on. The academic education component of many certification programs recognizes this work by often reducing experience requirements for college graduates.

Professional Education
Professional education, sponsored by associations, industry groups, vendors, and independent organizations, forms an important part of most certification programs. Workshops, seminars, conventions, and self-paced study are all recognized by certification programs for their importance in maintaining competence and staying current in a profession.

Contributions to the Profession
With many certification programs dropping any membership requirements, the professional/association contribution component provides both incentive and reward for individuals active in local, regional, and national association activities. This may also include writing about the profession, creating examination questions, or teaching in professional education venues.

Curriculum

Several certification programs include required professional education courses. These courses, often delivered by the sponsoring organization, cover core information considered necessary for competency within the field. The curriculum requirements differ from the prerequisite education requirements. The certification curriculum is part of the certification process, and professional or academic education is required before the certification process begins.

Special Requirements

Other professional qualification requirements may include research papers, portfolios, and performance exercises.

Examinations

The examination component, used in most programs, is usually the last step completed before actual certification. Frequently, the examination is objective-based and multiple-choice. Some programs use short-answer and essay formats. Most exams are proctored, and many are developed by professional testing companies or universities.

Fees/Costs

Certification costs vary widely. The examination costs may represent a small part of the financial commitment required to gain certification. However, the actual costs of certification—including professional education, testing fees, and study materials—are often much lower than college coursework.

Recertification

Recertification requires those already certified to stay current within the profession. Recertification often includes continued education and employment within the field. Not all programs require completing formal certification. Most programs require the payment of recertification or recurring fees; these items are not included in this book. Usually, certificants must accumulate a certain number of continuing education hours to recertify. A few programs require retesting.

Types of Certification

There are three basic types of certification: portfolio-based, competence-based, and curriculum-based.

Portfolio-Based Certification

Few certification programs regularly use a portfolio assessment method for certification. Candidates must provide evidence that they meet the certification program's minimum standards. Some programs require extensive documentation of professional experience and education within several competency areas. This method may be used for a short period of time to "grandfather" highly qualified individuals when a certification begins.

A small number of programs may be "portfolio" in name only; all that is required is association membership, an unqualified résumé, and a fee. These offer little value to anyone and should be avoided.

To evaluate portfolio-based certifications, you should consider the following:

- Can competency within the profession be adequately evaluated by reviewing the candidate's body of work?
- Does the required portfolio content reflect accepted industry practice?

Competency-Based Certification

These programs require candidates to demonstrate their expertise, mastery, or capability. True competency-based programs use examinations, professional education, and experience requirements based on a set of tasks identified through a job analysis. To earn certification, candidates must demonstrate their mastery of a common body of knowledge within their profession.

The critical requirement of competency-based certifications is the examination component. These examinations measure the mastery of knowledge that reflects job content. While it may be possible to study for this type of exam, most candidates need real-world experience to pass. These examinations are often criterion-referenced. A passing score is based on passing a certain percentage of questions based on areas of competency of knowledge, not on other candidates' scores.

To measure an individual's depth of professional knowledge, certification examinations must be based on job-related requirements, functions, and responsibilities. A certifying body must first decide *what* to test. However, job requirements vary from organization to organization, and even within organizations. The best way to select appropriate testing areas would be to survey a wide range of people within the profession.

These surveys, which are the basis for most competency-based certification examinations, are usually referred to as job analyses, task analyses, task surveys, and role-delineation studies. The analysis or survey separates, weighs, and defines all the tasks a person in a responsible position within the profession might do. By selecting people from different types of organizations, related job categories, and geographical locations, common task areas and performance levels are identified. While not everyone working within the profession performs all of the common tasks, most people will perform most of the tasks as part of their job.

Once a study identifies what people do within the profession, the knowledge required to perform those tasks must be identified. This means determining not only what someone needs to know, but how well someone should know it. Does a person need to be familiar with a concept, apply the concept to a situation, or use the concept in concert with other concepts to solve a problem? The results of this work are called the profession's **common body of knowledge**. Test questions are then written to this common body of knowledge. Tests are then validated, placed under test-control procedures, and updated regularly.

To evaluate a competency-based certification, you should consider the following:

- Does the program base examinations on a comprehensive body of knowledge created from task or job analysis?
- Does the program employ reasonable test-control procedures or use a third-party testing organization experienced in professional assessment?
- Is the program recognized, endorsed, or sponsored by the leading professional or industry association in the field?
- Do the qualification criteria reflect the relative importance each factor has towards developing qualified professionals?

Curriculum-Based Certification

Curriculum-based certifications are based on completing subject-based professional education. They differ from academic programs by focusing on defined, job-specific subjects rather than broader academic criteria. They differ from certificate programs by evaluating comprehension of material rather than only attendance. Many curriculum-based programs award certification upon passing examinations; the exams are based on self-study or workshop content.

The two industries with a majority of these programs are insurance and real estate. These professions have taken such a route for many reasons. The subjects are complex, with a constantly changing regulatory environment. Also, these industries already have state licensing requirements, so their programs recognize additional work and professional growth in the field.

Most programs use examinations combined with self-study or workshops. The professional curriculum may be created by academic groups or associations, or adapted from other sources. Some are based on a common body of knowledge. While it is important that the examinations adequately cover the coursework, it is just as important that the coursework follows standard or accepted industry practices. The curriculum and course design should be based on critical areas within the field.

To evaluate a curriculum-based certification, you should consider the following:

- Does the sponsoring organization have both professional and industry participation?
- Does the coursework use recognized resources (industry standards, accepted references)?
- Is there a course-based examination process, and does this process include proctored, properly controlled testing?

Who Certifies Certifications?

There are no universally recognized organization-evaluating certification programs. For most programs, association support and industry recognition is all the approval most certifications have. However, there are four sources of outside approval that may be useful in assessing certification programs.

The Council of Engineering Specialty Boards

130 Holiday Court, Suite 100
Annapolis, MD 21401
Phone: (410) 266-3766

The Council of Engineering and Scientific Specialty Boards (CESB) recognizes engineering, scientific, and technology certification programs meeting the highest standards of operation. The CESB recognizes only those related programs that have a fully developed body of knowledge or minimum level of skills and knowledge, use validated comprehensive examinations, and require thorough recertification.

The CESB evaluates a program's structure, financial resources, operation, public disclosure, and responsibilities. Member boards offer accredited certifications.

Member Boards

- American Academy of Environmental Engineers
- American Association of Cost Engineers
- American Society of Civil Engineers
- Board of Certified Safety Professionals
- Institute of Professional Environmental Practice
- National Academy of Forensic Engineers
- National Association of Corrosion Engineers
- National Institute for Certification in Engineering Technology

The National Commission for Certifying Agencies (NCCA)

1200 19th St. NW, Suite 300
Washington, DC 20036
Phone: (202) 857-1165

The National Commission for Certifying Agencies (NCCA) accredits certification agencies meeting stringent organizational and program requirements. Unlike the CESB, NCCA accreditation is open to all fields. The NCCA is sponsored by the National Organization for Competency Assurance (NOCA), an organization of certifying agencies. NCCA-accredited certifications must be national, nongovernmental, operated by a nonprofit agency, and complete at least two national examination administrations.

For NCCA accreditation, a certifying board must meet the following requirements:

1. Maintain administrative independence from any parent association or society.
2. Ensure that all programs are free of bias.
3. Require periodic recertification.
4. Determine pass/fail cutoff using psychometrically valid criteria.
5. Maintain disciplinary procedures.
6. Provide for the separation of the education and certification components of a program.
7. Provide alternative pathways to certification for nontraditional learners.
8. Have a public member on the governing board.
9. Show the reliability of test scores and pass-fail decisions.
10. As a minimum, perform content validation on the certification exams.

Over 30 certification programs are currently accredited by the NCCA, primarily in the allied health field. Contact NCCA for more information, their current list of accredited certification programs, or a copy of their accreditation standards.

The American Council on Education (ACE)

1 Dupont Circle
Washington, DC 20036

The American Council on Education (ACE) is an umbrella organization of U.S. colleges and universities. ACE acts as a forum for higher education issues and sponsors several programs involving alternative and non-traditional education. Two organizations within ACE review nontraditional education—including certification programs—and make college-credit recommendations. These recommendations are accepted by many colleges and universities. While not directly endorsing a certification program, an ACE recommendation indicates that an associated course or examination is equivalent to certain college coursework.

ACE's Center for Adult Learning and Educational Credentials, founded in 1942, provides college-credit recommendations for examination and experiential learning programs. The Center's Educational Credit by Examination program provides a stringent review of examination content, construction, delivery, and assessment. Specifically, reviews describe both program validity and technical accuracy. ACE recommends award of credit, by hour, in specific areas. ACE recommends college credit for the following certification examinations (unless otherwise noted, recommendations are for lower-division semester-hour credit):

Certification	Sponsor	ACE Credit Recommendations (semester hours)
Certified Payroll Professional (CPP)	American Payroll Association	11 hours total, covering payroll taxes, payroll accounting, business math, personnel administration, and accounting principles.
Certified Computer Programmer (CCP)	Institute for the Certification of Computer Professionals (ICCP)	Core exam = 17 hours covering introduction to computers, introduction to data base management, business organization, introduction to systems analysis, introduction to management, and associated disciplines. Specialty exams = 3 hours in the associated specialty.
Registered Professional Reporter (RPR)	National Court Reporters Association	21 hours covering legal terminology, court reporting procedures, English/office communications, dictation/transcription.
ASE Certified Technician	National Institute for Automotive Service Excellence	Each test: 2–6 hours in the related technical area.
Certified Professional Secretary (CPS)	Professional Secretaries International (PSI)	25 hours in accounting, business, management, communications, marketing, and office administration.

ACE's Program on Noncollegiate Sponsored Instruction (PONSI), established in 1974, evaluates and recommends credit for formal training in the workplace. Over 200 businesses, labor unions, industry groups, associations, and government agencies participate in this program. PONSI makes recommendations based on a review of course content, quality, administration, and validations procedures. PONSI also maintains the Registry of Credit Recommendations, providing students with a permanent record of training and colleges and universities with a transcript for review and credit award.

For certification programs, the certification itself is not assessed. What is assessed are the certification-related training courses used for initial certification or recertification. While ACE/PONSI credit recommendations are not endorsements of a particular certification, it does indicate the high quality of any underlying learning program. ACE/PONSI has recommended college credit for training sponsored by the following organizations:

- American Institute for Chartered Property Casualty Underwriters, sponsor of the Chartered Property Casualty Underwriter (CPCU) program
- American Bankers Association, sponsor of the Institute of Certified Bankers, which in turn sponsors these programs: Certified Corporate Trust Specialist (CCTS); Certified Trust and Financial Advisor (CTFA); Certified Financial Services Security Professional (CFSSP); and Certified Regulatory Compliance Manager (CRCM)
- Credit Union National Association, sponsor of the Certified Credit Union Executive (CCUE) program
- Health Insurance Association of America, sponsor of the Health Insurance Associate (HIA) and Managed Health Care Professional (MHP) programs
- Institute of Certified Travel Agents, sponsor of the Certified Travel Counselor (CTC) program
- Institute of Certified Professional Managers, sponsor of the Associate Certified Manager (ACM), Certified Manager (CM), and Certified Administrative Manager (CAM) programs
- Insurance Institute of America, sponsor of these Associate programs: Insurance Services (AIS); Management (AIM); Risk Management (ARM); Underwriting (AU); Loss Control Management (ALCM); Premium Auditing (APA); Research and Planning (ARP®); Insurance Accounting and Finance (AIAF); Marine Insurance Management (AMIM); Automation Management (AAM); Reinsurance (Are); Fidelity and Surety Bonding (AFSB); and Claims (AIC). The Institute also sponsors the Accredited Adviser in Insurance (AAI) program.
- Learning Tree International, sponsor of several vendor-independent certification programs
- National Association Medical Staff Services, sponsor of the Certified Medical Staff Coordinator (CMSC) program
- Society for Human Resource Management, sponsor of the Human Resource Certification Institute, which in turn sponsors the Professional in Human Resources (PHR) and Senior Professional in Human Resources (SPHR) programs

Defense Activity for Non-Traditional Education Support (DANTES)

6490 Saufley Field Road
Pensacola, FL 32509
Phone: (904) 452-1132

DANTES provides educational support to the Department of Defense. DANTES services includes developing educational counselors, sponsoring educational-technology and distance-education programs, and providing educational, career, and certification examinations to Department personnel worldwide. Endorsement by DANTES recognizes the growing importance of certification programs.

To help military personnel make the transition to civilian life, DANTES has evaluated the following certification programs for industry relevance, quality, and content validity. The following organizations' certification examinations are offered through DANTES:

- ABIH/BCSP Joint Committee, which sponsors the Certified Occupational Health and Safety Technologist (OHST), Certified Construction Health and Safety Technician (CHST), and Certified Safety Trained Supervisor—Construction (STS-Construction) programs
- American Nurses Credentialing Center (ANCC), which sponsors these programs: Registered Nurse, Certified in Nursing Administration Advanced (RN, CNAA); Registered Nurse, Certified in Nursing Administration (RN,CNA); Registered Nurse, Certified (RN,C); and Registered Nurse, Certified Specialist (RN,CS)
- American Society for Quality Control (ASQC), which sponsors the following programs: Certified Mechanical Inspector (CMI); Certified Quality Technician (CQT); Certified Reliability Engineer (CRE); Certified Quality Auditor (CQA); Certified Quality Manager (CQM); and Certified Quality Engineer (CQE)
- American Medical Technologists (AMT), which sponsors these programs: Registered Medical Assistant (RMA); Registered Dental Assistant (RDA); Medical Technologist (MT); Medical Laboratory Technician (MLT); and Registered Phlebotomy Technician (RPT)

10

- Board of Certified Safety Professionals (BCSP), which sponsors the Associate Safety Professional (ASP) and Certified Safety Professional (CSP) programs
- Electronics Technicians Association, International, which sponsors the Certified Electronics Technician (CET), Certified Satellite Installer (CSI), and Certified Customer Service Specialist (CSS) programs
- Institute of Certified Professional Managers (ICPM), which sponsors the Associate Certified Manager (ACM), Certified Manager (CM), and Certified Administrative Manager (C.A.M.) programs
- Institute for Personal Finance (IFP), which sponsors the Accredited Financial Counselor (AFC) program
- Institute for Certification of Computer Professionals (ICCP), which sponsors the Associate Computing Professional (ACP) and Certified Computing Professional (CCP) programs
- International Society for Clinical Laboratory Technology (ISCLT), which sponsors the Registered Medical Technologist (RMT), Registered Laboratory Technician (RLT), and Physician Office Laboratory Technician (POLT) programs
- Liaison Council on Certification for the Surgical Technologist (LCC-ST), which sponsors the CST Certified First Assistant (CST/CFA) and Certified Surgical Technologist (CST) programs
- National Institute for Certification in Engineering Technologies (NICET), which sponsors the Certified Engineering Technician (CET) and Certified Engineering Technologist (CT) programs
- National Board for Respiratory Care (NBRC), which sponsors the Registered Respiratory Therapist (RRT), Certified Respiratory Therapy Technician (CRTT), and Certified Pulmonary Function Technologist (CPFT) programs
- National Institute for the Certification of Healthcare Sterile Processing and Distribution Personnel (NICHSPDP), which sponsors the Certified Sterile Processing and Distribution Technician (CSPDT), Certified Sterile Processing and Distribution Supervisor (CSPDS), and Certified Sterile Processing and Distribution Manager (CSPDM) programs
- National Association of Radio and Telecommunications Engineers (NARTE), which sponsors the NARTE Certified Technician (NCT) and NARTE Certified Engineer (NCE) programs
- National Board for Respiratory Care (NBRC^{SM}), which sponsors the Registered Pulmonary Function Technologist (RPFT^{SM}) program
- National Institute of Automotive Service Excellence (ASE), which sponsors several automobile and truck technician certifications
- Professional Secretaries International, which sponsors the Certified Professional Secretary® (CPS®) program
- Society of Broadcast Engineers, Inc. (SBE), which sponsors these Certified programs: Professional Broadcast Engineer (CPBE); Broadcast Technologist (CBT); Broadcast Engineer Radio (CBRE); Broadcast Engineer TV (CBTE); Senior Broadcast Engineer Radio (CSRE); and Senior Broadcast Engineer TV (CSTE)

State/Local Licensing Boards

Many health, medical, real estate, insurance, and real estate certifications are recognized by state and local licensing boards. Many states may use certain voluntary certification examinations as part of a licensing process, especially in allied health fields. Other programs, especially curriculum-based certifications, may be recognized for continuing-education credit for regulated professions.

NATIONAL SKILLS STANDARDS

The United States is the only industrial nation without established, comprehensive skill standards for major occupations. Skill standards are sets of objective knowledge and performance requirements necessary to work within a broad section of an industry. Common standards allow skills to be portable: a worker certified in one setting or company can easily transfer to another. Several unsuccessful attempts were made by both industry and the government in the 1970s and 1980s to begin developing these standards.

The National Skills Standards Board, sponsored by the U.S. government, now brings together industry, labor groups, the U.S. Departments of Labor and Commerce, and educational institutions to form a coordinated effort towards developing and maintaining skill standards in this country. The skill standards define relevant skill clusters of major occupations that involve one or more industries and that share common skill requirements. Skill standards are competency-based, flexible, portable, and continuously updated and improved.

Established in 1994 by the Goals 2000: Educate America Act, the National Skills Standards Board serves as a catalyst to stimulate development and adoption of a voluntary national system of skill standards. The Board intends to create methods of assessing and certifying individuals meeting skill standards in a particular area. These standards will both form the basis of a workforce-skills enhancement strategy and facilitate the transition to high-performance work organizations.

The Goals 2000 Act defines a skill standard as "a standard that specifies the level of knowledge and competence required to successfully perform work-related functions within an occupational cluster." Skill standards recognize the development of high-performance work organizations focused on continuous improvement. Skill standards explicitly define the skills, knowledge, and abilities required by workers to support those workplace goals.

The National Skills Standards Board encourages and guides the creation and adoption of a national system of voluntary skill standards. The Board itself does not develop skill standards, but instead encourages the formation of industry-led voluntary partnerships to develop the skill standards. Participants include educational and professional organizations, corporations, unions, and government agencies.

Skill standards, as defined by the NSSB, must do the following:

1. Promote a highly flexible workforce by being based on broadly defined occupational categories within industries.
2. Respond to changing work organizations, technologies, and economy.
3. Use programs here and in other countries as benchmarks for a world-class level of industry performance.
4. Be free of any bias or discriminatory practice.
5. Be tied to assessable, competency-based outcomes.
6. Identify component reading, writing, and critical-thinking skills.
7. Be developed as a cooperative effort among all stakeholders, including labor, education, and business.
8. Be comparable with other industries, similar occupations, and geographic locations.
9. Use a structure readily understandable to users.
10. Provide tools to both qualify new hires and continuously upgrade employee skills.
11. Be applicable to a wide variety of work-based and school-based education and training service providers.
12. Be developed independent of any single training provider or type of training provider.

Benefits of Skill Standards

For employers, a standard set of skills for technical and entry-level workers provides guidelines for selection, hiring, and training.

For educational organizations, skill standards provide the basis for developing work-centered vocational curriculum. By following skills standards, publicly funded education and training programs are accountable by tying the achievement of specific, measurable performance outcomes to workplace requirements.

For individuals, skill standards can help provide access to high-skill, high-wage employment and career opportunities for those currently in, entering, or reentering the workforce.

Next Steps

Skill standards for the first 22 occupational clusters were completed at the end of 1995. The NSSB and the groups that developed these standards began building a support infrastructure for these standards in 1996. Educational curriculum, certifying bodies, and training standards will also be established. Organizations seeking to review or incorporate these standards, or to participate in ongoing acceptance and maintenance efforts, should contact the National Skills Standards Board at the following address or the coordinating organization for a particular occupational cluster.

National Skills Standards Board
1441 L St. NW
Washington, DC 20005
Phone: (202) 254-8628

Occupational Clusters

Advanced High-Performance Manufacturing

Organization
National Skill Standards Project for Advanced Manufacturing
National Coalition for Advanced Manufacturing (NACFAM)
1331 Pennsylvania Ave. NW, Suite 1410 North
Washington, DC 20004-1703

Agricultural Biotechnology

Organization
National FFA Center
5632 Mt. Vernon Memorial Highway
P.O. Box 15160
Alexandria, VA 22309-0160

Air Conditioning, Heating, and Refrigeration

Organization
Southern Association of Colleges and Schools
VTECS
1866 Southern Lane
Decatur, GA 30033-4097

Automobile, Autobody, Medium/Heavy Truck Technicians

Organization
National Automotive Technical Education Foundation (NATEF)
13505 Dulles Technology Drive
Herndon, VA 22071-3415

Bioscience

Organization
Education Development Center (EDC)
55 Chapel St.
Newton, MA 02158

Chemical Process Industries

Organization
American Chemical Society
1155 16th St. NW
Washington, DC 20016

Computer Aided Drafting and Design (CADD)

Organization
National Skill Standards Project for Advanced Manufacturing
National Coalition for Advanced Manufacturing (NACFAM)
1331 Pennsylvania Ave. NW, Suite 1410 North
Washington, DC 20004-1703

Electrical Construction

Organization
National Electrical Contractors Association
  (NECA)
3 Bethesda Metro Center, Suite 1100
Bethesda, MD 20814-5372

Electronics—AEA

Organization
American Electronics Association
5201 Great American Parkway
Box 54990
Santa Clara, CA 95054
Phone: (408) 987-4289

Electronics—EIF

Organization
Electronic Industries Foundation
919 18th St. NW
Washington, DC 20006

Grocery

Organization
Grocers Research and Education Foundation
1825 Samuel Morse Drive
Reston, VA 22090

Hazardous Materials Management Technology

Organization
Center for Occupational Research and
  Development (CORD)
601 Lake Air Drive
P.O. Box 21689
Waco, TX 76702-1689

Healthcare

Organization
National Consortium on Health Service and
  Technology Education
c/o WMU
1018A Trimpte Building
Kalamazoo, MI 49008

Heavy Highway/Construction and Environmental Remediation

Organization
Laborers—AGC Education and Training Fund
P.O. Box 37
37 Deerfield Road
Pomfret Center, CT 06259

Hospitality and Tourism

Organization
Council of Hotel, Restaurant, and Institutional
  Education (CHRIE)
1200 17th St. NW
Washington, DC 20036-3097
Phone: (202) 331-5990

Human Services

Organization
Human Services Research Institute
2335 Massachusetts Ave.
Cambridge, MA 02140

Industrial Laundry

Organization
Uniform and Textile Service Association
1730 M St. NW, Suite 610
Washington, DC 20036
Phone: (202) 938-5057

Machining/Metalworking

Organization
The Metalworking Industry Skills Standards
  Board
National Tool and Machining Association
9300 Livingston Road
Ft. Washington, MD 20744

Photonics

Organization
Center for Occupational Research and
  Development (CORD)
601 Lake Air Drive
Waco, TX 76710

Printing

Organization
Graphic Arts Technical Foundation (GATF)
4615 Forbes Ave.
Pittsburgh, PA 15213-3796

Retail Trade

Organization
National Retail Federation
710 Pennsylvania Ave. NW, Suite 710
Washington, DC 20004

Welding

Organization
American Welding Society
550 NW LeJeune Road
Miami, FL 33126

HOW TO USE THIS BOOK

Most program sponsors listed in this guidebook may be reached by mail, phone, fax, E-mail, or the Internet; each program description provides the specifics needed to contact the sponsor. The program information, based on questionnaire responses and other materials, is intended to give the reader a basic understanding of each certification. Most programs will send employers and prospective certificants more detailed information upon request.

To help you locate a particular certification, the Guide contains three separate listings:

- In the table of contents, certifications are organized by professional area and then keyword. If you are looking for various certifications within certain fields, check the table of contents first. For example, the Certified Compensation Professional (CCP) may be found under *Business and Management*, subheading *Human Resource Management*, and then keyword **Compensation** (underlined, as shown here).

- The index in Appendix A will help you locate a certification by designation. This index can help you identify a certification someone else is using that you may be unfamiliar with. The list is sorted alphabetically. For example, the Certified Compensation Professional would be found under *CCP*.

- The index in Appendix B will help you locate a certification based on keyword only. This is useful when you know exactly which field you are checking. The Certified Compensation Professional may be found under *Compensation Professional*.

You may find that the Guide does not list a particular certification that interests you. There may be any one of several reasons for the omission. Some certifications are inauthentic, actually membership or commercial gimmicks; such "certifications" are excluded from this book. Also excluded are small certification programs (those with less than 200 certificants in the past five years); dormant or discontinued programs; state licenses that are commonly mistaken for programs (usually these are found in environmental and real estate fields); and nontraditional health and specialized mental health/therapy certifications (whose inclusion was proscribed by conflicting state regulations and disagreement concerning national standards). A few sponsors and their programs were omitted because they did not wish to be listed, and others did not respond to requests for information.

The chances are, though, that you will find what you're looking for in this guidebook—accurate and complete information on certification programs that can help you to deal with changing workplace demands and to maintain a high measure of success in your professional life.

BUSINESS AND MANAGEMENT
Professional

CERTIFIED ARCHIVIST (C.A.)

Sponsor
Academy of Certified Archivists (ACA)
600 S. Federal St., Suite 504
Chicago, IL 60605
Phone: (312) 922-0140

Program Data
Certifying body: Independent board
Number certified: 850+
Organization members: 850+
Approximate certification costs: $275

Program Description
The Certified Archivist (C.A.) designation recognizes competence in archival management. Certification is based on passing an examination based on a role-delineation study.

Education/Experience
To sit for the examination, candidates must meet one of the following minimum professional education and experience requirements:

- Master's degree including or supplemented by nine semester hours of graduate archives administration study, and one year of qualifying professional experience
- Master's degree and two years of qualifying professional experience
- Bachelor's degree and three years of qualifying experience

Examinations
The examination is a 100-question, multiple-choice test developed by ACA and the Professional Testing Service. The test covers the entire scope of archival practice, such as papers, manuscripts, organizational and institutional records, and text, electronic, and photographic media. The specific examination areas are document selection; arrangement and description of documents; reference services and access to documents; preservation and protection of documents; outreach and promotion of documentary collections; program planning and assessment; and professional, ethical, and legal responsibility.

Recertification
Recertification is required every five years, and can be accomplished through retaking the examination or through professional development.

CERTIFIED, AUCTIONEER'S INSTITUTE (CAI®)

Sponsor
Auction Marketing Institute (AMI)
8880 Ballentine
Overland Park, KS 66214
Phone: (913) 541-8115
Fax: (913) 894-5281
E-mail: ami@netis.com
WWW: http://www.auctionweb.com/ami/

AMI publishes a directory of all CAI members.

Program Data
The CAI program is conducted in cooperation with the National Auctioneers Association (NAA) and Indiana University. AMI programs are accepted for continuing education credit by many state and local licensing boards.

Certifying body: Nonprofit professional education organization
Year certification began: 1978
Number certified: 1000
Organization members: 1000; CAIs automatically become members of the Institute.
Additional certifications: Accredited Auctioneer Real Estate (AARE); Graduate Personal Property Appraiser (GPPA)
Approximate certification costs: $2500

Program Description
The CAI designation is awarded to auctioneers who complete the Institute program held at Indiana University-Bloomington. Auctioneers attend a one-week program once a year for three years. Certification is based on meeting experiential requirements and completing all Institute coursework. A candidate must be a member of the NAA and meet any applicable state-licensing requirements. AMI has an active ethics board with decertification powers.

Education/Experience

To become a candidate, an auctioneer must have two years of full-time experience, be over the age of 21, and have a high school diploma. To receive the CAI designation, candidates must complete the three one-week sessions and submit an acceptable auction-summary report.

The CAI courses cover marketing and public relations, ethics, liquidations, and selling personal property and residential, agricultural, and commercial real estate. The courses are designed to help auctioneers in building skills and successful practices.

Examinations

The CAI courses include comprehensive examinations on the curriculum content. Exams are created by qualified instructors for the Institute.

Recertification

CAIs must maintain NAA membership and earn 24 hours of related continuing education every three years.

CHILD DEVELOPMENT ASSOCIATE (CDA)

Sponsor

The Council for Early Childhood Professional
  Recognition (CECPR)
1341 G St. NW, Suite 400
Washington, DC 20005
Phone: (800) 424-4310
Fax: (202) 265-9161

Program Data

The CDA program began with a federal government initiative in 1971. The Administration for Children, Youth, and Families subsidizes a portion of the program. The CDA credential is listed in child-care regulations in 46 states and DC as a teaching-staff or director qualification.

Certifying body: Independent credentialing
  organization
Year credentialing began: 1975
Number credentialed: 69,000
Approximate credentialing costs: $325,
  direct assessment; $1500 for P3

Program Description

The Child Development Associate (CDA) credential represents a unique collaboration between the federal government, which funds a portion of the program through grants, and child-care professionals. Holders of the CDA credential have met competency standards in six areas of early childhood education. CDAs work as caregivers and program directors in center-based, home visitor, and family day-care programs. CDAs are endorsed in center-based preschool, center-based infant/toddler, family day-care, or home visitor. CDAs may also receive a Spanish/English bilingual specialization.

Education/Experience

There are two ways to earn the CDA credential. Through direct assessment, a candidate can demonstrate current skills and knowledge. Candidates must be 18 or older, have a high school diploma, show 480 hours of experience, and have 120 hours of formal child-care education or training in 10 specific areas. Eligible candidates receive a formal observation of performance. A candidate prepares a resource file and provides questionnaires to parents with children under the candidate's care.

Curriculum

Candidates with insufficient education or experience may enter the CDA Professional Preparation Program (P3). Candidates over 18 and holding a high school diploma complete a one-year training program. The program consist of 480 hours of fieldwork and 120 hours of coursework. The program includes fieldwork with readings and exercises, coursework, and a final evaluation. Candidates then must complete an assessment similar to the direct assessment program.

Examinations

Candidates undergoing direct assessment must complete an oral interview and a two-hour multiple-choice examination. Candidates in the preparation program receive continued feedback prior to the final evaluation.

Recertification

Credential must be renewed every five years.

CERTIFIED CUSTOMER SERVICE SPECIALIST (CSS)

Sponsor

Electronics Technicians Association, International
  (ETA)
602 N. Jackson St
Greencastle, IN 46135
Phone: (317) 653-8262

Program Data

Certifying body: Association
Year certification began: 1966 (ETA certifications)
Number certified: 30,000 (all certifications)
Organization members: 1700
Additional programs: Certified Electronics Technician (CET); Certified Satellite Installer (CSI)
Approximate certification costs: $30

Program Description

The Certified Customer Service Specialist (CSS) designation recognizes frontline electronics technicians, electronics sales and marketing representatives, electronics support staff, and electronics technology consultants. This program ensures that sales, marketing, and other customer-contact technical staff are literate in electronics technology and knowledgeable in customer service skills. There are no membership or education requirements. Certification is based on passing an examination.

Examinations

The CSS examination covers basic electronics technology and customer support skills.

Recertification

None required.

CERTIFIED DISASTER RECOVERY PLANNER (CDRP)

ASSOCIATE DISASTER RECOVERY PLANNER (ADRP)

CERTIFIED MASTER DISASTER RECOVERY PLANNER (CMDRP)

Sponsor

Disaster Recovery Institute (DRI)
1810 Craig Road, Suite 125
St. Louis, MO 63146
Phone: (314) 434-2272
Fax : (314) 434-1260
WWW: http://www.dr.org/

Program Data

DRI has alliances with the Washington University in St. Louis, the University of Texas at Arlington, and the Canadian Centre for Emergency Preparedness.

Certifying body: Association
Year certification began: 1989

Program Description

The Disaster Recovery Institute's certification program recognizes planners skilled in business continuity and disaster recovery. Certification is based on examinations and experience validation. There are no membership requirements. DRI offers several educational and preparatory courses.

Education/Experience

Certified Disaster Recovery Planner (CDRP) candidates must have two years of experience as business continuity/disaster recovery planners and have two references that verify practical experience in at least three areas within the DRI common body of knowledge.

Candidates not meeting the CDRP requirements may, upon passing the examination, be awarded the Associate Disaster Recovery Planner (ADRP) designation.

Certified Master Disaster Recovery Planner (CMDRP) candidates must have five years of experience as business continuity/disaster recovery planners and have two references that verify practical experience in all areas within the DRI common body of knowledge.

Examinations

The DRI examination is based on the common body of knowledge. The exam covers project initiation and management; risk evaluation and control; business impact analysis; developing recovery strategies; emergency response; developing and implementing the plan; corporate awareness programs and training; testing and exercising the plan; and maintaining and updating the plan.

CERTIFIED ECONOMIC DEVELOPER® (CED®)

Sponsor

American Economic Development Council (AEDC)
9801 W. Higgins Road, Suite 540
Rosemont, IL 60018
Phone: (708) 692-9944
E-mail: aedc@interaccess.com
WWW: http://www.openweb.com/hqtrs/

Program Data

Certifying body: Association
Year certification began: 1971
Number certified: 623
Organization members: 2500
Approximate certification costs: $240 (members), $400 (nonmembers)

Program Description

The Certified Economic Developer® (CED®) recognizes professionals employed in a wide range of economic development activities. The field includes economic, industrial, and chambers of commerce executives, community and industrial planners and developers, bankers, and government officials. Certification is based on passing three examinations. There are no membership requirements.

Education/Experience

Eligibility to take the examination is determined using a point system. Candidates must have five years of full-time experience (five points) and earn an additional three points through experience, education, or AEDC membership.

Examinations

The CED requires passing three examinations: one essay, one short answer, and one oral. Exams are based on a task analysis. A study guide is provided to all candidates. The essay examination requires candidates to answer three essays selected from situations in different areas of economic development.

The short-answer test, which will include objective and fill-in questions, will cover financing; government regulations; industrial development theory; labor; land use and planning; marketing and prospect handling; organizations and leadership; real estate and site selection; research; and transportation.

The oral examination will evaluate both the ability to communicate and the depth of the candidate's practical knowledge.

Recertification

Recertification is required every three years through professional education.

CERTIFIED ELECTRONIC IMAGER (CEI)

Sponsor

Professional Photographers of America (PPA)
57 Forsyth St. NW, Suite 1600
Atlanta, GA 30303
Phone: (800) 786-6277
E-mail: 76231.2451@compuserve.com
WWW: http://www.ppa-world.org/

Program Data

Certifying body: Association
Additional certifications: Certified Professional Photographer (CPP)

Program Description

The Certified Electronic Imager (CEI) recognizes professional videographers whose work is judged to meet professional standards. Certification is based on a portfolio and passing a certification examination. Membership in PPA is required. Certification may be based on either business or consumer work.

Education/Experience

Candidates must be professionals available for assignment on a first-come, first-serve basis. Candidates must have either two years of professional experience or one year of experience and 60 college or photography-school semester hours. In addition, CEIs may receive qualification in a wide range of commercial, industrial, wedding/event, and computer-graphics classifications.

Candidates must submit a portfolio of four commercial assignments of no less than 30 seconds apiece.

Examinations

The two-hour, multiple-choice examination is designed to measure a candidate's knowledge of theory, composition, technique, terms, and business practices.

Recertification

CEIs must recertify every five years. Recertification is based on professional education and continued work. Candidates must accumulate 10 days of acceptable continuing education and submit a portfolio of work completed during the current certification cycle.

CERTIFIED PROFESSIONAL ESTIMATOR (CPE)

Sponsor

American Society of Professional Estimators
(ASPE)
11141 Georgia Ave., Suite 412
Wheaton, MD 20902
Phone: (301) 929-8848
E-mail: aspe@gate.vegas.com

Program Data

Certifying body: Association

Program Description

The Certified Professional Estimator (CPE) designation recognizes experienced construction estimators. Membership in ASPE is required. Certification is based on an examination and a technical paper.

Education/Experience

In order to sit for the CPE examination, a candidate must first have five years of professional experience. The technical paper must be submitted prior to taking the examination. A mandatory certification workshop is offered nationwide.

Examinations

The certification examination measures the candidate's knowledge of contract terms and conditions, cost calculations and reporting, ethics, and other areas critical to the estimating profession. The examination is based, in part, on the *ASPE Standard Estimating Practice Manual.*

Recertification

CPEs must recertify every three years. Recertification is based on continuing education and ASPE involvement.

CERTIFIED COST ESTIMATOR/ANALYST (CCEA)

Sponsor

Society of Cost Estimating and Analysis (SCEA)
101 S. Whiting St., Suite 201
Alexandria, VA 22304
Phone: (703) 751-8069

Program Data

Certifying body: Association
Year certification began: 1982
Number certified: 2175
Organization members: 825
Approximate certification costs: $85

Program Description

The Certified Cost Estimator/Analyst (CCEA) designation recognizes knowledgeable costing professionals with diverse backgrounds. CCEAs may work in fields such as cost analysis, estimating, budgeting, financial management, cost control, and value engineering. Certification is based on passing an examination. Membership in SCEA is not required. SCEA maintains an active ethics program.

Education/Experience

To qualify to sit for the examination, a candidate must meet one of these three requirements:

- Bachelor's degree or higher in a cost-estimating/related field or with 10 courses from the SCEA list, and two years of experience
- Associate's degree and five years of related experience
- Seven years of related experience

Examinations

The two-part examination is based on the Society's cost-analysis standard body of knowledge. Study guides, self-study materials, workshops, and preparatory classes are available. The first part is a 100-question, multiple-choice test covering general cost-estimating knowledge. This includes quantitative skills, contracting, cost estimating and analysis, procurement, and general management.

Due to the wide range of experiences and backgrounds professionals bring to cost estimating, the candidate chooses the second part of the exam from two specialty areas: cost estimating and cost analysis. Each option is a 50-question, multiple-choice test.

Recertification

CCEAs must recertify every five years. Recertification can be completed by either passing another examination or by accumulating points based on education, experience, and association participation. The current recertification rate is 26%.

CERTIFIED FORM SYSTEMS PROFESSIONAL (CFSP)

Sponsor

Business Forms Management Association
 (BFMA)
319 SW Washington St., Suite 710
Portland, OR 97204
Phone: (503) 227-3393
Fax: (503) 274-7667
E-mail: bfma@bfma.org
WWW: http://www.teleport.com/~bfma/

Program Data

Certifying body: Association-sponsored
 independent board
Year certification began: 1996
Number certified: New program
Organization members: 1200
Approximate certification costs: $285 (members),
 $395 (nonmembers)

Program Description

The Certified Form Systems Professional (CFSP)
designation recognizes individuals skilled in applying and integrating form systems. Candidates must
be familiar with both electronic and paper-based
systems. BFMA membership is not required.

Education/Experience

Candidates need to be proficient with electronic-
forms-design software and have five years of
forms-systems experience.

Examinations

The 250-question, multiple-choice examination
is administered by the Professional Testing Service
and covers process/workflow analysis, design and
development, manufacturing and technologies
principles, and forms management. Study groups
and reference materials are available.

Recertification

CFSPs must recertify every seven years. Recertification requirements are under discussion.

CERTIFIED FORMS CONSULTANT (CFC)

Sponsor

Document Management Industries Association
 (DMIA)
433 East Monroe Ave.
Alexandria, VA 22301
Phone: (703) 836-6225
Fax: (703) 836-2241
WWW: http://www.dmia.com/

Program Data

Certifying body: Association
Approximate certification costs: $250

Program Description

The Certified Forms Consultant (CFC) program
recognizes professionals involved with developing,
evaluating, and managing business forms and
systems. Certification is based on passing an
examination. There are no membership requirements.

Education/Experience

Candidates must have two or more years of
experience. Experience may be in one or several
areas, including forms control or management, and
forms development, marketing, or distribution.

Examinations

The DMIA has an extensive series of materials on
forms and form management, and recommends
their use in preparing for the CFC examination.
This includes the CFC Study Kit, three home-study
courses, the 12-volume Product Knowledge Series,
and a slide set. The CFC exam is comprised of
250 multiple-choice questions divided into five
sections:

- Business Forms Production and Materials
- Forms Design and Construction
- Business Systems
- Procedures, Products, and Technology
- Production and Packaging

Recertification

None.

CERTIFIED HOME ECONOMIST (CHE)

Sponsor

American Home Economics Association (AHEA)
1555 King St.
Alexandria, VA 22314
Phone: (703) 706-4600

Program Data

Certifying body: Association
Number certified: 8600+
Approximate certification costs: $150 (members),
$200 (nonmembers)

Program Description

The Certified Home Economist (CHE) designation recognizes home economics professionals working in any area of the field. Certification is based on passing an examination. Membership in AHEA is not required.

Education/Experience

Candidates must have either a bachelor's degree in home economics (or a related field), or a bachelor's degree in any field and two years of professional experience.

Examinations

Examinations are given through PLATO testing centers. The 150-question, multiple-choice examination covers the following areas: lifespan human development; the family system; family resource management; nutrition; impact of apparel and textiles; professional roles; and technology and the impact of change.

Recertification

CHEs must renew their certification every three years. Recertification is based on a point system. CHEs must accumulate 75 points. Examples: 1 point per professional workshop contact hour, 1 point per week of internship, 15 points per college semester hour beyond qualifying degree.

CERTIFIED INTERIOR DESIGNER (NCIDQ CERTIFIED)

Sponsor

National Council for Interior Design Qualification (NCIDQ)
50 Main St.
White Plains, NY 10606
Phone: (914) 948-9100

Program Data

The Council's members are the American Society of Interior Designers (ASID); Council of Federal Interior Designers (CFID); Institute of Business Designers (IBD); Institute of Store Planners (ISP); Interior Design Educators Council (IDEC); Interior Designers of Canada (IDC); and International Society of Interior Design (ISID). Many states and Canadian provinces use this program as part of their licensing or registration program for interior designers.

Certifying body: Association-sponsored
independent board
Number certified: 8000+
Approximate certification costs: $450

Program Description

The NCIDQ is the most widely recognized interior design certification in the country. Certification is based on passing the six-part examination. Candidates must meet the program's minimum education and experience requirements to take the examinations. There are no professional membership requirements.

Education/Experience

To be eligible for the exam, a candidate must meet one of the following requirements:

- Bachelor's degree (or equivalent) in interior design and two years of professional experience

- Three-year (or equivalent) certificate in interior design and three years of professional experience

- Two-year (or equivalent) certificate in interior design and four years of professional experience

Examinations

The six-part examinations are offered over the course of one weekend; they do not need to be attempted or passed at the same time. Candidates have five years to pass all examinations. The exam has a 75% pass rate. Hale Associates (Chicago) assists in test development. The exam questions are based on an extensive, independent job analysis performed by the Educational Testing Service (ETS). The exam parts and their contents are as follows:

- Identification and Application—a three-hour multiple-choice test

- Building and Barrier Free Codes—a 90-minute, multiple-choice test on building code concepts and their effects on public health and safety

- Problem-Solving—a 90-minute, multiple-choice exam requiring the candidate to review drawings and provide answers to a scenario

- Programming—a two-hour test consisting of two exercises, one on conducting a client interview and the other on creating a bubble diagram/schematic

- Three-Dimensional Exercise—a 90-minute test on applying interior design theory to a three-dimensional volume

- Project Scenario—a 90-minute test requiring the analysis of a written project scenario and its conversion into a space plan

Recertification

None. Some constituent members' states/provinces may require re-examination or continuing education independent of the NCIDQ.

CERTIFIED PROFESSIONAL MANUFACTURERS REPRESENTATIVE (CPMR)

CERTIFIED PROFESSIONAL FOOD BROKER (CPFB)

Sponsor

Manufacturers' Representatives Educational
  Research Foundation (MRERF)
P.O. Box 247
Geneva, IL 60134
Phone: (708) 208-1466
Fax: (708) 208-1475
WWW: http://www.era.org/pages/mrerf.htm

Program Data

Certifying body: Board created from a consortium of associations
Year certification began: 1989
Number certified: 400
Approximate certification costs: $1000

Program Description

The Certified Professional Manufacturers Representative (CPMR) and Certified Professional Food Broker (CPFB) designations recognize experienced representatives and brokers who have completed the three-level course of study. The designation awarded depends on the candidate's field; the classes are the same for both.

Education/Experience

To enter the program, a candidate have a high school diploma, be 25 or older, and have five years of professional experience in the field.

Curriculum

The required classes are presented at Indiana University and Arizona State University by industry experts and college instructors. Each in-residence level is 24 hours (one week), and ends with a four-hour examination. The courses are as follows:

Level 1/First Year—Building Professional Success; Preparing Effective Sales Presentations; Synergistic Selling; Successful Sales Formula; Developing the Sales Image of the Company; Effective Supplier Relationships; Measuring Product Line Profitability; Productivity Planning; Issues in Managing the Small Enterprise; and Listening Skills

Level 2/Second Year—Developing the Company's Resources; Managing the Entrepreneurial Enterprise; Developing and Managing New Principal Relationships; Building Your Customer Base; Developing Personal Communications Skills; Managing Yourself and Others; Developing a Sales Force; Team Building; Legal Concerns; and Listening Skills

Level 3/Third Year—Future Planning; Strategic Planning; Developing a Strategic Management Plan; Implementing Change; Strategic Marketing; Strategic Financial Planning; Developing a Succession Plan; and Taxes

Recertification

Under development.

CERTIFIED PROFESSIONAL PHOTOGRAPHER (CPP)

Sponsor

Professional Photographers of America (PPA)
57 Forsyth St. NW, Suite 1600
Atlanta, GA 30303
Phone: (800) 786-6277
E-mail: 76231.2451@compuserve.com
WWW: http://www.ppa-world.org/

Program Data

Certifying body: Association.
Additional certifications: Certified Electronic
  Imager (CEI)

Program Description

The Certified Professional Photographer (CPP)
recognizes photographers whose work is judged to
meet professional standards. Certification is based
on a portfolio and passing a certification examination. Membership in PPA is required. Certification may be based on either business or
consumer work.

Education/Experience

Candidates must be a professional available for
assignment on a first-come, first-serve basis.
Candidates must have either two years of professional experience or one year of experience and
60 college or photography-school semester hours.
After certification, CPPs may receive qualification in
a wide range of commercial, industrial, portrait, and
wedding classifications.

Candidates must submit a portfolio of 10 prints or
transparencies from 10 different job assignments
for evaluation.

Examinations

The two-hour, multiple-choice examination is
designed to measure a candidate's knowledge of
photography theory, composition, technique, terms,
and business practices.

Recertification

CPPs must recertify every five years. Recertification
is based on professional education and continued
work. Candidates must accumulate 10 days of
acceptable continuing education, and submit a
portfolio of work completed during the current
certification cycle.

CERTIFIED PLANNER (CP)

Sponsor

American Institute of Certified Planners (AICP)
1776 Massachusetts Ave. NW
Washington, DC 20036
Phone: (202) 872-0611
Fax: (202) 872-0643
WWW: http://www.planning.org/abtaicp/
  abtaicp.html

Program Data

The AICP is the certifying arm of the American
Planning Association (APA).

Certifying body: Association
Year certification began: 1968
Number certified: 9500
Organization members: 21,000
Approximate certification costs: $70–$115

Program Description

The Certified Planner designation recognizes APA
members experienced in analyzing, planning, and
influencing decisions concerning zoning, transportation, and land use; housing; capital improve-
ments; environmental protection; and economic
development. The AICP maintains an active ethics
program.

Education/Experience

To sit for the AICP examination APA members
must be currently employed in an acceptable
planning role and meet one of the following
requirements:

- Eight years of planning experience
- Four years of planning experience and a
  bachelor's degree
- Three years of planning experience and an
  AICP-recognized bachelor's degree in
  planning
- Two years of planning experience and an
  AICP-recognized graduate degree in
  planning

Examinations

The AICP examination is a 150-question, multiple-
choice test administered by the Educational Testing
Service (ETS). The current pass rate is 73%. The
exam covers these areas:

- Planning history, theory, and law
- Planning futures
- Plan-making methods, strategies, and
  techniques

- Functional topics, including land use, environment, public services, transportation, and urban design
- Plan implementation, including zoning, budgets, review functions, and intergovernmental relations
- Public interest, social justice, and AICP code of ethics

Recertification

None beyond maintaining AICP membership. The AICP has a voluntary Continuing Professional Development Program (CPDP) recognizing 60 contact hours of professional education over three years.

CERTIFIED QUALITY AUDITOR (CQA)

Sponsor

American Society for Quality Control (ASQC)
611 E. Wisconsin Ave.
Milwaukee, WI 53201
Phone: (800) 248-1946
Fax: (414) 272-1734
WWW: http://www.asqc.org/educat/cert.html

Program Data

Certifying body: Association
Year certification began: 1966 (first program)
Number certified: 50,000 (all programs)
Organization members: 130,000
Additional programs: Certified Mechanical Inspector (CMI); Certified Quality Engineer (CQE); Certified Quality Manager (CQM); Certified Quality Technician (CQT); Certified Reliability Engineer (CRE)

Program Description

The Certified Quality Auditor (CQA) designation recognizes individuals knowledgeable and proficient in determining quality systems adequacy and the principles and techniques of quality auditing. Certification is based on passing an examination. ASQC maintains an active ethics program. Candidates must demonstrate professionalism by holding any of the following:

- Professional Engineer (P.E.) registration
- ASQC (or foreign affiliate society) membership

- Membership in a society belonging to the American Association of Engineering Societies or the Accreditation Board for Engineering and Technology

Education/Experience

Candidates must have eight years of combined education and experience in at least one area of the CQA body of knowledge. At least three years must be in a decision-making technical, professional, or management position. An associate equals two years of experience, a bachelor's equals four years of experience, and a master's equals five years of experience.

Examinations

The 155-question, multiple-choice examination is based on the CQA body of knowledge and covers general knowledge, ethics, and audit administration; audit preparation; audit performance; audit reporting, corrective action, follow-up, and closure; and auditing tools and techniques.

CERTIFIED PROFESSIONAL SECRETARY® (CPS®)

Sponsor

Professional Secretaries International®
10502 NW Ambassador Drive
P.O. Box 20404
Kansas City, MO 64195-0404
Phone: (816) 891-6600
Fax: (816) 891-9118
E-mail: cps@psi.org
WWW: http://www.gvi.net/psi/

Program Data

The American Council on Education (ACE) recommends 32 semester hours for program completion.

Certifying body: Association
Year certification began: 1951
Number certified: 47,713
Organization members: 27,000
Approximate certification costs: $135

Program Description

The Certified Professional Secretary® (CPS®) designation recognizes experienced secretarial and administrative support professionals who complete the PSI's testing program. Certification is based on passing the three-part CPS examination.

Education/Experience

No experience is required to take the examination, but prior to certification a candidate must meet one of the following requirements:

- Two years of secretarial experience and a bachelor's degree
- Three years of experience and an associate's degree
- Four years of acceptable secretarial experience

Examinations

The multiple-choice CPS exam is divided into three parts, which may be taken separately or together.

Part 1—Finance and Business Law, including accounting, business law, and economics

Part 2—Office Systems and Administration, including business communications, office administration, and office technology

Part 3—Management, including behavioral science in business, human resource management, and organizations and management

Preparatory seminars are available.

Recertification

Those who applied on or after January 1, 1988 must recertify on a five-year cycle. Recertification is based on a point system. 120 points are needed to recertify.

CERTIFIED SPEAKING PROFESSIONAL (CSP)

Sponsor

National Speakers Association (NSA)
1500 S. Priest Drive
Tempe, AZ 85281
Phone: (602) 968-2552
Fax: (602) 968-0911

Program Data

Certifying body: Association
Year certification began: 1980
Number certified: 273
Organization members: 8554
Approximate certification costs: $225

Program Description

The Certified Speaking Professional (CSP) designation recognizes individuals who have a proven record as a professional speaker. Membership in the National Speakers Association (NSA) is mandatory. The CSP program is based on experience and endorsements; there is no examination requirement.

Education/Experience

Candidates document professional speaking experience and education from five of the previous six years. To receive the CSP designation, a candidate must meet the following requirements:

- Association membership—A candidate must have been a member of NSA for the previous three years.
- Clients—A candidate must have served at least 100 different clients (a special formula is available to speakers with substantial numbers of repeat clients).
- Presentations—A candidate must have given 250 fee-paid presentations with a minimum average gross speaking income of $50,000 per year.
- Testimonials—A candidate must provide testimonial letters from at least 20 separate clients.
- Professional education—Candidates must earn 32 credits of NSA professional education. Points are awarded as follows:
  - 8 credits per NSA convention
  - 4 credits per full registrant at NSA workshop, conference, or lab
  - 2 credits per day at NSA workshop, conference, or lab
  - 1 credit per year NSA chapter membership (maximum of 4)

Recertification

CPSs must renew certification every five years. Recertification is based on credits. In addition to the credits awarded for professional education (see above), CSPs may earn the following credits towards recertification:

- 1 credit per chapter presentation
- 1 credit per two NSA audio- or videotapes (maximum of eight credits)

ACCREDITED TRANSLATOR (ATA ACCREDITATION)

Sponsor

American Translators Association (ATA)
1800 Diagonal Road, Suite 220
Alexandria, VA 22314
Phone: (703) 683-6100
Fax: (703) 683-6122
E-mail: 73564,2032@compuserve.com
WWW: http://humanities.byu.edu/trg/
  ata/atahome.htm

Program Data

Certifying body: Association
Number certified: 1600
Organization members: 5500
Approximate certification costs: $100

Program Description

The ATA accredits a translator's competence to translate written material from one language into another. Accreditation is based on passing a proctored examination. Each accreditation is for a specific language and direction, either into that language from English, or into English from that language. Translators may be accredited in one or both directions. Language accreditation is in Arabic (into English only), Dutch, Finnish, French, German, Italian, Japanese, Polish, Portuguese, Russian, and Spanish. Membership in the ATA is required. A practice test program is offered and recommended by the ATA.

Examinations

The candidate is given five short written passages that cover five areas: general, literary, legal/commercial, scientific/medical, and semi-technical. Either two or three passages may be attempted, but two must be translated correctly for accreditation. The three-hour examination tests translation techniques and the ability to successfully translate meaning and intent.

Recertification

None.

CERTIFIED VALUE SPECIALIST (CVS) ASSOCIATE VALUE SPECIALIST (AVS) VALUE METHODOLOGY PRACTITIONER (VMP)

Sponsor

Society of American Value Engineers (SAVE)
60 Revere Drive, Suite 500
Northbrook, IL 60062
Phone: (847) 480-1730
Fax: (847) 480-9282
E-mail: 75321.223@compuserve.com
WWW: http://www.value-eng.com/

Program Data

Certifying body: Association

Program Description

The three certifications offered by the Society of American Value Engineers (SAVE) recognize professionals qualified to analyze the functions of a program, project, system, product, piece of equipment, building, facility, service; or to supply and improve performance, reliability, quality, safety, and life-cycle costs. SAVE membership is not required. SAVE offers extensive educational resources to candidates.

The Certified Value Specialist (CVS) designation recognizes experienced value-engineering practitioners.

The Associate Value Specialist (AVS) designation recognizes knowledgeable value-engineering practitioners with limited work experience.

The Value Methodology Practitioner (VMP) designation recognizes professionals who have gained experience in value-engineering methodology while primarily working in another field.

Education/Experience

CVS candidates must document at least two years of related experience.

AVS and VMP candidates must have minimal experience and document related value-engineering studies.

Curriculum

All candidates must complete a basic workshop approved by the SAVE certification board. The workshop is 20 hours of training and 20 hours of live project application and includes:

- Cost
- Creativity
- Evaluation/Implementation
- Function
- History, definitions, and job plans
- People-oriented topics

CVS candidates also must complete an advanced, 24-hour workshop covering:

- Administration
- Creativity
- Financial evaluation
- Function analysis
- Interpersonal skills
- Job plans
- Overview
- Project/Team structure
- Value management

Examinations

CVS candidates must complete a paper on a value-related subject and pass the CVS examination.

AVS and VMP candidates must pass a value theory examination.

Recertification

CVSs and VMPs must recertify every four years. The AVS designation is good for four years and cannot be renewed.

BUSINESS AND MANAGEMENT
Accounting and Finance

ACCREDITED IN ACCOUNTANCY/ ACCREDITED BUSINESS ACCOUNTANT^{SM}

Sponsor

Accreditation Council for Accountancy and
    Taxation^{SM} (ACAT)
1010 N. Fairfax St.
Alexandria, VA 22314
Phone: (703) 549-2228
WWW: http://www.nspa.org/act.html

Program Data

ACAT is affiliated with the National Society of Public Accountants (NSPA) and the National Endowment for Financial Education.

Certifying body: Association-sponsored
    independent board
Year certification began: 1973
Additional certifications: Accredited Tax
    Advisor^{SM}; Accredited Tax Preparer^{SM}

Program Description

The Accredited in Accountancy program recognizes individuals who provide accounting services to small businesses. In most states, the accreditation does not allow practitioners to certify audits. Accreditation is based on passing an examination. There are no membership or experience requirements.

Examinations

The six-hour accreditation examination covers the full range of financial and managerial accounting. NSPA offers a 40-hour preparatory correspondence course.

Recertification

Accreditation must be renewed every three years by accumulating 80 hours of professional education.

CERTIFIED CASH MANAGER (CCM)

Sponsor

Treasury Management Association (TMA)
7315 Wisconsin Ave., Suite 1250 West
Bethesda, MD 20814
Phone: (301) 907-2862
Fax: (301) 907-2864
E-mail: tma@tma-net.org
WWW: http://www.webplus.net/treasury/
    index.html

Program Data

Certifying body: Association
Number certified: 7000
Organization members: 9000+
Approximate certification costs: $406 (members),
    $596 (nonmembers)

Program Description

The Certified Cash Manager (CCM) designation recognizes professionals experienced in corporate cash management, including corporate finance officers, bankers (cash management department), and consultants to the cash management industry. Membership in the Treasury Management Association is not required. Candidates must meet one of the following requirements to take the CCM examination.

- Two years in a cash management-related position
- One year in a cash management position and an advanced business degree
- One year in a cash management position and two years teaching a related subject full time at a college/university
- Two years of teaching a related subject full time at a college/university and an advanced business degree
- Four years of teaching a related subject full time at a college/university

Finance and business majors may take the CCM exam after completing an approved curriculum in cash management. Passing the CCM exam awards students the CCM Associate designation. The CCM designation will be awarded upon completion of experience and education requirements.

Examination

The CCM examination is a four-hour, 200-question, multiple-choice test. The exam is administered by the Educational Testing Service (ETS), Princeton, NJ. The study guide for the exam is *The Essentials of Cash Management* (5th ed.), produced by the TMA. TMA sponsors exam-preparation materials and study groups. The examination covers:

- Accounts receivable/Credit management
- The banking system
- Bank relationship management
- Borrowing
- Cash concentration
- Collections
- Corporate financial function
- Disbursements
- Forecasting cash flows
- Foreign exchange
- Information management
- Interest rate management
- International cash management
- Investments
- The payment system

Recertification

CCMs must recertify every three years by earning 36 CCM renewal credits. Credits may be earned through formal and continuing education, association participation, independent study, and retaking the CCM exam.

CHARTERED ACCOUNTANT (C.A.)

Sponsor

Association of Chartered Accountants in the United States (ACAUS)
666 Fifth Ave., Suite 350
New York, NY 10103
Phone: (212) 713-5724
WWW: http://ourworld.compuserve.com/homepages/acaus/

Program Data

Number certified: 5000 (U.S.)

Program Description

The ACAUS represents the interests of accountants working in the United States and chartered by the following: Australian Institute of Chartered Accountants; Canadian Institute of Chartered Accountants; Institute of Chartered Accountants in England and Wales; Institute of Chartered Accountants in Ireland; Institute of Chartered Accountants of Scotland; New Zealand Institute of Chartered Accountants; and the South African Institute of Chartered Accountants.

C.A.s have expertise in both their own institute's country and in international accounting. Approximately 5000 C.A.s are currently based in the United States.

Education/Experience

The C.A. designation has criteria similar to the CPA educational and testing requirements.

CERTIFIED INTERNATIONAL FINANCIER (CIF)

Sponsor

International Society of Financiers (ISF)
P.O. Box 18508
Asheville, NC 28814
WWW: http://www.inet-serv.com/~isf/index.html#home

Program Data

Certifying body: Association
Year certification began: 1979

Program Description

The Certified International Financiers (CIF) designation recognizes members of the International Society of Financiers (ISF). Members must be professionally employed in managing major domestic or international transactions. Areas of expertise include real estate, commodities, syndication, offshore fund, trades, equipment, and finance. Membership is based on experience. There are no examination requirements. ISF maintains an active ethics program.

Education/Experience

Candidates must pass a screening process, which includes a review of professional activities, scope of responsibilities, and professional referrals. Those individuals passing this screen are accepted into ISF and awarded the CIF designation.

Recertification

None.

CERTIFIED FRAUD EXAMINER (CFE)

Sponsor

National Association of Certified Fraud Examiners
  (NACFE)
716 West Ave.
Austin, TX 78701
Phone: (800) 245-3321
Fax: (512) 478-9297

Program Data

Certifying body: Professional association
Number certified: 7000+
Organization members: 7000+
Approximate certification costs: $150–$200

Program Description

The Certified Fraud Examiner (CFE) designation recognizes experts in fraud and white-collar crime who are qualified to perform fraud examinations and forensic accounting. The average CFE has conducted 100 investigations. A CFE investigates fraud allegations, and assists in detecting and preventing fraud. Membership in NACFE is required. Certification is based on passing an examination.

Education/Experience

Candidates must have two years of experience in the field. Experience, if in the area of fraud and white-collar crime, may include academic/research, auditing and accounting, criminology and sociology, crime investigation, and loss prevention.

Examination

Candidates certifying through taking the Uniform CFE Examination receive a computer disk containing the examination. Candidates have 30 days to complete the 500-question, multiple-choice examination. A self-study course is available. The examination is divided into four sections:

- Financial Transactions
- Investigation
- Legal Elements of Fraud
- Criminology and Ethics

Candidates must pass all four sections. The pass rate is about 26% for all four section on the first attempt.

Recertification

Certification is maintained by accumulating 20 hours annually or 60 hours over three years of continuing education. Fifty percent must be fraud-related.

CERTIFIED HOSPITALITY ACCOUNTANT EXECUTIVE (CHAE)

Sponsor

International Association of Hospitality
  Accountants (IAHA)
9171 Capital of Texas Highway, Suite H-350
P.O. Box 203008
Austin, TX 78720
Phone: (512) 346-5680
Fax: (512) 346-5760
E-mail: iaha@iaha.org
WWW: http://www.iaha.org/

Program Data

Certifying body: Association
Year certification began: 1981
Number certified: 600+
Organization members: 3000
Approximate certification costs: $125 (members),
  $225 (nonmembers)

Program Description

The Certified Hospitality Accountant Executive (CHAE) designation recognizes experienced accountants in the hospitality industry. Certification is based on passing an examination. Membership in IAHA is not required.

Education/Experience

Candidates must meet minimum experience and education requirements to sit for the CHAE examination. Eligibility for certification is determined using a point system. Minimum points to qualify equal 100. Points are awarded for education (minimum 40; 40 per college degree, 1 per college credit, 1 per hour workshop/seminar), experience (10–30 each year depending on position), and IAHA membership (no minimum; 10 each year).

Examinations

The all-day CHAE examination covers both basic accounting theory and hospitality-specific issues. The examination includes basic accounting, managerial accounting, asset management, operations, and tax and law.

Recertification

CHAEs must renew their certification every two years through continuing education, association involvement, and professional experience.

CERTIFIED INSOLVENCY AND REORGANIZATION ACCOUNTANT (CIRA)

Sponsor

Association of Insolvency Accountants (AIA)
31312 Via Colina, Suite 101
Westlake Village, CA 91362
Phone: (818) 889-8317
Fax: (818) 889-5107

Program Data

The CIRA courses are recognized by state licensing and continuing education agencies.

Certifying body: Association
Year certification began: 1992
Number certified: 186
Organization members: 635
Approximate certification costs: $1500

Program Description

The Certified Insolvency and Reorganization Accountant (CIRA) designation recognizes experienced accountants who have completed the AIA's courses on insolvency and bankruptcy. Membership in the AIA is required. AIA maintains an active ethics program.

Education/Experience

To enroll in the CIRA courses, a candidate must be a Certified Public Accountant, Chartered Accountant, Certified Management Accountant, or have a bachelor's degree with four years of accounting experience. To be awarded the CIRA designation, a candidate must pass the required courses, demonstrate four years of accounting experience, and complete 4000 hours within the previous eight years of specialized experience in insolvency and reorganization.

Certification Course(s)

The CIRA program consists of three courses sponsored by the AIA. Each of the three CIRA courses are two and one-half days long; each are followed by a three-hour examination. The current pass rate is 80%. The three courses are as follows:

- Managing Turnaround and Bankruptcy Cases, including business failure causes, turnarounds and turnaround financing, pre-bankruptcy, managing bankruptcies, and the role and services provided by accountants

- Plan Development, including financial considerations, negotiations, funding, classes and interests, disclosures, taxes, and Chapters 11, 12, and 7

- Accounting, Financial Reporting, and Taxes, including reporting during reorganization and when emerging from Chapter 11, reorganization accounting, statements and accountants' reports, taxes, and the retention and responsibilities of accountants.

Examinations

The examinations, given at the end of each course, mirror the course content.

Recertification

Certification must be renewed every three years, and is based on continuing education. A CIRA must earn 60 hours of related continuing education within the certification period.

ASSOCIATE IN INSURANCE ACCOUNTING AND FINANCE (AIAF)

Sponsor

Life Office Management Association (LOMA)
2300 Windy Ridge Parkway, Suite 600
Atlanta, GA 30339
Phone: (770) 951-1770
Fax: (770) 984-0441
E-mail: education@loma.org
WWW: http://www.loma.org/

Insurance Institute of America (IIA)
720 Providence Road
Malvern, PA 19355
Phone: (800) 840-9576

Program Data

The National Program on Noncollegiate Sponsored Instruction (NPONSI) recommends college credit for the FLMI courses. The American Council on Education (ACE) recommends college credit for most AAI courses. Most states have approved FLMI and IIA courses as continuing-education credit hours for state agent licensing.

Certifying body: Association
Additional programs:
- LOMA—Associate, Customer Service (ACS®); Associate, Insurance Agency Administration (AIAA™); Associate in Research and Planning (ARP); Fellow, Life Management Institute (FLMI®); Master Fellow, Life Management Institute (FLMI/M®)
- IIA—Associate designations in the following programs: Accredited Adviser in Insurance (AAI®); Associate in Insurance Services (AIS); Automation Management (AAM®); Claims (AIC); Fidelity and Surety Bonding (AFSB); Loss Control Management (ALCM®); Management (AIM); Marine Insurance Management (AMIM®); Premium Auditing (APA®); Reinsurance (Are); Research and Planning (ARP®); Risk Management (ARM); Underwriting (AU)

Program Description

The Associate in Insurance Accounting and Finance (AIAF) designation recognizes professionals who have completed the educational program on life- and health-insurance accounting and finance. The Property and Casualty option is offered through IIA; the Life and Health Insurance option is offered jointly by LOMA and IIA. Membership in LOMA or IIA is not required.

Education/Experience

The program assumes previous knowledge of accounting and insurance principles, but there are no prerequisites. There are no experience or education prerequisites.

Curriculum

The causes are as follows:

Life Insurance Option

- FLMI Course 2—Life and Health Insurance Company Operations
- FLMI Course 9—Mathematics of Life and Health Insurance
- LOMA Course FA-1—Statutory Accounting for Life and Health Insurers
- IIA AIAF 112—Insurance Information Systems
- IIA AIAF 113—Insurance Company Finance

Property and Casualty Option (all IIA courses):

- Statutory Accounting for Property and Liability Insurers
- Insurance Information Systems

- Insurance Company Finance
- Insurance Operations, which examines internal and external insurance functions (CPCU course)—15 weeks.

Examination

The FLMI exams have approximately a 67% pass rate. Recent passing ratios for the IIA are approximately 70–72%. Exams are based on assigned texts and follow the content of the course.

Recertification

None.

CERTIFIED INTERNAL AUDITOR (CIA)

Sponsor

Institute of Internal Auditors (IIA)
249 Maitland Ave.
Altamonte Springs, FL 32701
Phone: (407) 830-7600
Fax: (407) 831-5171
E-mail: ciadirect@aol.com
WWW: http://www.rutgers.edu/
    Accounting/raw/iia/

Program Data

Certifying body: Association
Year certification began: 1973
Number certified: 21,000
Organization members: 51,000

Program Description

The Certified Internal Auditor (CIA) designation recognizes individuals performing an independent appraisal function within an organization. A CIA reviews financial activities, information reliability and integrity, policy and regulation compliance, and organizational goals, assets, and resources. CIAs may specialize in information systems, compliance, fraud, quality assurance, and environmental auditing. Certification is based on passing an examination. Membership in IIA is not required. The IIA maintains an active ethics program.

Education/Experience

In order to take the examination, a candidate must have a bachelor's degree and two years of experience in internal auditing.

Examinations

The four-part CIA examination program underwent a major revision in 1993, with new examinations going into effect in May 1994. Based on an extensive analysis and comprehensive study of the internal-auditing common body of knowledge, changes and additions to tested competencies and question formats were made. Each part is 210 minutes. The current pass rate is 45% per part and 31% for all parts at one sitting.

The CIA examination comprises the following:

Part 1—Internal Audit Process (combination of multiple-choice and essay), which focuses on internal auditing theory and practice. Major areas include auditing, professionalism and fraud detection, reporting, and investigation.

Part 2—Internal Audit Skills (combination of multiple-choice and essay), which tests reasoning and problem-solving skills, communications skills, and statistics and mathematical skills

Part 3—Management Control and Information Technology (multiple-choice), which covers business disciplines inherent to internal auditing, including organization and management, information technology, accounting, and quantitative methods as a management tool

Part 4: The Audit Environment (multiple-choice), which covers accounting, finance, and economics, and includes taxes, regulation, and marketing. In the future, this section may be adapted to specific regions or countries.

Recertification

CIAs must accumulate 80 Continuing Professional Development (CPD) hours every two years to maintain certification. Examples of the CPD awards are 15 per college semester, 1 per instructional hour, 1 per hour of association committee.

CERTIFIED INVESTMENT MANAGEMENT ANALYST (CIMA)

Sponsor

Investment Management Consultants Association (IMCA)
9101 E. Kenyon Ave., Suite 399
Denver, CO 80237
Phone: (303) 770-3377

Program Data

The CIMA program was developed in conjunction with the Wharton School at the University of Pennsylvania.

Certifying body: Association
Year certification began: 1988
Organization members: 1000
Approximate certification costs: $3850 (members), $4350 (nonmembers)

Program Description

The Certified investment Management Analyst (CIMA) designation recognizes experienced advisors and consultants in investment management consulting. CIMAs primarily advise corporations and organizations on fund plans, fund-planning management, endowments, and trusts. Certification is based on experience and a week-long class held at the Wharton School, University of Pennsylvania. IMCA maintains an active ethics program.

Education/Experience

All candidates must document three years of related experience. At least 50% of this experience must be in the consulting process. Acceptable experience includes:

- Asset allocation
- Designing, structuring, and implementing investment portfolios
- Manager selection and due diligence
- Performance measurement and monitoring
- Writing investment policies

Curriculum

The week-long program at the Wharton School covers:

- Asset allocation
- Beta coefficients
- Due diligence and manager selection
- Duration and convexity
- Ethics
- Historical returns
- International financial markets
- Investment policy
- Legal and regulatory environment
- Measuring return on portfolio
- Performance measurement and attribution
- Risk management

The program ends with a four-hour comprehensive examination.

Recertification

CIMAs must accumulate 40 hours of educational activity every two years to maintain certification.

CERTIFIED MANAGEMENT ACCOUNTANT (CMA)

Sponsor

Institute of Certified Management Accountants
(ICMA)
10 Paragon Drive
Montvale, NJ 07645
Phone: (800) 638-4427
Fax: (201) 573-8438
WWW: http://www.rutgers.edu/accounting/
raw/ima/cma.htm

Program Data

Certifying body: Association-sponsored
independent board
Year certification began: 1972
Number certified: 16,000+
Organization members: 85,000+
Approximate certification costs: $370

Program Description

The Certified Management Accountant (CMA) designation recognizes management accountants and financial managers. The program is affiliated with the Institute of Management Accountants (IMA), and membership in IMA is required. Certification is based on passing an examination. Approximately 70% of recent CMA candidates have been employed as industrial or commercial accountants; others have been government accountants, certified public accountants, and college administrative accountants. Employment in the areas of financial analysis, budgeting, auditing, and management-information-systems analysis also qualifies candidates for the CMA designation. ICMA maintains an active ethics board with decertification powers.

Education/Experience

Candidates must meet the following minimum requirements:

- Bachelor's degree or Certified Public Accountant

- Experience—not required to take the CMA examination. Two continuous years of professional experience must be completed either before or within seven years of the examination

Examinations

The CMA examination is in four parts, each of which may be taken separately. Candidates must attempt at least two parts of the four-part examination (unless only one is left) on one test date. Candidates must pass all four parts within a three-year period. The weighted average pass rate is approximately 40%; but only 13% of candidates pass all examinations in one sitting. The four parts are as follows:

Part 1—Economics, Finance, and Management. Topics covered include macro and micro-economics, management theory, the business environment, working capital, and communications.

Part 2—Financial Accounting, including financial statements, reporting, analysis, and external auditing

Part 3—Management Reporting, Analysis, and Behavior. Topics include measuring costs, strategic planning and budgeting, evaluating control and performance, and behavioral issues.

Part 4—Decision Analysis and Information Systems, including decision theory, decision analysis, information systems, and internal auditing

Ethics questions may appear in any part of the examination. Ethics questions are based on the IMA's standards of ethical conduct for management accountants.

Recertification

Recertification is based on continuing education; CMAs must earn 30 hours of approved continuing education every calendar year. The recertification rate is 85%.

CERTIFIED MUNICIPAL FINANCE ADMINISTRATOR (CMFA)

Sponsor

Municipal Treasurers' Association of the United
States and Canada (MTA US&C)
1229 Nineteenth St. NW
Washington, DC 20036
Phone: (202) 833-1017
Fax: (202) 833-0357

Program Data

Certifying body: Association
Number certified: 218
Organization members: 1500
Approximate certification costs: $150

Program Description

The Certified Municipal Finance Administrator credential recognizes individuals with experience, education, and achievement in the field of public finance. Active or affiliate membership in the Municipal Treasurers' Association of the United States and Canada (MTA US&C) is required.

Certification is based on a qualifying points system. To be eligible for certification, a candidate must be a municipal treasurer, a deputy or principal officer with public treasury responsibilities, or an eligible public treasurer (treasurer governmental entity other than a municipality with responsibilities closely related to those of a municipal treasurer). There are no examinations.

Total certification points required equals 100. Most categories have a maximum point total allowed.

Point examples:

- 50 points for a treasury-related bachelor's degree
- 15 points for an unrelated bachelor's degree
- 5 points per MTA US&C annual conference
- 4 points per year employed as a municipal treasurer
- 1 point per related college course quarter-hour

Recertification

Certification is for five years. A CMFA must maintain continuous membership in the MTA US&C and accumulate 50 certification points in the previous five years.

FELLOW, SOCIETY OF PENSION ACTUARIES (FSPA)

MEMBER, SOCIETY OF PENSION ACTUARIES (MSPA)

Sponsor

American Society of Pension Actuaries (ASPA)
4350 North Fairfax Drive, Suite 820
Arlington, VA 22203
Phone: (703) 516-9300
Fax: (703) 516-9308

Program Data

Certifying body: Professional society
Organization members: 3000

Additional programs: Associate Professional Member (APM); Certified Pension Consultant (CPC); Qualified Pension Administrator (QPA)
Approximate certification costs: $530 (MSPA), $1050 (FSPA—MSPA)

Program Description

The Member, Society of Pension Actuaries (MSPA) designation is an ASPA membership category that recognizes Enrolled Actuaries with three years of professional experience.

The Fellow, Society of Pension Actuaries (FSPA) designation is the highest ASPA membership category. It recognizes current holders of the Member, Society of Pension Actuaries (MSPA) designation who have completed the three required examinations.

Examinations

There are no independent examination requirements for the MSPA designation. Examinations are a part of the Enrolled Actuary certification.

The three examinations required for the FSPA designation are as follows:

- Advanced Actuarial Practice—A six-hour examination of problem-solving and essay questions. The areas covered include inflation impact on benefits; pension asset valuation and performance measurement; civil litigation; financial accounting; and consulting. Candidates need to be familiar with a wide range of federal regulations and acts, as well as IRS rulings and notices.

- Financial and Fiduciary Aspects of Qualified Plans—A four-hour, multiple-choice and short-answer examination which includes plan protection; accounting and financial reporting; plan assets; fiduciary standards; plan terminations; taxation; distribution; and estate planning

- Advanced Retirement Plan Consulting—A four-hour essay examination testing the candidate's depth of knowledge and ability to apply this knowledge to comprehensive pension problems

Recertification

All designated members of the ASPA must meet continuing-education requirements to maintain certification. MSPAs and FSPAs must earn 40 hours of continuing education every two years.

ASSOCIATE PROFESSIONAL MEMBER {PENSION ACTUARY} (APM)

Sponsor

American Society of Pension Actuaries (ASPA)
4350 North Fairfax Drive, Suite 820
Arlington, VA 22203
Phone: (703) 516-9300
Fax: (703) 516-9308

Program Data

Certifying body: Association
Organization members: 3000
Additional programs: Certified Pension Consultant (CPC); Fellow, Society of Pension Actuaries (FSPA); Member, Society of Pension Actuaries (MSPA); Qualified Pension Administrator (QPA)

Program Description

The APM designation is an ASPA membership category that recognizes attorneys, licensed CPAs, and enrolled agents who have three years of experience in pensions or pension-related services. There are no examination requirements.

Recertification

All designated members of the ASPA must meet continuing-education requirements to maintain certification. APMs must earn 40 hours of continuing education every two years.

QUALIFIED PENSION ADMINISTRATOR (QPA)

Sponsor

American Society of Pension Actuaries (ASPA)
4350 North Fairfax Drive, Suite 820
Arlington, VA 22203
Phone: (703) 516-9300
Fax: (703) 516-9308

Program Data

Certifying body: Association
Organization members: 3000
Additional programs: Associate Professional Member (APM); Certified Pension Consultant (CPC); Fellow, Society of Pension Actuaries (FSPA); Member, Society of Pension Actuaries (MSPA)
Approximate certification costs: $650

Program Description

The Qualified Pension Administrator (QPA) designation is an ASPA membership category that recognizes experienced professionals who have demonstrated the knowledge required for qualified plan administration.

Education/Experience

Candidates must document two years of professional experience prior to receiving the designation. Study courses are available but not required for the examinations. The QPA program was recently revised; the exam descriptions apply to current requirements.

Examinations

There are four examinations required for the QPA designation:

- Pension Administrator's Course—A self-study course ending in a take-home, open-book test. Questions include multiple-choice and short-answer, as well as case-study problems. The test covers the basics of plan administration, including types of plans; roles and responsibilities; trust accounting; IRD requirements; plan documents; and reporting and disclosure requirements.

- Qualification and Operation of Retirement Plans—A three-hour, multiple-choice examination which includes types of plans; qualifications; participation and distribution requirements; reporting and disclosure; taxes; fiduciary responsibilities; and investment vehicles and performance

- Administrative and Consulting Aspects of Defined Contribution Plans—A three-hour, multiple-choice examination which covers plans including profit-sharing; 401(k); employee stock ownerships (ESOP); and simplified employee pensions (SEP)

- Administrative and Consulting Aspects of Defined Benefit Plans—A three-hour, multiple-choice examination which covers benefit calculations; rules; terminations and changes; funding and accounting; and traditional plan variations

Recertification

All designated members of the ASPA must meet continuing-education requirements to maintain certification. QPAs must earn 40 hours of continuing education every two years.

ASSOCIATE IN PREMIUM AUDITING (APA®)

Sponsor

Insurance Institute of America (IIA)
720 Providence Road
P.O. Box 3016
Malvern, PA 19355
Phone: (800) 644-2101
Fax: (610) 640-9576

Program Data

The program has been developed in cooperation with the National Society of Insurance Premium Auditors (NSIPA). This and other IIA programs have been evaluated and recommended for college credit by the American Council on Education.

Certifying body: Independent education and certification organization

Additional programs: The IIA offers Associate designations in the following programs: Accredited Adviser in Insurance (AAI®); Associate in Insurance Services (AIS); Automation Management (AAM®); Claims (AIC); Fidelity and Surety Bonding (AFSB); Insurance Accounting and Finance (AIAF); Loss Control Management (ALCM®); Management (AIM); Marine Insurance Management (AMIM®); Reinsurance (ARe); Research and Planning (ARP®); Risk Management (ARM); Underwriting (AU)

Program Description

The Associate in Premium Auditing (APA®) designation recognizes professionals who have completed the six-course IIA program in insurance premium auditing. Weekly assignments are not graded or returned, but are designed to prepare the student to take the end-of-course examination. Courses can be either independent or group study. There are no education or experience requirements. Each course prepares candidates for an IIA examination. There is no recertification requirement.

Curriculum

The courses are as follows:

- Ethics, Insurance Perspectives, and Insurance Contract Analysis (CPCU course)—15 weeks
- Commercial Property Risk Management and Insurance (CPCU course)—15 weeks
- Commercial Liability Risk Management and Insurance (CPCU course)—15 weeks.
- Accounting and Finance, including basic accounting and property and casualty insurance company accounting requirements (CPCU course)—15 weeks
- Principles of Premium Accounting—13 weeks
- Premium Auditing Applications—13 weeks

CERTIFIED PUBLIC ACCOUNTANT (CPA)

Program Data

The Certified Public Accountant (CPA) designation is awarded by state certification boards; there is no national CPA certifying body. However, all states use the Uniform CPA Examination as a major portion of their certification process. This examination is developed and graded by the American Institute of Certified Public Accountants (AICPA), 1211 Avenue of the Americas, New York, NY 10036. Contact AICPA or the nearest state CPA board for further information.

BUSINESS AND MANAGEMENT
Financial Institutions

CHARTERED BANK AUDITOR (CBA™)

Sponsor

Bank Administration Institute (BAI) Foundation
One North Franklin, Suite 1000
Chicago, IL 60606
Phone: (800) 323-8552
Fax: (800) 375-5573
E-mail: info@bai.org
WWW: http://www.bai.org

Program Data

Certifying body: Association
Number certified: 4200+
Additional certifications: Certified Bank
    Compliance Officer (CBCO)
Approximate certification costs: $500

Program Description

The Chartered Bank Auditor (CBA™) designation recognizes bank internal auditors who have mastered the Bank Administration Institute's common body of knowledge for internal auditing.

Education/Experience

Candidates must have either a bachelor's degree and two years of experience, or a master's degree and six months of experience. Bank auditing experience may be gained at a financial institution, bank regulatory agency, public accounting firm (auditing financial institutions), or private bank-audit or examination firm.

Examinations

The CBA examination is in four parts, which may be taken at different times. All parts must be completed within four years. The pass rate is 75%. The BAI offers examination-review guides and preparatory courses. Each part has 100 multiple-choice questions. The examination parts are as follows:

Part 1—Accounting, including accounting principles, bank accounting, financial statements, and managerial accounting

Part 2—Auditing Principles and Bank Laws, including professional standards, internal controls, the audit function, audit techniques, and bank laws and regulations

Part 3—Auditing Practices, including using audit techniques; evaluating internal controls; the audit process; assets; income; liabilities; equity; and banking services

Part 4—General Business, including commercial law and the Uniform Commercial Code, economics, money markets, and general bank management

Recertification
None.

CERTIFIED BANK COMPLIANCE OFFICER (CBCO)

Sponsor

Bank Administration Institute (BAI) Foundation
One North Franklin, Suite 1000
Chicago, IL 60606
Phone: (800) 323-8552
Fax: (800) 375-5573
E-mail: info@bai.org
WWW: http://www.bai.org

Program Data

Certifying body: Association
Number certified: 650+
Additional certifications: Chartered Bank Auditor
    (CBA™)
Approximate certification costs: $500

Program Description

The Certified Bank Compliance Officer (CBCO) designation recognizes compliance officers, auditors, and examiners with experience and in-depth knowledge of bank regulation compliance. Compliance professionals oversee systems for assuring regulatory compliance. Certification is based on experience and passing an examination. Experience and educational requirements do not need to be met prior to taking the examination.

Education/Experience

Candidates need three years of compliance experience which may be earned at a financial institution or regulatory agency. Candidates may also meet the experience requirements through one year at a financial institution or regulatory agency, and two years at a bank consulting firm. Professional education requirements are 25 hours of acceptable compliance training.

Examinations

The CBCO examination is in four parts, each of which may be taken at different times. All parts must be completed within three years. The pass rate is 75%. The BAI offers examination-review guides and preparatory courses. New and revised regulations are integrated into the examination within six months of the announced change or implementation. The examination parts are as follows:

> Part 1—Fair Lending/Non-Consumer Compliance Issues
>
> Part 2—Credit Compliance/Real Estate Compliance
>
> Part 3—Operations and Deposit Issues Compliance
>
> Part 4—Compliance Program Development and Management Issues

Recertification

CBCOs must pay dues and attend 20 hours of acceptable compliance training annually. This annual training requirement reflects the ever-changing bank compliance field.

CERTIFIED COLLECTION AGENCY EXECUTIVE (CCAE)

Sponsor

Society of Certified Credit Executives (SCCE)
P.O. Box 419057
St. Louis, MO 63141
Phone: (314) 991-3030
Fax: (314) 991-3029

Program Data

The SCCE is the certification arm of the International Credit Association (ICA).

Certifying body: Association
Number certified: 5000 (all designations)
Additional certifications: Associate Credit Executive (ACE); Certified Consumer Credit Executive (CCCE); Certified Credit Bureau Executive (CCBE); Certified Financial Counseling Executive (CFCE); Credit Associate (CA)
Approximate certification costs: $200

Program Description

The Certified Collection Agency Executive (CCAE) designation recognizes management professionals in the collections industry. Membership in a recognized, credit-related association is required.

Education/Experience

Certification is based on meeting several criteria and passing an examination. The criteria are as follows:

- Current employment and five years of experience in a collection agency or the collections division of a credit reporting agency

- Service as an officer or other responsible position in a recognized, credit-related association

- Attendance at three approved, association-sponsored conferences, workshops, or other educational programs

- Demonstration of community involvement

Examinations

The 150-question, multiple-choice examination covers credit granting, credit reporting, debt collections, and consumer credit counseling. The exam is based on the International Credit Association's *Comprehensive Credit Manual*.

Recertification

CCAEs must recertify every three years. Recertification is based on continuing professional development and industry involvement.

CERTIFIED COLLECTION SALES PROFESSIONAL

Sponsor

American Collectors Association (ACA)
4040 W. 70th St.
Minneapolis, MN 55435
Phone: (612) 926-6547
Fax: (612) 926-1624
E-mail: acaintl@collector.com
WWW: http://www.member.com/aca/ acapub.html

Program Data

Certifying body: Association
Number certified: 3000+ (all designations)
Organization members: 3700 collection agencies
Additional certifications: Certified Collector

Program Description

The Certified Collection Sales Profession designation recognizes salespeople in telephone debt collection services. Candidates must work for a member agency. Certification is based on passing an examination.

Education/Experience

Candidates must have worked for the same employer for one year.

Curriculum

Candidates must complete the ACA's Sales and Marketing School and workplace motivation school.

Examinations

The comprehensive exam covers sales and motivational techniques.

Recertification

None.

CERTIFIED COLLECTOR

Sponsor

American Collectors Association (ACA)
4040 W. 70th St.
Minneapolis, MN 55435
Phone: (612) 926-6547
Fax: (612) 926-1624
E-mail: acaintl@collector.com
WWW: http://www.member.com/aca/
acapub.html

Program Data

Certifying body: Association
Number certified: 3000+ (all designations)
Organization members: 3700 collection agencies
Additional certifications: Certified Collection
Sales Professional

Program Description

The Certified Collector designation recognizes trained telephone-debt-collection professionals committed to professionalism and to regulatory compliance. Advanced certifications are available to Certified Collectors in several areas. Candidates must work for a member agency. Certification is based on passing an examination.

Education/Experience

Candidates must have worked for the same employer for one year.

Curriculum

Candidates must complete two in-depth ACA training courses:

- Fair Debt Collection Practices Act (FDCPA) School or the ACA's computer-based FDCPA course
- Professional Telephone Collector's Technique School or the computer-based equivalent

Advanced certifications for Certified Collectors are offered through additional ACA coursework:

- Advanced Certified Collector: Attend two ACA advanced training courses on communications, collections, and workplace motivation.
- Certified Skiptracer: Attend the Communications and Collections School and the Skiptracing School.
- Certified Supervisor: Attend the Supervisory Practices for Collection Agencies School and the Personnel Management School.

Examinations

The Certified Collector exam is a comprehensive test covering telephone collections, skiptracing, and the Fair Debt Collection Practices Act. The pass rate is 82.15%.

Recertification

None.

CERTIFIED CONSUMER CREDIT EXECUTIVE (CCCE)

Sponsor

Society of Certified Credit Executives (SCCE)
P.O. Box 419057
St. Louis, MO 63141
Phone: (314) 991-3030
Fax: (314) 991-3029

Program Data

The SCCE is the certification arm of the International Credit Association (ICA).

Certifying body: Association
Number certified: 5000 (all designations)
Additional certifications: Associate Credit Executive (ACE); Certified Collection Agency Executive (CCAE); Certified Credit Bureau Executive (CCBE); Certified Financial Counseling Executive (CFCE); Credit Associate (CA)
Approximate certification costs: $200

Program Description

The Certified Consumer Credit Executive (CCCE) designation recognizes management professionals in the credit-granting or credit services industry. Membership in a recognized, credit-related association is required.

Education/Experience

Certification is based on meeting several criteria and passing an examination. The criteria are as follows:

- Current employment and five years of experience in a credit-granting or credit services operation
- Service as an officer or other responsible position in a recognized, credit-related association
- Attendance at three approved, association-sponsored conferences, workshops, or other educational programs
- Demonstration of community involvement

Examinations

The 150-question, multiple-choice examination covers credit granting, credit reporting, debt collections, and consumer credit counseling. The exam is based on the International Credit Association's *Comprehensive Credit Manual.*

Recertification

CCCEs must recertify every three years. Recertification is based on continuing professional development and industry involvement.

CERTIFIED CORPORATE TRUST SPECIALIST™ (CCTS™)

Sponsor

Institute for Certified Bankers™ (ICB)
1120 Connecticut Ave. NW, Suite 600
Washington, DC 20036
Phone: (202) 663-5380

Program Data

The ICB is sponsored by the American Bankers Association (ABA).

Certifying body: Association
Additional programs: Certified Financial Services Security Professional™ (CFSSP™); Certified Regulatory Compliance Manager™ (CRCM™); Certified Trust and Financial Advisor™ (CTFA™)
Approximate certification costs: $600

Program Description

The Certified Corporate Trust Specialist (CCTS) designation recognizes experienced professionals in the corporate trust field. There are no professional membership requirements; certified individuals automatically become members of ICB. The ICB does not certify anyone who has signed a consent decree with any securities agency or has been found guilty of certain criminal acts.

Education/Experience

To earn the CCTS designation, a candidate must pass an examination and meet one of the following experience/education requirements:

- Eight years of experience and 30 hours of recognized professional education in the corporate trust field
- Five years of experience and 60 hours of recognized professional education in the corporate trust field
- Three years of experience and 90 hours of recognized professional education in the corporate trust field

Examinations

Examination-preparation materials come with enrollment. The examination covers:

- Core subjects in corporate trusts, including the Uniform Commercial Code; credit markets and instruments; Federal and state legal and regulatory issues; financial transactions; and the audit/compliance function
- Account and management, including trustee reporting and disclosure, documentation, and covenants
- Operations and systems, including agency functions; reporting; record-keeping; registration; trust accounting; transfers; and regulatory compliance

Recertification

Certification must be renewed every three years. Recertification is based on professional education, and CCTS holders must have 30 continuing-education hours in trust-related programs.

CREDIT ASSOCIATE (CA)

Sponsor

Society of Certified Credit Executives (SCCE)
P.O. Box 419057
St. Louis, MO 63141
Phone: (314) 991-3030
Fax: (314) 991-3029

Program Data

The SCCE is the certification arm of the International Credit Association (ICA).

Certifying body: Association
Number certified: 5000 (all designations)
Additional certifications: Associate Credit Executive (ACE); Certified Consumer Credit Executive (CCCE); Certified Collection Agency Executive (CCAE); Certified Credit Bureau Executive (CCBE); Certified Financial Counseling Executive (CFCE)
Approximate certification costs: $50

Program Description

The Credit Associate (CA) designation is the entry-level designation for the Society. Membership in a recognized, credit-related association is required.

Education/Experience

Certification is based on current employment and one year of experience in a credit-related position within a credit services organization, credit reporting or collection agency, or consumer credit counseling organization. There is no examination component.

Recertification

None.

CERTIFIED CREDIT BUREAU EXECUTIVE (CCBE)

Sponsor

Society of Certified Credit Executives (SCCE)
P.O. Box 419057
St. Louis, MO 63141
Phone: (314) 991-3030
Fax: (314) 991-3029

Program Data

The SCCE is the certification arm of the International Credit Association (ICA).

Certifying body: Association
Number certified: 5000 (all designations)
Additional certifications: Associate Credit Executive (ACE); Certified Collection Agency Executive (CCAE); Certified Consumer Credit Executive (CCCE); Certified Financial Counseling Executive (CFCE); Credit Associate (CA)
Approximate certification costs: $200

Program Description

The Certified Credit Bureau Executive (CCBE) designation recognizes management professionals in the credit reporting industry. Membership in a recognized, credit-related association is required.

Education/Experience

Certification is based on meeting several criteria and passing an examination. The criteria are as follows:

- Current employment and five years of experience in a credit reporting agency
- Service as an officer or other responsible position in a recognized, credit-related association
- Attendance at three approved, association-sponsored conferences, workshops, or other educational programs
- Demonstration of community involvement

Examinations

The 150-question, multiple-choice examination covers credit granting, credit reporting, debt collections, and consumer credit counseling. The exam is based on the International Credit Association's *Comprehensive Credit Manual*.

Recertification

CCBEs must recertify every three years. Recertification is based on continuing professional development and industry involvement.

ASSOCIATE CREDIT EXECUTIVE (ACE)

Sponsor

Society of Certified Credit Executives (SCCE)
P.O. Box 419057
St. Louis, MO 63141
Phone: (314) 991-3030
Fax: (314) 991-3029

Program Data

The SCCE is the certification arm of the International Credit Association (ICA).

Certifying body: Association
Number certified: 5000 (all designations)
Additional certifications: Certified Collection Agency Executive (CCAE); Certified Consumer Credit Executive (CCCE); Certified Credit Bureau Executive (CCBE); Certified Financial Counseling Executive (CFCE); Credit Associate (CA)
Approximate certification costs: $100

Program Description

The Associate Credit Executive (ACE) designation recognizes experienced professionals in credit-related industries. Membership in a recognized, credit-related association is required. There is no examination component.

Education/Experience

Certification is based on meeting these criteria:

- Current employment and three years of experience in a credit-related position within a credit services organization, credit reporting or collection agency, or consumer credit counseling organization.

- Attendance at one approved, association-sponsored conference, workshop, or other educational program.

Recertification

None.

CERTIFIED CREDIT UNION EXECUTIVE (CCUE)

Sponsor

Credit Union National Association, Inc. (CUNA)
CCUE Program
P.O. Box 431
Madison, WI 53701
Phone: (608) 231-4055
Fax: (608) 231-4253
E-mail: Talk2Us@CUNA.ORG.
WWW: http://www.cuna.org/

Program Data

The American Council on Education (ACE) Program on Noncollegiate-Sponsored Instruction (PONSI) recommends college course credit for 16 CCUE courses.

Certifying body: Trade association
Year certification began: 1975
Number certified: 1352
Organization members: CUNA members are credit unions; CCUEs are invited to join the Institute of Certified Credit Union Executives (400+ members)
Approximate certification costs: $2000

Program Description

The Certified Credit Union Executive (CCUE) designation recognizes credit union employees and volunteers who complete CUNA's 10-course training program in credit union management and operation. CUNA has an active ethics program.

Education/Experience

There are no prerequisites to entering the CUNA program. Certification is based on completing the CUNA course examinations. The courses prepare the candidate to take the associated examination. No coursework is graded. Candidates may use self-study, group study, credit-union-league courses, or participating colleges to help prepare for the examinations. These are the program courses:

- Introduction to Credit Unions—An introductory-level course covering the growth of the credit union movement, basic credit union organization and services, and NCUA-affiliated organizations

- Business Law—An advanced course covering the primary areas of business law

- Credit and Collections—An introductory course covering credit operations, credit decisions, collections, and business and government roles

- Economics and the Monetary System—An advanced course including macroeconomic theory and money and banking concepts. This includes monetary theory, the Federal Reserve System, financial institutions, and fiscal policy.

- Financial Management I—An advanced course concerning credit union financial management

- Management—An introductory course on basic management concepts, roles, and functions

- Personnel Administration—An introductory course including staffing; records management; evaluations; labor relations; training programs; and benefits

- Risk Management and Insurance—An intermediate-level course on evaluating risk, different insurance products and services, and insurance carrier selection

- Two electives to complete the CCUE course requirements

Examinations

Each course has a 100-question, multiple-choice examination covering material presented in the course.

Recertification

None.

CERTIFIED FINANCIAL COUNSELING EXECUTIVE (CFCE)

Sponsor

Society of Certified Credit Executives (SCCE)
P.O. Box 419057
St. Louis, MO 63141
Phone: (314) 991-3030
Fax: (314) 991-3029

Program Data

The SCCE is the certification arm of the International Credit Association (ICA).

Certifying body: Association
Number certified: 5000 (all designations)
Additional certifications: Associate Credit Executive (ACE); Certified Consumer Credit Executive (CCCE); Certified Collection Agency Executive (CCAE); Certified Credit Bureau Executive (CCBE); Credit Associate (CA)
Approximate certification costs: $200

Program Description

The Certified Financial Counseling Executive (CFCE) designation recognizes management professionals in the consumer budgeting and credit counseling industry. Membership in a recognized, credit-related association is required.

Education/Experience

Certification is based on meeting several criteria and passing an examination. These are the criteria:

- Current employment and five years of experience in a budgeting or consumer credit counseling service or organization

- Service as an officer or other responsible position in a recognized, credit-related association

- Attendance at three approved, association-sponsored conferences, workshops, or other educational programs

- Demonstration of community involvement

Examinations

The 150-question, multiple-choice examination covers credit granting, credit reporting, debt collections, and consumer credit counseling. The exam is based on the International Credit Association's *Comprehensive Credit Manual.*

Recertification

CFCEs must recertify every three years. Recertification is based on continuing professional development and industry involvement.

ACCREDITED FINANCIAL EXAMINER (AFE®)

Sponsor

Society of Financial Examiners® (SOFE®)
4101 Lake Boone Trail, Suite 201
Raleigh, NC 27607
Phone: (800) 787-SOFE

Program Data

SOFE has been designated the credentialing body for the state insurance department's classification system by the National Association of Insurance Commissioners (NAIC).

Certifying body: Association
Year certification began: 1981
Number certified: 1200
Organization members: 2000
Additional programs: Automated Examination Specialist (AES^{SM}); Certified Financial Examiner (CFE®)
Approximate certification costs: $1000

Program Description

The Accredited Financial Examiner (AFE®) is the first-level designation recognizing experienced financial examiners working in insurance, financial institution, and credit union industries. SOFE membership is required. SOFE maintains an active ethics program.

Education/Experience

Besides SOFE membership, candidates must meet the following requirements:

- Two years of insurance department or financial institution experience either as a financial examiner or financial analyst

- Bachelor's degree in a business-related area, computer science, or other acceptable area
- Education in core curriculum (accounting, business law, and computer information systems) either through college or industry coursework

Examinations

For certification, candidates must pass four SOFE examinations:

- Life and Health Insurance Fundamentals
- Life and Health Insurance Accounting
- Property and Liability Insurance Fundamentals
- Property and Liability Insurance Accounting

Textbooks and preparatory classes are available.

Recertification

AFEs are required to maintain SOFE membership and to participate in the continuing education program.

CERTIFIED FINANCIAL EXAMINER (CFE®)

Sponsor

Society of Financial Examiners® (SOFE®)
4101 Lake Boone Trail, Suite 201
Raleigh, NC 27607
Phone: (800) 787-SOFE

Program Data

SOFE has been designated the credentialing body for the state insurance department's classification system by the National Association of Insurance Commissioners (NAIC).

Certifying body: Association
Year certification began: 1981
Number certified: 1200
Organization members: 2000
Additional programs: Accredited Financial Examiner (AFE®); Automated Examination Specialist (AES℠)
Approximate certification costs: $800

Program Description

The Certified Financial Examiner (CFE®) is the second-level designation recognizing experienced financial examiners working in insurance, financial institution, and credit union industries. SOFE membership is required. SOFE maintains an active ethics program.

Education/Experience

Besides SOFE membership, candidates must meet the following requirements:

- Accredited Financial Examiner (AFE®) certification
- Three years of insurance department or financial institution experience either as a financial examiner or financial analyst
- College-level coursework in management

Examinations

For certification, candidates must pass three SOFE examinations.

- Analysis and Evaluation Procedures
- Examination Method and Management
- Reinsurance

Textbooks and preparatory classes are available.

Recertification

CFEs are required to maintain SOFE membership and to participate in the continuing education program.

CERTIFIED FINANCIAL SERVICES SECURITY PROFESSIONAL™ (CFSSP™)

Sponsor

Institute for Certified Bankers™ (ICB)
1120 Connecticut Ave. NW, Suite 600
Washington, DC 20036
Phone: (202) 663-5380

Program Data

The ICB is sponsored by the American Bankers Association (ABA).

Certifying body: Association
Additional certifications: Certified Corporate Trust Specialist™ (CCTS™); Certified Regulatory Compliance Manager™ (CRCM™); Certified Trust and Financial Advisor™ (CTFA™)
Approximate certification costs: $600

Program Description

The Certified Financial Services Security Professional™ (CFSSP™) designation recognizes experienced professionals responsible for their institution's security as defined in the Bank Protection Act. There are no professional membership requirements. To earn the CFSSP designation, a candidate must pass an examination, be employed by a financial institution, and either be appointed as the institution's security officer or spend 50% or more time in security. A CFSSP candidate cannot have a felony conviction. The ICB does not certify anyone who has signed a consent decree with any securities agencies or has been found guilty of certain criminal acts.

Education/Experience

Candidates must also meet one of the following requirements:

- High school diploma, and three years of security experience within a financial institution or three years of financial institution experience and three years of security experience

- Associate's degree, and two years of security experience within a financial institution or two years of financial institution experience and two years of security experience

- Bachelor's degree, and one year of security experience within a financial institution or one year of financial institution experience and one year of security experience

Examinations

Examination preparation materials are sent upon enrollment. The examination covers developing a security program, security devices, internal and external crimes, and investigations, including employee screening methods.

Recertification

Certification must be renewed every three years. Recertification is based on professional education, and CFSSP holders must have 24 continuing-education hours in ICB-approved security-related programs.

CERTIFIED MORTGAGE BANKER (CMB)

Sponsor

Mortgage Bankers Association of America (MBA)
1125 15th St. NW
Washington, DC 20005
Phone: (800) 793-6222
E-mail: info@mbaa.org
WWW: http://www.mbaa.org/

Program Data

Certifying body: Association
Other programs: Accredited Residential Underwriter (ARU)

Program Description

The Certified Mortgage Banker (CMB) designation recognizes experienced professionals in real estate finance.

Education/Experience

Candidates must be employed by an MBA member firm and have three years of experience. Certification is based on a point system and an examination. Candidates must have 150 points to take the CMB examination. Points are awarded for experience, education, MBA seminars and courses, and association/industry conferences. Point examples: 3 per year of experience (years 1–5), 15 per bachelor's degree, 10 per MBA correspondence course.

Examinations

The CMB examination is made up of several concentrations. Candidates must pass a Comprehensive Industry Issues section and any four of the following sections:

- Commercial Real Estate Loan Servicing and Administration
- Commercial Real Estate Lending
- Construction Lending and Administration
- Mortgage Instruments, Law, and Government Regulations
- Principles of Corporate Strategy for Residential Lenders
- Residential Loan Marketing and Investor Relations
- Residential Loan Origination and Underwriting
- Residential Loan Servicing and Administration

Recertification

None.

CERTIFIED REGULATORY COMPLIANCE MANAGER™ (CRCM™)

Sponsor

Institute for Certified Bankers™ (ICB)
1120 Connecticut Ave. NW, Suite 600
Washington, DC 20036
Phone: (202) 663-5380

Program Data

The ICB is sponsored by the American Bankers Association (ABA).

Certifying body: Association

Additional certifications: Certified Corporate Trust Specialist™ (CCTS™); Certified Financial Services Security Professional™ (CFSSP™); Certified Trust and Financial Advisor™ (CTFA™)

Approximate certification costs: $550

Program Description

The Certified Regulatory Compliance Manager™ (CRCM™) designation recognizes experienced professionals responsible for financial-institution regulatory compliance. There are no professional membership requirements; certified individuals automatically become members of ICB. The ICB does not certify anyone who has signed a consent decree with any securities agencies or has been found guilty of certain criminal acts.

Education/Experience

To earn the CRCM designation, a candidate must pass an examination and meet the following requirements:

- Three years of experience in a financial institution as a regulatory compliance manager
- Eighty hours of recognized professional education in the regulatory compliance field during the previous five years

Examinations

Examination preparation materials come with enrollment. The examination covers:

- Regulatory requirements for financial institutions
- Compliance enforcement, penalties, and administrative practices
- Management skills in regulatory compliance and proactive compliance monitoring

Recertification

Certification must be renewed every three years. Recertification is based on professional education, and CRCM holders must have 60 continuing-education hours in compliance-related programs, only 30 of which may come from an institution's programs.

ACCREDITED RESIDENTIAL UNDERWRITER (ARU)

Sponsor

Mortgage Bankers Association of America (MBA)
1125 15th St. NW
Washington, DC 20005
Phone: (800) 793-6222
E-mail: info@mbaa.org
WWW: http://www.mbaa.org/

Program Data

Certifying body: Association
Other programs: Accredited Residential Underwriter (ARU)

Program Description

The Accredited Residential Underwriter (ARU) designation recognizes underwriters competent in FHA, VA, and conventional home loans.

Education/Experience

Candidates must have one year of employment with an MBA member firm and three years of residential property experience.

Curriculum

Candidates must complete three correspondence courses or be HUD or VA approved underwriters. All candidates must complete the coursework for MBA's appraisal techniques and specialized techniques seminars. Certification is awarded upon passing a final comprehensive examination.

Recertification

None.

BUSINESS AND MANAGEMENT
Human Resource Management

CERTIFIED EMPLOYEE <u>BENEFIT</u> SPECIALIST (CEBS)

Sponsor

International Foundation of Employee Benefit
 Plans (IFEBP)
P.O. Box 1270
Brookfield, WI 53008-1270
Phone: (414) 786-6710
Fax: (414) 786-8650
E-mail: cebs@ifebp.org
WWW: http://www.ifebp.org/

Program Data

The CEBS program is co-sponsored by the Wharton School, University of Pennsylvania. All CEBS courses have been recommended for three semester upper-division semester credits by the American Council of Education.

Certifying body: Association
Year certification began: 1981
Number certified: 4700
Organization members: 34,000
Approximate certification costs: $2000

Program Description

The CEBS program participants come from all areas of employee benefits, including benefit managers, investment specialists, and insurance representatives. Certification is based on passing all 10 CEBS examinations. There are no membership or prerequisite requirements.

Examinations

Each examination is a 100-question, two-hour, multiple-choice test. Candidates may prepare for each exam through formal study, independent study, or study groups. Optional classes for each course are available at over 100 institutions, with an average course lasting 30 hours/12 weeks. Courses may also be completed through independent or group study. No coursework is turned in. The exams are as follows:

- Employee Benefit Concepts and Medical Care Benefits
- Life, Disability Income, and Other Welfare Benefit Plans
- Retirement Plans: Basic Features and Defined Contribution Approaches
- Retirement Plans: Defined Benefit Approaches and Plan Administration
- Contemporary Legal Environment of Employee Benefit Plans
- Accounting and Finance
- Asset Management
- Human Resources and Compensation Management
- Employee Benefit Plans and the Economy
- Contemporary Benefit Issues and Administration

Recertification

CEBSs are invited to join the International Society of Certified Employee Benefit Specialists (ISCEBS).

REGISTERED EMPLOYEE <u>BENEFITS</u> CONSULTANT (REBC)

Sponsor

National Association of Health Underwriters
 (NAHU)
1000 Connecticut Ave. NW, Suite 1111
Washington, DC 20036
Phone: (202) 223-5533
Fax : (202) 785-2274
WWW: http://www.nahu.org/contents.html

Program Data

Certifying body: Association
Organization members: 12,000
Additional programs: Registered Health
 Underwriter (RHU)
Approximate certification costs: $700 (members),
 $850 (nonmembers)

Program Description

The Registered Employee Benefits Consultant (REBC) designation recognizes experienced professionals who successfully complete the NAHU's study course/examination program in employee benefit plans. The program is supervised and administered by Northeastern University. The candidate must successfully complete two self-study courses and pass two examinations. Candidates who are not RHUs must also take the RHU II—Health Insurance course/examination. Membership in NAHU is not required for certification.

Education/Experience
Candidates must be designated as a Registered Health Underwriter (RHU) or have three years of insurance/employee benefit plans experience.

Curriculum
All courses end with a 100-question, multiple-choice exam. These are the two REBC courses:

- Employee Welfare Plans, including benefits concepts, risk management, types of benefits, major medical, and expenses

- Retirement and Additional Benefit Plans, including pensions and pension funding, benefit plan design/evaluation, and other plan programs

    Candidates not holding the RHU designation must complete: Health Insurance, including group insurance, government regulations, underwriting, different products and programs.

Recertification
REBCs must recertify every three years. Recertification is based on a point system. Points are awarded for continuing education, professional development, and association participation.

CERTIFIED BENEFITS PROFESSIONAL (CBP)

Sponsor
American Compensation Association (ACA)
14040 N. Northsight Blvd.
Scottsdale, AZ 85260
Phone: (602) 951-9191
Fax: (602) 483-8352
E-mail: qllr45a@prodigy.com
WWW: http://www.ahrm.org/aca/aca.htm

Program Data
Certifying body: Association
Year certification began: 1994
Number certified: New program
Organization members: 18,000
Additional programs: Certified Compensation Professional (CCP)
Approximate certification costs: $1400

Program Description
The Certified Benefits Professional (CBP) designation recognizes human resource professionals in the benefits area of the total compensation field. Certification is based on passing a series of examinations. ACA membership is not required.

Education/Experience
None required.

Examinations
ACA's body of knowledge model was validated by a research team from Rutgers University's Institute of Management and Labor Relations. The CBP program consists of nine examinations. Each examination is offered in conjunction with an optional two-day preparatory seminar. Candidates must pass nine examinations for certification, three of which are electives. The six required examinations are as follows:

- Fundamentals of Employee Benefit Programs

- Healthcare and Insurance Plans

- Principles of Accounting and Finance

- Quantitative Methods

- Retirement Plans

- Total Compensation Management

Recertification
Certification currency is based on continuing education. CBPs must earn 12 currency credits every three years.

CERTIFIED COMPENSATION PROFESSIONAL (CCP)

Sponsor
American Compensation Association (ACA)
14040 N. Northsight Blvd.
Scottsdale, AZ 85260
Phone: (602) 951-9191
Fax: (602) 483-8352
E-mail: qllr45a@prodigy.com
WWW: http://www.ahrm.org/aca/aca.htm

Program Data
Certifying body: Association
Year certification began: 1976
Number certified: 6000
Organization members: 18,000
Additional programs: Certified Benefits Professional (CBP)
Approximate certification costs: $1400

Program Description

The Certified Compensation Professional (CCP) designation recognizes human resource professionals in the direct-pay compensation field. Certification is based on passing a series of examinations. ACA membership is not required.

Education/Experience

None required.

Examinations

ACA's body of knowledge model was validated by a research team from Rutgers University's Institute of Management and Labor Relations. The CCP program consists of nine examinations. Each examination is offered in conjunction with an optional two-day preparatory seminar. Candidates must pass nine examinations for certification, three of which are electives. The six required examinations are as follows:

- Job Analysis, Job Documentation, and Job Evaluation
- Pay Structures, Pay Rate Determination, and Program Administration
- Principles of Accounting and Finance
- Quantitative Methods
- Regulatory Environments for Compensation Programs
- Total Compensation Management

Recertification

Certification currency is based on continuing education. CCPs must earn 12 currency credits every three years.

CERTIFIED EMPLOYEE ASSISTANCE PROFESSIONAL (CEAP®)

Sponsor

Employee Assistance Certification Commission (EACC)
Employee Assistance Professionals Association (EAPA)
2101 Wilson Blvd., Suite 500
Arlington, VA 22201
Phone: (703) 522-6272
Fax: (703) 522-4585

Program Data

Certifying body: Association-sponsored independent board
Organization members: 7000
Approximate cost of certification: $200 (members), $275 (nonmembers)

Program Description

The Certified Employee Assistance Professional (CEAP) designation recognizes experienced professionals working in an employee assistance program. Certification is based on passing an examination.

Education/Experience

Candidates must have three years of employee assistance experience and have worked 3000 hours in employee assistance programming. Membership in the EAPA is not required.

Examinations

The CEAP examination is administered for the EACC by the Professional Testing Corporation. The four-hour, 250-question, multiple-choice examination covers the following areas:

- Work organizations, including types of organizations; organizational dynamics; employee and labor relations; and policies towards troubled employees
- Human resources, including employment legislation and law; performance appraisals; collective bargaining; benefits; health; safety; and wellness
- Employee-assistance-program management and practice
- Employee-assistance-program services
- Addictions and chemical dependencies, including concepts, intervention, treatment, and rehabilitation

  Personal and psychological problems, including interviewing, assessments, crises management, and referrals.

Recertification

CEAPs must recertify every three years. Recertification is based on continuing education. One hundred hours of EAP-related, approved training is required; 60 of those hours must be in program management, practice, and services.

EMPLOYMENT AND TRAINING GENERALIST (ETG)

EMPLOYMENT AND TRAINING MASTER (ETM)

Sponsor

International Association of Personnel in
  Employment Security (IAPES)
1801 Louisville Road
Frankfort, KY 40601
Phone: (502) 223-4459
Fax: (502) 223-4127
E-mail: iapes@aol.com
WWW: http://www.psri.com/iapes/

Program Data

The IAPES examinations have been validated
through the U.S. Department of Labor's Test
Development Field Center system. The program is
endorsed by Interstate Conference of Employment
Security Agencies (ICESA).

Certifying body: Association
Year certification began: 1988
Organization members: 28,000

Program Description

The Employment and Training Generalist (ETG)
designation is the first level of the three-tier
Professional Development Program (PDP). The
PDP seeks to enhance competence and understanding of employment professionals, primarily
in the public sector. Certification is based
on passing an examination. Membership in IAPES
is not required. IAPES maintains an active ethics
program.

Four specialist designations make up the second
tier of the PDP. All candidates who have already
received their ETG designation are eligible. Each
specialty certification is based on passing an examination. These are the specialties:

- Employment Services Specialist (ESS)
- Job Training Specialist (JTS)
- Labor Market Information Specialist (LMIS)
- Unemployment Insurance Specialist (UIS)

The Master designation (ETM) is the top level of
the PDP, and recognizes professionals who have
completed all specialist examinations. There is no
separate exam for ETM.

Examinations

All PDP examinations are based on the PDP's
study guides. Each examination is a 100-question,
multiple-choice test. Exams and their study guides
are based on a developed core body of knowledge.

Recertification

None.

PROFESSIONAL IN HUMAN RESOURCES (PHR)

SENIOR PROFESSIONAL IN HUMAN RESOURCES (SPHR)

Sponsor

Human Resource Certification Institute (HRCI)
606 N. Washington St.
Alexandria, VA 22314
Phone: (703) 548-3440
Fax: (703) 836-0367
TDD: (703) 548-6999
E-mail: hrci@shrm.org
WWW: http://www.shrm.org/docs/HRCI.html

Program Data

HRCI was founded by the Society for Human
Resource Management (SHRM) to serve as its
certification body.

Certifying body: Association-sponsored
  independent board
Year certification began: 1976
Number certified: 15,000
Approximate certification costs: PHR—$175
  (members), $225 (nonmembers); SPHR—
  $300 (members), $350 (nonmembers)

Program Description

The Professional in Human Resources (PHR) and
Senior Professional in Human Resources (SPHR)
designations recognize professionals who demonstrate achievement of national standards in human
resources knowledge and comprehension. Certification is based on passing a professional examination.

Education/Experience

Employment experience must be in an exempt-
level position working primarily in the human
resources field. Experience may come from work
as a human resources practitioner, educator,
researcher, or consultant.

For the PHR designation, a candidate must have at least four years of HR experience (two years with a bachelor's, one year with a graduate degree).

For the SPHR designation, a candidate must at least eight years of HR experience (six years with a bachelor's, five years with a graduate degree).

Examinations
The 250-question, multiple-choice examinations are administered for HRCI by The Psychology Corporation. The PHR and SPHR examinations cover similar areas, but differ in both concentration and question level. PHR questions will be more on an operational or technical level, while SPHR questions will focus more on strategy and policy, and may include scenario-based questions. A full set of study materials is available to prepare for the exam. The exam areas are as follows:

- Business and human-resources-management practices
- Employee selection and placement
- Employee training and development
- Compensation and benefits
- Labor and employee relations
- Worker health and safety, and organizational security

Recertification
PHRs and SPHRs must recertify every three years, either by accumulating 60 contact hours of professional HR education, or by examination.

CERTIFIED HUMAN RESOURCES EXECUTIVE (CHRE®)

Sponsor
Educational Institute of the American Hotel and Motel Association (EI/AH&MA)
1407 S. Harrison Road, Suite 300
East Lansing, MI 48823
Phone: (800) 752-5527
Fax: (517) 353-5527
Toll-Free: 1-800-752-4567
E-mail: info@ei-ahma.org
WWW: http://www.ei-ahma.org

Program Data
Year certification began: 1969
Number certified: 15,000+

Organization members: 10,000
Additional certifications: Certified Engineering Operations Executive (CEOE®); Certified Food and Beverage Executive (CFBE®); Certified Hospitality Educator (CHE®); Certified Hospitality Housekeeping Executive (CHHE®); Certified Hospitality Sales Professional (CHSP®); Certified Hospitality Supervisor (CHS®); Certified Hospitality Technology Professional (CHTP®); Certified Hotel Administrator (CHA®); Certified Rooms Division Executive (CRDE®); Hospitality Skills Certification; Master Hotel Supplier (MHS®)
Approximate certification costs: $275 (AH&MA-member properties), $325 (nonmember properties)

Program Description
The Certified Human Resources Executive (CHRE®) recognizes experienced and knowledgeable human resources and personnel managers in the hospitality industry. Certification is based on passing an examination. AH&MA membership is not required.

Education/Experience
To sit for the CHRE examination, a candidate must be currently employed as a human resources manager at a hospitality property or hospitality corporation, and meet one of the following requirements:

- An associate's or higher human-resource-management or hospitality degree, or completion of the Educational Institute's five-course curriculum in human resource management, and two years of experience in a hospitality human-resource-management position
- Three years of experience in a hospitality human-resource-management position
- Currently an instructor teaching hospitality management, with two years of experience in this capacity, and two years of experience in human resource management

Examinations
The examination covers hospitality training, supervision, human resources, and law. The exam includes comprehensive coverage of labor regulations and law.

Recertification

CHREs must renew their certification every five years. Certification is based on a point system; 50 points are needed to recertify. Points are earned through professional experience, continuing education, professional involvement, and educational service.

MEMBER, OUTPLACEMENT INSTITUTE

FELLOW (PRACTITIONER), OUTPLACEMENT INSTITUTE

FELLOW (MANAGER), OUTPLACEMENT INSTITUTE

Sponsor

Outplacement Institute
P.O. Box 150759
San Rafael, CA 94915
Phone: (415) 459-2235
Fax: (415) 459-6298

Program Data

Endorsed by:

The Outplacement Institute is sponsored by the International Association of Career Management Professionals (IACMP) and the Association of Outplacement Consulting Firms (AOCF).

Certifying body: Association-sponsored independent board
Year certification began: 1995
Number certified: 260
Approximate certification costs: $200 (members), $290 (nonmembers)

Program Description

The Outplacement Institute's certification process evaluates the qualifications of outplacement professionals and endorses those candidates meeting all of the Institute's standards. Certification is based on portfolio review; there is no examination. Members must have 10 years of outplacement management experience. Fellows must have 15 years of outplacement management or consulting experience. The Outplacement Institute has an active ethics program.

Education/Experience

Candidates must demonstrate competency in outplacement through a portfolio-review process. A candidate's portfolio must include business education, outplacement experience, demonstrations of advancing the profession, and third-party endorsements.

Recertification

Membership must be renewed annually through continuing education.

REGISTERED ORGANIZATION DEVELOPMENT PROFESSIONAL (RODP)

REGISTERED ORGANIZATION DEVELOPMENT CONSULTANT (RODC)

Sponsor

The Organization Development Institute
11234 Walnut Ridge Road
Chesterland, OH 44026
Phone: (216) 461-4333
Fax: (216) 729-9319
E-mail: aa563@cleveland.freenet.edu

Program Data

Certifying body: Association
Year certification began: Not disclosed
Number certified: RODC—100; RODP—300
Organization members: 500
Approximate certification costs: $110–$150

Program Description

The Organization Development Institute registers organization development professionals in their International Registry of Organization Development Professionals. Membership is required for the registration. The O.D. Institute maintains an active ethics program.

Education/Experience

For the Registered Organization Development Professional (RODC) designation, members must feel that they are professionally qualified by training and experience and agree to follow the organization's code of ethics. Regular membership is $110.

For the Registered Organization Development Consultant (RODC), members must pass a written examination, provide two letters of recommendation from qualified O.D. consultants, and have either of the following: a doctorate in psychology or allied field plus two years of experience; a master's degree in psychology, business administration, or allied field plus four years of experience; or a bachelor's degree plus six years of experience.

Examinations
The RODC examination is under revision.

Recertification
None.

CERTIFIED PAYROLL PROFESSIONAL (CPP)

Sponsor
American Payroll Association (APA)
30 East 33rd St., 5th Floor
New York, NY 10016
Phone: (212) 686-2030

Program Data
The CPP examination has been reviewed by the American Council on Education (ACE), which recommends 11 undergraduate college credits for a passing score.

Certifying body: Professional association
Number certified: 2500 active
Organization members: 11,000

Program Description
The Certified Payroll Professional (CPP) designation recognizes professionals in payroll practice and management. Certification is based on passing an examination. APA membership is not required.

Education/Experience
To qualify to take the CPP examination, the candidate must have had direct involvement with payroll in three of the preceding five years. Reference materials to help prepare for the test are available from APA.

Examinations
The CPP examination was developed by the American Payroll Association (APA) with assistance from The Psychological Association, San Antonio, Texas. The Psychological Association administers the CPP examination for the APA.

The 200-question, multiple-choice test has a four-hour time limit. The CPP examination covers:

- Fundamentals of the practice of payroll, including federal regulations and legislation, benefits, deductions, record-keeping, and payment options
- Federal tax and social security
- Accounting
- Payroll systems
- General management

Recertification
The CPP must renew certification every five years. A CPP may either retake the certification examination, or meet the minimum of 120 contact hours of related continuing education during the five-year period.

CERTIFIED PENSION CONSULTANT (CPC)

Sponsor
American Society of Pension Actuaries (ASPA)
4350 North Fairfax Drive, Suite 820
Arlington, VA 22203
Phone: (703) 516-9300
Fax: (703) 516-9308

Program Data
Certifying body: Association
Organization members: 3000
Additional programs: Associate Professional Member (APM); Fellow, Society of Pension Actuaries (FSPA); Member, Society of Pension Actuaries (MSPA); Qualified Pension Administrator (QPA)
Approximate certification costs: $1000

Program Description
The Certified Pension Consultant (CPC) designation is an ASPA membership category recognizing experienced professionals who have demonstrated the knowledge required for consulting in various areas of qualified retirement and benefit programs.

Education/Experience
Candidates must document three years of professional pension-consulting experience prior to receiving the designation.

Examinations
Study courses are available but not required for the examinations. There are five examinations required for the CPC designation:

- Qualification and Operation of Retirement Plans—A three-hour, multiple-choice examination which includes types of plans; qualifications; participation and distribution requirements; reporting and disclosure; taxes, fiduciary responsibilities; and investment vehicles and performance

- Administrative and Consulting Aspects of Defined Contribution Plans—A three-hour, multiple-choice examination which covers plans including profit-sharing; 401(k); employee stock ownerships (ESOP); and simplified employee pensions (SEP)

- Administrative and Consulting Aspects of Defined Benefit Plans—A three-hour, multiple-choice examination which covers benefit calculations; rules; terminations and changes; funding and accounting; and traditional plan variations

- Financial and Fiduciary Aspects of Qualified Plans—A four-hour, multiple-choice and short-answer examination which includes plan protection; accounting and financial reporting; plan assets; fiduciary standards; plan terminations; taxation; distribution; and estate planning

- Advanced Retirement Plan Consulting—A four-hour essay examination testing the candidate's depth of knowledge and ability to apply this knowledge to comprehensive pension problems

Recertification

All designated members of the ASPA must meet continuing education requirements to maintain certification. CPCs must earn 40 hours of continuing education every two years.

CERTIFIED PERSONNEL CONSULTANT (CPC)

Sponsor

National Association of Personnel Services (NAPS)
3133 Mount Vernon Ave.
Alexandria, VA 22305
Phone: (703) 684-0180

Program Data

Certifying body: Association
Additional certifications: Certified Temporary-Staffing Specialist (CTS)
Approximate certification costs: $265 (members), $530 (nonmembers)

Program Description

The Certified Personnel Consultant (CPC) designation recognizes professionals in the permanent placement and recruiting industry. Certification is based on passing an examination. Membership in NAPS is not required.

Education/Experience

A candidate must have two years of experience as an owner, manager, partner, or consultant with a private placement firm.

Examinations

The three-hour certification examination is divided into two parts. The first part covers general knowledge of permanent placement consulting. The second part covers the topics of legal, regulatory, and business practices, including discrimination, contracts, background checks, and the Immigration Reform and Control Act. Training and reference material is sold by NAPS.

CERTIFIED PROFESSIONAL EMPLOYER SPECIALIST (CPES)

Sponsor

National Association of Professional Employer Organizations (NAPEO)
1735 North Lynn St., Suite 950
Arlington, VA 22209
Phone: (703) 524-3636
Fax: (703) 524-2303
E-mail: gco@napeo.com!
WWW: http://www.napeo.com/peo/index.html

Program Data

Certifying body: Association
Year certification began: 1994
Approximate certification costs: $200 (members), $500 (nonmembers)

Program Description

The Certified Professional Employer Specialist (CPES) designation recognizes individuals providing support or management services within an employee leasing or professional employer company. Certification is based on passing an examination. NAPEO membership is not required. NAPEO maintains an active ethics program.

Education/Experience

All candidates must have at least three years of staff or management experience within the employee leasing field. Eligibility is based on a point system; 100 points is required to sit for the CPES examination. Points must be earned in formal education, experience, and association to qualify.

Examinations

The CPES examination covers health insurance, human resources, orientation and training, payroll, and workers compensation. Study courses, training manuals, and video reviews are available.

Recertification

CPESs must meet all NAPEO-directed continuing education.

CERTIFIED QUALITY MANAGER (CQM)

Sponsor

American Society for Quality Control (ASQC)
611 E. Wisconsin Ave.
Milwaukee, WI 53201
Phone: (800) 248-1946
Fax: (414) 272-1734
WWW: http://www.asqc.org/educat/cert.html

Program Data

Certifying body: Association
Year certification began: 1966 (first program)
Number certified: 50,000 (all programs)
Organization members: 130,000
Additional programs: Certified Mechanical Inspector (CMI); Certified Quality Auditor (CQA); Certified Quality Engineer (CQE); Certified Quality Technician (CQT); Certified Reliability Engineer (CRE)

Program Description

The Certified Quality Manager (CQM) designation recognizes individuals knowledgeable in quality principles and standards in relation to organization and human resource management. Certification is based on passing an examination. ASQC maintains an active ethics program.

Examinations

The multiple-choice examination is based on the CQM body of knowledge and covers quality standards; organizations and their functions; quality needs and overall strategic plans; customer satisfaction and focus; project management; continuous improvement; human resource management; and training and education.

CERTIFIED RELOCATION PROFESSIONAL (CRP™)

SENIOR CERTIFIED RELOCATION PROFESSIONAL (SCRP™)

Sponsor

Employee Relocation Council (E-R-C)
1720 N St. NW
Washington, DC 20036
Phone: (202) 857-0857
E-mail: crp@erc.org
WWW: http://www.erc.org/erc.htm

Program Data

Certifying body: Association
Number certified: 3000+ (both designations)
Organization members: 1200 representatives from corporations, and approximately 10,000 individuals and companies in the relocation industry

Program Description

The Certified Relocation Professional (CRP™) and Senior Certified Relocation Professional (SCRP™) designations recognize professionals in the field of corporate relocation/employee transfer. A CRP/SCRP may be employed by a corporation in charge of handling employee transfers/corporate relocations, or by a provider of relocation services, including real estate and relocation counseling firms.

Education/Experience

To sit for the CRP examination, a candidate must have two years of relocation experience. To earn the SCRP designation, a CRP must earn points through E-R-C's service program.

Examinations

The CRP examination is based on a body of common knowledge gathered by relocation professionals in both corporations and relocation-related services. The pass rate is 65%. The CRP exam comes in three editions, one for each area of concentration in the field: real estate, appraisal, and general relocation. All editions cover the same knowledge areas, but emphasize the areas related to each concentration. The exam covers:

- Corporate relocation policy and issues
- Family relocation issues
- Relocation-related real estate
- Relocation-related appraising
- Relocation tax and legal issues

Recertification
CRPs and SCRPs are required to recertify every three years. Recertification is based on earning 30 credits of acceptable relocation-related continuing education.

CERTIFIED PROFESSIONAL RÉSUMÉ WRITER (CPRW)

Sponsor
Professional Association of Résumé Writers (PARW)
3637 Fourth St. North, Suite 330
St. Petersburg, FL 33704
Phone: (813) 821-2274

Program Data
Certifying body: Association
Approximate certification costs: $175

Program Description
The Certified Professional Résumé Writer (CPRW) designation recognizes members of the Professional Association of Résumé Writers (PARW) who have passed a certification examination. Candidates must submit two client résumés for evaluation.

Examinations
The certification examination is available to members by facsimile, on-line, or at the PARW convention. The test is based primarily on three texts: *The Perfect Résumé* by Tom Jackson, *The Overnight Résumé* by Donald Asher, and *How to Comply With Federal Employee Laws* by Sheldon London.

Recertification
None.

CERTIFIED ADMINISTRATOR OF SUGGESTION SYSTEMS (CASS)

CERTIFIED MANAGER OF SUGGESTION SYSTEMS (CMSS)

Sponsor
Employee Involvement Association (EIA)
1735 N. Lynn St., Suite 950
Arlington, VA 22209
Phone: (703) 524-3424
Fax: (703) 524-2303
WWW: http://www.eia.com/

Program Data
Certifying body: Association
Approximate certification costs: $150

Program Description
The Certified Administrator of Suggestion Systems (CASS) and Certified Manager of Suggestion Systems (CMSS) designations recognize employee involvement and suggestion systems professionals. EIA membership is required. Certification is based on passing an examination.

Education/Experience
Eligibility to sit for either examination is based on a point system. All CASS candidates must have at least two years of suggestion systems-related experience. All CMSS candidates must have at least three years of suggestion systems-related experience, with at least one year in management.

40 points needed for eligibility:

- Education: 40 per advanced degree; 30 per bachelor's degree; 20 per certification; 10 per high school diploma
- Experience: 8 per year as manager; 6 per year as administrator
- Association: 5 per conference; 3 per training course; additional point for leadership

Examinations
Both CASS and CMSS examinations are take-home, open-book tests. A certification textbook, from which all examination questions are derived, is provided for each candidate. Review workshops are available.

CMSS candidates must also complete a 1000-word professional paper.

Recertification

EIA certifications must be renewed every three years by earning 15 professional credits.

CERTIFIED TECHNICAL TRAINER (CTT)

Sponsor

Educational Testing Service (ETS)
P.O. Box 6541
Princeton, NJ 08541
Phone: (800) 258-4914
Fax: (609) 951-6240
E-mail: cttp@ets.org

Program Data

The CTT program was formed by a joint agreement between the Information Technology Training Association (ITTA) and the Computer Education Management Association (CEdMA). The exam is based on competencies defined by the International Board of Standards for Training Performance and Instruction (IBSTPI). Several major computer hardware and software companies also endorse the CTT program.

Certifying body: Independent board
Year certification began: 1995
Approximate certification costs: $145

Program Description

The Certified Technical Training (CTT) is a multi-vendor program recognizing skilled instructors. The program was developed by a team of expert instructors and leading computer hardware and software companies. Certification is based on a computer-based exam and an evaluation of a videotaped training session.

Education/Experience

Candidates must provide a videotape of an actual training session. The videotaped performance assessment is based on a 20-minute instructional performance. Supporting materials and background information should be provided with the videotape.

Examinations

The CTT knowledge exam is a 120-question, multiple-choice test based on 14 trainer competencies:

- Analyze course materials and learner information
- Assure preparation of the instructional site
- Establish and maintain instructor credibility
- Manage the learning environment
- Demonstrate effective communication skills
- Demonstrate effective presentation skills
- Demonstrate effective questioning skills
- Respond appropriately to needed clarification and feedback
- Provide positive reinforcement
- Use appropriate instructional methods
- Use media effectively
- Evaluate learner performance
- Evaluate delivery of instruction
- Report evaluation information

Recertification

None.

CERTIFIED TEMPORARY-STAFFING SPECIALIST (CTS)

Sponsor

National Association of Personnel Services (NAPS)
3133 Mount Vernon Ave.
Alexandria, VA 22305
Phone: (703) 684-0180

Program Data

Certifying body: Association
Additional programs: Certified Personnel Consultant (CPC)
Approximate certification costs: $265 (members), $530 (nonmembers)

Program Description

The Certified Temporary-Staffing Specialist (CTS) designation recognizes staffing professionals in the temporary-service industry. Certification is based on passing an examination. Membership in NAPS is not required.

Education/Experience

Candidates must be currently employed full time and have one year of experience in a temporary-service business.

Examinations

The three-hour certification examination is divided into two parts. The first part covers general knowledge of temporary-service operations. The second part covers the topics of legal, regulatory, and business practices, including equal-employment-opportunity requirements.

VOCATIONAL EXPERT (DIPLOMATE, FELLOW)

Sponsor

American Board of Vocational Experts (ABVE)
5700 Old Orchard Road, 1st Floor
Skokie, IL 60077
Phone: (708) 966-0074

Program Data

Certifying body: Independent, nonmembership certification organization
Number certified: 400

Program Description

The Diplomate and Fellow certifications are based on experience and passing the ABVE examination.

Education/Experience

Candidates must have a master's degree in human services, and three (Fellow) or seven (Diplomate) years of experience as a vocational expert.

Examinations

The ABVE exam covers psychological testing and psychology; vocational testing and work sampling; physical capabilities; job surveys and job analysis; job placement; and testimony and litigation.

Recertification

Certification is renewed annually and requires 14 contact hours of professional education.

BUSINESS AND MANAGEMENT
Legal

NATIONAL COURT REPORTERS ASSOCIATION CERTIFICATION PROGRAMS

Sponsor
National Court Reporters Association (NCRA)
8224 Old Courthouse Road
Vienna, VA 22182
Phone: (800) 272-6272
Fax: (703) 556-6291
E-mail: 72123,3102@compuserve.com
WWW: http://www.verbatimreporters.com/ncra/reporter/ncrahome.html

Program Data
Certifying body: Association
Year certification began: 1975
Number certified: 12,000
Organization members: 33,000

Program Description
NCRA certifies court reporters at several levels and in several specialties. These programs are designed to provide recognition and career path options to court reporters. All exams are based on a body of knowledge or task analysis. NCRA membership is required. NCRA maintains an active ethics program.

The certifications are listed below:

Court Reporting

- Registered Professional Reporter (RPR): Entry-level designation. Candidates must pass two exams: (1) a 100-question, written knowledge test covering reporting, transcript production, operating practices, and professional issues; (2) an entry-level skills test in court reporting.

- Registered Merit Reporter (RMR): Advanced-level designation. Candidates must be RPRs for three years. Candidates must pass two exams: (1) a written knowledge test covering reporting, transcript production, administration, and professional issues; (2) an advanced skills test in court reporting.

- Registered Diplomate Reporter (RDR): Top-level designation. Candidates must be RMRs for three years, hold two specialty certifications, and have a bachelor's degree. Candidates must pass a written knowledge test covering reporting, transcript production, administration, and professional issues.

Court Reporting Specialty

- Certified Manager of Reporting Services (CMRS). The CMRS designation recognizes individuals completing the two three-day program courses and an independent project. The courses cover management and management theory, personnel management, financial management, marketing, and technology.

- Certified Realtime Reporter (CRR). The CRR designation recognizes RPRs skilled at realtime reporting. Candidates must pass a five-minute realtime dictation exam.

- Certified Legal Video Specialist (CLVS). The CLVS designation recognizes court reporters who complete the CLVS workshop, pass a 100-question written test, and successfully complete a videotape production test.

Court Reporting Education Specialty

- Certified Reporting Instructor (CRI). The CRI designation recognizes court reporting instructors completing the 11-hour instructor orientation course.

- Certified Program Evaluator (CPE). The CPE designation recognizes individuals responsible for evaluating the quality of NCRA-approved education programs. Candidates must teach at an NCRA-approved program or hold RPR or CRI certification. The 10-hour program covers sensitivity training, evaluating reporting programs, and conducting an evaluation.

Recertification
Holders of RPR, RMR, RDR, and CRI designations must earn 30 professional education credits every three years. Other programs have no recertification requirements.

CERTIFIED LEGAL ASSISTANT (CLA)

CERTIFIED LEGAL ASSISTANT SPECIALIST (CLA SPECIALIST)

Sponsor

National Association of Legal Assistants (NALA)
1601 S. Main St., Suite 300
Tulsa, OK 74119
Phone: (918) 587-6828
E-mail: nala@mail.webtek.com
WWW: http://www.nala.org/

Program Data

Certifying body: Association
Year certification began: 1976
Number certified: 7740
Organization members: 15,000
Approximate certification costs: $250

Program Description

The Certified Legal Assistant (CLA) program is the only national certification program for paralegals. In addition to basic certification, CLAs may qualify as specialists in several areas. Membership in the NALA is not required for certification.

Education/Experience

A candidate must meet one of the following requirements to sit for the examination:

- Completion of legal assistant program that meets NALA requirements

- A bachelor's degree and one year of experience as a legal assistant

- A high school diploma, 20 hours of continuing legal education in the past two years, and seven years of experience as a legal assistant

Examinations

The CLA examination is a two-day series of tests in several areas. Study guides are available from NALA. The exam covers communications; ethics (including knowledge of American Bar Association rules of professional conduct); human relations and interviewing techniques; judgment and analytical ability; legal research; legal terminology; and substantive law (including selected legal specialties).

Specialty Certifications

CLAs may take specialty examinations in several areas. Each is a four-hour examination. Substantial experience in the specialty is expected in order to pass. The specialty exams are Bankruptcy Specialist; Civil Litigation Specialist; Probate and Estate Planning Specialist; Corporate and Business Law Specialist; Criminal Law and Procedure Specialist; Intellectual Property Specialist; and Real Estate Specialist.

Recertification

Recertification is required every five years, and is based on a point system. Points are awarded for continuing education, experience, and completion of specialty exams.

CERTIFIED LEGAL INVESTIGATOR® (CLI)

Sponsor

National Association of Legal Investigators, Inc. (NALI)
P.O. Box 3254
Alton, IL 62002
Phone: (618) 465-4400
Fax: (618) 465-1506

Program Data

Certifying body: Association
Year certification began: 1974
Number certified: 200
Organization members: 700
Approximate certification costs: $125 (members), $225 (nonmembers)

Program Description

The Certified Legal Investigator® (CLI) designation recognizes professionals who gather evidence and help attorneys prepare for litigation. Legal investigators are not private detectives; they work for an attorney rather than a private client. Certification is based on writing an acceptable white paper and passing an examination. Membership in NALI is not required.

Education/Experience

Candidates must meet the following requirements to qualify for certification:

- Be primarily involved in negligence investigations and be employed by a law firm or an investigative firm

- Be licensed (if required by state)
- Have two years of full-time experience or have completed 60 semester hours of college

The CLI white paper, turned in prior to taking the CLI examination, must exceed 1000 words, discuss an appropriate investigative subject selected by the candidate, and be in an article or thesis format.

Examinations

The certification examination includes both written and oral components. The examination content and pass rate were not released. NALI recommends several publications and manuals for use in preparing for the examination, including books on legal, traffic accident, and criminal investigation.

Recertification

Certification is maintained by completing four units of continuing education every two years.

Education/Experience

To take the ALS examination, a candidate must meet one of the following requirements: the NALS Basic Legal Course, the NALS Basic Course of Independent Study, or one year of professional experience.

Examinations

The six-hour, objective-question examination covers the following areas:

- Written communication comprehension and application
- Office administration, legal terminology, and accounting
- Ethics, human relations, and applied office procedures

Recertification

Certification is for five years, but may be extended an additional three years through 20 hours of continuing education annually.

ACCREDITED LEGAL SECRETARY (ALS)

Sponsor

National Association of Legal Secretaries®
  (NALS)
2250 E. 73rd St., Suite 550
Tulsa, OK 74136
Phone: (918) 493-3540
E-mail: nals@mail.webtek.com
WWW: http://www.nals.org/

Program Data

Certifying body: Association
Organization members: 16,000
Additional certifications: Certified Professional Legal Secretary (PLS)
Approximate certification costs: $75 (members), $100 (nonmembers)

Program Description

The Accredited Legal Secretary (ALS) designation is an entry-level recognition of legal support competence. Certification is based on passing an examination. NALS membership is not required. NALS maintains an active ethics program.

CERTIFIED PROFESSIONAL LEGAL SECRETARY (PLS)

Sponsor

National Association of Legal Secretaries®
  (NALS)
2250 E. 73rd St., Suite 550
Tulsa, OK 74136
Phone: (918) 493-3540
E-mail: nals@mail.webtek.com
WWW: http://www.nals.org/

Program Data

Certifying body: Association
Organization members: 16,000
Additional certifications: Accredited Legal Secretary (ALS)
Approximate certification costs: $150 (members), $200 (nonmembers)

Program Description

The Certified Professional Legal Secretary (PLS) recognizes individuals experienced in legal support. Certification is based on passing an examination. NALS membership is not required. To take the PLS examination, a candidate must have three years of professional experience.

Examinations

NALS sponsors a legal training course to help prepare for the examination. The examination is divided into seven parts: Accounting; Ethics; Exercise of Judgement; Legal Knowledge and Procedures; Legal Secretarial Skills; Office Procedures; and Written Communication Skills and Knowledge.

Recertification

PLSs must recertify every five years based on continuing education.

BUSINESS AND MANAGEMENT
Logistics, Packaging, and Purchasing

CERTIFIED ASSOCIATE CONTRACTS MANAGER (CACM)

Sponsor

National Contract Management Association (NCMA)
1912 Woodford Road
Vienna, VA 22182
Phone: (800) 344-8096
Fax: (703) 448-0939
E-mail: ncma@us.net
WWW: http://www.cyberserv.com/ncma/index.html

Program Data

Certifying body: Association
Year certification began: 1980
Number certified: 1300+
Organization members: 23,000
Additional certifications: Certified Professional Contracts Manager (CPCM)
Approximate certification costs: $90 (members), $120 (nonmembers)

Program Description

The CACM recognizes the mastery of contracting fundamentals for professionals working as the following: materials, procurement, and contracting managers; contract lawyers, negotiators, and auditors; buyers; contract writers; costs analysts; and expeditors. Membership in the NCMA is not required. Certification is based on experience and passing an examination. NCMA, through its local chapters, provides CPCM Preparation Workshops and study groups. Membership in the NCMA is not required. Certification is based on passing an examination; eligibility is determined by a point system.

Education/Experience

Candidates must accumulate seven points, with at least one point in each category area. Only college courses are accepted under formal education. Courses on acquisition counted under formal education will also count under acquisition education and training. Highest degree: Associate's degree equals 2 points; bachelor's degree equals 4 points; master's/doctorate equals 6 points. Acquisition Education and Training equals 1 point per course. Each course must be equivalent to 24 or more contact hours. Shorter courses may be combined. Correspondence courses and in-house training may also be evaluated for meeting these requirements.

Examinations

The exam is a multiple-choice, two-part test. NCMA encourages study groups, and has test-preparation aids available. The recent pass rate is 57%. Each part takes three hours. The exam covers the following areas:

- Competition and acquisition planning
- Contract management
- Contracting methods and contract types
- General contracting management
- Socioeconomic programs

Recertification

A CACM must recertify every five years. Recertification is through earning 60 contact hours of continuing education, with at least 10 hours completed in the last 18 months of the five-year period. College courses are counted as 15 contact hours per semester-credit hour. Lifetime certification is available to CACMs over the age of 60. The recertification rate is 80%.

CERTIFIED PROFESSIONAL CONTRACTS MANAGER (CPCM)

Sponsor

National Contract Management Association (NCMA)
1912 Woodford Road
Vienna, VA 22182
Phone: (800) 344-8096
Fax: (703) 448-0939
E-mail: ncma@us.net
WWW: http://www.cyberserv.com/ncma/index.html

Program Data

Certifying body: Association
Year certification began: 1974
Number certified: 4800+
Organization members: 23,000
Additional certifications: Certified Associate
  Contracts Manager (CACM)
Approximate certification costs: $120 (members),
  $160 (nonmembers)

Program Description

The CPCM designation recognizes experienced professionals managing contracts-related functions. Professionals in this field include materials, procurement, and contracting managers; contract lawyers, negotiators, and auditors; buyers; contract writers; costs analysts; and expeditors. Membership in the NCMA is not required. Certification is based on experience and passing an examination. NCMA, through its local chapters, provides CPCM Preparation Workshops and study groups.

Education/Experience

These are the requirements.

- Bachelor's degree. Waivers to this requirement are given in extraordinary circumstances.

- Minimum of two years of experience in contracting. A waiver to this requirement may be given to candidates with a master's degree in procurement or acquisition management.

All candidates must meet the following course/seminar requirements. Each course must be equivalent to 24 or more contact hours. Shorter courses may be combined. Correspondence courses, in-house training, teaching a procurement course, and credit for scholarly works may also be evaluated for meeting these requirements. Group 1—Procurement equals two courses; Group 2—Legal equals one course; Group 3—Financial equals one course; Group 4—Business/Procurement-related equals four courses.

Examinations

The CPCM is a one-day essay exam divided into two parts. The first part is a general examination on procurement and contracts management. The second part concentrates on specific areas of contract management: legal; financial; economic and accounting; production; contracting; logistics management; commercial purchasing; and state/local government procurement. Due to the varied backgrounds of contracts managers, this portion of the exam allows the candidate to select which areas to answer: three questions from one area, and one each from two other areas. The recent pass rate is 55%.

Recertification

A CPCM must recertify every five years. Recertification is through earning 60 contact hours of continuing education, with at least 10 hours completed in the last 18 months of the five-year period. College courses are counted as 15 contact hours per semester-credit hour. Lifetime certification is available to CPCMs over the age of 60. The recertification rate is 80%.

CERTIFIED PROFESSIONAL FLEET MANAGER (CPFM)

Sponsor

National Private Truck Council (NPTC)
66 Canal Center Plaza, Suite 600
Alexandria, VA 22314
Phone: (703) 683-1300

Program Data

Certifying body: Association-sponsored independent board
Year certification began: 1993
Number certified: 150+
Organization members: Corporate, 1300 private fleet organizations
Approximate certification costs: $150

Program Description

The Certified Professional Fleet Manager (CPFM) designation recognizes private fleet professionals who demonstrate essential skills and capabilities to safely and productively manage a company's private fleet operation. The Private Fleet Management Institute (PFMI) offers several preparatory programs for the examination.

Education/Experience

Candidates must have at least two years of experience. Eligibility is based on a point system. Ten points are needed for eligibility. Points: 1 per year of fleet management experience; 0.5 per year of general management; 2 per bachelor's degree; 4 per bachelor's degree with a transportation and logistics concentration.

Examinations

The five-part, seven-hour examination covers each of the four core bodies of knowledge for private fleet management. The fifth part is a comprehensive case analysis. The pass rate for the first year was 70%. These are the four core bodies:

- The Role of the Private Fleet, including value versus cost considerations, which includes costs, service, profit justification, and private fleet dynamics

- The Legal and Regulatory Environment of Today's Private Fleet, including tax law, regulations, and environmental, safety, and workplace laws

- Managing a Safe and Effective Private Fleet and Work Force

- Making Better Use of Private Fleet Resources, which includes fleet purchasing and maintenance, and productivity-improvement approaches, tools, techniques, and technologies

Recertification

Continued professional education.

CERTIFIED PROFESSIONAL LOGISTICIAN (C.P.L.)

Sponsor

Society of Logistics Engineers (SOLE)
8100 Professional Place, Suite 211
Hyattsville, MD 20785
Phone: (301) 459-8446
Fax: (301) 459-1522
E-mail: Solehq@aol.com
WWW: http://www.telebyte.com/sole/sole.html

Program Data

Certifying body: Association
Year certification began: 1974
Number certified: 1949
Organization members: 7500
Approximate certification costs: $75 (members), $150 (nonmembers)

Program Description

The Certified Professional Logistician (C.P.L.) designation recognizes professionals from all areas of logistics. Certification is based on passing an examination; candidates must meet minimum experience requirements to sit for the examination. Membership in SOLE is not required.

Education/Experience

The experience requirements are nine years of experience or teaching in logistics, with at least two years in each of two SOLE-designated logistics fields. College work and degrees may substitute for a portion of the experience requirement.

Examinations

The C.P.L. examination is divided into four parts, representing the four fields of logistics as divided by SOLE. Preparatory courses and materials are available, including a 62-module preparatory training course. The examination covers these parts:

- Systems Management, including system components, life cycle, and evaluation; logistics support and integration concepts; logistics planning and organization; proposals and contracts; and management concepts

- System Design and Development, including system engineering, review, and testing

- Acquisition and Production Support, including support requirements, pricing, control, and production support

- Distribution and Customer Support, including supply and material management, customer needs and requirements, and equipment phase-out

The pass rate is 30%.

Recertification

None.

PROFESSIONAL CERTIFIED IN MATERIALS HANDLING (PCMH)

PROFESSIONAL CERTIFIED IN MATERIALS MANAGEMENT (PCMM)

Sponsor

Materials Handling and Management Society (MHMS)
8720 Red Oak Blvd., Suite 224
Charlotte, NC 28217
Phone: (704) 525-4667
Fax: (704) 558-4753
E-mail: material.handling.industry@industry.net
WWW: http://www.industry.net/c-a/orgmain/mhi/mhms

Program Data

Certifying body: Association
Number certified: 250
Organization members: 1000
Approximate certification costs: $50 (members),
 $100 (nonmembers)

Program Description

The Professional Certified in Materials Handling (PCMH) and Professional Certified in Materials Management (PCMM) designations recognize individuals responsible for products and materials from procurement through delivery. Certification is based on passing an examination. Membership in MHMS is not required. MHMS sells a study guide and seven-volume learning system reference library.

Education/Experience

Candidates must meet one of the following options to sit for the examination:

- Three years of industry experience and a materials handling-related graduate degree

- Four years of industry experience and a bachelor's degree

- Six years of industry experience and an associate's degree

Two years of experience credit is given to candidates who are Registered Professional Engineers. However, a candidate must have at least three years of industry experience.

Examinations

PCMH—The three-hour, multiple-choice examination includes these areas: applications and systems planning; environmental control; industrial packaging; integrated computer applications; plant layout; safety; transportation; work measurements.

PCMM—The three-hour, multiple-choice examination includes these areas: in-plant handling; information systems/computer applications; inventory control; planning materials flow; production control; purchasing; traffic and distribution; value techniques

Recertification

PCMHs and PCMMs must recertify every three years. Recertification is based on a point system, with points awarded for professional experience, education, and association involvement. As an alternative, the current certification examination may be retaken.

MILITARY PACKAGING PROFESSIONAL (MPP)

Sponsor

School of Military Packaging Technology (SMPT)
ATTN: ATSZ-MPT
Aberdeen Proving Ground, MD 21005-5001
Phone: (410) 278-2254 / DSN 298-2254
Fax: (410) 278-2176 / DSN 298-2176
E-mail: XMCSMPTA@APG-9.APG.ARMY.MIL

Certifications can be verified by letter addressed to the Chairman, Packaging Sciences Department.

Program Data

The MPP program is co-sponsored and approved by the National Institute of Packaging, Handling, and Logistics Engineers (NIPHLE).

Certifying body: Independent certifying
 organization formed in association between
 NIPHLE and SMPT
Year certification began: 1990
Number certified: 212
Organization members: Nonmembership

Program Description

The Military Packaging Professional (MPP) designation recognizes professionals who have completed an educational program on military packaging. The program is open to military personnel, Department of Defense civilian employees, non-Department agencies, and employees of private contractors bidding or planning to bid on military contracts. The school offers study guides and courses. Five years of related experience is required for certification. There is no examination component. Candidates are awarded the MPP certification based on the judgment of a review board that considers the following: completion of the school's three packaging courses and completion of six other relevant courses.

Curriculum

The core courses are as follows:

- Defense Preservation and Intermediate Protection

- Defense Packing and Unitization

- Defense Packaging Design

Electives include six additional courses on packaging. SMPT courses may be resident, on-site, or correspondence. Other service or civilian courses related to military packaging may be accepted as electives upon petition to SMPT.

Recertification
None.

CERTIFIED PACKAGING PROFESSIONAL (CPP)

CERTIFIED PROFESSIONAL IN TRAINING {PACKAGING} (CPIT)

Sponsor
Institute of Packaging Professionals (IoPP)
481 Carlisle Drive
Herndon, VA 22070
Phone: (703) 318-8970
Fax: (703) 318-0310
WWW: http://www.packinfo-world.org/US/iopp.html

Program Data
Certifying body: Professional association
Year certification began: 1972
Number certified: 350
Organization members: 7000
Approximate certification costs: $75 (members), $175 (nonmembers)

Program Description
The Certified Packaging Professional (CPP) designation is based on passing an examination and submission of a technical paper. Membership in IoPP is not required. The IoPP offers a study guide to help prepare for the examination. The Certified Professional in Training (CPIT) designation recognizes college seniors and recent graduates in appropriate technology who pass the CPP examination but who do not have sufficient experience.

Education/Experience
To sit for the CPP examination, a candidate must meet one of the following options:

- Six years of professional experience
- Two years of professional experience and a bachelor's degree in packaging technology. One additional year of credit will be given for a postgraduate degree.

The technical paper component tests both the candidate's professional knowledge and ability to communicate. The paper is completed after the candidate passes the examination, and will cover an area of packaging. A previously published paper or U.S. patent (within the previous 12 months) may be substituted for the paper.

Examinations
Examinations are based on consultant recommendations, and the test questions are written by academia and consultants. Candidates may take either the Consumer, Commercial/Distribution, or Military versions of the open-book, multiple-choice examination. There is a mail-in examination option.

The pass rate is 90%.

Recertification
CPPs must recertify twice at five-year intervals. Recertification is based on either meeting the professional activities requirements (based on a point system) or taking the recertification examination. CPPs must maintain employment in the field to recertify. After the second recertification, CPPs are certified for life.

- Points required for recertification: 60
- Point examples:
  - 10 for advanced degree
  - 3 per year employed
  - 2 per positional promotion
  - 1 per year of professional society membership
  - ½ per hour professional education course

Recertification rate: 80%

CERTIFIED IN PRODUCTION AND INVENTORY MANAGEMENT (CPIM®)

CERTIFIED FELLOW IN PRODUCTION AND INVENTORY MANAGEMENT (CFPIM™)

Sponsor
American Production and Inventory Control Society (APICS™)
500 W. Allendale Road
Falls Church, VA 22046
Phone: (800) 444-2742
WWW: http://www.apics.org

Program Data

Certifying body: Association
Number certified: Not released. 60,000 examinations are given annually.
Organization members: 70,000
Additional programs: Certified in Integrated Resource Management (CIRC™)
Approximate certification costs: $260 (members), $375 (nonmembers)

Program Description

The Certified in Production and Inventory Management (CPIM®) designation is based on passing five of six CPIM examinations. There are no experience or membership requirements. APICS offers a wide range of reference books, guides, workshops, and in-house program materials to prepare for the examinations.

The Certified Fellow in Production and Inventory Management (CFPIM) is given for passage of all six CPIM exams and meeting a minimum point level of 100 points. Points are given for high examination scores, presentations, publications, and instructing courses.

Examinations

The CPIM examinations are administered by Educational Testing Service (ETS). Five out of the six 100-question, multiple-choice examinations must be passed for the CPIM designation. The examinations are as follows:

- Inventory Management, including objectives, policies, systems, techniques, and distribution planning and control

- Just-in-Time, including basic concepts; human resources; Total Quality Control; techniques; integration; applications; and considerations unique to just-in-time

- Master Planning, including forecasting concepts and techniques; servicing orders; production and resource planning; and master-scheduling concepts, considerations, requirements, and implementation

- Material and Capacity Requirements Planning, including concepts; data sources and requirements; and planning characteristics, mechanics, implementation, and measurement

- Production Activity Control, including suppliers; capacity and priority control; lead time; and reporting and measurement

- Systems and Technologies, including strategies and choices; configuration and integration of production and inventory management functions; implementation; and performance measurement

Recertification

None.

CERTIFIED PURCHASING PROFESSIONAL (CPP)

CERTIFIED PURCHASING EXECUTIVE (CPE)

Sponsor

American Purchasing Society, Inc. (APS)
11910 Oak Trail Way
Port Richey, FL 34668
Phone: (813) 862-7998
Fax: (813) 862-8199

Program Data

Certifying body: Association
Year certification began: 1970
Number certified: 2350
Approximate certification costs: $189 (members), $225 (nonmembers)

Program Description

The Certified Purchasing Professional (CPP) and Certified Purchasing Executive (CPE) designations recognize buyers, purchasing agents, purchasing managers and executives. Certification is based on a point system. Candidates usually take the written examination. APS may make exceptions for applicants with extensive experience or for other acceptable examinations already taken. Membership is not required for certification.

Education/Experience

Eligibility is determined by a point system. In addition, candidates must provide proof of financial responsibility (including personal credit references) upon application. APS investigates candidate background references prior to certification.

Examinations

The exam includes general purchasing, accounting, technical and legal aspects of purchasing, negotiating, and economics. The pass rate is 92%. Study materials and seminars are available through APS.

Candidates are tested on the following knowledge areas:

- Mathematical ability, particularly the ability to use percentage calculations, to understand and use averages, and to use other statistical calculations
- Negotiations, as exhibited by an understanding of applied psychology and communications skills
- Business law, particularly when related to contracts and commercial transactions
- Purchasing management, including knowledge of current administrative and management practices in purchasing operations
- Purchasing operations, including the areas of economics, marketing, accounting, and finance as they apply to purchasing operations
- Engineering, particularly elementary areas of engineering related to purchasing activities

Recertification

Reapplication is needed every five years. A CPP must accumulate 15 or more points, and a CPE must accumulate 25 points.

CERTIFIED PROFESSIONAL PUBLIC BUYER (CPPB)

Sponsor

Universal Public Purchasing Certification Council
11800 Sunrise Valley Drive, Suite 1050
Reston, VA 22091
Phone: (703) 715-9400
Fax: (703) 715-9897
WWW: http://www.nigp.org/nigp/nigphome.htm

Program Data

The Council is made up of the National Institute of Governmental Purchasing (NIGP) and the National Association of State Purchasing Officials (NASPO).

Certifying body: Association-sponsored independent board

Number certified: 5000

Additional programs: Certified Public Purchasing Officer (CPPO)

Approximate certification costs: $100 (members), $150 (nonmembers)

Program Description

The Certified Professional Public Buyer (CPPB) designation recognizes purchasing, procurement, contract administration, and logistics professionals in the public sector. Certification is based on passing an examination. There are no membership requirements.

Education/Experience

Candidates must meet one of the following requirements:

- High school diploma, NIGP General and Public Purchasing seminar, the NIGP Materials Management seminar, and four years of purchasing experience, with at least two in the public sector
- Associate's degree in purchasing (or a related field) or bachelor's degree and the NIGP General and Public Purchasing and Materials Management seminars, and three years of purchasing experience, with at least two in the public sector
- Bachelor's degree in purchasing (or a related field) or advanced degree and two years of public purchasing experience

Examinations

The CPPB examination is a two-part, four-hour written test covering purchasing-related technical, operational, organizational, and coordination areas. Optional three-day NIGP General and Public Purchasing and Materials Management seminars cover the examination content. The two-part examination includes administration; competitive bidding; contracting; legal and commercial code requirements; logistics; organization and management; purchasing methods; quality assurance; records management; source selection; specifications and standards.

Recertification

Certification must be renewed every five years and is based on a point system for professional development and education. CPPBs with 15 years of experience may request lifetime certification at age 62 or retirement.

CERTIFIED PUBLIC PURCHASING OFFICER (CPPO)

Sponsor

Universal Public Purchasing Certification Council
11800 Sunrise Valley Drive, Suite 1050
Reston, VA 22091
Phone: (703) 715-9400
Fax: (703) 715-9897
WWW: http://www.nigp.org/nigp/nigphome.htm

Program Data

The Council is made up of the National Institute of Governmental Purchasing (NIGP) and the National Association of State Purchasing Officials (NASPO).

Certifying body: Association-sponsored independent board
Additional programs: Certified Professional Public Buyer (CPPB)

Education/Experience

Candidates must meet one of the following requirements:

- High school diploma, NIGP General and Public Purchasing seminar, NIGP Materials Management seminar, and five years of purchasing experience, with at least four in the public sector and two in a supervisory position

- Associate's degree in purchasing (or a related field) or bachelor's degree and the NIGP General and Public Purchasing and Materials Management seminars and four years of purchasing experience, with at least three in the public sector and two in a supervisory position

- Bachelor's degree in purchasing (or a related field) or advanced degree and three years of purchasing experience, with at least two in the public sector and two in a supervisory position

Examinations

The CPPO examination is a three-part, six-hour written test covering purchasing management, business and public administration, and purchasing-related organization and coordination. Candidates holding the CPPB designation are exempt from the third part of the examination, which covers purchasing-related organization and coordination. Optional three-day NIGP Public Procurement Management (two parts), General and Public Purchasing, and Materials Management seminars cover the examination content.

Recertification

Certification must be renewed every five years, based on a point system for professional development and education. CPPOs with 15 years of experience may request lifetime certification at age 62 or retirement.

CERTIFIED PURCHASING MANAGER (C.P.M.)

Sponsor

National Association of Purchasing Managers (NAPM)
2055 East Centennial Circle
P.O. Box 22160
Tempe, AZ 85285-2160
Phone: (800) 888-6276
Fax: (602) 752-7890
WWW: http://www.napm.org/

Program Data

The C.P.M. program is endorsed by 179 affiliated organizations worldwide, including the following national associations: National Association of Educational Buyers; National Purchasing Institute; Insurance Company and Bank Purchasing Management Association; National Minority Suppliers Development Council; and Newspaper Publishing Management Association.

Certifying body: Association
Year certification began: 1974
Number certified: 26,000+
Organization members: 40,000+
Additional programs: Accredited Purchasing Practitioner (A.P.P.)
Approximate certification costs: $270 (NAPM/Allied members), $480 (nonmembers). Computer testing is an additional $80.

Program Description

The Certified Purchasing Manager (C.P.M.) designation recognizes experienced professionals in purchasing and materials management. Certification is based on experience, education, and passing an examination. Membership in NAPM is not required.

Education/Experience

Besides passing the C.P.M. exam, candidates must meet these requirements:

- Have five years of purchasing/materials management/supply management experience or three years of experience and a four-year degree
- Earn 35 C.P.M. points through any of the following: professional work experience that is primarily purchasing/supply management in nature; a college degree; specific college courses; seminars and continuing education; and contributions to the profession

Examinations

The C.P.M. examination consists of four multiple-choice modules. The pass rate for each exam module is approximately 55%. The exam content is based on a 1990 job analysis determining the important tasks or duties of the typical purchasing manager, along with the knowledge, skills, and abilities needed to perform those tasks. The exam modules are as follows:

Module 1—Purchasing, which covers purchase request review and analysis; soliciting and evaluating competitive bids; analyzing suppliers; negotiations; and contracts

Module 2—Administration, which includes defining goals and objectives; developing policies and procedures; records; and human resources

Module 3—Supply, which covers material flow, inventories, and cost control

Module 4—Current issues, including forecasting and strategies; external and internal relationships; computerization; and environmental issues

Recertification

Recertification is required every five years and is based on a point system. Point awards for college coursework and professional education are similar to the initial point system described above. In addition, Module 4 of the C.P.M. exam may be retaken for six points, and after that module has been passed, Module 2 or 3 may be taken for six points. Lifetime certification may be granted for C.P.M.s at age 55 or over with 15 years of experience.

ACCREDITED PURCHASING PRACTITIONER (A.P.P.)

Sponsor

National Association of Purchasing Managers (NAPM)
2055 East Centennial Circle
P.O. Box 22160
Tempe, AZ 85285-2160
Phone: (800) 888-6276
Fax: (602) 752-7890
WWW: http://www.napm.org/

Program Data

Certifying body: Association
Year certification began: 1996
Number certified: New program
Organization members: 40,000+
Additional programs: Certified Purchasing Manager (C.P.M.)

Program Description

The Accredited Purchasing Practitioner (A.P.P.) program is for entry-level buyers who are primarily engaged in tactical and operational areas, and for persons with procurement responsibilities but working outside the purchasing department. Membership in NAPM is not required.

Education/Experience

Candidates must have either at least two years of work experience or one year of work experience plus an associate's degree. Purchasing or materials management can be a secondary component of a candidate's job, but such experience must include purchasing/materials management work that is of a professional nature.

Examinations

Candidates must pass two modules from NAPM's C.P.M. examination:

Module 1—Purchasing, which covers purchase request review and analysis; soliciting and evaluating competitive bids; analyzing suppliers; negotiations; and contracts

Module 4—Current issues, including forecasting and strategies; external and internal relationships; computerization; and environmental issues

Recertification

Reaccreditation is required every five years and is based on a point system. Lifetime certification may be granted for A.P.P.s at age 55 or over with 15 years of experience.

CERTIFIED IN TRANSPORTATION AND LOGISTICS (CTL)

Sponsor

American Society of Transportation and Logistics, Inc. (AST&L)
216 East Church St.
Lock Haven, PA 17745
Phone: (717) 748-8515
Fax: (717) 748-9118

Program Data

Certifying body: Association
Year certification began: 1946
Number certified: Not disclosed
Organization members: Not disclosed
Approximate certification costs: $175

Program Description

The Certified in Transportation and Logistics (CTL) designation recognizes professionals in the traffic, transportation, logistics, and physical distribution fields. The CTL designation reflects certified membership status in the AST&L; membership is required for certification. Candidates must be 21 for certified member status. Certification is based on passing or meeting the waiver requirements for four examinations and a research paper. AST&L sells study guides for the examinations. AST&L maintains an active ethics board with decertification powers.

Education/Examinations

Tests are a combination of short-answer and multiple-choice questions. Tests may be waived. The examination pass rate is confidential. Life experience may be considered for exemption of any examination.

Recertification

None.

BUSINESS AND MANAGEMENT
Management

CERTIFIED ARCHITECTURAL ADMINISTRATOR (CAA)

Sponsor
Society of Architectural Administrators (SAA)
c/o American Institute of Architects
1735 New York Ave. NW
Washington, DC 20006

Program Data
Certifying body: Professional association
Approximate certification costs: $140

Program Description
The Certified Architectural Administrator (CAA) designation recognizes experienced administrative professionals working in the architectural industry. A candidate must be a corporate member of the SAA to pursue certification. A corporate member works in an administrative position for a licensed and practicing architect. The SAA is an affiliate of the American Institute of Architects.

Education/Experience
Certification is based on a point system; there is no examination. All candidates must have a high school diploma. Forty-five points must be earned in these categories:

- Experience—Ten points are awarded for either of the following: ten years of experience (five in an architectural firm); or an associate's degree with five years of experience in an architectural firm; or a bachelor's degree and three years of experience in an architectural firm.

- Continuing Education—A minimum of 10 points is required. One point is awarded per eight hours of attendance at recognized seminars, workshops, and college/university classes.

- Professional Association Activity—A minimum of 10 points is required. One to three points are awarded for service in an associated professional organization as an officer, committee member, or program speaker.

Recertification
None.

CERTIFIED ASSOCIATION EXECUTIVE (CAE)

Sponsor
American Society of Association Executives (ASAE)
1575 Eye St. NW
Washington, DC 20005
Phone: (202) 626-2772
Fax: (202) 289-4049
E-mail: cae@asae.asaenet.org
WWW: http://www.asaenet.org/

Program Data
Certifying body: Association
Year certification began: 1960
Number certified: 2300
Approximate certification costs: $385 (members), $480 (nonmembers)

Program Description
The Certified Association Executive (CAE) designation recognizes paid, professional association-management executives. Certification is based on passing an examination. ASAE membership is not required. Course guides, study courses, and books are available.

Education/Experience
Eligibility for the examination is determined using a point system.

- Minimum points required: 500
- Point examples:
  - 100 for a bachelor's degree
  - 1 point per contact hour of professional education

Examinations
The CAE examination is made up of 16 sections and a case study based on required readings. Test questions are a combination of objective, short-answer, and essay. The examination pass rate is 85%. The 1995 examination covered the following areas:

- Association planning, evaluation, and human resources
- Association structure, finance, and parent/chapter relations
- Credential and codes of ethics

- Fund raising
- Legislation, regulation, and government relations
- Management information systems
- Meetings and conventions
- Membership, education, marketing, and public relations
- Research and statistics

Recertification

Candidates recertify four years after initial certification and every three years afterwards. Recertification is based on a point system. Points are earned through participation in leadership activities, and writing and speaking on association management issues. No points are awarded for continued employment.

CERTIFIED AUTOMOTIVE FLEET MANAGER (CAFM)

Sponsor

National Association of Fleet Administrators, Inc. (NAFA)
100 Wood Ave. South, Suite 310
Iselin, NJ 08830
Phone: (908) 494-8100
Fax: (908) 494-6789

Program Data

Certifying body: Association
Year certification began: 1988
Number certified: 142
Organization members: 3400+
Approximate certification costs: $700 (members), $1100 (nonmembers)

Program Description

The Certified Automotive Fleet Manager (CAFM) credential recognizes professionals experienced in managing fleets of vehicles for corporations, utilities, and government agencies. Membership in NAFA is not required.

Education/Experience

To be eligible to sit for the CAFM examination, a candidate must have at least two years of experience as an automotive fleet manager or assistant.

Examinations

The CAFM exam consists of several multiple-choice sections and a take-home case study. To help a candidate prepare for the examination, NAFA makes available a comprehensive study guide, reference readings, videos, and textbooks. NAFA also sponsors preparation seminars, and many local chapters sponsor CAFM study groups. The objective portion of the exam covers these areas:

- Accounting and finance
- Computerization
- Insurance
- Law
- Management
- Safety
- Vehicle acquisition and marketing
- Vehicle technology and maintenance

The case study is completed after exam completion and is returned within a specific time period.

Recertification

Recertification is conducted through a point system based primarily on professional contributions. CAFMs must recertify every five years. Lifetime certification is given to CAFMs when they reach age 60.

CERTIFIED EMERGENCY MANAGER (CEM)

Sponsor

National Coordinating Council on Emergency Management (NCCEM)
7297 Lee Highway, Unit N
Falls Church, VA 22042
Phone: (703) 533-7672
Fax: (703) 241-5603

Program Data

Program development has been supported by the Federal Emergency Management Agency (FEMA) and the National Emergency Management Association (NEMA).

Certifying body: Association-sponsored independent board
Year certification began: 1993
Number certified: 488
Organization members: 1700
Approximate certification costs: $325

Program Description

The Certified Emergency Manager (CEM) designation recognizes professionals in emergency management, disaster response, and civil defense. The National Coordinating Council on Emergency Management (NCCEM) draws members from government, industry, and volunteer organizations. Certification is through peer review, which includes a management essay.

Education/Experience

All candidates must put together a credentials portfolio for the peer-review process. This portfolio must include three professional references, including the candidate's current supervisor. Candidates must also demonstrate six contributions to the emergency management profession through speaking, writing, professional association involvement, and other activities. Candidates must document meeting the following minimum education and experience requirements:

- Experience (either one of the below)
  - Three years of emergency management experience
  - Two years of emergency management experience and a bachelor's degree in emergency management
- Formal Education:
  - 1995/before: Bachelor's degree or 45 college semester credits in approved areas
  - 1996/after: Bachelor's degree with college credits in approved areas
- Continuing Education: 100 classroom hours in emergency management, and 100 classroom hours in general management. No more than 25 hours may be in one topic.

Examinations

The management essay is not a true examination but an essential part of the peer-review process. The applicant will be given scenarios, to which he or she must provide narrative responses. Three different versions are available, depending on which area of the profession the candidate works:

- Private Industry
- Local Emergency Management
- Military Disaster Preparedness

Recertification

CEMs must recertify every five years. For the first recertification, CEMs must pass a multiple-choice test. Since this is a new program, subsequent recertification requirements have not been defined.

CERTIFIED ENERGY MANAGER (CEM)

Sponsor

Association of Energy Engineers® (AEE)
4025 Pleasantdale Road, Suite 420
Atlanta, GA 30340
Phone: (770) 447-5083
Fax: (770) 446-3969
WWW: http://www.aeecenter.org

Program Data

The U.S. Agency for International Development has sponsored the CEM program in Eastern European countries.

Certifying body: Association
Year certification began: 1981
Number certified: 3000
Organization members: 8000
Additional programs: Certified Cogeneration Professional (CCP); Certified Demand-Side Management Professional (CDSM); Certified Indoor Air Quality Professional (CIAQP); Certified Lighting Efficiency Professional (CLEP)

Program Description

The Certified Energy Manager (CEM) designation recognizes experienced energy engineering and management professionals. Certification is based on passing an examination. Membership in AEE is not required.

Education/Experience

To take the CEM examination, candidates must be an engineering graduate or P.E. with three years of professional experience, have a business or related bachelor's or associate's degree with five to eight years of professional experience, or have 10 years professional experience.

Examinations

The four-hour, multiple-choice CEM examination is an open-book test where the candidate selects sections based on proficiency and experience. A two-day preparation course is presented by AEE.

Recertification

None.

CERTIFIED FRANCHISE EXECUTIVE (CFE™)

Sponsor

International Franchise Association (IFA)
1350 New York Ave. NW, Suite 900
Washington, DC 20005-4709
Phone: (202) 628-8000
Fax: (202) 628-0812
E-mail: franchise@msn.com
WWW: http://www.entremkt.com/ifa/

Program Data

Certifying body: Association
Year certification began: 1994
Organization members: 32,000
Approximate certification costs: $2000+

Program Description

The Certified Franchise Executive (CFE) designation recognizes franchise principles and management reaching the IFA's requirements in experience and education. IFA membership is required. Certification is based on education and association-sponsored education. There is no examination component.

Education/Experience

Qualifications are based on a point system; 3500 points are required for certification. Of these, 2000 must be from IFA-related programs. Point examples: 100 per day IFA programs; 300 per year of experience; 500 per bachelor's degree.

Recertification

None.

CERTIFIED FUND RAISING EXECUTIVE (CFRE)

ADVANCE CERTIFIED FUND RAISING EXECUTIVE (ACFRE)

Sponsor

National Society of Fund Raising Executives (NSFRE)
1101 King St., Suite 700
Alexandria, VA 22314
Phone: (703) 684-0410
Fax: (703) 684-0540
E-mail: cert@nsfre.org
WWW: http://www.nsfre.org

Program Data

Certifying body: Association
Number certified: 3100
Organization members: 14,000+

Program Description

The Certified Fund Raising Executive (CFRE) designation recognizes paid fund-raising professionals. Volunteer fund-raising experience does not count towards meeting the society's requirements. Membership in the NSFRE is not required. Certification is based on examination. The Advance designation recognizes experienced, skilled fund-raising professionals. NSFRE maintains an active ethics program.

Education/Experience

CFRE candidates must be employed as fund-raising executives and have five years of experience as full-time fund-raising professionals or fund-raising consultants.

ACFRE candidates must have completed one CFRE recertification, have 10 years of experience, hold a bachelor's degree, demonstrate active association participation, attend two national fund-raising conferences, and accumulate 24 hours of senior-level continuing education.

Examinations

The CFRE examination was developed by the NSFRE Foundation and the Professional Examination Service. The pass/fail rate is 94%. The multiple-choice exam covers fund-raising planning, volunteer leadership, public relations and marketing, proposals and solicitations, management, and ethics.

ACFRE candidates must complete a written examination, a review of a portfolio of developmental materials, and an oral evaluation.

Recertification

CFREs must be recertified every three years through continuing education, experience, and professional service.

ACFREs are certified for life.

CERTIFIED GRAPHICS ARTS EXECUTIVE (CGAE)

Sponsor

National Association of Printers and
Lithographers (NAPL)
780 Palisade Ave.
Teaneck, NJ 07666
Phone: (201) 342-0700
Fax: (201) 692-0286
E-mail: info@napl.org
WWW: http://www.napl.org/

Program Data

The NAPL's Management Institute is presented at Northwestern University.

Certifying body: Association
Number certified: 450 (all designations)
Organization members: 3000
Additional certifications: Certified Business Planning Executive (CBPE); Certified Sales and Marketing Executive (CSME); Certified Production Management Executive (CPME)

Program Description

The National Association of Printers and Lithographers (NAPL) certification program recognizes printing industry managers completing one or more six-day, in-residence Management Institute courses at Northwestern University. Candidates should work in a management position within the industry.

Curriculum

The Management Institute courses are taught by a combination of industry experts and university instructors. About 90% of the managers and executives attending a course complete it. Membership in NAPL is not required. The courses guide students through creating and executing a business plan, and use case studies, projects, and group study.

- The Certified Business Planning Executive (CBPE) designation recognizes printing management professionals who have completed the six-day Business Planning course.

- The Certified Sales and Marketing Executive (CSME) designation recognizes printing management professionals who have completed the six-day Sales and Marketing course.

- The Certified Production Management Executive (CPME) designation recognizes printing management professionals who have completed the six-day Production Management course.

- The Certified Graphics Arts Executive (CGAE) designation recognizes printing management professionals who have completed all three of the six-day courses of NAPL's Management Institute.

Recertification

None.

CERTIFIED GRAPHICS COMMUNICATIONS MANAGER (CGCM)

Sponsor

International Publishing Management Association (IPMA)
1205 W. College Ave.
Liberty, MO 64068
Phone: (816) 781-1111
Fax: (816) 781-2790
E-mail: ipmainfo@ipma.org.
WWW: http://www.ipma.org/certification.html

Program Data

Certifying body: Association
Year certification began: 1976
Organization members: 2300+
Additional certifications: Certified Mail Manager (CMM)
Approximate certification costs: $225 (members), $450 (nonmembers)

Program Description

The Certified Graphics Communications Manager (CGCM) designation recognizes experienced in-house graphics arts and printing managers.

Education/Experience

To be eligible to sit for the CGCM examination, candidates must have five years of experience in in-house graphics management.

Examinations

The seven-part examination is made up of 360 multiple-choice and five essay questions. IPMA sells a CGCM study guide. The exam takes about five and one-quarter hours. Partial retakes are allowed. All sections must be passed for certification. The pass rate is 48% on the first attempt. The exam covers computer skills, financial management, general management, personnel management, production management, skills application (essay), and technical skills.

Recertification

Certification must be renewed every five years and is based on a professional-development credits system. Credits are earned through association membership, conferences, and seminars, and writing or lecturing on mail management.

CERTIFIED IN INTEGRATED RESOURCE MANAGEMENT (CIRC™)

Sponsor

American Production and Inventory Control
   Society (APICS™)
500 W. Allendale Road
Falls Church, VA 22046
Phone: (800) 444-2742
WWW: http://www.apics.org

Program Data

Certifying body: Association
Organization members: 70,000
Additional programs: Certified Fellow in
   Production and Inventory Management
   (CFPIM™); Certified in Production and
   Inventory Management (CPIM®)
Approximate certification costs: $525 (members),
   $825 (nonmembers)

Program Description

The Certified in Integrated Resource Management (CIRC™) is a business generalist designation recognizing individuals who have passed the five program-module examinations. Each module is a self-study program designed to prepare candidates for the examinations. There are no experience or membership requirements.

Examinations

The CIRC examinations are administered by the Educational Testing Service (ETS). The first four examinations, which may be taken in any order, are 125-question, multiple-choice tests. The Integrated

Enterprise Management examination has multiple-choice, short-answer, and essay questions. The examinations are as follows:

- Customers and Products, including product design, marketing, and service
- Logistics, including production and inventory control, procurement, and distribution
- Manufacturing Processes, including facilities management, process design and development, and production
- Support Functions, including TQM, human resources accounting and finance, information systems, and relationships
- Integrated Enterprise Management, including personal and teamwork skills; integrating functions; the enterprise; the environment; and history

Recertification

None.

CERTIFIED LAUNDRY/LINEN MANAGER (CLLM)

Sponsor

National Association of Institutional Linen
   Management (NAILM)
2130 Lexington Road, Suite H
Richmond, KY 40475
Phone: (606) 624-0177

Program Data

Certifying body: Association
Number certified: 200
Organization members: 1500+
Additional certifications: Registered
   Laundry/Linen Director (R.L.L.D.)

Program Description

The Certified Laundry/Linen Manager (CLLM) designation recognizes institutional laundry and linen supervisors and managers. Certification is based on completing a series of correspondence courses and a final examination. Membership in NAILM is not required.

Education/Experience

Candidates must have a high school diploma and meet one of the following experience requirements: one year as laundry/linen manager, two years as assistant or associate laundry/linen manager, or three years as laundry/linen supervisor.

Curriculum

The eight CLLM courses are as follows: Accounting; Chemistry; Equipment; Infection Control; Linen Management; Management; Production; and Textiles.

Examinations

Candidates must pass a comprehensive final examination based on the curriculum.

Recertification

CLLMs recertify every three years by accumulating 45 hours of acceptable continuing education.

REGISTERED LAUNDRY/LINEN DIRECTOR (R.L.L.D.)

Sponsor

National Association of Institutional Linen
  Management (NAILM)
2130 Lexington Road, Suite H
Richmond, KY 40475
Phone: (606) 624-0177

Program Data

The program is offered by the American Laundry and Linen College, sponsored by NAILM on the campus of Eastern Kentucky University.

Certifying body: Association
Number certified: 450
Organization members: 1500+
Additional certifications: Certified Laundry/Linen
  Manager (CLLM)
Approximate certification costs: $3000
  (members), $3525 (nonmembers)

Program Description

The Registered Laundry/Linen Director (R.L.L.D.) designation recognizes graduates of the American Laundry and Linen College. The on-site, three-part program focuses on industry-specific, executive-level laundry/linen operations. Membership in NAILM is not required.

Education/Experience

Candidates must have a high school diploma; there are no experience requirements.

Curriculum

The courses, which include peer interaction, daily quizzes, and industry involvement, are as follows:

Part 1—A one-week course including team dynamics; linen basics; safety; infection control; washroom chemistry; drycleaning; and a group project

Part 2—A two-week course covering team dynamics; interpersonal relations; human resources and training management; communication; equipment; and a group project

Part 3—A two-week program on cost accounting; computers; human resources; writing; infection control; and a group project

Recertification

RLLDs must accumulate 45 hours of continuing education every two years.

CERTIFIED MAIL AND DISTRIBUTION SYSTEMS MANAGER (CMDSM)

Sponsor

Mail Systems Management Association (MSMA)
J.A.F. Building, Box 2155
New York, NY 10116
Phone: (800) 955-MSMA

Program Data

Certifying body: Association
Year certification began: 1989
Number certified: 139
Organization members: 1700
Approximate certification costs: $175 (members),
  $225 (nonmembers)

Program Description

The Certified Mail and Distribution Systems Manager (CMDSM) program recognizes the development of the specialized management field of professional mail-systems management. Membership in the MSMA is not required for certification. The certification program covers the following: professionals in positions of mail-services management; supervisors of distribution, messenger, shipping, receiving, or fulfillment; administrative or facilities managers responsible for mail/distribution; and vendors and consultants in the mail management field.

Education/Experience

Eligibility to take the CMDSM examination is based on meeting work-experience and management-expertise requirements. Work experience and management expertise are evaluated on a point system.

Examinations

The examination currently consists of 135 multiple-choice questions and five essays. The majority of the questions are specific to the industry; the rest are general management questions. The exam content is designed so that anyone meeting the requirements for certification would have been exposed, through supervisory or management experience, to the topics of finance, human resources, and general management. A review course for the certification examination is offered. The pass rate is 85%.

Recertification

None.

CERTIFIED MAIL MANAGER (CMM)

Sponsor

International Publishing Management Association (IPMA)
1205 W. College Ave.
Liberty, MO 64068
Phone: (816) 781-1111
Fax: (816) 781-2790
E-mail: ipmainfo@ipma.org.
WWW: http://www.ipma.org/certification.html

Program Data

Certifying body: Association
Year certification began: 1976
Organization members: 2300+
Approximate certification costs: $225 (members), $450 (nonmembers)

Program Description

The Certified Mail Manager (CMM) designation recognizes in-plant mail management professionals.

Education/Experience

To be eligible to sit for the CMM examination, candidates must have five years of experience in in-house mail management.

Examinations

The six-part examination is made up of 360 multiple-choice questions and takes approximately four and one-half hours. IPMA sells a CMM study guide. The pass rate is 48% on the first attempt. All sections must be passed for certification. The exam covers computer skills; financial management; general management; personnel management; general mail management; and technical skills.

Recertification

Certification must be renewed every five years and is based on a professional development credits system. Credits are earned through association membership, conferences, and seminars, and writing or lecturing on mail management.

CERTIFIED MANAGEMENT CONSULTANT (CMC)

Sponsor

Institute of Management Consultants (IMC)
521 Fifth Ave., 35th floor
New York, NY 10175
Phone: (212) 697-8262
Fax: (212) 949-6571
E-mail: imccr@aol.com
WWW: http://www.well.com/user/business/imc.html

Program Data

Certifying body: Association
Year certification began: 1968
Organization members: 2600

Program Description

The Institute of Management Consultants (IMC) recognizes experienced members with the Certified Management Consultant (CMC) designation. Certification is based on experience, an interview, and an ethics exam.

Education/Experience

Candidates must have a bachelor's degree or equivalent training. Candidates must have, as a minimum, three years of consulting experience. Actual qualification is based on a point system evaluating education, experience, and professional activities.

Examinations
Candidates must pass an ethics exam and undergo an interview process.

Recertification
IMC membership must be maintained.

CERTIFIED MANAGER (CM)

CERTIFIED ADMINISTRATIVE MANAGER (C.A.M.)

ASSOCIATE CERTIFIED MANAGER (ACM)

Sponsor

Institute of Certified Professional Managers (ICPM)
James Madison University
Harrisonburg, VA 22807
Phone: (800) 568-4120
Fax: (703) 568-3587
E-mail: ADM_ICPM@jmu.edu

Program Data

Certifying body: Independent board
Year certification began: 1975
Number certified: 6000
Approximate certification costs: $230 (CM), $405 (C.A.M.)

Program Description

The Certified Manager (CM) designation recognizes management professionals and management as a profession. The Certified Administrative Manager (C.A.M.) recognizes experienced office administration managers. The National Management Association and the International Management Council helped form the Institute of Certified Professional Managers (ICPM) in 1974. The ICPM Board of Regents has representatives from universities, professional organizations, and major corporations.

Education/Experience

Eligibility to sit for the CM examination is based on a point system. Candidates must meet the total point requirements and the minimum point requirements in two categories. Candidates who meet the minimum point requirements in only one of the two areas are, upon passing of the examination, awarded the designation Associate Certified Manager (ACM).

Candidates for the C.A.M. designation must meet all of the CM eligibility requirements and also have two years of experience in an office-environment administrative position.

Examinations
The three CM multiple-choice examinations may be taken together or separately and are each two hours long. ICPM sells study guides for independent or group study, and provides an extensive bibliography for study. These are the examinations:

Area 1—Personal Skills, covering professionalism; personal organization; self-development; and the managerial personality

Area 2—Administrative Skills, covering planning objectives; scheduling; implementation of the plan; control process; and administrative knowledge

Area 3—Interpersonal Skills, covering leadership; employer/employee relationships; motivation; interpersonal relationships; and group dynamics

Two additional examinations are required for the C.A.M. designation: Financial Management and Information/Office Systems Management.

Recertification
Certification must be renewed every five years. The ACM, CM, or C.A.M. must complete 50 hours of management education, which may include academic coursework, in-house training, management-related CEUs, instructor/teacher of management, and self-study. An ACM, upon completion of the needed point requirements, will be upgraded to CM.

CERTIFIED PROFESSIONAL CONSULTANT (CPC)

Sponsor

The Consultants Institute (TCI)
1290 Palm Ave.
Sarasota, FL 34236
Phone: (914) 952-9290
Fax: (914) 379-6024
WWW: American Consultants League

Program Data

The Consultants Institute is a division of the American Consultants League.

Certifying body: Association
Year certification began: 1968
Number certified: 925
Organization members: 1000+
Approximate certification costs: Not disclosed

Program Description

The Certified Professional Consultant (CPC) designation recognizes professionals who have successfully completed the Consultants Institute (TCI) program. Certification is based on completing TCI's CPC courses; there are no educational or experience requirements.

Examinations

There are six at-home courses in the CPC program. Each course includes an open-book, unproctored test which is mailed to TCI, graded, and returned. Failed tests may be retaken at no charge. The pass rate is 91%. The courses are as follows: Becoming a Consultant; Protecting Yourself Legally; Avoiding Malpractice; Bookkeeping and Accounting; Setting Fees; and Marketing and Public Relations

Recertification

None.

CERTIFIED PROFESSIONAL SERVICES MANAGER (CPM)

Sponsor

Professional Services Management Association (PSMA)
4726 Park Road, Suite A
Charlotte, NC 28209
Phone: (704) 521-8890

Program Data

Certifying body: Association
Approximate certification costs: $75 plus membership fees

Program Description

The Certified Professional Services Manager (CPM) designation recognizes managers in professional services firms. Certification is based on a point system. Membership in PSMA is required. The program, managed by the Professional Services Management Institute (PSMI) within PSMA, confers certification with endorsements in general management, finance and accounting, marketing, operations, and human resources.

Education/Experience

PSMA separates each education and experience category into several subrequirements for acceptable qualifying points. Both the general management and specialized endorsements award the CPM designation. Education and experience must meet very specific minimum requirements in practice management, finance/accounting, marketing, operations, and human resources categories for each category/endorsement. Contact PSMI for further information on these requirements.

Recertification

None.

PROJECT MANAGEMENT PROFESSIONAL (PMP)

Sponsor

Project Management Institute (PMI)
130 S. State Road
Upper Darby, PA 19082
Phone: (610) 734-3330
Fax: (610) 734-3266
E-mail: PMIEO@ix.netcom.com
WWW: http://www.pmi.org/

Program Data

Certifying body: Association
Year certification began: 1984
Number certified: 3810
Approximate certification costs: $175 (members), $275 (nonmembers)

Program Description

The Project Management Professional (PMP) designation recognizes individuals skilled in multidisciplinary project management. A candidate must display a professional commitment to project management through educational, work, and professional background. Membership in the PMI is not required for certification. PMI requires candidates to subscribe to the Project Management Profession code of ethics and has an active ethics board with decertification powers.

Education/Experience

A point system is used to qualify candidates for certification. Candidates with less than the required number of points may still take the examination, but are not certified until the minimum point requirement is met. The required point totals must be reached within seven years of passing the examination. Points are awarded for academic and professional education, professional experience, and association participation.

Point examples:

- 15 points for a bachelor's degree (highest earned)
- 5 points per year employed as a supervisor of professionals
- 5 points for a paper published on project management
- 1 point per continuing education unit

Examinations

The Project Management Institute has developed the Project Management Body of Knowledge (PMBOK), divided into eight functional areas. The six-hour, 40-minute exam is based on the PMBOK. Current certificants write the examination questions based on the PMBOK, and the test is assembled to ensure psychometric validity. PMI offers study guides, self-study materials, and workshops for candidates. The examination's elements are as follows:

- Project Scope Management
- Project Quality Management
- Project Cost Management
- Project Contract/Procurement Management
- Project Time Management
- Project Risk Management
- Project Human Resources Management
- Project Communications Management

Recertification

PMP certification must be renewed every seven years through professional experience and education acceptable to the PMI. Recertification is based on a point system, and PMPs who do not reach the 95-point minimum must retake the certification exam.

CENTER FOR INTERNATIONAL PROJECT AND PROGRAM MANAGEMENT (CIPPM®)

Sponsor

Center for International Project and Program
  Management (CIPPM®)
123 Charles
Jackson, MI 49203
E-mail: CIPPM@free.org
WWW: http://ireland.iol.ie/~mattewar/CIPPM/
  index.html

Program Data

The International Standards Organisation (ISO) has approved CIPPM certification for ISO 9000-4 (Quality Systems—Guide to Dependability Program Management), ISO 9004-2 (Quality Systems Elements—Guidelines for Services), and ISO 10006 Draft (Guideline to Quality in Project Management).

Certifying body: Association
Year certification began: 1987
Organization members: 6900
Approximate certification costs: $125

Program Description

The CIPPM® certifies individuals, organizations, and corporate entities in project management. Membership is required. The CIPPM designation indicates that the certificant meets the Institute's standards of professionalism, ethical conduct, and quality in project management. Certification is based on knowledge and practice. The CIPPM ethical conduct standards form the cornerstone of certification. There are no examination requirements.

Education/Experience

The CIPPM designation requires certificants to adhere to all ethical guidelines, protect clients, avoid dual-role contracts, and provide written guarantees. Certificants must demonstrate adherence to continuous quality improvement (Deming) and ISO 9000.

CERTIFIED ADMINISTRATOR OF PUBLIC PARKING (CAPP)

Sponsor

Institutional and Municipal Parking Congress
  (IMPC)
P.O. Box 7167
Fredericksburg, VA 22404

Program Data

The certification is presented in cooperation with the University of Virginia.

Certifying body: Association
Organization members: 1200

Program Description

The Certified Administrator of Public Parking (CAPP) program recognizes parking management professionals in both government and institutions. The certification program combines an education/experience point system, prerequisite courses, and an examination.

Education/Experience

A candidate must meet a minimum point system in order to sit for the examination.

- Minimum points needed: 105
- Point examples:
  - 1 per year of parking staff experience
  - 5 per bachelor's degree
  - 5 per IMPC seminar
  - 20 per IMPC five-day course

Curriculum

The IMPC certification courses are held in conjunction with IMPC conferences and seminars, and are recognized by the University of Virginia. One five-day course is mandatory. Certification is not possible without taking a selection of other courses.

Examinations

The CAPP comprehensive exam was developed by the University of Virginia Division of Continuing Education.

Recertification

Certification must be renewed every three years. CAPPs must accumulate 12 points based on continuing education and association participation.

CERTIFIED RECORDS MANAGER (CRM)

Sponsor

Institute of Certified Records Managers (ICRM)
ICRM Secretary
P.O. Box 8188
Prairie Village, KS 66208
Phone: (800) 825-4276
WWW: http://www.arma.org/hp/hq/crminfo.html

Program Data

Acts as the official certifying body for the Association of Records Managers and Administrators (ARMA) and the Nuclear Information Records Management Association (NIRMA).

Certifying body: Independent board
Year certification began: 1975
Number certified: 615
Recertification rate: 90%
Approximate certification costs: $320

Program Description

The Certified Records Manager (CRM) designation recognizes experienced professionals responsible for an organization's records program. Records managers are responsible for active and inactive records systems, and related disciplines such as archives, computerization, micrographics, and optical disk technology. ICRM maintains an active ethics program.

Education/Experience

A candidate must have a bachelor's degree (or substitute) and three years of acceptable work experience in at least three of the following records management/administration areas:

- Active records systems
- Inactive records systems
- Records and information management and technology
- Records appraisal, retention, and disposition
- Records creation and use
- Records program management
- Records protection

Acceptable experience may come from developing, implementing, or managing records systems, or teaching college courses in records management. Consultants and vendors must have at least two clients describe their work in writing. Specialized equipment operations and traditional librarian functions are not acceptable. While this designation is not intended for medical records personnel, medical records experience may be accepted based on the actual tasks performed. Two years of additional experience may be substituted for one year of education, evaluated on a case-by-case basis, up to 11 years of experience for high school graduates.

Examinations

There are six parts to the CRM examination. The first five parts are multiple-choice and may be taken either individually or all together. Part 6 is an essay examination and may be taken only after the first five are successfully completed. Study materials and workshops are available from ARMA. These are the exam parts:

- Management Principles and the Records Management Program
- Records Creation and Use
- Records Systems, Storage, and Retrieval
- Records Appraisal, Retention, Protection, and Disposition
- Equipment, Supplies, and Technology
- Case Studies (essays)

Recertification

CRMs must recertify every five years. The CRM certification maintenance program was revised during 1993; CRMs are required to accumulate 100 contact hours or equivalent of acceptable continuing education. The current recertification rate is 90%.

CERTIFIED SERVICE EXECUTIVE (CSE)
ASSOCIATE SERVICE EXECUTIVE (ASE)
LIFETIME CERTIFIED SERVICE EXECUTIVE (LCSE)

Sponsor

National Association of Service Managers (NASM)
1030 W. Higgins Road, Suite 109
Hoffman Estates, IL 60195
Phone: (708) 310-9930
Fax: (708) 310-9934
E-mail: nasm@starnetinc.com
WWW: http://www.starnetinc.com/nasm/ brochure.html

Program Data

Certifying body: Association
Number certified: 250 (all programs)
Organization members: 850
Approximate certification costs: $100

Program Description

The NASM programs are designed to recognize experienced managers and executives in the service industry. The NASM also sponsors the Service Management Executive Development Program in conjunction with the University of Wisconsin-Madison. The NASM certifications are designed to provide a continuing ladder of progression to service executives.

Education/Experience

Eligibility to sit for exams is based on a point system. NASM membership is not required.

Examinations

The certification examinations are self-administered. NASM considers the exam broad enough to avoid penalizing candidates for lacking experience in a specific area. The exam tests the candidate's awareness and understanding of concepts, principles, and practices in the field of management, with particular emphasis on service-management topics and concerns. The exam has 100 multiple-choice and true/false questions and 10 essay questions. The candidate must answer five of the 10 essay questions. The pass/fail rate is 95%.

Recertification

The ASE designation cannot be renewed. An ASE must reach CSE within seven years, or lose the ASE designation.

The CSE designation must be renewed after three years. To be recertified, the CSE must earn 36 additional points. CSEs actually only need to recertify once. By the time recertification is needed a second time, the CSE has had the designation for six years and is eligible for Lifetime Certified Service Executive (LCSE). The required points for LCSE are the same as recertification for CSE.

CERTIFIED SHOPPING CENTER MANAGER (CSM)

Sponsor

International Council of Shopping Centers (ICSC)
665 Fifth Ave.
New York, NY 10022
Phone: (212) 421-8181
Fax: (212) 421-6464
WWW: http://www.icsc.org

Program Data

Certifying body: Association
Number certified: 2200+
Organization members: 30,000
Additional certifications: Certified Marketing
   Director (CMD)
Approximate certification costs: $400 (members),
   $800 (nonmembers)

Program Description

The Certified Shopping Center Manager (CSM) designation recognizes professionals in shopping center management. Certification is based on passing an examination. Membership in the ICSC is not required.

Education/Experience

To qualify for certification, an applicant must meet one of the following requirements:

- Employment as a shopping center manager for four years
- Three years of experience and the ICSC Management I and II certificate programs
- Three years of experience, college coursework equivalent to the Management I certificate program with a 'C' or better, and the ICSC Management II certificate program

Examinations

The examination was developed by ICSC and the Center for Occupational and Professional Assessment division of the Educational Testing Service (ETS). A review course for the exam is offered. The exam is given at Michigan State University in two sessions. The morning session is a multiple-choice test covering these areas: operations; leasing; accounting; retailing/merchandising; marketing and PR; insurance; and law. The afternoon session is called an "in-basket" examination, which simulates a set of problems typical of a medium-sized shopping center. The candidate is scored based on responses to the simulated problems.

Recertification

None.

BUSINESS AND MANAGEMENT
Marketing and Public Relations

ACCREDITED BUSINESS COMMUNICATOR (ABC)

Sponsor

International Association of Business
    Communicators (IABC)
One Hallidie Plaza, Suite 600
San Francisco, CA 94102
Phone: (415) 433-3400
Fax: (414) 362-8762
E-mail: service_centre@iabc.com
WWW: http://www.iabc.com//homepage.htm

Program Data

Accrediting body: Association
Year accreditation began: 1973
Number accredited: 900
Organization members: Not disclosed
Approximate accreditation costs: $225
    (members), $400 (nonmembers)

Program Description

The Accredited Business Communicator (ABC)
program is designed for experienced organizational
communicators and communications managers.
Membership in the IABC is not required. Accreditation is based on a portfolio and an examination.
The IABC sponsors accreditation workshops to
help candidates prepare for their portfolio submission and exams. The IABC maintains an active
ethics board with decertification powers.

Education/Experience

Candidates must have a total of nine years'
combined education and communications experience to apply for accreditation. Once the experience and education requirements are verified, the
candidate must next submit a portfolio of completed communications projects. This portfolio is
evaluated and scored for professional expertise
and understanding of the communications planning
process. If the portfolio is judged acceptable, the
candidate then takes the ABC examination.

Examinations

The four-part examination uses two types of
questions. Some questions target knowledge
essential to all areas of business communication.
Other questions provide several options for
answering based on the candidate's specific job
background. Essential skills covered include the
following: budgets; ethics; evaluating communications effectiveness; investor/shareholder
communications; management skills; media relations; oral presentation; organizational culture; project management; and written communication.

The first written exam section covers general
knowledge of organizational communication. The
second section requires the candidate to develop a
complete communication program based on a
given scenario. The third section tests organizational communication philosophy, including communication management and ethics. The last
section of the test is an oral exam during which the
candidate must present a solution to a given
communications problem.

Recertification

None. Nonmembers must pay a $250 annual
administrative fee to maintain accreditation.

CERTIFIED BUSINESS COMMUNICATOR (CBC)

Sponsor

Business Marketing Association
150 N. Wacker Drive, Suite 1760
Chicago, IL 60606
Phone: (800) 664-4BMA
Fax: (312) 409-4266
E-mail: bma@marketing.org.
WWW: http://www.usa.net/bma/default.html

Program Data

Certifying body: Professional association
Number certified: 2100
Year certification began: 1978
Approximate certification costs: $200 (members),
    $325 (nonmembers)

Program Description

The Certified Business Communicator (CBC) designation recognizes business-to-business marketing communications professionals. Certification is based on passing an examination. Membership in BMA is not required; nonmembers receive one year's membership upon certification.

Education/Experience

To sit for the examination, a candidate must have eight years of experience in marketing communications. Up to four years of college work may be used as experience in meeting this requirement.

Examinations

The multiple-choice certification examination is designed to test all areas of business marketing communication. The recent pass rate was 81%. The exam is prepared with the assistance of the Professional Testing Service, which administers the examination. The examination covers advertising and PR agencies; advertising measurement and accountability; creative fundamentals (copy, graphics, printing, audiovisuals); legal and ethical considerations; media selection and evaluation; planning and budgeting; and marketing communications (catalogs, direct mail, exhibits, inquiry management, interactive media, PR, presentations, sales literature, telemarketing).

Recertification

Certification must be renewed every five years. Candidates can either maintain continuous membership in BMA, pass another examination, or demonstrate continued professional education and development.

Program Description

The Certified Rural Electric Communicator (CREC) designation recognizes skilled and experienced communications professionals working in the rural electric field. Certification is based on a portfolio and an examination. The portfolio is made up of work samples taken from one to five categories. A minimum of 1000 out of the maximum of 1650 points is needed to go on to the examination.

Education/Experience

To be eligible for certification, a candidate must meet these requirements:

- Work for a rural electric cooperative distribution system, generation and transmission system, or a rural electric organization
- Currently spend 50% or more work time using mass communication skills, and have had these responsibilities for at least one year
- Have three years of experience (or one plus a bachelor's degree) as a communicator

Examinations

The four-hour certification exam covers general rural electric knowledge, and internal, public, and mass communication. Test questions include multiple-choice, short-answer, essay, and writing/editing problems. A maximum of 1500 points may be earned on the exam. The portfolio and exam points are then added together. A total of 2400 is needed for certification.

Recertification

None.

CERTIFIED RURAL ELECTRIC COMMUNICATOR (CREC)

Sponsor

Council of Rural Electric Communicators (CREC)
4301 Wilson Blvd.
Arlington, VA 22203
Phone: (703) 907-5500

Program Data

The Council is a professional advisory group to the National Rural Electric Cooperative Association.

Certifying body: Association
Number certified: 200
Approximate certification costs: $200

CERTIFIED MANAGER OF EXHIBITS (CME)

Sponsor

International Exhibitors Association (IEA)
5501 Backlick Road, Suite 105
Springfield, VA 22151
Phone: (703) 941-3275
Fax: (703) 941-8275
E-mail: iea@ieabbs.org
WWW: http://ieabbs.org/member.htm

Program Data

Certifying body: Association
Approximate certification costs: $150

er of Exhibits (CME) desig-
rienced professionals in the
ustry. Membership in IEA is
on is based on evaluation of
ion, experience, education,
nation.

e

f recommendation, and a
score of 70 are required to
nation. Candidates need a
s of experience, five shows,
rs of continuing education.
or experience, professional
conferences.

to public.

ne attendance at TS² is re-
ME must earn 1.0 CEU from

TING DIRECTOR (CMD)

of Shopping Centers (ICSC)

WWW: http://www.icsc.org

Program Data

Certifying body: Association
Number certified: 1400
Organization members: 30,000
Additional programs: Certified Shopping Center
   Manager (CSM)
Approximate certification costs: $400 (members),
   $800 (nonmembers)

Program Description

The Certified Marketing Director (CMD) designation
recognizes professionals in shopping center promotion and marketing. Membership in the ICSC is
not required.

Education/Experience

To qualify, an applicant must meet one of the
following requirements:

- Employment as a shopping center marketing
  director for four years
- Completion of the ICSC Marketing I and II
  certificate programs, and employment as a
  shopping center marketing director for three
  years
- Completion of college coursework equivalent
  to the Marketing I Certificate program with a
  'C' or better, completion of the ICSC Marketing II certificate program, and employment
  as a shopping center marketing director for
  three years

Examinations

The examination was developed by ICSC and the
Center for Occupational and Professional Assessment division of the Educational Testing Service
(ETS). A review course for the exam is offered. The
exam is given at Michigan State University in two
sessions. The morning session is a multiple-choice
test covering marketing, product development,
merchandising, communications, media planning,
and administration. The afternoon session is called
an "in-basket" examination, which simulates a set
of marketing and promotion problems typical of a
medium-sized shopping center. The candidate is
scored based on responses to the simulated
problems.

Recertification

None.

CERTIFIED MARKETING EXECUTIVE (CME)

Sponsor

Sales and Marketing Executives International
   (SMEI)
Statler Office Tower
Cleveland, OH 44115
Phone: (800) 999-1414
Fax: (216) 771-6652
E-mail: smeihq@smei.org
WWW: http://www.smei.org/

Program Data

Certifying body: Association
Organization members: 6000
Additional certifications: Certified Sales Executive
   (CSE)
Approximate certification costs: $500 (members),
   $600 (nonmember)

Program Description

The Certified Marketing Executive (CME) designation recognizes experienced sales management professionals. Certification is based on passing an examination. Membership in SMEI is not required.

Education/Experience

Candidates must meet minimum experience and education requirements. Eligibility for the examination is determined using a point system. Candidates are awarded points for experience, academic and professional education, and association participation.

Examinations

The CME examination is prepared and scored by the Fogelman College of Business and Economics, Memphis State University. The exam includes:

- Analyses
- Computers
- Concepts
- Consumer behavior
- International, industrial, brand and product marketing
- Marketing auditing
- Organization
- Planning
- Promotion
- Regulation
- Research
- Staffing
- Systems

Recertification

A CME must renew certification every five years; recertification is based on a point system. A CME may also pass a reexamination for certification renewal.

MARKETING PROFESSIONAL (MP)

SENIOR MARKETING PROFESSIONAL (SMP)

FELLOW MARKETING PROFESSIONAL (FMP)

Sponsor

Society for Marketing Professional Services (SMPS)
99 Canal Center Plaza, Suite 320
Alexandria, VA 22314
Phone: (703) 549-6117

Program Data

Certifying body: Association
Organization members: 3300

Program Description

The Society for Marketing Professional Services (SMPS) certification program recognizes skilled individuals responsible for new business development at architectural firms, engineering firms, and other professional services companies. The program uses three tiers to identify levels of professional competency. Certification is based on passing an examination.

Education/Experience

Candidates qualify for a particular certification level based on a point system. A typical candidate will meet the following criteria:

- Marketing Professional—Proficient in basic marketing skills, with three to five years of industry experience
- Senior Marketing Professional—Proficient in marketing management, services, and/or business development, with eight to 10 years of industry experience
- Fellow Marketing Professional—Demonstrates leadership in the profession, as well as proficient in all areas of marketing services

Examinations

Competency exams are required for all levels. Content not released.

Recertification

Biannual, based on accumulation of points for professional education and participation.

ACCREDITED IN PUBLIC RELATIONS (APR)

Sponsor

Public Relations Society of America (PRSA)
33 Irving Place
New York, NY 10003
Phone: (212) 995-2230
Fax: (212) 995-0757
E-mail: hdq@prsa.org
WWW: http://www.prsa.org/

Program Data

Certifying body: Association
Year certification began: 1965
Number certified: 4110
Organization members: 16,000
Approximate certification costs: $200

Program Description

The Accredited in Public Relations (APR) designation recognizes experienced public relations professionals with broad knowledge and skills. Membership in PRSA is required. Certification is based on passing an examination.

Education/Experience

Candidates must have five years of public relations experience to sit for the examination.

Examinations

The APR examination has both a written and an oral component. The exam is based on an extensive PR body of knowledge developed by PRSA. The day-long written examination has two parts: general knowledge and case history/application. The exam includes public relations theories; societal factors; planning; research; evaluation; media relations; crisis management; and law and professional ethics. The case history portion of the exam presents problems for candidates to solve. The one-hour oral component consists of a series of structured questions. The pass rate is 70%.

Recertification

Accreditation must be maintained on a three-year cycle; maintenance is based on continued experience, education, and association activities.

CERTIFIED SALES EXECUTIVE (CSE)

Sponsor

Sales and Marketing Executives International (SMEI)
Statler Office Tower
Cleveland, OH 44115
Phone: (800) 999-1414
Fax: (216) 771-6652
E-mail: smeihq@smei.org
WWW: http://www.smei.org/

Program Data

Certifying body: Association
Organization members: 6000
Additional certifications: Certified Marketing Executive (CME)
Approximate certification costs: $500 (members), $600 (nonmembers)

Program Description

The Certified Sales Executive (CSE) designation recognizes professionals experienced in sales management. Certification is based on passing an examination. Membership in SMEI is not required.

Education/Experience

Candidates must meet minimum experience and education requirements. Eligibility for examination is determined using a point system. Candidates are awarded points for experience, academic and professional education, and association participation.

Examinations

The CSE examination is prepared and scored by the Fogelman College of Business and Economics, Memphis State University. The exam includes the following:

- Recruiting, training, supervision, compensation, and evaluation of sales representatives
- Product and service development and pricing
- Computers
- Legal aspects
- Market analysis
- Telemarketing/direct, industrial, and wholesaler selling

Recertification

A CSE must renew certification every five years; recertification is based on a point system. A CSE may also pass a reexamination for certification renewal.

BUSINESS AND MANAGEMENT
Security

CERTIFIED CONFIDENTIALITY OFFICER (CCO)

Sponsor

Business Espionage Controls and
    Countermeasures Association (BECCA)
P.O. Box 55582
Seattle, WA 98155
Phone: (206) 364-4672
Fax: (206) 367-3316
E-mail: 76731.474@compuserve.com
WWW: http://ourworld.compuserve.com/
    homepages/william_johnson_5/

Program Data

Certifying body: Association
Year certification began: 1990
Approximate certification costs: $700

Program Description

The Certified Confidentiality Officer (CCO) designation recognizes professionals responsible for protecting intellectual property assets in corporate environments. BECCA developed the CCO program in response to a research project co-sponsored by the U.S. Departments of Labor and Education. Since many corporations assign responsibility for controls and countermeasures programs to various departments, BECCA used the U.S. Department of Personnel Management Factor Evaluation System to create a standardized job description for confidentiality officers. BECCA maintains an active ethics program. Certification is based on completing five training modules.

Education/Experience

All candidates must have experience in the confidentiality field, either as a confidentiality officer or a manager responsible for confidentiality programs. Candidates must meet one of the following requirements:

- Ten years of experience
- Bachelor's degree and five years of experience

- Master's degree and four years of experience
- Doctoral degree and three years of experience

Curriculum

Candidates entering the CCO program must complete five training modules. At the end of each module, the candidates complete a confidentiality survey of their workplace or other acceptable location. Each survey is graded as pass/fail, with unacceptable surveys returned with comments for repeating the assignment. The five CCO modules are as follows:

- Introduction to Business Espionage Controls and Countermeasures
- Electronic Eavesdropping
- Computers
- Pretext Interviews
- Undercover Operations

Recertification

All CCOs must continue to contribute to the profession every year. BECCA offers several opportunities to CCOs for continuing education and contribution.

CERTIFIED PROTECTION OFFICER (CPO)

Sponsor

International Foundation for Protection Officers
    (IFPO)
Bellingham Business Park
4200 Meridian, Suite 200
Bellingham, WA 98226
Phone: (206) 733-1571

Program Data

Certifying body: Association
Year certification began: 1986
Number certified: 4100
Organization members: 1100
Additional programs: Certified Security
    Supervisor (CSS)
Approximate certification costs: $100

Program Description

The Certified Protection Officer (CPO) designation recognizes private security and protection professionals. The CPO program may be taken either individually, or offered through an employer. Certification is based on passing an examination. Two security professionals must act as references. Membership in the IFPO is not required.

Examinations

Candidates study the *Protection Officer Training Manual*, published by Butterworth-Heinemann, and complete an unsupervised mid-term and proctored final examination. The average completion time is three to four months. The pass rate is 78%.

Recertification

None.

CERTIFIED PROTECTION PROFESSIONAL (CPP)

Sponsor

American Society for Industrial Security (ASIS)
1655 North Fort Myer Drive, Suite 1200
Arlington, VA 22209
Phone: (703) 522-5800
Fax: (703) 243-4954
WWW: http://biz.swcp.com/coach/asis/

Program Data

Certifying body: Association-sponsored independent board
Year certification began: 1977
Number certified: 3000+
Organization members: 25,000
Approximate certification costs: $200

Program Description

The Certified Protection Professional (CPP) designation recognizes security practitioners involved in the protection of assets in the public or private sector. CPPs may work for corporations, criminal justice system, government intelligence, or investigative agencies. CPPs may be involved in security, asset protection, or loss-control systems, programs, or services. ASIS maintains an active ethics board with decertification powers. Certification is based on passing an examination; candidates must meet the minimum education and experience requirements to take the examination.

Education/Experience

Candidates must meet one of the following criteria:

- Ten years of experience
- Eight years of experience and an associate's degree
- Seven years of experience and a bachelor's degree
- Six years of experience and a master's degree
- Five years of experience and a doctoral degree

All candidates must also be endorsed by a CPP in good standing and pledge to maintain the CPP standards of conduct.

Examinations

The CPP examination covers 10 mandatory and four candidate-selected specialty areas. The exam content and percentage of questions from each area are based on an extensive role-delineation project that evaluated the task percentages of actual practitioners. The multiple-choice questions, which are based on practices as well as theory, emphasize the concepts, principles, or facts that have widespread application or significance in the solution of problems encountered by practitioners in all areas of security. ASIS provides all candidates with an extensive bibliography to help prepare for the examination. A two-day preparation workshop is available. The specialty areas covered are listed below.

Mandatory areas (200 questions, 3½ hours):

- Emergency Planning, including plan development, implementation, and types of emergencies
- Investigations, including resources, methods, reports, and types
- Legal Aspects, including civil liability, civil rights, contracts, fair employment, due process, and criminal justice
- Personnel Security, including employment and retention standards, screening, and disciplinary actions
- Physical Security, including barriers; facilities; devices and equipment; lighting; security systems; and alarms
- Protection of Sensitive Information, including control and identification of sensitive information

- Security Management, involving the application of general management techniques to security, and including financial, personnel, organization, and communications management, management systems, countermeasures, and vulnerability assessment
- Substance Abuse, including abuser identification and disposition, prevention programs, and abused substances
- Loss Prevention, including risk assessment, countermeasures, and policies
- Liaison, covering internal and external relations

Specialty areas (candidates choose four), each of which includes laws, regulations, and standards, and program development and implementation for area-unique problems (25 questions each):

- Banking and Financial Institutions
- Computer Security
- Credit Card Security
- Defense Industrial Security Program
- Educational Institutions Security
- Fire Resources Management
- Health Care Institutions Security
- Manufacturing Security
- Nuclear Power Security
- Public Utility Security
- Restaurant and Lodging Security
- Retail Security
- Transportation and Cargo Security
- Oil and Gas Industrial Security
- Telephone and Telecommunications Security

Recertification

CPPs must recertify every three years. Certification is based in a credit system; candidates must earn nine credits to recertify. The recertification rate is 85%.

PERSONAL PROTECTION SPECIALIST (PPS)

Sponsor

Executive Protection Institute
Arcadia Manor
Route 2, Box 3645
Berryville, VA 22611
Phone: (540) 955-1128

Program Data

Shenandoah University grants three course credits for certification.

Certifying body: Association-sponsored independent board
Year certification began: 1978
Number certified: 1000+
Organization members: Personal Protection Specialists are nominated to the Nine Lives Associates (NLA)
Additional programs: Certified Security Trainer (C.S.T.) through the Academy of Security Educators and Trainers (ASET)
Approximate certification costs: $2900

Program Description

The Personal Protection Specialist credential is earned through an on-site seven-day program on executive/VIP protection. Candidates receive a background and police check.

Curriculum

The course is 110 hours of training followed by a comprehensive written examination. The training covers all areas of personal protection, including driving, weapons use, planning, special events, and procedures.

Examinations

Content not disclosed. The pass rate is 85%.

Recertification

Under review; may be in place in near future.

CERTIFIED SECURITY SUPERVISOR (CSS)

Sponsor

International Foundation for Protection Officers (IFPO)
Bellingham Business Park
4200 Meridian, Suite 200
Bellingham, WA 98226
Phone: (206) 733-1571

Program Data

Certifying body: Association
Year certification began: 1986
Number certified: 790
Organization members: 1100
Additional programs: Certified Protection Officer (CPO)
Approximate certification costs: $125

Program Description

The Security Supervisor Program, leading to the CSS certification, is a distance-learning program for protection officer supervisors. Membership in the IFPO is not required.

Curriculum

The *Security Supervisor Training Manual,* published by Butterworth-Heinemann, is used as the study text. During the course, candidates complete several true/false and multiple-choice tests, and complete 15 simulated workplace scenarios. In the scenarios, candidates describe their recommended course of action, backing up their actions with the course material. Upon successful completion of the program, the candidate may then apply to IFPO for certification.

The study text covers these areas: leadership development; motivation and supervision; management and the management function; time management; effective communication; delegation and authority; complaints and grievances; training skill development; safety attitude development; community/public relations; and ethics.

Examinations

Candidates must score at least 70% on both the written and the scenario portions of the course.

Recertification

None.

CERTIFIED SECURITY TRAINER (C.S.T.)

Sponsor

Academy of Security Educators and Trainers
(ASET)
Route Two, Box 3644
Berryville, VA 22611
Phone: (540) 955-1129

Program Data

Certifying body: Association
Year certification began: 1981
Organization members: 500
Other certifications: Personal Protection Specialist (Executive Protection Institute program)

Program Description

The Certified Security Trainer (C.S.T.) designation recognizes individuals creating and presenting security training. Certification is a three-part process. ASET requires a background check and the completion of qualifying essay questions in security training.

Curriculum

Candidates selected for continuation then attend a seven-day assessment/evaluation program at the Executive Protection Institute. Each candidate completes written and oral tests, training exercises, and personal interviews. Each candidate presents three training sessions to the certification board. The assessment program has a 95% pass rate. ASET maintains an active ethics board with decertification powers.

Recertification

None.

INSURANCE AND PERSONAL FINANCE
Insurance

ASSOCIATE, INSURANCE AGENCY ADMINISTRATION (AIAA™)

Sponsor
Life Office Management Association (LOMA)
2300 Windy Ridge Parkway, Suite 600
Atlanta, GA 30339
Phone: (770) 951-1770
Fax: (770) 984-0441
E-mail: education@loma.org
WWW: http://www.loma.org/

Program Data
The National Program on Noncollegiate Sponsored Instruction (NPONSI) recommends college credit for the FLMI courses. Most states have approved FLMI courses as continuing-education credit hours for state agent licensing.

Certifying body: Association

Additional programs: Associate, Customer Service (ACS®); Associate in Insurance Accounting and Finance (AIAF); Associate in Research and Planning (ARP); Fellow, Life Management Institute (FLMI®); Master Fellow, Life Management Institute (FLMI/M®)

Program Description
The Associate, Insurance Agency Administration (AIAA) designation recognizes administrative non-sales employees in agency, regional, and insurance home offices.

Education/Experience
There are no prerequisites.

Curriculum
Each course prepares the candidate for an objective-question examination. Courses need not be taken in order. Credit for certain courses may be granted to holders of other insurance-related designations. These are the courses/examinations:

- FLMI Course 1—Principles of Life and Health Insurance
- FLMI Course 2—Life and Health Insurance Company Operations
- FLMI Course 4—Marketing Life and Health Insurance
- ACS CS-1—Foundations of Customer Service
- AIAA 200—Agency Administration

Examinations
Examinations, either paper or on-line, are taken after the completion of each course. The exams have approximately a 67% pass rate. Exams are based on assigned texts and follow the content of the course.

Recertification
None.

ACCREDITED ADVISER IN INSURANCE (AAI®)

Sponsor
Insurance Institute of America (IIA)
720 Providence Road
P.O. Box 3016
Malvern, PA 19355
Phone: (800) 644-2101
Fax: (610) 640-9576

Program Data
The Accredited Adviser in Insurance (AAI®) program was developed with the Independent Insurance Agents of America (IIAA). The IIA programs have been evaluated and recommended for college credit by the American Council on Education.

Certifying body: Independent education and certification organization

Additional programs: The IIA offers Associate designations in the following programs: Insurance Services (AIS); Automation Management (AAM®); Claims (AIC); Fidelity and Surety Bonding (AFSB); Insurance Accounting and Finance (AIAF); Loss Control Management (ALCM®); Management (AIM); Marine Insurance Management (AMIM®); Premium Auditing (APA®); Reinsurance (Are); Research and Planning (ARP®); Risk Management (ARM); and Underwriting (AU)

Program Description

The Accredited Adviser in Insurance (AAI®) designation recognizes professionals who have completed the three-course IIA program. The program is recommended for agency managers and field representative supervisors. Weekly assignments are not graded or returned, but are designed to prepare the student to take the end-of-course examination. Courses can be either independent or group study. There are no education or experience requirements. Each course prepares candidates for an IIA examination.

Curriculum

The curriculum consists of the following:

- Principles of Insurance Production, including insurance sales, legal liability, personal lines, and commercial insurance
- Multiple-Lines Insurance Production
- Agency Operations and Sales Management

Recertification

Accreditation must be renewed every three years through continuing education.

ASSOCIATE IN CLAIMS (AIC)

Sponsor

Insurance Institute of America (IIA)
720 Providence Road
P.O. Box 3016
Malvern, PA 19355
Phone: (800) 644-2101
Fax: (610) 640-9576

Program Data

The National Association of Independent Insurance Adjusters (NAIIA) assisted in the development of the AIC program. The IIA programs have been evaluated and recommended for college credit by the American Council on Education.

Certifying body: Independent education and certification organization

Additional programs: The IIA offers Associate designations in the following programs: Accredited Adviser in Insurance (AAI®); Associate in Insurance Services (AIS); Automation Management (AAM®); Fidelity and Surety Bonding (AFSB); Insurance

Accounting and Finance (AIAF); Loss Control Management (ALCM®); Management (AIM); Marine Insurance Management (AMIM®); Premium Auditing (APA®); Reinsurance (Are); Research and Planning (ARP®); Risk Management (ARM); and Underwriting (AU)

Program Description

The Associate in Claims (AIC) designation recognizes professionals who have completed the four-course IIA claims program. Each course is 13 weeks long. The program is recommended for claims adjusters, supervisors and examiners, and others working with property-loss and liability claims. Weekly assignments are not graded or returned, but are designed to prepare the student to take the end-of-course examination. Courses can be either independent or group study. There are no education or experience requirements. Each course prepares candidates for an IIA examination. There is no recertification requirement.

Curriculum

The curriculum consisted of the following:

- The Claims Environment, a basic overview of the claims process and types
- Workers Compensation and Medical Aspects of Claims
- Property Loss Adjusting
- Liability Claims

ASSOCIATE, LIFE AND HEALTH CLAIMS (ALHC)

Sponsor

International Claim Association (ICA)
(Program Administration)
Life Office Management Association
5770 Powers Ferry Road
Atlanta, GA 30327
Phone: (770) 951-1770

Program Data

Certifying body: Association
Number certified: 6900+
Organization members: The 400+ members of ICA are licensed or chartered life and health insurance companies.

Program Description

The Associate, Life and Health Claims (ALHC) designation recognizes claims professionals who successfully complete the ICA's six-course program. Courses consist of assigned text; no coursework is submitted by the student. The courses prepare the candidate for the examinations.

Curriculum

The program is divided into two parts; the introductory course segment and the ICA course segment.

Candidates have three options for fulfilling the introductory course requirement. All introductory courses are sponsored by other organizations. The three options are as follows:

- Option 1—FLMI Insurance Education Program, sponsored by LOMA
  - Course 1—Principles of Life and Health Insurance
  - Course 2—Life and Health Insurance Company Operations
- Option 2—The American College (Bryn Mawr, PA) CLU Program
  - Course 1—Individual Life and Health Insurance
  - Course 2—Group Benefits
- Option 3—CLU Program, The Life Underwriters Association of Canada

The ICA Course Segment is made up of the following four courses:

- Medical and Dental Aspects of Claims, including medical terms and disorders, substance abuse, dental insurance, and dental services
- Life and Health Insurance Law, including contracts and agency; legal remedies; settlements; taxes; regulations; and the legal aspects of life and health policies
- Claim Administration, including the claims process; coverage and misrepresentation; types of claims and their administration; and claims examinations and payments
- Management of Claims Operations, including management theories, organizational dynamics, claims staff/personnel management, and claims operations management

Recertification

None.

CERTIFIED CLAIMS ASSISTANCE PROFESSIONAL (CCAP)

Sponsor

National Association of Claims Assistance
  Professionals, Inc. (NACAP)
5328 S. Main St., Suite 102
Downers Grove, IL 60515
Phone: (708) 963-3500
Fax: (708) 936-1997
WWW: http://www.nacap.org/

Program Data

Certifying body: Association
Additional programs: Certified Electronic Claims
  Professional (CECP)
Approximate certification costs: $250

Program Description

The Certified Claims Assistance Professional (CCAP) designation recognizes individuals acting as consumer ombudsmen to assisting clients with claims to health insurance providers. A CCAP may complete and submit health insurance forms, track payments, assist in challenging denied claims, and maintain insurance-related financial records. Certification is based on passing an examination. NACAP membership is required.

Education/Experience

To sit for the CCAP exam, a candidate must meet either the minimum education standard *or* the minimum experience standard.

- Minimum education standard: Hold either a current agent or broker's license, an acceptable, related professional certification, or an associate's degree or higher in a related field
- Minimum experience standard: Two years of acceptable claims assistance experience, or three years of acceptable claims handling experience in an approved environment

Examinations

The CCAP exam is a two-part, multiple-choice test; 120 questions on core topics, and 40 questions on CCAP-specific topics. All test questions are reviewed by a Technical Advisory Committee with representatives from Aetna Life and Casualty; American Medical Association; Health Care Financing Administration; Veteran's Administration; Cooperative Healthcare Networks; NEIC; and Medical Electronic Data Exchange.

The exam covers the following:

Core—Claims Processing Management; Claims-Related Formulas and Calculations; Claims-Related Terminology; Client Rights and Entitlement Concepts; Health Care Provider Responsibilities; Reimbursement Concepts; Third-Party Payer Systems

CCAP Specialty—Administrative Appeals Process; Basic Insurance Concepts; Obtaining Additional Information; Organizing and Maintaining Client Data; Reconciling Payment to Claims

Recertification
CCAPs must meet all NACAP membership and continuing-education requirements.

CERTIFIED ELECTRONIC CLAIMS PROFESSIONAL (CECP)

Sponsor
National Association of Claims Assistance
  Professionals, Inc. (NACAP)
5328 S. Main St., Suite 102
Downers Grove, IL 60515
Phone: (708) 963-3500
Fax: (708) 936-1997
WWW: http://www.nacap.org/

Program Data
Certifying body: Association
Additional programs: Certified Claims Assistance
  Professional (CCAP)
Approximate certification costs: $250

Program Description
The Certified Electronic Claims Professional (CECP) designation recognizes third-party claims billers providing electronic claim and other transaction services.

Certification is based on passing an examination. NACAP membership is required.

Education/Experience
To sit for the CECP exam, a candidate must meet either the minimum education standard *or* the minimum experience standard.

- Minimum education standard: Hold either a current agent or broker's license, an acceptable professional certification, or an associate's degree or higher in a related field

- Minimum experience standard: Two years of business experience in electronics claims processing, or three years of acceptable experience in an approved environment.

Examinations
The CECP exam is a two-part, multiple-choice test; 120 questions on core topics, and 40 questions on CECP-specific topics. All test question are reviewed by a Technical Advisory Committee with representatives from Aetna Life and Casualty; American Medical Association; Health Care Financing Administration; Veteran's Administration; Cooperative Healthcare Networks; NEIC; and Medical Electronic Data Exchange.

The exam covers:

Core—Claims Processing Management; Claims-Related Formulas and Calculations; Claims-Related Terminology; Client Rights and Entitlement Concepts; Health Care Provider Responsibilities; Reimbursement Concepts; Third Party Payer Systems

CECP Specialty—Claims Submission Methods; Computer Knowledge; Data Security; Editing; Auditing and Reporting; Transmission Methods

Recertification
CECPs must meet all NACAP membership and continuing education requirements.

ASSOCIATE, CUSTOMER SERVICE (ACS®)

Sponsor
Life Office Management Association (LOMA)
2300 Windy Ridge Parkway, Suite 600
Atlanta, GA 30339
Phone: (770) 951-1770
Fax: (770) 984-0441
E-mail: education@loma.org
WWW: http://www.loma.org/

Program Data
The National Program on Noncollegiate Sponsored Instruction (NPONSI) recommends college credit for the FLMI courses. Most states have approved FLMI courses as continuing-education credit hours for state agent licensing.

Certifying body: Association
Number certified: 50,000
Additional programs: Associate in Insurance Accounting and Finance (AIAF); Associate, Insurance Agency Administration (AIAA™); Associate in Research and Planning (ARP); Fellow, Life Management Institute (FLMI®); Master Fellow, Life Management Institute (FLMI/M)

Program Description

The Associate, Customer Service (ACS) designation recognizes individuals who have completed the educational program offered by the Life Office Management Association (LOMA) on life/health-insurance customer service. Membership in LOMA is not required.

Education/Experience

There are no experience or education prerequisites.

Curriculum

The designation is awarded upon completion of the five-course program. Each course prepares candidates for an examination. Courses need not be taken in order. Credit for certain courses may be granted to holders of other insurance-related designations. Four of the five courses are required courses in the Fellow, Life Management Institute (FLMI) program. The courses areas are as follows:

- FLMI Course 1—Principles of Life and Health Insurance
- FLMI Course 2—Life and Health Insurance Company Operations
- FLMI Course 3—Legal Aspects of Life and Health Insurance
- FLMI Course 4—Marketing Life and Health Insurance
- ASC Course CS1—Foundations of Customer Service

Examinations

The examinations, either paper or on-line, are taken after the completion of each course. The exams have approximately a 67% pass rate. Exams are based on assigned texts and follow the content of the course.

Recertification

None.

ACCREDITED CUSTOMER SERVICE REPRESENTATIVE (ACSR)

Sponsor

Independent Insurance Agents of America (IIAA)
P.O. Box 1497
127 S. Peyton St.
Alexandria, VA 22314
Phone: (703) 683-4422
WWW: http://www.iiaa.iix.com

Program Data

Certifying body: Association
Number certified: 6450+
Organization members: 280,000+

Program Description

The Accredited Customer Service Representative (ACSR) designation recognizes customer service representatives in the insurance field. Certification is based on completing a series of modules and examinations. There are no minimum requirements. The ACSR may receive their designation for Personal Lines, Commercial Lines, or both.

Curriculum

Each module is presented in a one-day training session, which ends in an examination. A self-study option has been developed. These are the modules:

- Core Modules (required for both designations): Error and Omissions Loss Control and Professional Development and Account Management
- Personal Lines designation courses: Homeowners Coverages, Automobile Coverages, and Related Coverages
- Commercial Lines designation courses: Commercial Property, Commercial Liability, Auto and Garage Policies, and Related Coverages

Recertification

Recertification requires six hours of continuing education annually.

ASSOCIATE IN FIDELITY AND SURETY BONDING (AFSB)

Sponsor

Insurance Institute of America (IIA)
720 Providence Road
P.O. Box 3016
Malvern, PA 19355
Phone: (800) 644-2101
Fax: (610) 640-9576

Program Data

Program was developed with the National Association of Surety Bond Producers (NASBP) and the Surety Association of America (SAA). The IIA programs have been evaluated and recommended for college credit by the American Council on Education.

Certifying body: Independent education and certification organization

Additional programs: The IIA offers Associate designations in the following programs: Accredited Adviser in Insurance (AAI®); Insurance Services (AIS); Automation Management (AAM®); Claims (AIC); Insurance Accounting and Finance (AIAF); Loss Control Management (ALCM®); Management (AIM); Marine Insurance Management (AMIM®); Premium Auditing (APA®); Reinsurance (Are); Research and Planning (ARP®); Risk Management (ARM); Underwriting (AU)

Program Description

The Associate in Fidelity and Surety Bonding (AFSB) designation recognizes professionals who have completed the five-course IIA program covering the fidelity and surety bond industry. Weekly assignments are not graded or returned, but are designed to prepare the student to take the end-of-course examination. Courses can be either independent or group study. There are no education or experience requirements. Each course prepares candidates for an IIA examination. There is no recertification requirement.

Curriculum

The courses are as follows:

- Management (CPCU course)—A 15-week course covering basic management concepts and how they apply in insurance organizations

- Accounting and Finance (CPCU course)—A 15-week course including basic accounting and property- and casualty-insurance company accounting requirements
  - Principles of Suretyship—13 weeks
  - Contract Surety—13 weeks
  - Fidelity and Noncontract Surety—13 weeks

HEALTH INSURANCE ASSOCIATE (HIA)

Sponsor

Health Insurance Association of America (HIAA)
555 13th St. NW, Suite 600 East
Washington, DC 20004-1109
Phone: (202) 823-1853

Program Data

The American Council on Education (ACE) recommends both undergraduate and graduate credit for certification courses.

Certifying body: Trade association educational arm
Year certification began: 1988
Number certified: 12,000 (all programs)
Additional programs: Managed Healthcare Professional (MHP)
Approximate certification costs: $300 (member company), $425 (nonmember company)

Program Description

The Health Insurance Associate (HIA) designation recognizes insurance professionals who have completed the HIAA's course of study. Certification is based on passing a series of examinations. Enrollment is primarily through an insurance company, which provides test proctors. There are no experience or education requirements.

Curriculum

The courses, which may be taken as either self-study or group study, prepare the candidate for the examination(s). The course fee covers enrollment, examination, and any certificate earned. Course materials must be purchased separately. The following five courses are needed for HIA certification:

- Group Life and Health

  Group A—provides information on group insurance concepts and history; medical and other coverages; marketing; underwriting; pricing; insurance contracts

Group B—provides information on administration; examination; claim processing; experience refunds; federal and state regulation; financial reports; Canadian insurance

Group C—provides information on group plan structure; cost management; funding; retirement; group universal life; disability and rehabilitation; long-term care; computers; current issues

- Individual Health

Individual A—provides information on history; markets and marketing; disability income and medical expense insurance; contracts; underwriting; policy issue; service

Individual B—provides information on claims; regulation; pricing; reports; investments; computers; cost control; current issues

Examinations
Each course requires a two-and-one-half hour, multiple-option test covering the associated course content.

Recertification
None.

REGISTERED HEALTH UNDERWRITER (RHU)

Sponsor
National Association of Health Underwriters (NAHU)
1000 Connecticut Ave. NW, Suite 1111
Washington, DC 20036
Phone: (202) 223-5533
Fax : (202) 785-2274
WWW: http://www.nahu.org/contents.html

Program Data
Certifying body: Association
Organization members: 12,000
Additional certifications: Registered Employee Benefits Consultant (REBC)
Approximate certification costs: $1000 (members), $1300 (nonmembers)

Program Description
The Registered Health Underwriter (RHU) designation recognizes professionals who successfully complete the NAHU's study course/examination program in health and disability insurance. There are no education or experience prerequisites. The program is supervised and administered by Northeastern University. Candidates must successfully complete three self-study courses and pass three examinations. A separate Canadian RHU program, consisting of two self-study courses and examinations, is also offered. Membership in NAHU is not required for certification.

Curriculum
All courses end with a 100-question, multiple-choice exam. These are the three courses:

- Disability Income, including different products and programs; rates; actuarial functions; claims and legal functions; taxation; and marketing

- Health Insurance, including group insurance; government regulations; underwriting; different products and programs

- Advanced Applications of Disability and Health Insurance, including cost controls; cafeteria plans; HMOs; PPOs; major medical; business expenses; long- and short-term disability salary continuation; and long-term care insurance

Recertification
RHUs must recertify every three years. Recertification is based on a point system. Points are awarded for continuing education, professional development, and association participation.

CERTIFIED INSURANCE COUNSELOR (CIC)

Sponsor
Society of Certified Insurance Counselors (Society of CIC)
P.O. Box 27027
Austin, TX 78755
Phone: (800) 633-2165
Fax: (512) 343-2167
E-mail: alliance@scic.com
WWW: http://www.zilker.net/business/alliance/ cic/index.htm

Program Data
The Society of CIC is a member of the National Alliance for Insurance Education and Research.

Certifying body: Association
Year certification began: 1969
Number certified: 20,000

Program Description

The Certified Insurance Counselor (CIC) designation recognizes insurance professionals who have completed the Society's educational program. Membership in the Society of CIC is not required. Candidates meeting the minimum experience requirements are eligible to attend the five CIC institutes. Candidates who successfully complete all of these three-day institutes receive the CIC designation.

Education/Experience

Candidates must meet one of the following requirements:

- Two years of insurance industry experience
- Two years as college/university insurance instructor
- Be a licensed insurance agent, broker, or solicitor

Curriculum

Each institute ends with a comprehensive written examination on the topics presented. The examination must be passed to receive institute credit. The topic categories are as follows:

- Commercial Property, which includes property coverages, endorsements, time element coverages, and inland marine coverages
- Commercial Casualty, which includes workers' compensation, general liability, business auto, and excess liability and umbrella coverages
- Personal Lines, which includes automobile, homeowners, and related coverages; condominiums and umbrella coverages
- Agency Management, which includes planning, human resources, finances, law, and ethics. This institute combines classroom and group learning situations.
- Life and Health, which includes life, disability, and health insurance basics; marketing; and tailoring life and health products to individual and business requirements

Recertification

A CIC must attend one Society of CIC-sponsored seminar program or institute each year to maintain certification.

CERTIFIED INSURANCE EXAMINER (CIE)
ACCREDITED INSURANCE EXAMINER (AIE)

Sponsor

Insurance Regulatory Examiners Society (IRES)
130 N. Cherry, Suite 202
Olathe, KS 66061
Phone: (913) 768-4700

Program Data

Certifying body: Association
Organization members: 1000

Program Description

The Certified Insurance Examiner (CIE) and Accredited Insurance Examiner (AIE) designations recognize members of IRES who have completed a series of industry courses.

Education/Experience

Members must be employed by or contracting with an insurance regulatory agency and review insurance-company operations or products.

Curriculum

IRES offers no courses of its own; all required courses come from industry offerings. Both designations have two educational paths: Property and Casualty, and Life and Health.

The AIE Property and Casualty path comprises the following courses offered by the Insurance Institute of America (IIA):

- Accounting and Finance
- Business Research Methods
- Commercial Insurance
- Insurance Company Operations
- Management
- Personal Lines Underwriting
- The Claims Person and the Public
- The Legal Environment of Insurance

The CIE Property and Casualty path comprises the AIE (property and casualty) designation courses and the following Life Management Institute (LOMA) courses:

- Information Management in Insurance Companies
- Life and Health Insurance Company Operations
- Marketing Life and Health Insurance
- Principles of Life and Health Insurance

The AIE Life and Health path comprises the following Life Management Institute (LOMA) courses:

- Accounting in Life and Health Insurance Companies
- Claim Administration
- Information Management in Insurance Companies
- Legal Aspects of Life and Health Insurance
- Life and Health Insurance Company Operations
- Management of Organizations and Human Resources
- Marketing Life and Health Insurance
- Principles of Life and Health Insurance

The CIE Life and Health path comprises the AIE (life and health) designation courses and the following Insurance Institute of America (IIA) courses:

- Business Research Methods
- Insurance Company Operations
- Principles of Insurance
- The Legal Environment of Insurance

Recertification
Under development.

CERTIFIED INSURANCE REHABILITATION SPECIALIST (CIRS)

Sponsor
Certification of Insurance Rehabilitation
  Specialists Commission (CIRSC)
1835 Rohlwing Road, Suite E
Rolling Meadows, IL 60008
Phone: (708) 818-1967

Program Data
CIRSC is a sponsoring organization of the Foundation for Rehabilitation Certification, Education, and Research.

Appointing organizations: Case Management Society of America (CMSA); Insurance Rehabilitation Study Group (IRSG); National Association of Rehabilitation Professionals in the Private Sector (NARPPS); National Council on Rehabilitation Education (NCRE); National Council of Self-Insurers (NCSI); National Rehabilitation Counseling Association (NRCA); Vocational Evaluation and Work Adjustment Association (VEWAA)
Certifying body: Independent board
Year certification began: 1983
Number certified: 4500
Approximate certification costs: $290

Program Description
The Certified Insurance Rehabilitation Specialist (CIRS) practitioners provide direct assistance to disabled individuals receiving benefits from a disability compensation system. CIRSs may counsel and may evaluate psychological, social, medical, and vocational needs and options. Certification is based on passing an examination and meeting minimum educational standards. There are no membership requirements.

Education/Experience
To sit for the CIRS examination, candidates must meet one of the following requirements:

- Registered Nurse (RN) or Certified Rehabilitation Counselor (CRC) with two years of acceptable experience
- Master's degree or doctorate and two to five years of acceptable experience, depending on courses taken
- Bachelor's degree with major in rehabilitation and three years of acceptable experience
- Bachelor's degree (or higher) and five years of acceptable experience

Examinations
The 300-question, one-day, multiple-choice examination covers job placement and vocational assessment, case management and human disabilities, rehabilitation services and care, forensic rehabilitation, and disability legislation (including OSHA and ADA).

Recertification
CIRSs must renew certification every five years by accumulating 80 clock hours of acceptable continuing education, or retake the CIRS examination.

ASSOCIATE IN INSURANCE SERVICES (AIS)

Sponsor

Insurance Institute of America (IIA)
720 Providence Road
P.O. Box 3016
Malvern, PA 19355
Phone: (800) 644-2101
Fax: (610) 640-9576

Program Data

The IIA programs have been evaluated and recommended for college credit by the American Council on Education.

Certifying body: Independent education and certification organization

Additional programs: The IIA offers Associate designations in the following programs: Accredited Adviser in Insurance (AAI®); Automation Management (AAM®); Claims (AIC); Fidelity and Surety Bonding (AFSB); Insurance Accounting and Finance (AIAF); Loss Control Management (ALCM®); Management (AIM); Marine Insurance Management (AMIM®); Premium Auditing (APA®); Reinsurance (Are); Research and Planning (ARP®); Risk Management (ARM); Underwriting (AU)

Program Description

The Associate in Insurance Services (AIS) recognizes individuals completing the IIA's services program. Each course is 13 weeks long. Weekly assignments are not graded or returned, but are designed to prepare the student to take the end-of-course examination. Courses can be either independent or group study. There are no education or experience requirements. Each course prepares candidates for an IIA examination. There is no recertification requirement.

Curriculum

The curriculum includes the following:

* IIA Program in General Insurance
* Delivering Insurance Services

Examination

Each examination mirrors the program content. Recent passing ratios are approximately 70–72%.

Recertification

None.

CERTIFIED INSURANCE SERVICE REPRESENTATIVE (CISR)

Sponsor

Society of Certified Insurance Service
  Representatives (Society of CISR)
P.O. Box 27028
Austin, TX 78755
Phone: (800) 633-2165
Fax: (512) 346-4672
E-mail: alliance@scic.com
WWW: http://www.zilker.net/business/alliance/
  cisr/index.htm

Program Data

The Society of CISR is a member of the National Alliance for Insurance Education and Research.

Certifying body: Association
Number certified: 5100+

Program Description

The Certified Insurance Service Representative (CISR) designation recognizes insurance service professionals who have completed the Society's educational program for customer service. Membership in the Society of CISR is not required.

Education/Experience

Current employment in an agency, insurance company, or insurance-related business is required.

Curriculum

Certification is based on completing the five one-day CISR classroom courses. Each course in the CISR program ends with a one-hour examination. The courses are as follows:

* Insuring Personal Residential Property
* Insuring Personal Auto Exposures
* Introduction to Commercial Property Coverages
* Introduction to Commercial Casualty Insurance
* Agency Operations

Credit for courses from other associations' programs may be accepted as replacements for CISR courses.

Recertification

CISR certification must be updated annually. There are four update options: Attend any one CISR course, any Advanced Lecture Series one-day course, any Certified Insurance Counselor institute (fulfills update option for two years), or attend a Dynamics of Service program.

LIMRA® LEADERSHIP INSTITUTE FELLOW (LLIF)

Sponsor

LIMRA® International
P.O. Box 208
Hartford, CT 06141
Phone: (860) 688-3358
E-mail: jberlin@limra.com
WWW: http://tccn.com/limra-international/ home.htm

Program Data

Certifying body: Association
Number certified: 200
Approximate certification costs: $1200

Program Description

The LIMRA® Leadership Institute Fellow (LLIF) designation is conferred jointly by LIMRA and Babson College (Wellesley, MA), and recognizes insurance executives who have completed the on-site Strategies for Executive Advancement Program series. Each of the four programs is one week long, with additional projects. Each program includes workshops and formal presentations. Organizations participating in this program include Milliman & Robertson (independent consulting actuaries) and Manus Associates (strategic leadership).

Curriculum

The courses are as follows:

Part 1—Marketing Strategies. Examines the marketing elements of an insurance or financial services company. Provides the tools for analyzing and advancing marketing performance.

Part 2—Financial Disciplines. Examines financial operations in different insurance lines, and explores the roles other disciplines play in insurance and financial services companies.

Part 3—Executive Effectiveness. Analyzes strategic leadership and management style/characteristics and how they have an impact on organization's functions. Provides a framework for embracing and implementing personal change.

Part 4—Managing the Financial Services Enterprise. Provides a comprehensive understanding of strategy and change from the CEO's point of view. This includes business unit, corporate, and cultural change; quality and innovation; and managing change, service, and quality.

Recertification
None.

FELLOW, LIFE MANAGEMENT INSTITUTE (FLMI®)
MASTER FELLOW, LIFE MANAGEMENT INSTITUTE (FLMI/M®)

Sponsor

Life Office Management Association (LOMA)
2300 Windy Ridge Parkway, Suite 600
Atlanta, GA 30339
Phone: (770) 951-1770
Fax: (770) 984-0441
E-mail: education@loma.org
WWW: http://www.loma.org/

Program Data

The National Program on Noncollegiate Sponsored Instruction (NPONSI) recommends college credit for the FLMI courses. Most states have approved FLMI courses as continuing-education credit hours for state agent licensing.

Certifying body: Association
Number certified: 50,000
Additional programs: Associate, Customer Service (ACS®); Associate in Insurance Accounting and Finance (AIAF); Associate, Insurance Agency Administration (AIAA™); Associate in Research and Planning (ARP)
Approximate certification costs: $600 (members), $1100 (nonmembers)

Program Description

The Fellow, Life Management Institute (FLMI) designation recognizes professionals who have completed the university-level educational program offered by the Life Office Management Association (LOMA) on life and health insurance. Membership in LOMA is not required.

Education/Experience

While designed for non-sales insurance professionals and professionals providing services to the insurance community, there are no experience or education prerequisites.

Curriculum

The designation is awarded upon completion of the 10-course program (nine required courses and one elective). Each course prepares the candidate for an objective-question examination. Courses need not be taken in order. Credit for certain courses may be granted to holders of other insurance-related designations. These are the courses/examinations:

- Principles of Life and Health Insurance
- Life and Health Insurance Company Operations
- Legal Aspects of Life and Health Insurance
- Marketing Life and Health Insurance
- Management of Organizations and Human Resources
- Information Management of Health Insurance Companies
- Accounting in Life and Health Insurance Companies
- Economics and Investments
- Mathematics of Life and Health Insurance
- Elective, one of several FLMI courses

The Master Fellow, Life Management Institute (FLMI/M) designation is an advanced program for FLMIs. This designation is awarded to professionals who complete the additional courses and examinations. All courses except the Strategic Management course are from the FLMI elective list.

These are the required courses:

- Management Science
- Managerial Accounting
- Financial Management or Life Insurance Investments
- Three approved courses from FLMI electives
- Strategic Management course, the program capstone course, with a two-part examination that includes essay, objective questions, and a case study

Examinations

Examinations, either paper or on-line, are taken after the completion of each course. The exams have approximately a 67% pass rate. Exams are based on assigned texts and follow the content of the course.

Recertification

None.

LIFE UNDERWRITER TRAINING COUNCIL FELLOW (LUTCF)

Sponsor

Life Underwriter Training Council (LUTC)
7625 Wisconsin Ave.
Bethesda, MD 20814
Phone: (301) 913-5882

Program Data

Certifying body: Association-sponsored independent board
Number certified: 42,000
Approximate certification costs: $800

Program Description

The Fellow (LUTCF) designation recognizes members of the National Association of Life Underwriters (NALU) who complete four LUTC courses.

Education/Experience

Candidates must be engaged in the insurance industry.

Curriculum

All courses are semester-length classroom courses. One of the four courses must be either the Personal Insurance or Business Insurance course. Candidates must pass a final examination for course credit. Other available courses include:

- Advanced Business Planning
- Disability Income
- Fundamentals of Financial Services
- Multiline Skills Course
- Personal Estate and Retirement Planning
- Professional Growth

Recertification

None.

CHARTERED LIFE UNDERWRITER (CLU)

Sponsor

The American College (AC)
270 S. Bryn Mawr Ave.
Bryn Mawr, PA 19010
Phone: (215) 526-1490

Program Data

The American College is accredited by the Middle States Association of Colleges and Schools.

Certifying body: College
Year certification began: 1927
Number certified: 76,000
Organization members: Nonmembership. Upon certification, individuals are encouraged to join the American Society of CLU & ChFC® (35,000 members), with headquarters located on the campus. For information, call (215) 526-2500.
Additional programs: Chartered Financial Consultant (ChFC)
Approximate certification costs: $3000

Program Description

The Chartered Life Underwriter (CLU) designation recognizes professionals in insurance and financial planning. A CLU advises in estate, financial, and retirement planning, employee benefit planning, and business/tax planning.

Education/Experience

While many CLUs are insurance agents and underwriters, the designation is open to any individual with three years of acceptable business experience.

Examinations

Certification is based on passing a series of examinations based on self-study courses. Formal classes, study groups, and agency classes may also be options. These are the self-study courses:

- Fundamentals of Estate Planning
- Fundamentals of Financial Planning
- Group Benefits
- Income Taxation
- Individual Life and Health Insurance
- Investments
- Life Insurance Law
- Planning for Retirement Needs
- Two electives

All examinations follow the associated course content. The two-hour, multiple-choice test may be taken either as paper and pencil or on computer at test centers.

Recertification

Recertification is required for CLUs who matriculated after June 30, 1989, and other CLUs who voluntarily elect to participate. CLUs must accumulate 60 hours of acceptable education every two years. Examples of hour awards: 1 per 50 minutes of instruction, 45 hours for a nationally recognized designation, and 15 hours per college-semester-credit hour.

ASSOCIATE IN LOSS CONTROL MANAGEMENT (ALCM®)

Sponsor

Insurance Institute of America (IIA)
720 Providence Road
P.O. Box 3016
Malvern, PA 19355
Phone: (800) 644-2101
Fax: (610) 640-9576

Program Data

IIA programs have been evaluated and recommended for college credit by the American Council on Education.

Certifying body: Independent education and certification organization
Additional programs: The IIA offers Associate designations in the following programs: Accredited Adviser in Insurance (AAI®); Insurance Services (AIS); Automation Management (AAM®); Claims (AIC); Fidelity and Surety Bonding (AFSB); Insurance Accounting and Finance (AIAF); Management (AIM); Marine Insurance Management (AMIM®); Premium Auditing (APA®); Reinsurance (Are); Research and Planning (ARP®); Risk Management (ARM); Underwriting (AU)

Program Description

The Associate in Loss Control Management (ALCM®) designation recognizes professionals who have completed the six-course IIA program in loss control. Weekly assignments are not graded or returned, but are designed to prepare the student to take the end-of-course examination. Courses can be either independent or group study. There are no education or experience requirements. Each course prepares candidates for an IIA examination. There is no recertification requirement.

Curriculum

The courses are as follows:

- Ethics, Insurance Perspectives, and Insurance Contract Analysis (CPCU course)—15 weeks

- Insurance Operations (CPCU course)—
  15 weeks
- Management (CPCU course)—A 15-week course covering basic management concepts and how they apply in insurance organizations
- Accident Prevention—13 weeks
- Property Protection—13 weeks
- Occupational Health and Hygiene—
  13 weeks

MANAGED HEALTHCARE PROFESSIONAL (MHP)

Sponsor

Health Insurance Association of America (HIAA)
555 13th St. NW, Suite 600 East
Washington, DC 20004-1109
Phone: (202) 823-1853

Program Data

The American Council on Education (ACE) recommends both undergraduate and graduate credit for certification courses.

Certifying body: Trade association educational
  arm
Year certification began: 1988
Number certified: 12,000 (all programs)
Additional programs: Health Insurance Associate
  (HIA)
Approximate certification costs: $300 (member
  company), $425 (nonmember company)

Program Description

The Managed Healthcare Professional (MHP) designation recognizes insurance professionals who have completed the HIAA's course of study. Certification is based on passing a series of examinations. Enrollment is primarily through an insurance company, which provides test proctors. There are no education or experience requirements.

Curriculum

The courses, which may be taken as either self-study or group study, prepare the candidate for the examination(s). The course fee covers enrollment, examination, and any certificate earned. Course materials must be purchased separately. The following five courses are needed for MHP certification:

- Managed Care Parts A and B—provide an in-depth look at the development, structure, and organization of managed care, as well as its operation and administration
- Long-Term Care—provides information on issues related to the needs, costs and financing of long-term care

and either

- Group Life and Health Parts A and B—provide information on group insurance concepts and history; medical and other coverages; marketing; underwriting; pricing; insurance contracts; administration; examination; claim processing; experience refunds; federal and state regulation; financial reports; and Canadian insurance

or

- Individual Health Parts A and B—provide information on history; markets and marketing; disability income and medical expense insurance; contracts; underwriting; policy issues and service; claims; regulation; pricing; reports; investments; computers; cost control; and current issues

Examinations

Each course requires a two-and-one-half hour, multiple-option test (except for Long-Term Care, which has a time limit of one-and-one-quarter hours) covering the associated course content.

Recertification

None.

ASSOCIATE IN MANAGEMENT (AIM)

Sponsor

Insurance Institute of America (IIA)
720 Providence Road
P.O. Box 3016
Malvern, PA 19355
Phone: (800) 644-2101
Fax: (610) 640-9576

Program Data

Endorsements: The IIA programs have been evaluated and recommended for college credit by the American Council on Education.

Certifying body: Independent education and
  certification organization
Additional programs: The IIA offers Associate
  designations in the following programs:

Accredited Adviser in Insurance (AAI®); Insurance Services (AIS); Automation Management (AAM®); Claims (AIC); Fidelity and Surety Bonding (AFSB); Insurance Accounting and Finance (AIAF); Loss Control Management (ALCM®); Marine Insurance Management (AMIM®); Premium Auditing (APA®); Reinsurance (Are); Research and Planning (ARP®); Risk Management (ARM); Underwriting (AU)

Program Description

The Associate in Management (AIM) designation recognizes professionals who have completed the three-course IIA management program. This program is recommended for upper- and middle-management insurance professionals, including those beginning their first management position. Weekly assignments are not graded or returned, but are designed to prepare the student to take the end-of-course examination. Courses can be either independent or group study. There are no education or experience requirements. Each course prepares candidates for an IIA examination. There is no recertification requirement.

Curriculum

The courses are as follows:

- Management (CPCU course)—A 15-week course covering basic management concepts and how they apply in insurance organizations

- Human Resource Management—A 12-week course

- Organizational Behavior in Insurance—A 12-week course

ASSOCIATE IN MARINE INSURANCE MANAGEMENT (AMIM®)

Sponsor

Insurance Institute of America (IIA)
720 Providence Road
P.O. Box 3016
Malvern, PA 19355
Phone: (800) 644-2101
Fax: (610) 640-9576

Program Data

Program was developed with assistance from the Inland Marine Underwriters Association (IMUA) and the American Institute of Marine Underwriters (AIMU). The IIA programs have been evaluated and recommended for college credit by the American Council on Education.

Certifying body: Independent education and certification organization

Additional programs: The IIA offers Associate designations in the following programs: Accredited Adviser in Insurance (AAI®); Insurance Services (AIS); Automation Management (AAM®); Claims (AIC); Fidelity and Surety Bonding (AFSB); Insurance Accounting and Finance (AIAF); Loss Control Management (ALCM®); Management (AIM); Premium Auditing (APA®); Reinsurance (Are); Research and Planning (ARP®); Risk Management (ARM); Underwriting (AU)

Program Description

The Associate in Marine Insurance Management (AMIM®) designation recognizes professionals who have completed the six-course IIA program in marine insurance. Weekly assignments are not graded or returned, but are designed to prepare the student to take the end-of-course examination. Courses can be either independent or group study. There are no education or experience requirements. Each course prepares candidates for an IIA examination. There is no recertification requirement.

Curriculum

The courses are as follows:

- Ethics, Insurance Perspectives, and Insurance Contract Analysis (CPCU course)—15 weeks

- Insurance Operations (CPCU course)—15 weeks

- The Legal Environment of Insurance (CPCU course)—15 weeks

- Management (CPCU course)—A 15-week course covering basic management concepts and how they apply in insurance organizations

- Ocean Marine Insurance

- Inland Marine Insurance

CHARTERED PROPERTY CASUALTY UNDERWRITER (CPCU®)

Sponsor
American Institute for Chartered Property
   Casualty Underwriters (AICPCU)
720 Providence Road
P.O. Box 3016
Malvern, PA 19355
Phone: (800) 644-2101
Fax: (610) 640-9576

Program Data
The CPCU program has been evaluated and recommended for college credit by the American Council on Education.

Certifying body: Independent industry education
   and certifying organization
Number certified: 36,000
Organization members: The American Institute is
   nonmembership. Those receiving their desig-
   nation are invited to join the Society of the
   CPCU.
Approximate certification costs: $900

Program Description
The Chartered Property Casualty Underwriter (CPCU®) designation recognizes experienced insurance professionals who have completed the 10 courses in the CPCU curriculum.

Education/Experience
Candidates must, within the five years prior to the award of CPCU, show that they have 36 months of acceptable insurance experience.

Curriculum
The CPCU program consists of nine required courses and one elective. Each course prepares the candidate for the course examination. The nine required courses are 15 weeks long, and may be completed in group or independent study. Course credit is based solely on passing the associated examination. There is no recertification require-ment. The courses are as follows:

- Accounting and Finance
- Commercial Liability Risk Management and Insurance
- Commercial Property Risk Management and Insurance
- Economics
- Ethics, Insurance Perspectives, and Insurance Contract Analysis

- Insurance Operations
- Management
- Personal Risk Management and Insurance
- The Legal Environment of Insurance
- Elective

ASSOCIATE IN REINSURANCE (ARe)

Sponsor
Insurance Institute of America (IIA)
720 Providence Road
P.O. Box 3016
Malvern, PA 19355
Phone: (800) 644-2101
Fax: (610) 640-9576

Program Data
Program was developed with the Reinsurance Section of the Society of Chartered Property and Casualty Underwriters (Society of CPCU) and the Brokers and Reinsurance Markets Association. The IIA programs have been evaluated and recom-mended for college credit by the American Council on Education.

Certifying body: Independent education and
   certification organization
Additional programs: The IIA offers Associate
   designations in the following programs:
   Accredited Adviser in Insurance (AAI®);
   Insurance Services (AIS); Automation
   Management (AAM®); Claims (AIC); Fidelity
   and Surety Bonding (AFSB); Insurance
   Accounting and Finance (AIAF); Loss Control
   Management (ALCM®); Management (AIM);
   Marine Insurance Management (AMIM®);
   Premium Auditing (APA®); Research and
   Planning (ARP®); Risk Management (ARM);
   Underwriting (AU)

Program Description
The Associate in Reinsurance (ARe) designation recognizes professionals who have completed the four-course IIA program on the reinsurance busi-ness. Weekly assignments are not graded or returned, but are designed to prepare the student to take the end-of-course examination. Courses can be either independent or group study. There are no education or experience requirements. Each course prepares candidates for an IIA examination. There is no recertification requirement.

Curriculum

The courses are as follows:

- Management (CPCU course)—A 15-week course covering basic management concepts and how they apply in insurance organizations

- Accounting and Finance, including basic accounting and property- and casualty-insurance company accounting requirements (CPCU course)—15 weeks

- Principles of Reinsurance

- Reinsurance Practices

ASSOCIATE IN RESEARCH AND PLANNING (ARP)

Sponsors

Life Office Management Association (LOMA)
2300 Windy Ridge Parkway, Suite 600
Atlanta, GA 30339
Phone: (770) 951-1770
Fax: (770) 984-0441
E-mail: education@loma.org
WWW: http://www.loma.org/

Insurance Institute of America (IIA)
720 Providence Road
Malvern, PA 19355
Phone: (800) 644-2101

Program Data

The National Program on Noncollegiate Sponsored Instruction (NPONSI) recommends college credit for the FLMI courses. The American Council on Education (ACE) recommends college credit for most IIA courses. Most states have approved FLMI and IIA courses as continuing-education credit hours for state agent licensing.

Certifying body: Association
Additional certifications:

- LOMA—Associate, Customer Service (ACS®); Associate, Insurance Agency Administration (AIAA™); Associate in Research and Planning (ARP); Fellow, Life Management Institute (FLMI®); Master Fellow, Life Management Institute (FLMI/M®)

- IIA—Associate designations in the following programs: Accredited Adviser in Insurance (AAI®); Insurance Services (AIS); Automation Management (AAM®); Claims (AIC); Fidelity and Surety Bonding (AFSB); Insurance Accounting and Finance (AIAF); Loss Control Management (ALCM®); Management (AIM); Marine Insurance Management (AMIM®); Premium Auditing (APA®); Reinsurance (Are); Risk Management (ARM); Underwriting (AU)

Program Description

The Associate in Research and Planning (ARP) designation recognizes professionals who have completed the educational program on life- and health-insurance research and planning. The Property and Casualty option is offered through IIA; the Life Insurance option is offered jointly by the Life Office Management Association (LOMA) and the Insurance Institute of America (IIA). Membership in LOMA or IIA is not required.

Education/Experience

While designed for non-sales insurance professionals and professionals providing services to the insurance community, there are no experience or education prerequisites.

Curriculum

The courses prepare the candidate for passing examinations. Candidates may choose one of two course paths. These are the courses/examinations:

Life Insurance Option

- FLMI Course 1—Principles of Life and Health Insurance

- FLMI Course 2—Life and Health Insurance Company Operations

- FLMI Course 4—Marketing Life and Health Insurance

- FLMI Course 8—Economics and Investments

- IIA ARP Course 101—Business Research Methods

- IIA ARP Course 1-2—Strategic Planning for Insurers

Property and Casualty Option (all IIA courses)

- Ethics, Insurance Perspectives, and Insurance Contract Analysis (CPCU course)—15 weeks

- Insurance Operations, which examines internal and external insurance functions (CPCU course)—15 weeks

- Economics, which covers general macro- and micro-economics and how economic forces affect insurance operations (CPCU course)—15 weeks

- Insurance Issues and Professional Ethics—15 weeks

- Business Research Methods
- Strategic Planning for Insurers

Recertification
None.

ASSOCIATE IN RISK MANAGEMENT (ARM)

Sponsor

Insurance Institute of America (IIA)
720 Providence Road
P.O. Box 3016
Malvern, PA 19355
Phone: (800) 644-2101
Fax: (610) 640-9576

Program Data

The IIA programs have been evaluated and recommended for college credit by the American Council on Education.

Additional programs: The IIA offers Associate designations in the following programs: Accredited Adviser in Insurance (AAI®); Insurance Services (AIS); Automation Management (AAM®); Claims (AIC); Fidelity and Surety Bonding (AFSB); Insurance Accounting and Finance (AIAF); Loss Control Management (ALCM®); Management (AIM); Marine Insurance Management (AMIM®); Premium Auditing (APA®); Reinsurance (Are); Research and Planning (ARP®); Underwriting (AU)

Program Description

The Associate in Risk Management (ARM) designation recognizes professionals who have completed the IIA's three-course risk management program. Each course is 13 weeks long. Weekly assignments are not graded or returned, but are designed to prepare the student to take the end-of-course examination. Courses can be either independent or group study. There are no education or experience requirements. Each course prepares candidates for an IIA examination. There is no recertification requirement.

Curriculum

The courses are as follows:

- Essentials of Risk Management
- Essentials of Risk Control
- Essentials of Risk Financing

ASSOCIATE IN UNDERWRITING (AU)

Sponsor

Insurance Institute of America (IIA)
720 Providence Road
P.O. Box 3016
Malvern, PA 19355
Phone: (800) 644-2101
Fax: (610) 640-9576

Program Data

The IIA programs have been evaluated and recommended for college credit by the American Council on Education.

Certifying body: Independent education and certification organization

Additional programs: The IIA offers Associate designations in the following programs: Accredited Adviser in Insurance (AAI®); Insurance Services (AIS); Automation Management (AAM®); Claims (AIC); Fidelity and Surety Bonding (AFSB); Insurance Accounting and Finance (AIAF); Loss Control Management (ALCM®); Management (AIM); Marine Insurance Management (AMIM®); Premium Auditing (APA®); Reinsurance (Are); Research and Planning (ARP®); Risk Management (ARM)

Program Description

The Associate in Underwriting (AU) designation recognizes professionals who have completed the IIA's four-course program in personal and commercial lines. Each course is 13 weeks long. Weekly assignments are not graded or returned, but are designed to prepare the student to take the end-of-course examination. Courses can be either independent or group study. There are no education or experience requirements. Each course prepares candidates for an IIA examination. There is no recertification requirement.

Curriculum

The courses are as follows:

- Principles of Property and Liability Underwriting
- Personal Lines Underwriting
- Commercial Liability Underwriting
- Commercial and Multiple-Lines Underwriting

INSURANCE AND PERSONAL FINANCE
Financial Advising

ENROLLED AGENT (EA)

Sponsor

Internal Revenue Service
Department of the Treasury

For information, contact:

Association of Enrolled Agents (AEA)
200 Orchard Ridge Drive, Suite 302
Gaithersburg, MD 20878
Phone: (301) 212-9608
Fax: (301) 990-1611
E-mail: naea1@aol.com

Program Data

Certifying body: U.S. Government
Year certification began: 1884
Number certified: 33,000

Program Description

The Enrolled Agent (EA) designation recognizes a tax professional licensed by the U.S. government to represent taxpayers before all administrative levels of the Internal Revenue Service (attorneys and Certified Public Accountants are licensed by individual states). EAs can also advise, represent, and prepare tax returns. EAs are bound by Federal ethical guidelines. All EAs undergo an IRS background check.

The Association of Enrolled Agents (AEA) is one of several professional associations for Enrolled Agents; membership is not required. The AEA will answer questions and refer clients to EAs.

Education/Experience

There are no prerequisites.

An individual employed by the IRS for five years in a position responsible for applying and interpreting IRS codes and regulations may be enrolled without taking the IRS exam.

Examinations

EAs must pass a two-day IRS examination covering individual, corporate, partnership, estate, and trust taxes. The exam also includes procedures and ethics.

Recertification

An EA must earn 72 hours of continuing professional education every three years to stay enrolled.

CERTIFIED TRUST AND FINANCIAL ADVISOR™ (CTFA™)

Sponsor

Institute for Certified Bankers™ (ICB)
1120 Connecticut Ave. NW, Suite 600
Washington, DC 20036
Phone: (202) 663-5380

Program Data

The ICB is sponsored by the American Bankers Association (ABA).

Certifying body: Association
Additional certifications: Certified Corporate Trust Specialist™ (CCTS™); Certified Financial Services Security Professional™ (CFSSP™); Certified Regulatory Compliance Manager™ (CRCM™)
Approximate certification costs: $600

Program Description

The Certified Trust and Financial Advisor™ (CTFA™) designation recognizes experienced professionals in the personal trust and financial advisement field. There are no professional membership requirements; certified individuals automatically become members of ICB. The ICB does not certify anyone who has signed a consent decree with any securities agency or has been found guilty of certain criminal acts.

Education/Experience

To earn the CTFA designation, a candidate must pass an examination, be employed by a financial institution, and meet one of the following requirements:

- Ten years of personal trust experience in a bank or trust company
- A bachelor's degree and five years of personal trust experience in a bank or trust company

- A graduate of an acceptable school program on personal trust and three years of personal trust experience in a bank or trust company

Examinations

Examination preparation materials come with enrollment. The examination covers:

- Tax law as it affects personal income, trusts, and estates
- Fiduciary law and accounting, including trusts and probate
- Personal finance, including planning, insurance, and analysis
- Personal investments, including vehicles, risk, and portfolio management

Recertification

Certification must be renewed every three years. Recertification is based on professional education. CTFAs must have 45 continuing-education hours in qualified programs. At least six hours must come from each area of the trust and financial advisement field: tax law, fiduciary law, personal finance, and personal investments.

PERSONAL FINANCIAL SPECIALIST (CPA/PFS)

Sponsor

American Institute of Certified Public Accountants (AICPA)
Personal Financial Planning Division
P.O. Box 2206
Jersey City, NJ 07303
Phone: (800) 862-4272
WWW: http://www.aicpa.org/

Program Data

AICPA develops and grades the Uniform Certified Public Accountant Examination used for state CPA licensure.

Certifying body: Association
Number certified: 800+
Organization members: 330,000

Program Description

The Personal Financial Specialist (PFS) designation recognizes Certified Public Accountants (CPAs) who specialize in personal financial planning. AICPA membership and a CPA certificate are required. Certification is based on passing an examination.

Education/Experience

A candidate must be currently licensed as a CPA and have three years (250 hours per year) of experience in personal financial planning.

Examinations

The six-hour PFS examination is 75% objective questions, 25% a case study. The pass rate is 75%. A study bibliography is provided. The test includes estate planning; investments; managing risk; personal financial-planning process; personal income-tax planning; planning for retirement; professional responsibilities and standards. The case study tests the candidate's ability to apply concepts and knowledge to a specific situation.

Recertification

A CPA/PFS must recertify every three years by maintaining AICPA membership and CPA certificate, performing 750 hours of personal financial planning, and accumulating 72 hours of professional education in financial planning.

CHARTERED FINANCIAL ANALYST (CFA®)

Sponsor

Association for Investment Management and
    Research (AIMR)
5 Boar's Head Lane
P.O. Box 3668
Charlottesville, VA 22903
Phone: (800) 247-8132
Fax: (804) 980-9755
E-mail: info@aimr.com
WWW: http://www.aimr.com/aimr.html

Program Data

Certifying body: Professional association
Year certification began: 1963
Number certified: 20,000
Organization members: 27,000
Approximate certification costs: $1000

Program Description

The Chartered Financial Analyst (CFA®) designation recognizes experienced security analysts, portfolio managers, and other investment professionals. A CFA has demonstrated a wide range of knowledge that allows him or her to bring a balanced approach to investments and adapt to a rapidly evolving profession. Certification is based on passing three examinations and meeting the minimum education and experience requirements. AIMR has an extensive and proactive ethics program based on the AIMR code of ethics and standards of professional conduct. AIMR membership is required.

Education/Experience

To sit for the first examination, a candidate must have a bachelor's degree or experiential equivalent. Three years of acceptable experience, along with passing the three certification examinations, is required before the charter is awarded.

Examinations

The CFA program has three examinations. They must be taken in order, and only one may be taken per year. Candidates spend approximately 160 hours preparing for each test; group study is encouraged.

Level 1 (pass rate 62%) covers investment valuation and management tools and inputs. Using multiple choice, problems, and short essay, the candidate is tested on ethics and standards; quantitative methods; economic and financial state analysis; asset valuation; and portfolio management.

Level 2 (pass rate 67%) uses problems and short essays to test applying the concepts found in the Level 1 exam. It also includes asset valuation techniques and case studies, and industry and company analysis.

Level 3 (pass rate 77%) uses problems and short essays to test advanced areas of portfolio management, including risk, portfolio categories, implementation, and performance measurement.

Recertification

CFA charterholders are expected to participate in AIMR's continuing education program.

CHARTERED FINANCIAL CONSULTANT (CHFC)

Sponsor

The American College (AC)
270 S. Bryn Mawr Ave.
Bryn Mawr, PA 19010
Phone: (215) 526-1490

Program Data

The American College is accredited by the Middle States Association of Colleges and Schools.

Certifying body: College
Year certification began: 1982
Number certified: 26,000
Organization members: Nonmembership. Upon certification, individuals are encouraged to join the American Society of CLU & ChFC® (35,000 members), with headquarters located on the campus. For information, call (215) 526-2500.
Additional programs: Chartered Financial Consultant (ChFC)
Approximate certification costs: $3000

Program Description

The Chartered Financial Consultant (ChFC) designation recognizes financial planning professionals. A ChFC advises in income-tax planning, wealth accumulation, and investments.

Education/Experience

While many ChFCs are insurance agents and underwriters, the designation is open to any individual with three years of acceptable business experience.

Examinations

Certification is based on passing a series of examinations based on self-study courses. Formal classes, study groups, and agency classes may also be options. The self-study courses are as follows:

- Financial Decision Making at Retirement
- Financial Planning Applications
- Fundamentals of Estate Planning
- Fundamentals of Financial Planning
- Income Taxation
- Individual Life and Health Insurance
- Investments
- Wealth Accumulation Planning
- Two electives

All examinations follow the associated course content. The two-hour, multiple-choice test may be taken either as paper and pencil or on computer at test centers.

Recertification

Recertification is required for ChFCs who matriculated after June 30, 1989, and other ChFCs who voluntarily elect to participate. ChFCs must accumulate 60 hours of acceptable education every two years. Examples of hour awards: 1 per 50 minutes of instruction, 45 hours for a nationally recognized designation, and 15 hours per college-semester-credit hour.

ACCREDITED FINANCIAL COUNSELOR (AFC)

Sponsor

Association for Financial Counseling and
  Planning Education (AFCPE)
3900 East Camelback Road, Suite 200
Phoenix, AZ 85018
Phone: (602) 912-5331
Fax: (602) 957-4828
E-mail: theadmin@indirect.com
WWW: http://www.hec.ohio-state.edu/hanna/
  afcpe/index.htm

Program Data

Certifying body: Association
Year accreditation began: 1993
Number certified: 100+
Organization members: 500 (AFCPE)
Additional programs: Accredited Housing
  Counselor (AHC), Certified Housing Counselor
  (CHC)
Approximate accreditation costs: $500

Program Description

The Accredited Financial Counselor (AFC) designation recognizes financial advisors trained to educate clients in sound financial principles, to assist in developing strategies to meet a client's financial goals, and to help clients overcome financial challenges.

Education/Experience

Anyone working as a financial counselor or educator for at least two years is eligible to enter the AFC program. Candidates must provide at least three letters of reference. Acceptable counseling experience includes one-on-one counseling with clients; developing or delivering education and training programs for financial counselors; supervising financial counselors; or acting as an education director for a financial counseling organization.

Curriculum

A candidate must complete two self-study courses, which include a text and study guide. The two AFC courses are as follows:

- Personal Finance, which includes an analysis of financial services, estate, and retirement planning. The course emphasizes personal-financial-management mechanics, techniques, and strategies. Candidates learn the appropriate processes of personal and family financial management.

- Financial Counseling, which includes counseling, budgeting, debt reduction, collections, bankruptcies, and government assistance programs. The course also covers the counseling process and techniques on advising clients.

Examinations

Each course ends with a proctored, 100-question, multiple-choice examination covering the curriculum content.

Reaccreditation

AFCs must earn 20 hours of acceptable continuing education every year to maintain their designation.

CERTIFIED FINANCIAL PLANNER® (CFP®)

Sponsor

Certified Financial Planners Board of Standards
1660 Lincoln St., Suite 3050
Denver, CO 80264
Phone: (303) 830-7543
Fax: (303) 860-7388
E-mail: cfp1brd@ix.netcom.com

Program Data

Recognized by: NCCA
Certifying body: Independent board
Year certification began: 1972
Number certified: 30,750
Organization members: Nonmembership
Approximate certification costs: $450

Program Description

The Certified Financial Planner® (CFP®) designation recognizes financial planners who meet CFP Board of Standards education, experience, examination, and ethics requirements. The successful candidate then receives a license to use the CFP designation. The CFP Board of Standards maintains an ethics board with decertification powers.

Education/Experience

All candidates must complete a 180-hour financial planning course of study with an institution registered with the CFP Board or equivalent. The instructional hours may be classroom, distance learning, or correspondence. The required curriculum includes the fundamentals of financial planning; employee benefits; insurance; investments; retirement; and estate planning. CFPs need a bachelor's degree and three years of experience. Certain degrees reduce the experience requirement.

Examinations

The 10-hour, two-day, multiple-choice examination has a pass rate of 53%. Approximately two-thirds of the examination questions require analysis, synthesis, and evaluation to answer correctly. The exam, based on an in-depth job analysis, includes client assessments; estates; ethics; functions of financial planning; income tax and tax planning; insurance analysis; investment and legal environment; investments; and retirement planning.

Recertification

CFP licensees must pay an annual $75 licensing fee and earn 30 hours of acceptable continuing education every two years to maintain certification. The recertification rate is 98%.

REGISTERED FINANCIAL PLANNER (RFC)

Sponsor

International Association of Registered Financial Planners (IARFP)
P.O. Box 504
Chesterfield, MO 63006
Phone: (800) 532-9060
E-mail: admin@iarfc.investing.com
WWW: http://www.iarfc.investing.com/reception.htm

Program Data

Certifying body: Association
Number certified: 630
Approximate certification costs: $175

Program Description

The Registered Financial Planner (RFC) designation recognizes active and experienced financial planners. Certification is based on professional credentials and experience. There are no examination requirements. The IARFP maintains an active ethics program.

Education/Experience

An RFC must document an active financial planning practice. Candidates must have four years of full-time financial planning experience, have a bachelor's or graduate degree in a related field, hold an acceptable designation or degree in financial planning, and qualify for at least one securities license. Candidates must meet their state's licensing requirements for life/health insurance.

Recertification

RFCs must complete 40 hours of continuing education annually.

CERTIFIED FUND SPECIALIST (CFS)

Sponsor

Institute of Certified Fund Specialists (ICFS)
7911 Herschel Ave., Suite 201
La Jolla, CA 92037-4413
Phone: (800) 848-2029
Fax: (619) 454-4660
E-mail: icfs@icfs.com
WWW: http://millennianet.com/icfs/

Program Data

ICFS coursework is recognized as professional continuing education by most state departments of insurance and accountancy.

Certifying body: For-profit corporation
Approximate certification costs: $725

Program Description

The Certified Fund Specialist (CFS) designation recognizes individuals completing the Institute's 60-hour mutual fund and annuity curriculum. The ICFS maintains an active ethics program. There are no prerequisites or membership requirements.

Curriculum

The CFS program is a 60-hour home-study course. The course materials include a study guide, videotapes, an audiotape, and two investment books. The course covers annuities; dollar-cost averaging; introduction to mutual funds; market indexes; modern portfolio theory; mutual fund categories; reducing risk; retirement plans; selecting mutual funds; systematic withdrawal plans; taxes on distributions; time value of money; and titling assets.

Examinations

The two-hour, 100-question comprehensive CFS examination is administered through the National Association of Security Dealers (NASD) PROCTOR® Certification Testing Centers.

Recertification

The ICFS requires annual continuing education.

CERTIFIED HOUSING COUNSELOR (CHC)

ACCREDITED HOUSING COUNSELOR (AHC)

Sponsor

Association for Financial Counseling and
  Planning Education (AFCPE)
3900 East Camelback Road, Suite 200
Phoenix, AZ 85018
Phone: (602) 912-5331
Fax: (602) 957-4828
E-mail: theadmin@indirect.com
WWW: http://www.hec.ohio-state.edu/hanna/
  afcpe/index.htm

Program Data

Certifying body: Association
Year accreditation began: 1993
Number certified: 100+
Organization members: 500 (AFCPE)
Additional programs: Accredited Financial
  Counselor (AFC)
Approximate accreditation costs: $290 (AHC),
  $715 (CHC)

Program Description

The Accredited Housing Counselor (AHC) and Certified Housing Counselor (CHC) designations recognize financial counselors providing housing and money management counseling to low, moderate, and middle income families seeking to obtain, maintain, or retain adequate housing.

The AHC program is designed for para-professionals; the CHC program is a professional-level certification.

Education/Experience

AHC candidates must have six months of counseling experience and provide one letter of reference.

CHC candidates must have three years of counseling experience and provide three letters of reference.

Curriculum

The AHC program is a basic course taught in a structured classroom environment. The course includes counseling skills, and the management of cash, credit, debt, taxes, and risk. Candidates also receive training on housing options, affordability factors, mortgages, housing legislation, and moratoriums (HUD assignment, VA refunding, foreclosures, etc.).

The CHC program is based on completing three college-level courses, either in-class or self-study.

- Personal Finance, which includes an analysis of financial services, estate, and retirement planning. The course emphasizes personal-financial-management mechanics, techniques, and strategies. Candidates learn the appropriate processes of personal and family financial management.

- Debt Management and Counseling Techniques, which includes advanced counseling skills, debt management, collections, and government assistance programs

- Housing Principles and Practices, which focuses on the residential housing market. The course emphasizes residential appraisals and property values; real estate contracts; financing and mortgage underwriting; taxes; and public policy issues.

Examinations

- Candidates must pass a comprehensive examination at the end of the AHC course.

- CHC candidates must pass a proctored, 100-question, multiple-choice examination at the end of each CHC course.

Recertification

AHCs and CHCs must earn 20 hours of acceptable continuing education every year to maintain their designation.

REGISTERED INVESTMENT ADVISER (RIA)

Sponsor

Securities and Exchange Commission (SEC)
450 Fifth St. NW
Washington, DC 20549
Phone: (202) 942-7040

Program Data

Certifying body: Government
Year certification began: 1940
Approximate certification costs: $150

Program Description

Under the Investment Advisers Act of 1940, most professionals providing investment advice must register with the Securities Exchange Commission (SEC). The act requires advisers to give clients and potential clients a written disclosure describing the adviser's compensation, background, and business practices. This information must also be filed with the SEC. The SEC also requires registered advisers to maintain records. The term *Registered Investment Adviser* is derived from these registration requirements.

Most states have additional registration requirements; SEC registration does not exempt financial advisers from state licensing requirements.

Education/Experience

There are no federal qualifications standards for registration. The SEC must accept an applicant except when an applicant has been convicted of certain crimes or otherwise banned from providing financial advice by regulatory actions.

CHARTERED MARKET TECHNICIAN (CMT)

Sponsor

Market Technicians Association (MTA)
One World Trade Center, Suite 4447
New York, NY 10048
Phone: (212) 912-0995
WWW: http://www.mta-usa.org/~lensmith/

Program Data

Certifying body: Association
Organization members: 650
Approximate certification costs: $1000

Program Description

The Chartered Market Technician (CMT) program recognizes bond, commodity, currency, equity, futures, and options professionals skilled in technical analysis. Certification is based on passing two examinations and completing a research paper. MTA membership is required. MTA has an active ethics program.

Education/Experience

Candidates should be actively employed in the field.

Examinations

MTA has developed a self-study program and provides a reading list for exam preparation. The Level I exam is a multiple-choice test evaluating entry-level competence. The Level II exam is essay-based and evaluates competence in one or more areas of expertise. Candidates passing both exams then must write an original research paper for publication.

Recertification

CMTs must complete continuing professional education to remain certified.

ACCREDITED TAX ADVISOR℠

Sponsor

Accreditation Council for Accountancy and
Taxation℠ (ACAT)
1010 N. Fairfax St.
Alexandria, VA 22314
Phone: (703) 549-2228
WWW: http://www.nspa.org/act.html

Program Data

ACAT is affiliated with the National Society of Public Accountants (NSPA) and the National Endowment for Financial Education.

Certifying body: Association-sponsored independent board
Year certification began: 1973
Additional certifications: Accredited in Accountancy/Accredited Business Accountant℠; Accredited Tax Preparer℠

Program Description

The Accredited Tax Advisor℠ designation recognizes financial services professionals qualified to do tax planning. Certification is based on completing Certified Financial Planner courses and passing certification examinations. CFP courses are primarily directed to independent study and prepare the candidate for the examinations.

Education/Experience

Candidates must also have an undergraduate degree, a related professional designation, or experience acceptable to the College to enroll in the program. Prior to accreditation, a candidate must meet one of the following requirements:

- Master's in Tax Accounting or LLM in taxation
- Bachelor's degree and one year of professional tax-preparation experience

- Two years of professional tax-preparation experience

Curriculum

The total course schedule is approximately 24 months in length. It includes the following:

- Advanced Estate Planning
- Case Studies in Tax Planning
- Qualified Retirement Plans
- Tax Planning for the Highly Compensated
- Tax Planning for the Owners of a Closely Held Business
- Tax Practice

Examinations

All courses except the Case Studies course have a three-hour, 75-question, multiple-choice examination covering the course content. Case Studies in Tax Planning includes short-answer and essay formats.

Recertification

An Accredited Tax Advisor must earn 60 hours of continuing professional education every three years.

ACCREDITED TAX PREPARER℠

Sponsor

Accreditation Council for Accountancy and
　Taxation℠ (ACAT)
1010 N. Fairfax St.
Alexandria, VA 22314
Phone: (703) 549-2228
WWW: http://www.nspa.org/act.html

Program Data

ACAT is affiliated with the National Society of Public Accountants (NSPA) and the National Endowment for Financial Education.

Certifying body: Association-sponsored
　independent board
Year certification began: 1973
Additional certifications: Accredited Tax
　Advisor℠; Accredited in Accountancy/
　Accredited Business Accountant℠

Program Description

The Accredited Tax Preparer℠ designation recognizes tax professionals qualified to prepare tax returns for both individuals and businesses. Certification is based on completing the Certified Financial Planner courses and passing certification

examinations. CFP courses are primarily directed to independent study and prepare the candidate for the examinations.

Education/Experience

Candidates must also have one year of professional tax-preparation experience prior to the award of the Accredited Tax Preparer mark.

Curriculum

The curriculum comprises the following two courses:

Tax Preparer I: Individual Tax Returns—an in-depth course on individual tax returns, filing, computerized return preparation, and preparer responsibilities. Candidates who complete the course and pass the examination are qualified to prepare individual returns and all associated schedules. The course ends with a three-hour, 75-question, multiple-choice examination.

Tax Preparer II: Partnership, Corporation and Fiduciary Tax Returns—an in-depth course on business income-tax returns. Candidates study the full range of partnership returns and rules, corporate tax reporting, S corporations, and formations and liquidations. The course also covers estate-tax and trust-tax requirements. The course ends with a three-hour, 75-question, multiple-choice examination.

Recertification

An Accredited Tax Preparer must earn 60 hours of continuing professional education every three years.

CERTIFIED TAX PREPARER (CTP)

CERTIFIED TAX PREPARER SPECIALIST (CTPS)

CERTIFIED TAX PREPARER MASTER (CTPM)

Sponsor

Institute of Tax Consultants (ITC)
7500-212 SW, Suite 205
Edmonds, WA 98026
Phone: (206) 774-3521
Fax: (206) 672-0461

Program Data

The ITC program is recognized by the American Society of Tax Professionals (ASTP).

Certifying body: Independent board
Year certification began: 1979
Number certified: 500+
Approximate certification costs: $100

Program Description

The Certified Tax Preparer or Certified Tax Practitioner (CTP) designation recognizes tax preparation professionals. Enrolled agents and CPAs certified by ITC are considered "practitioners" rather than preparers under Internal Revenue Service rules. Enrolled agents and CPAs may be granted the CTP designation without taking the examination. The Specialist and Master designations recognize preparers/practitioners with advanced expertise in one or more areas (see *Examinations*). Membership in a national association focusing on taxes is "encouraged." The ITC has an active ethics program.

Education/Experience

A CTP candidate must have graduated from a program on either post-secondary accounting or income tax, and must have worked three of the preceding four years in the field.

Examinations

The CTP examination is an open-book, 250-question, multiple-choice test that also includes a comprehensive written problem. The exam covers personal income taxes and is based on IRS publications. The CTP examination has a 70% pass rate.

The Certified Tax Preparer Specialist (CTPS) designation recognizes CTPs with at least one year's experience who pass one of five specialty examinations. The CTPS examinations are 200-question, multiple-choice tests that include a comprehensive problem on the tested specialty. Specialty examinations are available in these areas:

- Partnerships
- C & S corporations
- Exempt organizations
- Tax planning
- Estates, trusts, gifts, and fiduciaries

The Certified Tax Preparer Master (CTPM) designation recognizes preparers with additional experience and training. A CTPM candidate must have passed three specialty examinations. Candidates complete an in-depth research paper; upon acceptance, the Master designation is awarded.

Recertification

Certification must be renewed every two years. Renewal is based on continuing education; 60 contact hours of tax-related education is required. CTPSs must accumulate five additional hours during the renewal period for each specialty. The CTPM designation has no renewal requirements.

The recertification rate is 80%.

REAL ESTATE AND APPRAISAL
Appraisal

CERTIFIED BUSINESS APPRAISER (CBA)

Sponsor

Institute of Business Appraisers, Inc. (IBA)
112 S. Federal Highway, Suite 6
P.O. Box 1447
Boynton Beach, FL 33425
Phone: (407) 732-3202

Program Data

Certifying body: Professional association
Number certified: 150
Organization members: 2000
Approximate certification costs: $200

Program Description

The Certified Business Appraiser (CBA) accreditation recognizes business appraisers who have demonstrated a high level of competence. Membership in the IBA is required. Accreditation is based on passing an examination and demonstrating competence through submission of two business appraisal reports. The candidate must submit business appraisal reports he or she has prepared for clients. The reports are judged on the compliance to the IBA's Business Appraisal Standards to ensure a candidate can perform competent original appraisals The Institute sells a basic business appraisal self-study course that can help prepare a candidate for the examination.

Examinations

The three-and-one-half-hour examination is made up of multiple-choice, short-answer, and problem-solving questions. The test covers the full range of business appraisal and evaluation.

Recertification

Continued work in the field and a review of work product are required.

CERTIFIED COMMERCIAL REAL ESTATE APPRAISER (CCRA)

Sponsor

National Association of Real Estate Appraisers (NAREA)
8383 East Evans Road
Scottsdale, AZ 85260
Phone: (602) 948-8000
Fax: (602) 998-8022
E-mail: narea@iami.org.
WWW: http://www.iami.org/narea.html

Program Data

Certifying body: Association
Additional certifications: Certified Real Estate Appraiser (CREA); Registered Professional Member (RPM)
Approximate cost of certification: $265

Program Description

The Certified Commercial Real Estate Appraiser (CCRA) designation is a membership category in NAREA. Certification is based on experience. There are no exam requirements. Candidates must pledge to follow the NAREA code of ethics.

Education/Experience

Candidates must have a general real-property state license or certificate.

Recertification

None.

GENERAL APPRAISER, APPRAISAL INSTITUTE (MAI)

Sponsor

Appraisal Institute (AI)
875 N. Michigan Ave., Suite 2400
Chicago, IL 60611-1980
Phone: (312) 335-4100
Fax: (312) 335-4400
E-mail: aimail@realworks.com
WWW: http://www.realworks.com/ai

Program Data

Certifying body: Association
Year certification began: 1980
Number certified: 5700 (all designations)
Organization members: 12,000
Additional programs: Residential Appraisal,
   Appraisal Institute (SRA)

Program Description

The MAI designation recognizes Appraisal Institute members experienced in commercial and industrial properties. Certification is based on completing several requirements. The Appraisal Institute maintains an active ethics program.

Education/Experience

All candidates must meet the following requirements for the MAI designation:

- One year as an AI candidate member
- Bachelor's degree
- 4500 documented hours of specialized appraisal experience in work relating to real estate, other than one-to-four family properties. Experience may be in either real estate valuation, real estate evaluation, or appraisal-report review.

Candidates must also submit one demonstration report.

Curriculum

Candidates must attend the Standards of Professional Practice and Report Writing and Valuation Analysis courses.

Examinations

All MAI examinations have preparatory courses. Candidates not holding state appraiser licensure or certification must compete additional requirements.

Candidates must pass at least seven general appraiser examinations, including Standards of Professional Practice; Advanced Income Capitalization; Highest & Best Use and Market Analysis; Advanced Sales Comparison and Cost Approaches; Report Writing; and Valuation Analysis and Advanced Applications.

Candidates must also pass a comprehensive general-appraiser examination.

Recertification

MAIs must pass a Standards of Professional Practice exam every five years.

GENERAL ACCREDITED APPRAISER (GAA)
RESIDENTIAL ACCREDITED APPRAISER (RAA)

Sponsor

National Association of REALTORS® (NAR)
Appraisal Section
430 North Michigan Ave.
Chicago, Illinois 60611-4087
Phone: (800) 874-6500
Fax: (312) 329-8576
E-mail: apprupdate@aol.com
WWW: http://www.realtor.com

Program Data

Certifying body: Association
Number certified: New program
Organization members: 14,000
Additional programs: Accredited Residential Manager (ARM®); Certified International Property Specialist (CIPS); Certified Real Estate Brokerage Manager (CRB); Certified Residential Specialist (CRS®); Counselor of Real Estate (CRE); Graduate, REALTOR® Institute (GRI); Leadership Training Graduate (LTG); REALTOR® Association Certified Executive (RCE); Society of Industrial and Office REALTORS® (SIOR®)

Program Description

The General Accredited Appraiser (GAA) and Residential Accredited Appraiser (RAA) designations recognize experienced state-certified/licensed appraisers. Candidates take continued coursework through NAR.

ACCREDITED MACHINERY AND EQUIPMENT APPRAISER (AMEA)

CERTIFIED MACHINERY AND EQUIPMENT APPRAISER (CMEA)

Sponsor

Association of Machinery and Equipment
   Appraisers (AMEA)
1110 Spring St.
Silver Spring, MD 20910
Phone: (301) 587-9335
Fax: (301) 588-7830
E-mail: amea@amea.org
WWW" http://www.mdna.org/amea/home.html

Program Data

Certifying body: Association
Organization members: 300
Approximate certification costs: $400 (AMEA),
 $800 (CMEA)

Program Description

The Accredited Machinery and Equipment Appraiser (AMEA) and the Certified Machinery and Equipment Appraiser (CMEA) designations recognize individuals who buy, sell, and appraise used machinery and equipment. Membership in AMEA is required. Designation award is based on course attendance, examination, and a work sample.

Education/Experience

Candidates must be employed and have two years of experience with a member firm of the Machinery Dealers National Association (MDNA).

Curriculum

AMEA candidates must attend the Introduction to Appraising Machinery and Equipment course and an AMEA Code of Ethics seminar. An acceptable appraisal complying with AMEA standards is also required.

CMEA candidates hold the AMEA designation for two years. Candidates must complete the Research and Analysis in Appraising Machinery and Equipment course and submit an acceptable appraisal.

Examinations

The AMEA examination covers the AMEA code of ethics. The CMEA examination content was not disclosed.

Recertification

AMEAs and CMEAs must renew accreditation every two years by continuing employment and membership, attending two acceptable seminars annually, and submitting a completed appraisal.

REGISTERED MORTGAGE UNDERWRITER (RMU)

Sponsor

National Association of Review Appraisers and
 Mortgage Underwriters (NARA/MU)
8383 East Evans Road
Scottsdale, AZ 85260
Phone: (602) 948-3000
Fax: (602) 998-8022
E-mail: nara@iami.org
WWW: http://www.iami.org/nara.html

Program Data

Certifying body: Association
Additional certifications: Certified Review
 Appraiser (CRA)
Organization members: 4800+
Approximate registration costs: $265

Program Description

The Registered Mortgage Underwriter (RMU) designation recognizes membership in NARA/MU. Certification is based on experience. There are no examination requirements.

Education/Experience

Candidates need two years of mortgage underwriting experience.

Recertification

None.

GRADUATE PERSONAL PROPERTY APPRAISER (GPPA)

Sponsor

Auction Marketing Institute (AMI)
8880 Ballentine
Overland Park, KS 66214
Phone: (913) 541-8115
Fax: (913) 894-5281
E-mail: ami@netis.com
WWW: http://www.auctionweb.com/ami/

Program Data

Certifying body: Nonprofit professional education
 organization.
Year certification began: 1996
Number certified: New program
Organization members: 1000 (holders of the CAI
 designation)
Additional certifications: Accredited Auctioneer
 Real Estate (AARE); Certified, Auctioneer's
 Institute (CAI®)

Program Description

The Graduate Personal Property Appraiser (GPPA) designation recognizes appraisal professionals completing the Auction Marketing Institute (AMI) two-part appraisal course. Certification is based on meeting experiential requirements and completing all Institute coursework. GPPAs must maintain membership in AMI. AMI has an active ethics board with decertification powers.

Education/Experience

To become candidates, individuals must have two years of full-time experience, be over the age of 21, and have a high school diploma. To receive the GPPA designation, candidates must complete the GPPA course, conduct 10 appraisals in the selected speciality area, and submit an acceptable appraisal report.

Curriculum

The first part of the GPPA course covers responsibility of the appraiser; identification; USPAP; factors affecting value; valuation; functions of an appraisal; report writing; responsibility to client; definitions; risk reduction; and marketing appraisal services.

Candidates select a product-specific section of the second-level. The sections are as follows:

- Personal Property, Antiques, and Collectibles
- Commercial Equipment
- Forestry, Construction, and Farm Equipment

Recertification

Not released.

REGISTERED PROFESSIONAL MEMBER (RPM)

Sponsor

National Association of Real Estate Appraisers (NAREA)
8383 East Evans Road
Scottsdale, AZ 85260
Phone: (602) 948-8000
Fax: (602) 998-8022
E-mail: narea@iami.org.
WWW: http://www.iami.org/narea.html

Program Data

Certifying body: Association
Additional certifications: Certified Commercial Real Estate Appraiser (CCRA); Certified Real Estate Appraiser (CREA)
Approximate cost of registration: $135

Program Description

The Registered Professional Member (RPM) designation is a membership category in NAREA. The RPM designation is for professionals in real estate who do not have a state appraisal license. Certification is based on experience. There are no exam requirements. Candidates must pledge to follow the NAREA code of ethics.

Education/Experience

Candidates must have one year of experience in the real estate field.

Recertification

None.

CERTIFIED REAL ESTATE APPRAISER (CREA)

Sponsor

National Association of Real Estate Appraisers (NAREA)
8383 East Evans Road
Scottsdale, AZ 85260
Phone: (602) 948-8000
Fax: (602) 998-8022
E-mail: narea@iami.org.
WWW: http://www.iami.org/narea.html

Program Data

Certifying body: Association
Additional certifications: Certified Commercial Real Estate Appraiser (CCRA); Registered Professional Member (RPM)
Approximate certification costs: $215

Program Description

The Certified Real Estate Appraiser (CREA) designation is a membership category in NAREA. Certification is based on experience. There are no exam requirements. Candidates must pledge to follow the NAREA code of ethics.

Education/Experience

Candidates must meet one of three options for certification: real property appraiser state license/certificate; residential real property state license/certificate; or general real property state license/certificate.

Recertification

None.

REAL PROPERTY REVIEW APPRAISER (RPRA)

Sponsor

American Society of Farm Managers and Rural
 Appraisers (ASFMRA)
950 S. Cherry St., Suite 508
Denver, CO 80222
Phone: (303) 758-3513
Fax: (303) 758-0190
E-mail: 71630,1172 (Compuserve)

Program Data

The Advanced Rural Appraisal course meets the
education requirements for state appraiser and
broker licensing in many states.

Certifying body: Professional society
Accrediting body: Association
Year accreditation began: 1935
Number Accredited: 1065
Organization members: 2122
Additional programs: Accredited Farm Manager
 (AFM); Accredited Rural Appraiser (ARA)
Approximate accreditation costs: $2300

Program Description

The Real Property Review Appraiser (RPRA)
designation is a membership category in ASFMRA
and recognizes review appraisers with specialized
education and experience in rural property.

Education/Experience

Candidates must have a bachelor's degree or
equivalent, one year of appraisal review experience, and hold a current state General Appraiser
certification. Candidates must submit appraisal
reviews meeting ASFMRA standards.

Curriculum

Candidates must complete the following courses or
approved equivalents:

- Fundamentals of Rural Appraisal—A 38-
  hour, entry-level course covering appraisal
  concepts and foundations; valuation; legal
  and area descriptions; finance and cost;
  income; and sales comparison approaches.
  The ASFMRA ethics and standards of
  professional appraisal practice are also
  covered in this course.

- Standards of Professional Appraisal Practice
  and Code of Ethics—An 18½-hour course
  providing an in-depth examination of ethics
  and practices. Examples from actual
  appraisal situations are included.

- Report Writing School—A 24-hour course
  focusing on grammar and report organization; professional standards and content
  requirements in report writing; and the
  selection of style, presentation, and graphics

- Principles of Rural Appraisal—A 42½-hour
  course covering practical application of the
  appraisal process to rural-appraisal
  problems

- Eminent Domain—A 20-hour, intermediate
  course covering condemnation appraisals;
  just compensation; zoning; easements;
  appraiser relationships within the judicial
  process; and current trends

- Advanced Rural Appraisal—A 43½-hour
  comprehensive review of the appraisal
  process. This course includes advanced
  application of depreciation, capitalization,
  and market adjustments as they apply to
  rural situations.

- Valuation of Natural Resources—A specialized course in evaluating the current and
  potential worth of a property's natural
  resources. Full course description not
  released.

- Advanced Technical Review of Appraisals—
  A 45-hour course on commercial, industrial,
  and agricultural narrative reports. The course
  uses reports from different properties and
  shows how to complete a review report; also
  included are unique problems in rural appraisals and current regulatory requirements.
  This course is designed for independent fee
  appraisers, government reviewers, Federal
  lenders, and private lending institutions.

Examinations

The accreditation examination consists of case-
study problems and a written test including
appraisal practices and theories, ethics, and general agriculture. The pass rate is 85%.

Recertification

All accredited and professional members of
ASFMRA must earn 60 continuing-education credits every three years to maintain certification.

RESIDENTIAL APPRAISAL, APPRAISAL INSTITUTE (SRA)

Sponsor

Appraisal Institute (AI)
875 N. Michigan Ave., Suite 2400
Chicago, IL 60611-1980
Phone: (312) 335-4100
Fax: (312) 335-4400
E-mail: aimail@realworks.com
WWW: http://www.realworks.com/ai

Program Data

Certifying body: Association
Year certification began: 1980
Number certified: 5700 (all designations)
Organization members: 12,000
Additional programs: General Appraiser, Appraisal Institute (MAI)

Program Description

The SRA designation recognizes Appraisal Institute members experienced in residential (one-to-four family) properties. Certification is based on completing several requirements. The Appraisal Institute maintains an active ethics program.

Education/Experience

All candidates must meet the following requirements for the SRA designation:

- One year as an AI Candidate member

- Bachelor's degree

- 3000 hours of specialized appraisal experience in one-to-four family properties. Experience may be in either real estate valuation, real estate evaluation, or appraisal report review.

Candidates must also submit one demonstration report.

Curriculum

Candidates must attend the Standards of Professional Practice course.

Examinations

All SRA examinations have preparatory courses. Candidates not holding state appraiser licensure or certification must compete additional requirements.

Candidates must pass at least four residential appraiser examinations: Standards of Professional Practice; Advanced Residential Form and Narrative Report Writing; Residential Income Capitalization; and Residential Cost Approach.

Candidates must also pass a comprehensive residential-appraiser examination.

Recertification

None.

CERTIFIED REVIEW APPRAISER (CRA)

Sponsor

National Association of Review Appraisers and Mortgage Underwriters (NARA/MU)
8383 East Evans Road
Scottsdale, AZ 85260
Phone: (602) 948-3000
Fax: (602) 998-8022
E-mail: nara@iami.org
WWW: http://www.iami.org/nara.html

Program Data

Certifying body: Association
Organization members: 4800+
Additional certifications: Registered Mortgage Underwriter (RMU)
Approximate certification costs: $265

Program Description

The Certified Review Appraiser (CRA) designation recognizes membership in NARA/MU. Certification is based on experience. There are no examination requirements. The designation has two categories: CRA and CRA-Administrative.

Education/Experience

The CRA designation is given to members who hold a current state appraiser license or certificate.

The CRA-Administrative designation is given to members with five years of experience in appraisal review, but who do not hold a state license or certificate. Members in this designation are not authorized to change a valuation.

Recertification

None.

ACCREDITED RURAL APPRAISER (ARA)

Sponsor

American Society of Farm Managers and Rural Appraisers (ASFMRA)
950 S. Cherry St., Suite 508
Denver, CO 80222
Phone: (303) 758-3513
Fax: (303) 758-0190
E-mail: 71630,1172 (Compuserve)

Program Data

The Advanced Rural Appraisal course meets the education requirements for state appraiser and broker licensing in many states.

Accrediting body: Association
Year accreditation began: 1935
Number accredited: 1065
Organization members: 2122
Additional programs: Accredited Farm Manager (AFM); Real Property Review Appraiser (RPRA)

Program Description

The Accredited Rural Appraiser (ARA) designation recognizes real estate appraisers with specialized education and experience in rural property. Accreditation is based on completing several courses and passing the associated examinations.

Education/Experience

Candidates must have a bachelor's degree or equivalent, and five years of rural appraisal experience. Candidates must submit one rural-appraisal report meeting ASFMRA standards.

Curriculum

Candidates must complete the following courses or approved equivalents:

- Fundamentals of Rural Appraisal—A 38-hour, entry-level course covering appraisal concepts and foundations; valuation; legal and area descriptions; finance and cost; income; and sales comparison approaches. The ASFMRA ethics and standards of professional appraisal practice are also covered in this course.

- Standards of Professional Appraisal Practice and Code of Ethics—An 18½-hour course providing an in-depth examination of ethics and practices. Examples from actual appraisal situations are included.

- Report Writing School—A 24-hour course focusing on grammar and report organization; professional standards and content requirements in report writing; and the selection of style, presentation, and graphics

- Principles of Rural Appraisal—A 42½-hour course covering practical application of the appraisal process to rural-appraisal problems

- Eminent Domain—A 20-hour, intermediate course covering condemnation appraisals; just compensation; zoning; easements; appraiser relationships within the judicial process; and current trends

- Advanced Rural Appraisal—A 43½-hour comprehensive review of the appraisal process. This course includes advanced application of depreciation, capitalization, and market adjustments as they apply to rural situations.

Examinations

The accreditation examination consists of case-study problems and a written test including appraisal practices and theories, ethics, and general agriculture.

Reaccreditation

All accredited and professional members of ASFMRA must earn 60 continuing-education credits every three years to maintain accreditation.

REAL ESTATE AND APPRAISAL
Facilities Management

CERTIFIED BUILDING SERVICE EXECUTIVE (CBSE)

Sponsor

Building Service Contractors Association
  International (BSCAI)
10201 Lee Highway, Suite 225
Fairfax, VA 22030
Phone: (703) 359-7090

Program Data

Certifying body: Association
Number certified: 250
Organization members: 2600
Additional programs: Registered Building Service
  Manager (RBSM)
Approximate certification cost: $350 (members),
  $700 (nonmembers)

Program Description

Building service contractors provide cleaning, facility maintenance, and janitorial services to building owners and managers. The Certified Building Service Executive (CBSE) designation recognizes experienced executives in building-service contracting firms. Certification is based on passing an examination. Membership in the Building Service Contractors Association International (BSCAI) is not required.

Education/Experience

To sit for the CBSE examination, the candidate must hold an executive position in a building-service contracting firm; have been in the field for five years; and have worked in management for three years.

Examinations

The CBSE examination includes human resources; law; accounting; insurance; taxes; customer and public relations; trade practices; safety; bidding and estimating; inspection and rating; purchasing; quality control; and warehousing. BSCAI sells a preparatory package, audio and video training materials, and publications.

Recertification

CBSE certification must be renewed every three years using a point system. Forty professional credits must be earned, which may come from BSCAI membership, educational programs, industry education programs, and conventions and conferences.

REGISTERED BUILDING SERVICE MANAGER (RBSM)

Sponsor

Building Service Contractors Association
  International (BSCAI)
10201 Lee Highway, Suite 225
Fairfax, VA 22030
Phone: (703) 359-7090

Program Data

Certifying body: Association
Number certified: 300
Organization members: 2600
Additional certifications: Certified Building Service
  Executive (CBSE)
Approximate certification costs: $175

Program Description

Building service managers supervise cleaning, facility maintenance, and janitorial services for building owners and managers. The Registered Building Service Manager (RBSM) designation recognizes experienced managers in building service and supervisors in building service contracting. Membership in the Building Service Contractors Association International (BSCAI) is not required.

Education/Experience

In order to sit for the RBSM examination, the candidate must be a building service manager/supervisor with one year of experience.

Examinations

The RBSM examination includes human resources management; cleaning and restoration; janitorial technology and chemistry; quality assurance; and safety, fire, and security. BSCAI makes exam-preparation materials available.

Recertification

RBSM certification must be renewed every two years. Recertification is based on completion of a "knowledge review" examination.

CERTIFIED DEMAND-SIDE MANAGEMENT PROFESSIONAL (CDSM)

Sponsor

Association of Energy Engineers® (AEE)
4025 Pleasantdale Road, Suite 420
Atlanta, GA 30340
Phone: (770) 447-5083
Fax: (770) 446-3969
WWW: http://www.aeecenter.org

Program Data

Certifying body: Association
Number certified: New program
Organization members: 8000
Additional programs: Certified Cogeneration Professional (CCP); Certified Energy Manager (CEM); Certified Indoor Air Quality Professional (CIAQP); Certified Lighting Efficiency Professional (CLEP)

Program Description

The Certified Demand-Side Management Professional (CDSM) designation recognizes non-technical managers working in the energy management field. Certification is based on passing an examination. Membership in AEE is not required.

Education/Experience

To take the CDSM examination, candidates must have a business or related bachelor's or associate's degree with demand-side experience.

Examinations

The four-hour, multiple-choice CDSM examination is an open-book test. A two-day preparation course is presented by AEE.

Recertification

None.

FACILITIES MANAGEMENT ADMINISTRATOR (FMA)

Sponsor

Building Owners and Managers Association (BOMA) International
1201 New York Ave. NW, Suite 300
Washington, DC 20005
Phone: (800) 235-2664
Fax: (202) 371-0101
E-mail: genmail@bomi-edu.org
WWW: http://www.boma.org/bomihome.htm

Program Data

The American Council on Education (ACE) recommends college credit for BOMI Institute courses.

Certifying body: Association-sponsored independent board
Number certified: 13,000 (all programs)
Additional programs: Real Property Administrator (RPA); Systems Maintenance Administrator (SMA); Systems Maintenance Technician (SMT)

Program Description

The Facilities Management Administrator (FMA) program is offered through the BOMI Institute. The FMA designation recognizes individuals completing the BOMI Institute's curriculum. BOMA has an active ethics program. There are no education or experience requirements.

Curriculum

FMA courses are offered through classroom study, self-study, accelerated review, and corporate classes. Candidates must complete eight courses for certification: Ethics Is Good Business Seminar; The Design, Operation, and Maintenance of Building Systems, Parts I and II; Facilities Management and the Work Environment; Technologies for Facilities Management; Facilities Planning and Project Management; Real Estate Investment and Finance; and Environmental Health and Safety Issues.

Recertification

None. Certificants are encouraged to join the Society of Property Professionals (SPP) and participate in continuing education opportunities.

CERTIFIED FACILITIES MANAGER (CFM)

Sponsor

International Facilities Management Association
  (IFMA)
1 East Greenway Plaza, Suite 1100
Houston, TX 77046
Phone: (713) 623-4362
Fax: (713) 623-6124

Program Data

Certifying body: Association
Year certification began: 1992
Number certified: 1400+
Organization members: 13,000+
Approximate certification costs: $350

Program Description

The Certified Facilities Manager (CFM) designation recognizes skilled facilities managers and individuals from affiliated fields. Certification is based on passing an examination created from an extensive job analysis and built around eight facilities-management competency areas. The IFMA will investigate professional complaints against a CFA and take disciplinary action if warranted. IFMA membership is not required for certification.

Education/Experience

Currently, candidates must meet one of the following requirements to take the CFM examination:

- Four years of experience, a related degree, and continuing education
- Five years of experience, unrelated degree, and continuing education
- Eight years of experience, and some post-secondary and continuing education

Because the examination is based on experiential competencies rather than knowledge competencies, candidates without experience in at least six of the eight competency areas would not be expected to pass the examination. IFMA offers an examination handbook and a 36-page experience assessment tool that candidates should complete before taking the examination. Study resources for those candidates requiring additional professional education are provided. Local IFMA chapters offer additional resources.

Examinations

The CFM examination is a criterion-based, objective test designed to assess competence, not knowledge. The examination questions are written by certificants and academia in consultation with the testing company, Hale Associates. The pass rate is 70%. The four-part, six-hour, multiple-choice examination covers:

- Communication
- Facility function
- Finance
- Human and environmental factors
- Operations and maintenance
- Planning and project management
- Quality assessment and innovation
- Real estate

Recertification

CFMs must recertify every three years. Recertification is based on a point system. Candidates must earn points in four main categories, each of which has a 60-point maximum. Point examples:

- Practice
  - 20 points per year of full-time facility management employment
- Continuing Education
  - 20 points per year enrolled in a facility management degree program
  - 20 points per three-day facilities management conference
  - 6 points per one-day seminar
- Professional Involvement
  - 5 points per year of membership in a related professional association
  - 5 points for proctoring a CFM examination
- Development of the Profession
  - 20 points per year of task-force/committee work helping develop the profession
  - 30 points per published article or research report

CERTIFIED EXECUTIVE HOUSEKEEPER (C.E.H.)

REGISTERED EXECUTIVE HOUSEKEEPER (R.E.H.)

Sponsor

National Executive Housekeepers Association (N.E.H.A.)
1001 Eastwind Drive, Suite 301
Westerville, OH 43081
Phone: (800) 200-6342
Fax: (614) 895-1248

Program Data

N.E.H.A. is a member of the International Association for Continuing Education and Training. The Training and Certification Program is accepted for 30 credit hours at Newport University. Over 85 schools offer the N.E.H.A. certification program. N.E.H.A. maintains a position-referral service for employers.

Certifying body: Professional association
Year certification began: 1960
Number certified: 1600 (current)
Organization members: 7000
Approximate certification costs: Varies depending on certification route

Program Description

An executive housekeeper, as defined by the N.E.H.A., is a middle manager responsible for directing housekeeping programs in commercial, institutional, medical, or industrial facilities. This includes managing staff and budgets. N.E.H.A. maintains an active ethics board with decertification powers.

The Certified Executive Housekeeper (C.E.H.) designation is based on completing an educational program either independently or at one of the schools offering the certification program. The Registered Executive Housekeeper (R.E.H.) designation recognizes work beyond the Certified level.

Education/Experience—C.E.H.

A high school diploma or equivalent, one year of experience in institutional housekeeping management, and N.E.H.A. associate membership is required for certification.

There are three ways to earn C.E.H. status:

- Complete the 330-hour C.E.H. program offered through over 85 colleges and schools. Most of the hours (270) are in Personnel Management, Communications, Housekeeping Techniques, Environmental Controls, Behavioral Sciences, and Introduction to Business. Sixty hours are in selected electives.

- Complete the Collegiate Program option, requiring 60 hours of college coursework at a regionally accredited college or university. Transcripts are submitted to N.E.H.A. for acceptance. Thirty-nine hours must be in classes required by the N.E.H.A., with 21 hours in unrestricted electives.

- Complete the N.E.H.A. Training and Certification Program, a self-study program of two series. The pass rate for this program is 80%.

Education/Experience–R.E.H.

To earn R.E.H. status, a candidate must complete one year as an Associate member of N.E.H.A. or as a Certified Executive Housekeeper and have a Bachelor of Science or Arts degree from an accredited college or university. The 60 semester hours required under the Collegiate Program for Certification must be included.

Recertification

Recertification is required for both programs. Membership in N.E.H.A. is required to maintain certification. Every two years, a C.E.H./R.E.H. must complete two CEUs or two college-credit hours in business management or areas related to executive housekeeping. The recertification rate is 80%.

CERTIFIED INDOOR AIR QUALITY PROFESSIONAL (CIAQP)

Sponsor

Association of Energy Engineers® (AEE)
4025 Pleasantdale Road, Suite 420
Atlanta, GA 30340
Phone: (770) 447-5083
Fax: (770) 446-3969
WWW: http://www.aeecenter.org

Program Data

Certifying body: Association
Number certified: New program
Organization members: 8000
Additional programs: Certified Cogeneration Professional (CCP); Certified Demand-Side Management Professional (CDSM); Certified Energy Manager (CEM); Certified Lighting Efficiency Professional (CLEP)

Program Description

The Certified Indoor Air Quality Professional (CIAQP) designation recognizes experienced indoor-air-quality experts with proven on-the-job skills and subject expertise. CIAQPs work both on improving "sick building" situations and on maintaining healthy indoor-air-quality environments. Certification is based on passing an examination. Membership in AEE is not required.

Education/Experience

Engineering graduate or Registered Professional Engineer and three years of related professional experience. Other candidates may need additional experience.

Examinations

The four-hour, multiple-choice CIAQP examination is an open-book test. A two-day preparation course is presented by AEE.

Recertification

None.

CERTIFIED INSPECTOR (ICBO)

Sponsor

International Conference of Building Officials
  (ICBO)
5360 S. Workman Mill Road
Whittier, CA 90601
Phone:(310) 699-0541
Fax: (310) 692-2845
WWW: http://www.icbo.org/

Program Data

The ICBO programs are also offered by the International Association of Plumbing and Mechanical Officials (IAPMO).

Certifying body: Association
Number certified: 25,000 for all ICBO
  certifications
Organization members: 20,000
Additional certifications: Certified Plans Examiner

Program Description

The ICBO programs recognize inspectors passing examinations on various U.S. building-related codes. Certifications are based on passing examinations. There are no prerequisites. Many local and state governments recognize ICBO certifications.

A Certified Building Inspector ensures that buildings under construction meet codes and specifications, advise on construction and code requirements, inspect existing buildings for dangerous or illegal conditions, and document code violations.

A Certified Electrical Inspector inspects electrical installations during and after construction to ensure compliance and identify hazardous or illegal conditions.

A Certified Mechanical Inspector is responsible for heating, cooling, ventilating, and refrigeration systems, and heat-producing appliances.

A Certified Plumbing Inspector evaluates plumbing, sewage, and water transport systems.

A Certified Combination Inspector is responsible for inspecting both residential and commercial buildings for electrical, plumbing, mechanical, and building-systems-code compliance. This is automatic when either the Certified Building and Certified Electrical Inspector designation or the Certified Plumbing and Certified Mechanical Inspector designation are maintained.

A Certified Combination Dwelling Inspector is responsible for inspecting those same areas in one- and two-family dwellings.

Specialty inspector certifications are based on passing the ICBO examination. The specialties are Certified Reinforced Concrete Inspector; Certified Prestressed Concrete Inspector; Certified Structural Masonry Inspector; Certified Structural Steel and Welding Inspector; and Certified Spray-Applied Fireproofing Inspector.

Examinations

Except for the specialty exams, the ICBO exams are open-book. Except for general knowledge and plan-reading questions, the tests evaluate the candidate's ability to use specific codes.

Certified Building Inspector—Uniform Building Code. The examination covers building classifications; carpentry inspections; concrete inspections; construction requirements; exit requirements; fire safety and protection; footings, foundations, and site drainage; inspection practices; insulation, vents, and access inspections; masonry inspections; roofing inspections; and sheathing and wall coverings inspections.

Certified Electrical Inspector—National Electrical Code. The exam covers design and protection of wiring; equipment; general inspections; special occupancies; equipment and conditions; and wiring materials and methods.

Certified Mechanical Inspector—Uniform Mechanical Code. The exam covers appliances; cooling and refrigeration; ducts and ventilation; heating systems; materials and methods; and venting.

Certified Plumbing Inspector—Uniform Plumbing Code

Certified Combination Dwelling Inspector—Uniform Building Code; Uniform Mechanical Code; Uniform Plumbing Code; National Electrical Code; and Uniform Swimming Pool, Spa, and Hot Tub Code. The exam covers carpentry inspections; concrete-slab inspections; electrical inspections; footings, foundations, and site drainage; inspection practices; insulation, vents, and access inspections; layout, stairs, doors, and windows inspections; masonry inspections; plumbing inspections; roofing inspections; and swimming pool/spa inspections.

Specialty inspector examination—Each exam includes both an open-book and a closed-book examination (except Spray-Applied Fireproofing; closed-book only). The exam questions cover both basic industry standards and specialized references for specific areas.

Recertification

Recertification involves passing an open-book, take-home examination on codes and standards changes every three years.

CERTIFIED PARKING FACILITY MANAGER (CPFM)

Sponsor

National Parking Association (NPA)
1112 16th St. NW, Suite 300
Washington, DC 20036
Phone: (202) 296-4336

Program Data

Certifying body: Association
Year certification began: 1993
Approximate certification costs: $300 (members), $900 (nonmembers)

Program Description

The Certified Parking Facility Manager (CPFM) designation recognizes both private and public parking-facility supervisors and managers. Membership in the NPA is not required. Certification is based on passing an examination.

Education/Experience

Candidates must be employed in a supervisory or managerial position in the parking industry.

Examinations

The certification examination covers the three major areas within the body of knowledge a parking manager would need to perform effectively. The areas are as follows:

- Customer relations, including service, safety, security, and damage claims
- Employee supervision, including training and dealing with skill deficiencies and behavior problems
- Facility operations, including cleaning, maintenance, equipment, and cash handling

Recertification

Certification will be renewed every three years through professional development and continuing education.

CERTIFIED PLANS EXAMINER

Sponsor

International Conference of Building Officials (ICBO)
5360 S. Workman Mill Road
Whittier, CA 90601
Phone:(310) 699-0541
Fax: (310) 692-2845
WWW: http://www.icbo.org/

Program Data

Certifying body: Association
Number certified: 25,000 (all ICBO certifications)
Organization members: 20,000
Additional certifications: Certified Inspector (ICBO)

Program Description

The Certified Plans Examiner certification is based on passing the ICBO examination. A plans examiner ensures, through reviewing plans and specifications, compliance with nonstructural considerations of the building code. They may also advise others on nonstructural requirements, assist building inspectors, and maintain records. There are no prerequisites.

Examinations

The Certified Plans Examiner examination is an open-book examination. The pass rate for ICBO examinations is confidential. Except for general knowledge and plan-reading questions, the exam questions reference the Uniform Building Code. The exam includes building classification, exiting requirements, fire protection, regulations, and types of construction.

Recertification

Recertification involves passing an open-book, take-home examination on codes and standards changes every three years.

CERTIFIED PLANT ENGINEER (CPE)

Sponsor

Association for Facilities Engineering (AFE)
8180 Corporate Park Drive, Suite 305
Cincinnati, OH 45242
Phone: (513) 489-2473
Fax: (513) 247-7422
E-mail: aipe@ix.netcom.com
WWW: http://www.afe.org/

Program Data

Certifying body: Professional association
Year certification began: 1976
Number certified: 4000+
Organization members: 8000+
Approximate certification costs: $175 (members), $295 (nonmembers)

Program Description

The Association for Facilities Engineering (AFE) was formerly known as the American Institute of Plant Engineers (AIPE).

The Certified Plant Engineer (CPE) designation recognizes experienced plant engineers and managers of industrial, commercial, or institutional facilities. Membership in AFE is not required. AFE offers study guides, self-study materials, and examination preparatory classes.

Education/Experience

A candidate with a bachelor's degree in engineering or a related field must have either six years of experience in plant engineering or four years of experience in plant engineering management to sit for the examination.

A candidate without a degree, or with a degree outside of the engineering field, must have either eight years of plant engineering or six years of experience in plant engineering management to sit for the examination.

A candidate who is a registered PE with four years of experience in plant engineering is exempt from the certification examination requirement.

Examinations

The CPE examination is an open-book, multiple-choice test. Test questions are written by certificants, academia, and consultants and based on a comprehensive plant-engineering body of knowledge. Candidates are tested on their comprehensive skills in mechanical, electrical, civil, and environmental engineering. The exam also covers specific plant-engineering topics: electrical systems; administration and supervision; mechanical systems, controls, and instrumentation; energy management; economics; maintenance; and OSHA/safety. Candidates are presented with operational/scenario questions and asked to determine the correct solution to the described situation. The pass rate is 75%.

Recertification

CPEs must renew their certification every five years. Recertification is based on the following point system.

- Points needed for recertification: 8
- Points examples:
  - 1 point per year of plant engineering employment
  - 1 point per plant-engineering course of at least 10 contact hours
  - ½ point per plant-engineering course of between five and 10 contact hours.

The recertification rate is 50%.

REAL PROPERTY ADMINISTRATOR (RPA)

Sponsor

Building Owners and Managers Association
  (BOMA) International
1201 New York Ave. NW, Suite 300
Washington, DC 20005
Phone: (800) 235-2664
Fax: (202) 371-0101
E-mail: genmail@bomi-edu.org
WWW: http://www.boma.org/bomihome.htm

Program Data

The American Council on Education (ACE) recommends college credit for BOMI Institute courses.

Certifying body: Association-sponsored independent board
Number certified: 13,000 (all programs)
Additional programs: Facilities Management Administrator (FMA); Systems Maintenance Administrator (SMA); Systems Maintenance Technician (SMT)

Program Description

The Real Property Administrator (RPA) program is offered through the BOMI Institute. The RPA designation recognizes experienced property managers completing the BOMI Institute's curriculum. BOMA has an active ethics program.

Education/Experience

Candidates must have three years of experience as a property manager.

Curriculum

RPA courses are offered through classroom study, self-study, accelerated review, and corporate classes. Candidates must complete eight courses for certification. The five core courses are Ethics Is Good Business; Design, Operation, and Maintenance of Building Systems, Parts I and II; Law for Property Managers; Real Estate Investment and Finance; and Environmental Health and Safety Issues. Candidates must also complete two electives from the BOMI RPI catalog.

Recertification

None. Certificants are encouraged to join the Society of Property Professionals (SPP) and participate in continuing education opportunities.

SYSTEMS MAINTENANCE TECHNICIAN (SMT)

SYSTEMS MAINTENANCE ADMINISTRATOR (SMA)

Sponsor

Building Owners and Managers Association (BOMA) International
1201 New York Ave. NW, Suite 300
Washington, DC 20005
Phone: (800) 235-2664
Fax: (202) 371-0101
E-mail: genmail@bomi-edu.org
WWW: http://www.boma.org/bomihome.htm

Program Data

The American Council on Education (ACE) recommends college credit for BOMI Institute courses.

Certifying body: Association-sponsored independent board
Number certified: 13,000 (all programs)
Additional programs: Facilities Management Administrator (FMA); Real Property Administrator (RPA)

Program Description

The Systems Maintenance Technician (SMT) and Systems Maintenance Administrator (SMA) programs are offered through the BOMI Institute. The SMT and SMA designations recognize individuals completing the BOMI Institute's curriculum. BOMA has an active ethics program. There are no education or experience requirements.

Curriculum

For the SMT designation, candidates must complete the following six courses: Ethics Is Good Business Seminar; Boilers, Heating Systems, and Applied Mathematics; Refrigeration Systems and Accessories; Air Handling, Water Treatment, and Plumbing Systems; Electrical Systems and Illumination; and Building Control Systems.

For the SMA designation, candidates must complete the SMT curriculum and the following three courses: Building Design and Maintenance; Energy Management; and Supervision.

Examinations

Courses are offered through classroom study, self-study, accelerated review, and corporate classes.

Recertification

None. Certificants are encouraged to join the Society of Property Professionals (SPP) and participate in continuing education opportunities.

CERTIFIED UNIFORM FIRE CODE INSPECTOR

Sponsor

International Fire Code Institute (IFCI)
5360 Workman Mill Road
Whittier, CA 90601
Phone: (310) 699-0124

Program Data

The International Fire Code Institute is co-sponsored by the International Association of Fire Chiefs (IAFC), the International Conference of Building Officials (ICBO), and the Western Fire Chiefs Association (WFCA).

Certifying body: Association-sponsored
  independent board
Additional certifications: Underground Storage
  Tank Certification

Program Description

The Certified Uniform Fire Code Inspector certification is based on passing the IFCI examination. A fire code inspector inspects new and existing fire prevention, detection, and control systems and measures. There are no prerequisites or qualifications for the examination.

Examinations

The Certified Uniform Fire Code Inspector examination is an open-book examination. The pass rate for IFCI examinations is confidential. The exam questions reference the Uniform Building Code and the Uniform Fire Code. The examination includes:

- Inspections
- Fire Safety
- Flammable and hazardous materials
- Special occupancies inspections
- Special processes and equipment

Recertification

Recertification involves passing an open-book, take-home examination on codes and standards changes every three years.

REAL ESTATE AND APPRAISAL
Property Management

CERTIFIED APARTMENT MANAGER (CAM)

Sponsor

National Apartment Association (NAA)
201 North Union St., Suite 200
Alexandria, VA 22314
Phone: (703) 518-6141
E-mail: postmaster@naahq.Com

Program Data

The CAM program is recognized by the U.S. Department of Housing and Urban Development.

Certifying body: Association
Organization members: 26,000
Additional certifications: Certified Apartment Maintenance Technician (CAMT); Certified Apartment Property Supervisor (CAPS)

Program Description

The Certified Apartment Manager (CAM) designation recognizes professional on-site managers who complete NAA's comprehensive training program.

Education/Experience

Candidates must have two years of apartment management experience and 40 elective credits of professional/academic education for certification.

Curriculum

Candidates have two years to complete NAA's CAM program. These are the program requirements:

- Complete the Survey of Apartment Management—a 30-hour course.
- Complete the Advanced Apartment Management—a 33-hour block of six specialized courses.
- Complete an Apartment Community Analysis.

Recertification

CAMs must earn five continuing-education credits every year.

CERTIFIED APARTMENT PROPERTY SUPERVISOR (CAPS)

Sponsor

National Apartment Association (NAA)
201 North Union St., Suite 200
Alexandria, VA 22314
Phone: (703) 518-6141
E-mail: postmaster@naahq.Com

Program Data

Certifying body: Association
Organization members: 26,000
Additional certifications: Certified Apartment Maintenance Technician (CAMT); Certified Apartment Manager (CAM)

Program Description

The Certified Apartment Property Supervisor (CAPS) designation recognizes supervisors responsible for multiple properties and large staffs.

Education/Experience

Two years of multiple properties experience or CAM certification is required for certification.

Curriculum

Candidates must complete NAA's CAPS 156-hour program of study. The courses are Administrative Control; Finance and Economics; Human Resources; Maintenance; Marketing; Mid-Management Overview; and Property Evaluation.

Recertification

None.

PROFESSIONAL COMMUNITY ASSOCIATION MANAGER (PCAM®)

ASSOCIATION MANAGEMENT SPECIALIST (AMS®)

Sponsor

Community Associations Institute (CAI)
1630 Duke St.
Alexandria, VA 22314
Phone: (703) 548-8600
WWW: http://www.caionline.com

Program Data

Certifying body: Association
Number certified: 800 (both certifications)
Approximate certification costs: $3800
   (members), $4900 (nonmembers)

Program Description

The Professional Community Association Manager (PCAM) designation recognizes experienced community association professionals completing an extensive professional management development program. The Association Management Specialist (AMS) designation recognizes experienced professionals completing the first part of the program. Membership is not required. CAI maintains an active ethics program.

Education/Experience

PCAM candidates must have three years of professional experience for certification. AMS candidates must have two years of professional experience for certification.

Curriculum

The professional management development program consists of seven two-day courses. AMS candidates must complete the first course; PCAM candidates must complete all courses. These are the courses: The Essentials of Community Association Management; Facilities Management; Association Communications; Community Leadership; Community Governance; Risk Management; and Financial Management.

The AMS designation is awarded upon course completion. PCAM candidates, upon completion of all coursework, must complete an in-depth case study of an actual community association.

Recertification

PCAM certification must be renewed through continuing professional education.

CERTIFIED IN PROFESSIONAL DOWNTOWN MANAGEMENT

Sponsor

National Main Street Center
National Trust for Historic Preservation
1785 Massachusetts Ave. NW
Washington, DC 20036
Phone: (202) 673-4219
Fax: (202) 673-4050
WWW: http://home.worldweb.net/trust/

Program Data

Certifying body: Association
Year certification began: 1993
Number certified: 40 (100+ enrolled)
Organization members: 260,000
Approximate certification costs: $2100

Program Description

The Main Street Certification Institute in Professional Downtown Management provides training in managing historic downtown revitalization programs. Professionals certified by the Institute include managers of Main Street programs, historic preservation planners, and city managers.

Education/Experience

Candidates are accepted on a competitive basis determined by professional background and current responsibilities. For admission into the program, an applicant must provide professional references and proof of two years of related experience. Candidates must complete all classes within five years.

Curriculum

The certification program is made up of four classes:

- Design, including architecture, public spaces, research, building codes, and review procedures
- Economic restructuring, including real estate development, demographics, surveys, public finance, and office and housing development

- Organization, including fund-raising, accounting, volunteer development, and operations
- Promotion, including graphics, tourism, targeting markets, and logistics

Examinations
Each class concludes with a three-hour, open-book examination.

Recertification
None.

ACCREDITED FARM MANAGER (AFM)

Sponsor
American Society of Farm Managers and Rural
  Appraisers (ASFMRA)
950 S. Cherry St., Suite 508
Denver, CO 80222
Phone: (303) 758-3513
Fax: (303) 758-0190
E-mail: 71630,1172 (Compuserve)

Program Data
Accrediting body: Association
Year accreditation began: 1935
Number accredited: 1065
Organization members: 2122
Additional programs: Accredited Rural Appraiser
  (ARA); Real Property Review Appraiser
  (RPRA)
Approximate accreditation costs: $1800

Program Description
The Accredited Farm Manager (AFM) designation recognizes professionals trained to assist farm owners, banks, attorneys, farm purchasers, and rural property managers. ASFMRA maintains an active ethics board with enforcement powers. Accreditation is based on completing several courses and passing the associated examinations.

Education/Experience
Candidates must have a bachelor's degree or equivalent, and five years of farm management experience. Candidates must submit one farm-management report meeting ASFMRA standards.

Candidates must complete the following courses:

- Principles of Farm Management—An introductory course covering both technical and managerial subjects. This six-day course ends with a three-hour examination.

- Code of Ethics and Standards of Professional Practice—Covers standards of practice and ASFMRA ethics. This two-day course ends in a one-hour examination.

- Report Writing School—Teaches writing skills needed to complete management reports, including technical writing and the ASFMRA's management report guidelines. This three-day course ends with a one-hour examination.

- Advanced Farm Management—A six-day course designed for experienced farm managers. The course covers a wide range of environmental, financial, and planning subjects. Lotus 1-2-3® is used for problems and case studies. The course ends with a two-hour examination.

Examinations
The final accreditation examination includes a dry lab field problem; a written examination including management practices and theories, ethics, and general agriculture; and an oral examination covering all areas of farm management.

Reaccreditcation
All accredited and professional members of ASFMRA must earn 60 continuing-education credits every three years to maintain accreditation.

CERTIFIED PROFESSIONAL PROPERTY SPECIALIST (CPPS)

CERTIFIED PROFESSIONAL PROPERTY ADMINISTRATOR (CPPA)

CERTIFIED PROFESSIONAL PROPERTY MANAGER (CPPM)

CONSULTING FELLOW {PROPERTY} (CF)

Sponsor
National Property Manager Association, Inc.
  (NPMA)
380 Main St., Suite 290
Dunedin, FL, 34698
Phone: (813) 736-3788
Fax: (813) 736-6707
E-mail: npma@gate.net
WWW: http://www.npma.org/

Program Data

Certifying body: Professional association
Organization members: 2500
Approximate certification costs: $70 plus
   membership costs

Program Description

The Certified Professional Property Specialist (CPPS) is the entry-level certification for the NPMA's four-tier program. Certification is based on completing three of NPMA's 14 certification examinations. Membership in NPMA is required.

The Certified Professional Property Administrator (CPPA) is the second-level certification, requiring passage of all 14 examinations and three years of acceptable experience.

The Certified Professional Property Manager (CPPM) is the third-level certification, requiring passage of a comprehensive CPPM examination beyond the 14 certification examinations. Six years of acceptable experience is also required.

The Consulting Fellow (CF) designation recognizes CPPMs with additional experience, education, and leadership. Certification is based on a point system, with 16 out of a possible 30 points needed.

Examinations

Only the examination titles were released by NPMA. The examinations are Acquisition; Contract Completion; Disposition; Maintenance; Physical Inventory; Property Audits; Property; Consumption; Real Property; Receiving and Identification; Records; Reporting; Storage and Movement; Subcontract Administration; Utilization.

Recertification

CPPSs and CFs have no recertification requirements. CPPAs and CPPMs must recertify every five years. Recertification is based on participating in three of eight approved activities.

CERTIFIED PUBLIC HOUSING MANAGER (PHM)

Sponsor

National Association of Housing and
   Redevelopment Officials (NAHRO)
630 Eye St. NW
Washington, DC 20001-3736
Phone: (202) 289-3500
Fax: (202) 289-8181
E-mail: nahro@nahro.org
WWW: http://www.nahro.org/

Program Data

Certifying body: Association
Number certified: 15,000
Organization members: 3000
Approximate certification costs: $700

Program Description

The Public Housing Manager certification program recognizes property managers who demonstrate the knowledge and skills to manage public housing. Certification is based on passing an examination and review exercise. NAHRO membership is not required. There are no experience or education requirements.

Curriculum

Candidates attend a three-day seminar on public housing management, and then take the PHM examination for certification. The two-part testing program was developed by NAHRO and the Educational Testing Service (ETS) based on an extensive job analysis. Both the multiple-choice examination and the review exercise cover the following areas: maintenance and security; occupancy cycle; tenant services and relations; management; and administration. The review exercise requires the candidate to take the role of a public housing authority manager and respond to simulated work conditions.

Recertification

None.

ACCREDITED RESIDENTIAL MANAGER (ARM®)

Sponsor

Institute of Real Estate Management (IREM)
430 N. Michigan Ave.
Chicago, IL 60610
Phone: (800) 837-0706
E-mail: tmillon@irem.org
WWW: http://www.irem.org/

Program Data

IREM is an affiliated institute of the National Association of REALTORS® (NAR).

Certifying body: Association
Number certified: 10,000

Additional programs: Certified International Property Specialist (CIPS); Certified Real Estate Brokerage Manager (CRB); Certified Residential Specialist (CRS®); Counselor of Real Estate (CRE); General Accredited Appraiser (GAA); Graduate, REALTOR® Institute (GRI); Leadership Training Graduate (LTG); REALTOR® Association Certified Executive (RCE); Residential Accredited Appraiser (RAA); Society of Industrial and Office REALTORS® (SIOR®)

Program Description

The Accredited Residential Manager (ARM®) designation recognizes on-site residential property managers completing the Institute's education program. There are no association membership requirements. Certification is based on completing the required education and experience requirements.

Education/Experience

The candidate must be a high school graduate.

The required residential management experience is based on the unit size and types; from 24 to 48 months. Time requirements are cut in half if under direct supervision of a Certified Property Manager (CPM). Candidates must currently spend 50% of the time managing property.

Curriculum

Candidates must complete one of the following courses: Successful Site Management; Successful Management of Government Assisted and Public Housing; or Housing Management Training for Nonprofits.

Recertification

ARMs must be reaccredited every two years. Reaccreditation is based on continued experience, education, or pursuit of CPM designation.

REAL ESTATE AND APPRAISAL
Real Estate

REALTOR® ASSOCIATION CERTIFIED EXECUTIVE (RCE)

Sponsor

National Association of REALTORS® (NAR)
430 N. Michigan Ave.
Chicago, IL 60611
Phone: (312) 329-5972
WWW: http://www.realtor.com

Program Data

Certifying body: Association
Additional programs: Accredited Residential Manager (ARM®); Certified International Property Specialist (CIPS); Certified Real Estate Brokerage Manager (CRB); Certified Residential Specialist (CRS®); Counselor of Real Estate (CRE); General Accredited Appraiser (GAA); Graduate, REALTOR® Institute (GRI); Leadership Training Graduate (LTG); Residential Accredited Appraiser (RAA); Society of Industrial and Office REALTORS® (SIOR®)

Program Description

The REALTOR® Association Certified Executive (RCE) designation recognizes association professionals who have proficiency and knowledge of both general association management and real estate association requirements. Certification is based on a written examination.

Education/Experience

A candidate must be currently employed by NAR or by a local or state REALTOR association, subsidiary, or multiple-listing service. In order to qualify to sit for the RCE examination, a candidate must have attended one NAR EO Institute, and have three years of experience with EO or five years of experience with REALTOR as an association staff specialist.

Examinations

The multiple-choice and short-answer RCE examination includes association planning and budgeting; staffing; public relations; professional standards and ethics; laws and regulations; and multiple listings.

Recertification

None.

ACCREDITED AUCTIONEER REAL ESTATE (AARE)

Sponsor

Auction Marketing Institute (AMI)
8880 Ballentine
Overland Park, KS 66214
Phone: (913) 541-8115
Fax: (913) 894-5281
E-mail: ami@netis.com
WWW: http://www.auctionweb.com/ami/

Program Data

AMI's AARE courses are accepted for continuing education credits by many state licensing boards.

Certifying body: Nonprofit professional education organization
Year certification began: 1992
Number certified: 100
Organization members: 1000 (holders of the CAI designation)
Additional certifications: Certified, Auctioneer's Institute (CAI®); Graduate Personal Property Appraiser (GPPA)
Approximate certification costs: $2000

Program Description

The Accredited Auctioneer Real Estate (AARE) designation recognizes experienced real estate auctioneers who complete the Auction Marketing Institute's (AMI's) education program. Certification is based on meeting experiential requirements and completing all Institute coursework. National Auctioneers Association (NAA) membership is required, and candidates must meet any applicable state-licensing requirements. AMI has an active ethics board with decertification powers.

Education/Experience

The AARE courses may be taken as seminars by any interested individual. However, to earn the AARE designation, candidates must have a high school diploma, hold a current state license in real estate, and conduct 10 real estate auctions within three years of completing the AARE coursework. Courses include both practical scenarios and case studies.

The four AARE courses are as follows:

- Principles of Auction Marketing, including customer/client concerns, appraisals, law, and standards of practice
- Marketing Real Estate at Auction, including residential, agricultural, commercial, and industrial property; gaining clients; and government contracting
- Financial Analysis of Real Estate Auction Marketing, including investment calculations, holding periods, and taxes
- Planning an Auction Event, including pre-auction marketing, marketing campaigns, preparation, and closing

Recertification

AAREs are required to earn 24 hours of approved continuing education every three years. Continued licensure and membership in AMI and NAA are required to maintain the designation.

MASTER OF CORPORATE REAL ESTATE (MCR)

ASSOCIATE OF CORPORATE REAL ESTATE (ACR)

Sponsor

International Association of Corporate Real Estate Executives (NACORE)
440 Columbia Drive, Suite 100
West Palm Beach, FL 33409
Phone: (407) 683-8111
Fax: (407) 697-4853
WWW: http://www.nacore.org/

Program Data

Certifying body: Association
Number certified: 280
Approximate certification costs: $150

Program Description

The Master of Corporate Real Estate (MCR) recognizes corporate real estate professionals and is awarded through NACORE's Institute for Corporate Real Estate. The Associate designation (ACR) is awarded to service providers meeting the MCR requirements. Certification is based on experience

and education. Eligibility for certification is determined through a point system. NACORE membership is required. Requirements are as follows:

- Graduate degree; bachelor's degree in real estate and five years of experience; or high school diploma and ten years of experience
- Three years of professional experience (beyond years used for the education requirement)
- Four NACORE courses, selected from several offered, on different aspects of corporate real estate
- Completion of a case study/research paper or attendance at a capstone course
- Accumulation of 50 points based on NACORE courses, additional education, and NACORE participation

Recertification

It is necessary to maintain NACORE membership and to meet the MCR/ACR continuing education requirements.

COUNSELOR OF REAL ESTATE (CRE®)

Sponsor

American Society of Real Estate Counselors (REC)
430 N. Michigan Ave.
Chicago, IL 60611
Phone: (312) 329-8427
Fax: (312) 329-8881
E-mail: cre@interaccess.com
WWW: http://www.cre.org/

Program Data

The American Society of Real Estate Counselors is associated with the National Association of REALTORS® (NAR).

Certifying body: Association
Year certification began: 1953
Number certified: 1000
Additional programs: Accredited Residential Manager (ARM®); Certified International Property Specialist (CIPS); Certified Real Estate Brokerage Manager (CRB); Certified Residential Specialist (CRS®); General Accredited Appraiser (GAA); Graduate, REALTOR® Institute (GRI); Leadership Training Graduate (LTG); REALTOR®

Association Certified Executive (RCE); Residential Accredited Appraiser (RAA); Society of Industrial and Office REALTORS® (SIOR®)

Program Description

The Counselor of Real Estate (CRE) designation is given to all members of the American Society of Real Estate Counselors. To be eligible for membership, a candidate must provide services in real estate counseling on a fee or salary basis. Candidates invited to become a member are expected to demonstrate leadership and commitment to counseling. No examinations or classes are required.

Education/Experience

A candidate needs 10 years of practical experience; post-baccalaureate credentials may be substituted if the candidate has acted as a real estate counselor in three of the previous 10 years. In most cases, NAR (or state or local board) membership is required.

Recertification

None.

REGISTERED ENVIRONMENTAL PROPERTY ASSESSOR (REPA)

ASSOCIATE ENVIRONMENTAL PROPERTY ASSESSOR (AEPA)

Sponsor

National Registry of Environmental
   Professionals℠ (NREP℠)
P.O. Box 2068
Glenview, IL 60025
Phone: (708) 724-6631
Fax: (708) 724-4223

Government and industry professionals may locate professionals in the Official Registry of Environmental Professionals; contact NREP for more information.

Program Data

NREP credentials are endorsed by the Society of Environmental Management. The Resolution Trust Corporation, Department of Energy, U.S. Air Force, and U.S. Army recognize certain NREP certifications in bid proposals.

Certifying body: Independent board (professional registration)
Year registration began: 1988
Number certified: Not disclosed
Organization members: Nonmembership
Additional programs: Associate Environmental Professional (AEP); Certified Environmental Auditor (CEA); Registered Environmental Laboratory Technologist (RECT); Registered Environmental Manager (REM); Registered Environmental Professional (REP); Registered Environmental Scientist (RES)
Approximate certification costs: $50 (AEP; government employee), $75 (RELT), $90 (AEPA; CEA; REP; REPA; RES), $150 (REM)

Program Description

The Registered Environmental Property Assessor (REPA) registration recognizes experienced professionals who inspect and evaluate environmental risk in real property. REPAs are competent to evaluate current environmental conditions and redial costs in both developed and undeveloped residential and commercial real estate.

The Associate Environmental Property Assessor (AEPA) designation is awarded to entry-level professionals who pass the REPA exam but do not meet the required experience or education requirements. AEPAs are awarded the REPA upon meeting the experience and education requirements.

The National Registry of Environmental Professionals (NREP) seeks to provide a consolidated, recognized recognition program for environmental practitioners. Three official advisory boards have responsibility for examination and career development, and are made up of representatives from leading universities, officials from U.S. government agencies, and major corporations. The NREP maintains documentation on all registrants, and will validate qualifications upon written request. NREP has an active ethics board with decertification powers.

Education/Experience

REPA candidates must have three years of experience related to environmental property transfer assessments. REPA candidates must hold a bachelor's degree in an environmentally related discipline or hold an Associate Environmental Professional (AEP) designation.

AEPA candidates have no experience or education requirements.

Examinations

Examination questions are based on an academic review and written by academia and consultants. The NREP's Board of Environmental Educators, Board of Environmental Regulatory Officials, and Board of Industrial Environmental Managers provide guidance on test content. Refresher workshops are available through NREP-endorsed university programs and private training providers. NREP provides a list of recommended reading to applicants. Exams are open-book. The pass rate is 70% for all NREP exams.

The four-hour, multiple-choice examination covers the following:

- Developing an auditable environmental risk inventory
- Document analysis
- Federal environmental laws
- Health effects of environmental contamination
- Pollutant control and transport mechanisms
- Sampling theory and techniques
- Site history analysis

Recertification

Registration must be renewed annually, and REPAs and AEPAs must demonstrate continued professional education. NREP maintains records of CEUs and continuing professional training.

The recertification rate is 90%.

GRADUATE, REALTOR® INSTITUTE (GRI)

Sponsor

National Association of REALTORS® (NAR)
430 N. Michigan Ave.
Chicago, IL 60610
Phone: (312) 329-3282
WWW: http://www.realtor.com

Program Data

Certifying body: Association
Additional programs: Accredited Residential Manager (ARM®); Certified International Property Specialist (CIPS); Certified Real Estate Brokerage Manager (CRB); Certified Residential Specialist (CRS®); Counselor of Real Estate (CRE); General Accredited Appraiser (GAA); Leadership Training

Graduate (LTG); REALTOR® Association Certified Executive (RCE); Residential Accredited Appraiser (RAA); Society of Industrial and Office REALTORS® (SIOR®)

Program Description

The Graduate, REALTOR Institute (GRI) designation recognizes real estate professionals who have completed 90-plus classroom hours of instruction. The GRI courses are developed by National Association of REALTORS (NAR), but customized and delivered by each state association.

Curriculum

Here is a sample curriculum from the New York State Board of REALTORS:

- Delivering Effective Real Estate Services to the Consumer
- Real Estate Legal Issues: Not Knowing Can Be Dangerous
- Financing for Today's Homebuyer
- Introduction to Investment Real Estate
- New and Existing Home Construction
- Real Property Valuation

CERTIFIED INTERNATIONAL PROPERTY SPECIALIST (CIPS)

Sponsor

National Association of REALTORS® (NAR)
International Section
430 N. Michigan Ave.
Chicago, IL 60611
Phone: (800) 874-6500
WWW: http://38.248.210.12:80/international/ intr_edu.htm

Program Data

Certifying body: Association
Year certification began: 1993
Number certified: 325
Organization members: 1500 (International section)
Additional programs: Accredited Residential Manager (ARM®); Certified Real Estate Brokerage Manager (CRB); Certified Residential Specialist (CRS®); Counselor of Real Estate (CRE); General Accredited Appraiser (GAA); Graduate, REALTOR®

Institute (GRI); Leadership Training Graduate (LTG); REALTOR® Association Certified Executive (RCE); Residential Accredited Appraiser (RAA); Society of Industrial and Office REALTORS® (SIOR®)
Approximate certification costs: $1200

Program Description
The Certified International Property Specialist (CIPS) designation recognizes real estate professionals with training and experience in international property transactions. Membership is not required. Certification is based on required course completion, experience, and a point system.

Education/Experience
Candidates must submit descriptive transaction sheets on three transactions involving a foreign citizen or country.

Candidates must also earn elective points.

- Elective points needed: 100
- Point examples:
  - 25 per NAR-associated designation
  - 25 per master's degree
  - 20 per bachelor's degree
  - 10 per language fluency
  - 10 per overseas business trip
  - 5 per NAR course

Curriculum
Candidates must complete the following one- to two-day courses:

- Essentials of International Real Estate
- Europe and International Real Estate
- Asia Pacific and International Real Estate
- The Americas and International Real Estate
- Investment and Financial Analysis in International Real Estate

Recertification
None.

SOCIETY OF INDUSTRIAL AND OFFICE REALTORS® (SIOR®)

Sponsor
Society of Industrial and Office REALTORS® (SIOR®)
700 11th St. NW, Suite 510
Washington, DC 20001
Phone: (202) 737-1150
E-mail: webmaster@sior.com
WWW: http://sior.com

Program Data
Sponsor: Association
Number certified: 1400
Organization members: 2000
Additional programs: Accredited Residential Manager (ARM®); Certified International Property Specialist (CIPS); Certified Real Estate Brokerage Manager (CRB); Certified Residential Specialist (CRS®); Counselor of Real Estate (CRE); General Accredited Appraiser (GAA); Graduate, REALTOR® Institute (GRI); Leadership Training Graduate (LTG); REALTOR® Association Certified Executive (RCE); Residential Accredited Appraiser (RAA)

Program Description
The Society of Industrial and Office REALTORS® (SIOR®) recognizes members who possess the minimum experience, skill, and knowledge to meet all commercial client requirements. Membership is required.

Education/Experience
Candidates must be engaged as an industrial or office broker or salesperson, with seven years of professional experience. Candidates need to meet local chapter minimum dollar volume/transaction requirements.

Curriculum
Candidates must complete the following two- and three-day courses:

- Fundamentals of Industrial Real Estate Brokerage
- Fundamentals of Office Real Estate Brokerage

- Mastering Lease and Contract Negotiation (industrial members only)
- Intermediate Commercial Brokerage Techniques (office members only)
- Expanding Commercial Real Estate Skills and Techniques.

Recertification
None.

LEADERSHIP TRAINING GRADUATE (LTG)

Sponsor

Women's Council of REALTORS® (WCR)
430 N. Michigan Ave.
Chicago, IL 60611
Phone: (312) 329-8483

Program Data

WCR is an affiliated institute of the National Association of REALTORS® (NAR).

Certifying body: Association
Organization members: 14,000
Additional programs: Accredited Residential Manager (ARM®); Certified International Property Specialist (CIPS); Certified Real Estate Brokerage Manager (CRB); Certified Residential Specialist (CRS®); Counselor of Real Estate (CRE); General Accredited Appraiser (GAA); Graduate, REALTOR® Institute (GRI); REALTOR® Association Certified Executive (RCE); Residential Accredited Appraiser (RAA); Society of Industrial and Office REALTORS® (SIOR®)

Program Description
The Leadership Training Graduate (LTG) designation recognizes real estate professionals with training and experience in leadership. Membership or affiliation with the National Association, Local Board, or State Association of REALTORS® (NAR), and of the Women's Council of REALTORS® (WCR), is required. Certification is based on completing courses, completing an oral interview, and meeting the required association work.

Education/Experience
Candidates must earn 100 points through experience and local, state, and association-related activities. Point examples include 20 per NAR-related designation; 10 per year association committee membership; 5 per year manager or principle broker.

Curriculum
The LTG courses are as follows:
- Excellence in Communication
- Personal and Professional Power
- Group Dynamics and Meeting Management
- Leadership Through High Performance

The oral interview follows the completion of all required courses; candidates will discuss the skills learned through the courses and how they have applied these skills.

Recertification
None.

CERTIFIED REAL ESTATE BROKERAGE MANAGER (CRB)

Sponsor

Real Estate Brokerage Managers Council
430 N. Michigan Ave.
Chicago, IL 60611
Phone: (800) 621-8738
Fax: (312) 329-8882
E-mail: mcinfo@CRB.com
WWW: http://www.crb.com/courses.html

Program Data

The Managers Council is an affiliate of the National Association of REALTORS (NAR).

Certifying body: Association
Year certification began: 1968
Number certified: 10,000+
Additional programs: Accredited Residential Manager (ARM®); Certified International Property Specialist (CIPS); Certified Residential Specialist (CRS®); Counselor of Real Estate (CRE); General Accredited Appraiser (GAA); Graduate, REALTOR® Institute (GRI); Leadership Training Graduate (LTG); REALTOR® Association Certified Executive (RCE); Residential Accredited Appraiser (RAA); Society of Industrial and Office REALTORS® (SIOR®)

Program Description
The Certified Real Estate Brokerage Manager (CRB) designation recognizes real estate professionals who complete the Council's highly specialized program. Membership in the National Association of REALTORS is required. Certification is based on completing courses.

Education/Experience

Candidates have five years to complete the program; prior to certification they must have two consecutive years of applicable experience.

Curriculum

Candidates must complete 18 credits through Managers Council coursework and professional experience.

Courses are available in changing markets, marketing, technology, finance, and productivity/human resources. The four-day Decision Making capstone course uses a computer-based simulation to implement skills learned in previous courses.

Recertification

None.

DISTINGUISHED REAL ESTATE INSTRUCTOR (DREI)

Sponsor

Real Estate Educators Association (REEA)
11 S. La Salle St., Suite 1400
Chicago, IL 60603
Phone: (312) 201-0101
WWW: http://www.holonet.net/realed

Program Data

Certifying body: Professional association (REEA membership required)
Year certification began: 1984
Number certified: Not disclosed
Organization members: Not disclosed
Approximate certification costs: $175 plus membership

Program Description

The Distinguished (formerly Designated) Real Estate Instructor (DREI) designation recognizes members of REEA who have demonstrated both industry knowledge and instructional skill. Certification is based on a teaching skills evaluation and written examination. Candidates must have at least three years of industry-related experience and 200 hours as a real estate instructor. Eligibility for certification is determined using a point system.

Examinations

The 120-question comprehensive examination covers broker-level real estate knowledge and instructional methodology.

The teaching skills evaluation is based on a videotape of an instructional session. Candidates are evaluated on real estate knowledge, verbal presentation, instructional environment, teaching aids used, and instructional quality.

Both the examination and the teaching skills evaluation are based on the REEA's Generally Accepted Principles of Education. The REEA has defined several categories of education, and each candidate must demonstrate mastery of each category. These categories are Knowledge, Andragogy, Speech, Teaching Aids, and Learning Environment.

Recertification

DREIs must renew certification every three years based on a point system. Eighty-five points are required, with required minimums in experience and real estate education.

HOSPITALITY AND TRAVEL

CERTIFIED CATERING EXECUTIVE (CCE)

Sponsor
National Association of Catering Executives
  (NACE)
60 Revere Drive, Suite 500
Northbrook, IL 60062
Phone: (708) 480-9080

Program Data
The CCE examination was developed in conjunction with the University of Nevada, Las Vegas, and Florida International University.

Certifying body: Association
Number certified: 100+
Organization members: 2600+
Approximate certification costs: $200 (members), $275 (nonmembers)

Program Description
The Certified Catering Executive (CCE) designation recognizes experienced executives within the catering industry. Certification is based on passing an examination. NACE membership is not required.

Education/Experience
Eligibility for the certification examination is determined using a point system. Thirty points are required.

- Point examples:
  - 10 per hotel or restaurant management degree
  - 1 per year of catering-manager employment
  - 1 per hour of professional education
  - 1 per year of NACE membership

Examinations
NACE recommends several texts for study. The examination content and pass/fail rate are confidential.

Recertification
None.

CERTIFIED CLUB MANAGER (CCM)
MASTER CLUB MANAGER (MCM)

Sponsor
Club Managers Association of America (CMAA)
1733 King St.
Alexandria, VA 22314
Phone: (703) 739-9500
Fax: (703) 739-1234
E-mail: cmaa@cmaa.org
WWW: http://www.cmaa.org/

Program Data
Certifying body: Association
Number certified: 1000+
Organization members: 5000+

Program Description
The Certified Club Manager (CCM) designation recognizes experienced professionals in private club management. In addition to its certification programs, the CMAA offers a series of courses through its Business Management Institute (BMI). These courses are used for certification, but are independent of the certification process. Active membership in the CMAA is required for certification.

Education/Experience
Candidates must meet one of the following minimum education requirements:

- Option 1—Hospitality degree and
  - Attendance at one CMAA Annual Conference
  - Three years of active CMAA status
  - Completion of two CMAA-endorsed workshops
  - Completion of BMI III
- Option 2—College degree and
  - Attendance at one CMAA Annual Conference
  - Four years of active CMAA status
  - Completion of four CMAA-endorsed workshops
  - Completion of BMI II and BMI III

- Option 3—No degree and
  - Attendance at one CMAA Annual Conference
  - Five years of active CMAA status
  - Completion of six CMAA-endorsed workshops
  - Completion of BMI I, BMI II, and BMI III

If a candidate meets the minimum education requirements, eligibility is determined using a point system. Minimum points equal 300. Point examples: 2 per year of CMAA membership; 1 per contact hour; 1 per three-hour college credit.

CCMs may enter into the Honor Society by earning 400 additional credits beyond certification (minimum of 150 from CMAA-endorsed education programs), maintaining a total of seven years of active membership in CMAA, and completing BMI IV.

Master Club Manager (MCM) is a new program. MCM candidates must have the following: the CCM designation and Honor Society membership; 200 credits beyond Honor Society (minimum of 100 from CMAA-endorsed education programs); a total of 11 years of active membership in CMAA; completion of BMI V; and completion of Professional Data Form and Monograph.

Examinations
The CCM examination was revised in 1993, developed in conjunction with the Educational Institute of the American Hotel and Motel Association and others. Reference textbooks are available. However, the exam is based on competency areas, not the textbooks. The exam comprises 400 questions and an essay/case study, and covers the following competency areas: private clubs—operation, management, and human resources; recreational activity management; food and beverage operations; accounting and finance in private clubs; communications and marketing; building and facilities management; and external and governmental influences (regulatory agencies, IRS, club law, labor law, and liquor liability).

Recertification
Recertification requires 200 credits beyond credit total at certification or entrance into the Honor Society.

CERTIFIED CORPORATE TRAVEL EXECUTIVE (CCTE)

Sponsor
National Business Travel Association (NBTA)
1650 King St., Suite 401
Alexandria, VA 22314
Phone: (703) 684-0836
Fax: (703) 684-0263
E-mail: info@nbta.org
WWW: http://www.nbta.org/nbta/

Program Data
The CCTE program is conducted under the auspices of the Cornell University School of Hotel Administration.

Certifying body: Association
Organization members: 1600
Approximate certification costs: $3100 (members), $5000 (nonmembers)

Program Description
The Certified Corporate Travel Executive (CCTE) program recognizes business-travel-management professionals completing the NBTA training courses. Certification is based on completing coursework. The program takes two years to complete.

Education/Experience
To begin the program, candidates must have two years of business travel industry experience.

Curriculum
The CCTE program consists of two one-week residence courses, five elective courses, a work project, and a final examination. The two courses cover automation and information systems; business travel law; finance systems and management; negotiation and purchasing; and travel industry operations. Electives include the areas of managing the information; travel patterns and needs; travel industry ethics; leadership and management; meeting facilitation; using internal corporate resources; and increasing compliance. The work project is an in-depth research project applying coursework learning to real-world work experience. The final examination covers information learned through CCTE coursework.

Recertification
CCTEs must annually complete professional education requirements to maintain certification.

AMERICAN CULINARY FEDERATION CERTIFICATION PROGRAM

Sponsor

American Culinary Federation Education Institute
(ACFEI)
P.O. Box 3466
10 San Bartola Road
St. Augustine, FL 32085
Phone: (904) 824-4468

Program Data

Certifying body: Association
Number certified: 6000 (all certifications)
Organization members: The American Culinary
Federation, 24,000+

Program Description

The American Culinary Federation certifies cooks
and chefs based on education and experience.
Membership is required. Certification is based on a
point system.

The designations are as follows:

Certified Cook (CC)/Certified Pastry Cook
(CPC)—Candidates must have either completed
an ACFEI apprenticeship program; completed a
culinary trade school program and acquired
three years of industry experience; or passed the
ACFEI written examination. Candidates must
have completed acceptable courses in nutrition,
sanitation, and supervisory development.

Certified Working Chef (CWC)/Certified Working
Pastry Chef (CWPC)—Candidates must have
completed acceptable courses in nutrition, sanitation, and supervisory development, and have
five years of experience.

Certified Executive Chef (CEC)/Certified Executive Pastry Chef (CEPC)—Recognizes highly
skilled and experienced culinarians. Candidates
must have completed acceptable courses in
nutrition, sanitation, and supervisory development, and have nine years of acceptable experience.

Certified Master Chef (CMC)/Certified Master
Pastry Chef (CMPC)—The highest certification
given by the ACF, certification is by review.

Certified Culinary Educator (CCE)—Recognizes
experienced culinarians with additional training
and experience as professional instructors.
Candidates must already hold either a Certified
Working Chef (CWC) or a Certified Working
Pastry Chef (CWPC) designation.

Recertification

Certification must be renewed every five years.
Renewal is based on accumulating approved
continuing-education hours.

CERTIFIED DESTINATION MANAGEMENT EXECUTIVE (CDME)

Sponsor

International Association of Convention and
Visitor Bureaus (IACVB)
2000 L St. NW, Suite 702
Washington, DC 20036
Phone: (202) 296-7888
Fax: (202) 296-7889
E-mail: gbarrett@cais.com
WWW: http://www.iacvb.org/iacvb.html

Program Data

Program was developed in conjunction with the
University of Calgary World Tourism Education and
Research Centre and Purdue University.

Certifying body: Association
Approximate certification costs: $5500

Program Description

The Certified Destination Management Executive
(CDME) recognizes senior convention and visitors-
bureau executives completing the Executive Program in Destination Management. IACVB membership is not required.

Education/Experience

Most candidates are convention/visitors-bureau
CEOs. Individuals in a senior management position
and nominated by their CEO, or individuals completing 32 hours of IACVB-approved professional
education, may also enroll.

Curriculum

The CDME program consists of three core
courses. These three-day courses include take-
home assignments which are evaluated before
course credit is awarded. Candidates must also
complete two approved electives. A comprehensive
exam covering the core course material is required
for certification.

Recertification

None.

CERTIFIED ENGINEERING OPERATIONS EXECUTIVE (CEOE®)

Sponsor

Educational Institute of the American Hotel and
Motel Association (EI/AH&MA)
1407 S. Harrison Road, Suite 300
East Lansing, MI 48823
Phone: (800) 752-5527
Fax: (517) 353-5527
E-mail: info@ei-ahma.org
WWW: http://www.ei-ahma.org

Program Data

Year certification began: 1969
Number certified: 15,000+
Organization members: 10,000
Additional certifications: Certified Food and
Beverage Executive (CFBE®); Certified
Hospitality Educator (CHE®); Certified
Hospitality Housekeeping Executive (CHHE®);
Certified Hospitality Sales Professional
(CHSP®); Certified Hospitality Supervisor
(CHS®); Certified Hospitality Technology
Professional (CHTP®); Certified Hotel Admin-
istrator (CHA®); Certified Human Resources
Executive (CHRE®); Certified Rooms Division
Executive (CRDE®); Hospitality Skills
Certification; Master Hotel Supplier (MHS®)
Approximate certification costs: $275 (AH&MA-
member properties), $325 (nonmember
properties)

Program Description

The Certified Engineering Operations Executive
(CEOE®) recognizes experienced property operations and engineering managers in the hospitality
industry. Certification is based on passing an examination. AH&MA membership is not required.

Education/Experience

To sit for the CEOE examination, candidates must
be currently employed as a director or chief of
engineering/property operations in a lodging hospitality company and meet the following requirements.

- Prerequisites (any one of the below)
  - Five years of hospitality property operations
    and maintenance experience
  - A technical license related to building
    operations
  - A post-secondary building operations
    certificate or diploma related to building
    relations

- Enrollment options (any one of the below)
  - An associate's degree or higher
    engineering or hospitality degree, or
    completion of the Educational Institute's
    five-course curriculum in engineering
    operations, and two years of experience in
    a hospitality engineering/property
    operations position
  - Three years of experience as a director or
    chief of hospitality engineering/property
    operations
  - Currently an instructor teaching hospitality
    management, with two years of experience
    in this capacity, and two years of experi-
    ence in hospitality engineering/property
    operations management

Examinations

The CEOE examination covers a wide range of
areas needed by engineering/property operations
management, including facilities management,
energy and water management, technical operations, and supervision.

Recertification

CEOEs must renew their certification every five
years. Certification is based on a point system;
50 points are needed to recertify. Points are earned
through professional experience, continuing
education, professional involvement, and educational service.

CERTIFIED FESTIVAL EXECUTIVE (CFE)

Sponsor

International Festival and Events Association
(IFEA)
P.O. Box 2950
Port Angeles, WA 98362
Phone: (360) 457-4695
Fax: (360) 452-4695
E-mail: ifea@festivals.com
WWW: http://ifea.com/

Program Data

The program was developed in cooperation with
the Restaurant, Hotel, and Tourism Management
Institute at Purdue University.

Certifying body: Association
Year certification began: 1983

Program Description

The Certified Festival Executive (CFE) program recognizes individuals experienced in managing and administering special events and festivals. Certification is based on completing the CFE curriculum. IFEA membership is required.

Education/Experience

Candidates must have four years of full-time experience in festival management. Prior to certification, candidates must have attended four IFEA conventions within the previous six years, attend a regional or other approved seminar, and speak at a seminar or IFEA convention.

Curriculum

The one-day CFE sessions at Purdue include marketing, communications, program development, and financial management. To complete the certification program, candidates must write a publication-ready festival management paper.

Recertification

None.

CERTIFIED FOOD AND BEVERAGE EXECUTIVE (CFBE®)

Sponsor

Educational Institute of the American Hotel and
  Motel Association (EI/AH&MA)
1407 S. Harrison Road, Suite 300
East Lansing, MI 48823
Phone: (800) 752-5527
Fax: (517) 353-5527
E-mail: info@ei-ahma.org
WWW: http://www.ei-ahma.org

Program Data

Year certification began: 1969
Number certified: 15,000+
Organization members: 10,000
Additional certifications: Certified Engineering Operations Executive (CEOE®); Certified Hospitality Educator (CHE®); Certified Hospitality Housekeeping Executive (CHHE®); Certified Hospitality Sales Professional (CHSP®); Certified Hospitality Supervisor (CHS®); Certified Hospitality Technology Professional (CHTP®); Certified Hotel Administrator (CHA®); Certified Human Resources Executive (CHRE®); Certified Rooms Division Executive (CRDE®); Hospitality Skills Certification; Master Hotel Supplier (MHS®)
Approximate certification costs: $275 (AH&MA-member properties), $325 (nonmember properties)

Program Description

The Certified Food and Beverage Executive (CFBE®) designation recognizes experienced food and beverage managers in the hospitality industry. Certification is based on passing an examination. AH&MA membership is not required.

Education/Experience

To sit for the CFBE examination, candidates must be currently employed as an executive-level manager administering hotel food and beverage, a facility director, or an executive chef at hospitality property or hospitality corporation. Candidates must meet one of the following requirements:

- An associate's or higher hospitality degree, or completion of the Educational Institute's five-course curriculum in food and beverage management, and two years of experience in a hospitality food and beverage management position

- Three years of experience in a hospitality food and beverage management position

- Currently an instructor teaching hospitality management, with two years of experience in this capacity, and two years of experience in food and beverage management

Examinations

The examination covers every area of hospitality food and beverage management, including sanitation, food service and controls, bar management, production, purchasing, and supervision. Applicable laws and regulations are also covered.

Recertification

CFBEs must renew their certification every five years. Certification is based on a point system; 50 points are needed to recertify. Points are earned through professional experience, continuing education, professional involvement, and educational service.

FOODSERVICE MANAGEMENT PROFESSIONAL (FMP)

Sponsor

Educational Foundation of the National
  Restaurant Association
250 South Wacker Drive, Suite 1400
Chicago, IL 60606
Phone: (800) 765-2122
Fax: (312) 715-1010
WWW: http://www.restaurant.org/educate/
  educate.htm

Program Data

Certifying body: Association-sponsored
  independent board
Approximate certification costs: $250
  (examination only; courses additional)

Program Description

The Foodservice Management Professional (FMP)
designation recognizes experienced foodservice
management professionals who successfully pass
the comprehensive FMP examination. There are no
association membership requirements.

Education/Experience

Candidates must be currently employed as a foodservice manager or corporate executive, a foodservice corporate trainer, or hospitality educator.
Candidates must also meet one of the following:

- Ten years of foodservice management
  experience, with a minimum of five years
  in a unit manager or corporate executive
  position, and either one FMP Review Session
  or one Management Development course.

- Five years of foodservice management
  experience, with a minimum of three years
  in a unit manager or corporate executive
  position, and either three Management
  Development courses or a bachelor's or
  associate's degree and one Management
  Development course

- Three years of foodservice management
  experience, with a minimum of one year in a
  unit manager or corporate executive position,
  and either:
  - A bachelor's or associate's degree with a
    foodservice or hospitality-related major
  - A bachelor's or associate's degree with a
    business-related major and one Founda-
    tion foodservice operations course

- Completion of the Management
  Development Diploma Program
- Completion of the Management Institute
- Three years as full-time foodservice
  corporate trainer (three or more units),
  and two years of foodservice management
  experience
- Three years as hospitality or foodservice
  school instructor, and two years of
  foodservice management experience

Examinations

The three-hour examination covers five major
areas of foodservice management: Accounting
and Finance; Administration; Human Resources;
Marketing; and Operations.

Recertification

FMPs must recertify every three years. Recertification is based on a point system, with points
awarded for continuing professional education and
development, professional experience, and involvement with the industry.

CERTIFIED FOOD EXECUTIVE (CFE)
CERTIFIED FOOD MANAGER (CFM)

Sponsor

International Food Service Executives Association
  (IFSEA)
1100 S. State Road 7, Suite 103
Margate, FL 33068
Phone: (954) 977-0767
Fax: (954) 977-0874
E-mail: hq@ifsea.org
WWW: http://paradise.net/~lance/ifsea.html

Program Data

Certifying body: Association
Number certified: 600 (both programs)
Organization members: 3000
Approximate certification costs: CFE—$80
  (members), $150 (nonmembers); CFM—$60
  (members), $130 (nonmembers)

Program Description

The CFE/CFM program recognizes food service
professionals who demonstrate a commitment to
the profession through experience and education.
Membership in IFSEA is not required. There is no
examination; certification is based solely on
experience/education point system. Points used for
CFM may later be used for CFE.

Recertification

Recertification is required every five years, based on points.

CERTIFIED HOSPITALITY EDUCATOR (CHE®)

Sponsor

Educational Institute of the American Hotel and
 Motel Association (EI/AH&MA)
1407 S. Harrison Road, Suite 300
East Lansing, MI 48823
Phone: (800) 752-5527
Fax: (517) 353-5527
E-mail: info@ei-ahma.org
WWW: http://www.ei-ahma.org

Program Data

Year certification began: 1969
Number certified: 15,000+
Organization members: 10,000
Additional certifications: Certified Engineering
 Operations Executive (CEOE®); Certified Food
 and Beverage Executive (CFBE®); Certified
 Hospitality Housekeeping Executive (CHHE®);
 Certified Hospitality Sales Professional
 (CHSP®); Certified Hospitality Supervisor
 (CHS®); Certified Hospitality Technology
 Professional (CHTP®); Certified Hotel Admin-
 istrator (CHA®); Certified Human Resources
 Executive (CHRE®); Certified Rooms Division
 Executive (CRDE®); Hospitality Skills
 Certification; Master Hotel Supplier (MHS®)
Approximate certification costs: $600

Program Description

The Certified Hospitality Educator (CHE®)
designation recognizes hospitality instructors in
both academic and industrial settings. Certification
is a multi-step process.

Education/Experience

The candidates must first document their industry
and instructional experience. English fluency is
required for this program. The minimum educational and professional experience is described
below:

- Academic instructors—A bachelor's degree;
 current employment and two years of experience as a hospitality educator; and two years
 of experience, with one year supervisory/
 managerial, in the hospitality industry

- Industry instructors—Current employment,
 either full or part time, as a hospitality
 instructor, and five years of experience,
 with two years supervisory/managerial, in
 the hospitality industry

The next step is to prepare and complete work for
the mandatory CHE Workshop. The candidate then
will attend the four-day workshop, where instructional skills and techniques will be taught and
discussed. On the fourth day, candidates will take
the two-hour CHE examination, which covers the
materials taught in the workshop. The last step is
the post-workshop presentation. The candidate will
give and videotape an instructional session, which
will then be evaluated by the Educational Institute.

Examinations

The CHE examination covers information given
during the four-day CHE Workshop, including
instructional theory, presentations, and evaluation
of instruction.

Recertification

CHEs must renew their certification every five years
through instructional experience, professional
involvement, and continuing education.

CERTIFIED HOSPITALITY HOUSEKEEPING EXECUTIVE (CHHE®)

Sponsor

Educational Institute of the American Hotel and
 Motel Association (EI/AH&MA)
1407 S. Harrison Road, Suite 300
East Lansing, MI 48823
Phone: (800) 752-5527
Fax: (517) 353-5527
E-mail: info@ei-ahma.org
WWW: http://www.ei-ahma.org

Program Data

Year certification began: 1969
Number certified: 15,000+
Organization members: 10,000
Additional certifications: Certified Engineering
 Operations Executive (CEOE®); Certified Food
 and Beverage Executive (CFBE®); Certified
 Hospitality Educator (CHE®); Certified
 Hospitality Sales Professional (CHSP®);
 Certified Hospitality Supervisor (CHS®);
 Certified Hospitality Technology Professional

(CHTP®); Certified Hotel Administrator (CHA®); Certified Human Resources Executive (CHRE®); Certified Rooms Division Executive (CRDE®); Hospitality Skills Certification; Master Hotel Supplier (MHS®)

Approximate certification costs: $260 (AH&MA-member properties), $310 (nonmember properties)

Program Description

The Certified Hospitality Housekeeping Executive (CHHE®) designation recognizes experienced housekeeping managers in the hospitality industry. Certification is based on passing an examination. AH&MA membership is not required.

Education/Experience

To sit for the CHRE examination, candidates must be currently employed as a housekeeping manager, executive housekeeper, or director of housekeeping operations at a hospitality property or hospitality corporation. Candidates must also meet one of the following requirements:

- An associate's or higher hospitality degree, or completion of the Educational Institute's five-course curriculum in housekeeping management, and two years of experience in a hospitality housekeeping management position

- Three years of experience in a hospitality housekeeping management position

- Currently an instructor teaching hospitality management, with two years of experience in this capacity, and two years of experience in hospitality housekeeping management

Examinations

The CHHE examination covers the technical and managerial skills needed for effective hospitality housekeeping management, including security, human resources/personnel, purchasing, law, and cleaning/housekeeping technology.

Recertification

CHHEs must renew their certification every five years. Certification is based on a point system; 50 points are needed to recertify. Points are earned through professional experience, continuing education, professional involvement, and educational service.

CERTIFIED HOSPITALITY SALES PROFESSIONAL (CHSP®)

Sponsor

Educational Institute of the American Hotel and Motel Association (EI/AH&MA)
1407 S. Harrison Road, Suite 300
East Lansing, MI 48823
Phone: (800) 752-5527
Fax: (517) 353-5527
E-mail: info@ei-ahma.org
WWW: http://www.ei-ahma.org

Program Data

Year certification began: 1969
Number certified: 15,000+
Organization members: 10,000
Additional certifications: Certified Engineering Operations Executive (CEOE®); Certified Food and Beverage Executive (CFBE®); Certified Hospitality Educator (CHE®); Certified Hospitality Housekeeping Executive (CHHE®); Certified Hospitality Supervisor (CHS®); Certified Hospitality Technology Professional (CHTP®); Certified Hotel Administrator (CHA®); Certified Human Resources Executive (CHRE®); Certified Rooms Division Executive (CRDE®); Hospitality Skills Certification; Master Hotel Supplier (MHS®)
Approximate certification costs: $275 (AH&MA-member properties), $325 (nonmember properties)

Program Description

The Certified Hospitality Sales Professional (CHSP®) designation recognizes experienced hotel and motel salespeople. Certification is based on passing an examination. AH&MA membership is not required.

Education/Experience

To sit for the CHSP examination, candidates must be currently employed in hospitality sales (a position with at least 50% sales responsibility) and meet one of the following requirements:

- A two-year (at least) hospitality or sales/marketing degree

- Completion of the EI's five-course Marketing and Sales Management program

- Two years of qualifying experience

Examinations

The CHSP examination covers the tourism and hospitality industry, hospitality services marketing, hospitality sales, and convention services.

Recertification

CHSPs must renew their certification every five years. Certification is based on a point system; 50 points are needed to recertify. Points are earned through professional experience, continuing education, professional involvement, and educational service.

HOSPITALITY SKILLS CERTIFICATION

Sponsor

Educational Institute of the American Hotel and
   Motel Association (EI/AH&MA)
1407 S. Harrison Road, Suite 300
East Lansing, MI 48823
Phone: (800) 752-5527
Fax: (517) 353-5527
E-mail: info@ei-ahma.org
WWW: http://www.ei-ahma.org

Program Data

The program for Front Desk Agents is sponsored by MasterCard International.

Year certification began: 1969
Number certified: 15,000+
Organization members: 10,000
Additional certifications: Certified Engineering Operations Executive (CEOE®); Certified Food and Beverage Executive (CFBE®); Certified Hospitality Educator (CHE®); Certified Hospitality Housekeeping Executive (CHHE®); Certified Hospitality Sales Professional (CHSP®); Certified Hospitality Supervisor (CHS®); Certified Hospitality Technology Professional (CHTP®); Certified Hotel Administrator (CHA®); Certified Human Resources Executive (CHRE®); Certified Rooms Division Executive (CRDE®); Master Hotel Supplier (MHS®)

Program Description

The Hospitality Skills Certification program recognizes front desk employees, room attendants, and food and beverage servers. Candidates completing the program are registered in their specific skill category. The program includes a skill assessment and a training program customized for the candidate's property. There are no prerequisites.

Curriculum

Each program includes a handbook with job knowledge sections, task lists, task breakdowns, and job tips. Upon completion, candidates are awarded one of the following designations:

- Registered Front Desk Agent
- Registered Room Attendant
- Registered Restaurant Server

Recertification

None.

CERTIFIED HOSPITALITY SUPERVISOR (CHS®)

Sponsor

Educational Institute of the American Hotel and
   Motel Association (EI/AH&MA)
1407 S. Harrison Road, Suite 300
East Lansing, MI 48823
Phone: (800) 752-5527
Fax: (517) 353-5527
E-mail: info@ei-ahma.org
WWW: http://www.ei-ahma.org

Program Data

Year certification began: 1969
Number certified: 15,000+
Organization members: 10,000
Additional certifications: Certified Engineering Operations Executive (CEOE®); Certified Food and Beverage Executive (CFBE®); Certified Hospitality Educator (CHE®); Certified Hospitality Housekeeping Executive (CHHE®); Certified Hospitality Sales Professional (CHSP®); Certified Hospitality Technology Professional (CHTP®); Certified Hotel Administrator (CHA®); Certified Human Resources Executive (CHRE®); Certified Rooms Division Executive (CRDE®); Hospitality Skills Certification; Master Hotel Supplier (MHS®)
Approximate certification costs: Varies depending on workshops/education

Program Description

The Certified Hospitality Supervisor (CHS®) designation is designed for those either starting their hospitality career or those who have gained experience as a first-line hospitality supervisor. Certification is based on passing an examination. AH&MA membership is not required.

Education/Experience

To qualify to sit for the CHS examination, candidates have two options:

- CHS Plan A—designed for entry-level hospitality supervisors starting their careers. A candidate must be employed for three months as a qualifying supervisor or become employed and work in a position within one year of taking the CHS examination.

  A candidate must also complete one of the following:

  - El's Supervisory Skills Builder, a nine-workbook series
  - El's Hospitality Supervision course
  - Hospitality Human Resources Management course

- CHS Plan B—designed for those already in a qualifying supervisory position with nine months of hospitality supervisory experience

Qualifying supervisory positions require that a candidate supervise two or more subordinates and contribute to hiring and firing decisions. Supervision must make up 20% or more of the position.

Examinations

The CHS examination covers common hospitality-supervisory decisions, problems, and goals.

Recertification

CHSs must renew their certification every five years. Certification is based on a point system; 50 points are needed to recertify. Points are earned through professional experience, continuing education, professional involvement, and educational service.

CERTIFIED HOSPITALITY TECHNOLOGY PROFESSIONAL (CHTP®)

Sponsor

Educational Institute of the American Hotel and Motel Association (EI/AH&MA)
1407 S. Harrison Road, Suite 300
East Lansing, MI 48823
Phone: (800) 752-5527
Fax: (517) 353-5527
E-mail: info@ei-ahma.org
WWW: http://www.ei-ahma.org

Program Data

The CHTP program was developed in conjunction with the International Association of Hospitality Accountants (IAHA).

Year certification began: 1994
Organization members: 10,000
Additional certifications: Certified Engineering Operations Executive (CEOE®); Certified Food and Beverage Executive (CFBE®); Certified Hospitality Educator (CHE®); Certified Hospitality Housekeeping Executive (CHHE®); Certified Hospitality Sales Professional (CHSP®); Certified Hospitality Supervisor (CHS®); Certified Hotel Administrator (CHA®); Certified Human Resources Executive (CHRE®); Certified Rooms Division Executive (CRDE®); Hospitality Skills Certification; Master Hotel Supplier (MHS®)

Program Description

The Certified Hospitality Technology Professional (CHTP®) designation recognizes professionals managing technical systems unique to the hospitality industry. Certification is based on passing an examination. Neither IAHA nor AH&MA membership is required.

Education/Experience

Candidates qualify to take the CHTP examination based on a point system. Points are awarded for the following:

- Formal and professional education (40 points minimum: 40 per degree; 1 per college credit; 1 per hour professional education)
- Work experience (40 minimum: positional responsibilities worth 10–40 points per year)
- Association membership (no minimum: 10 per year)

Examinations

The exam covers all areas of hospitality technology, including telecommunications, clubs, hotel systems, and safety.

Recertification

CHTPs must renew their certification every five years through professional experience, continuing education, professional involvement, and educational service.

CERTIFIED HOTEL ADMINISTRATOR (CHA®)

Sponsor

Educational Institute of the American Hotel and
   Motel Association (EI/AH&MA)
1407 S. Harrison Road, Suite 300
East Lansing, MI 48823
Phone: (800) 752-5527
Fax: (517) 353-5527
E-mail: info@ei-ahma.org
WWW: http://www.ei-ahma.org

Program Data

Year certification began: 1969
Number certified: 15,000+
Organization members: 10,000
Additional certifications: Certified Engineering
   Operations Executive (CEOE®); Certified Food
   and Beverage Executive (CFBE®); Certified
   Hospitality Educator (CHE®); Certified
   Hospitality Housekeeping Executive (CHHE®);
   Certified Hospitality Sales Professional
   (CHSP®); Certified Hospitality Supervisor
   (CHS®); Certified Hospitality Technology
   Professional (CHTP®); Certified Human
   Resources Executive (CHRE®); Certified
   Rooms Division Executive (CRDE®); Hospitality
   Skills Certification; Master Hotel Supplier
   (MHS®)
Approximate certification costs: $375 (AH&MA-
   member properties), $425 (nonmember
   properties)

Program Description

The Certified Hotel Administrator (CHA®) designation recognizes experienced hospitality professionals who are general managers, owner/
operators, or corporate hospitality executives.
Certification is based on passing an examination.
AH&MA membership is not required.

Education/Experience

In order to sit for the CHA examination, a candidate
must meet one of the following requirements:

- Associate's or higher hospitality degree (or
  EI's Hospitality Management Diploma) and
  current employment and two years of experience in a qualifying hospitality position

- Current employment and three years of
  experience in a qualifying hospitality position

Examinations

The CHA examination covers managing both
human resources and property, and includes
employment and property law. A comprehensive

study guide is provided upon registration. The
examination may be taken in conjunction with a
group certification review class.

Recertification

CHAs must renew certification every five years.
Recertification is through approved continuing
education and professional activities (60 points).
CHA holders may apply for emeritus status (lifetime) if they retire at age 65 or older, or have
25 years in the industry. One five-year cycle must
be completed.

CERTIFIED HOTEL SALES EXECUTIVE (CHSE)

Sponsor

Hospitality Sales and Marketing Association
   International (HSMAI)
21 N. Rosborough Ave.
Ventnor, NJ 08406
Phone: (609) 823-7211
Fax: (609) 822-9234
E-mail: bghsmai@aol.com
WWW: http://www.hsmai.org

Program Data

Certifying body: Association
Organization members: 3700
Approximate certification costs: 75$ (members),
   $150 (nonmembers)

Program Description

The Certified Hotel Sales Executive (CHSE)
designation recognizes experienced sales and
marketing professionals in the lodging industry.
Membership in HSMAI is not required. Certification
is based on an examination.

Education/Experience

Eligibility for the certification examination is
determined using a point system. Qualification
minimum equals 250 points.

- Point examples:
  - 60 per bachelor's degree in hotel
    administration
  - 15 per year of lodging sales experience
  - 10 per Certified Meeting Planner (CMP)
    designation
  - 5 per HSMAI correspondence course

Examinations

The examination component is made up of a written test and a research paper. The three-hour exam has 50 multiple-choice and five essay questions covering the following areas: customer organizations; direct selling and advertising procedures; internal sales and servicing; legal concerns; market trends; marketing plan; sales office management; sales philosophy; sales-marketing responsibilities; sales-operations relationships; and future trends.

The 1500-word research paper is based on an approved proposal and graded on relevance, style, research, and proper construction.

Recertification

None.

MASTER HOTEL SUPPLIER (MHS®)

Sponsor

Educational Institute of the American Hotel and
  Motel Association (EI/AH&MA)
1407 S. Harrison Road, Suite 300
East Lansing, MI 48823
Phone: (800) 752-5527
Fax: (517) 353-5527
E-mail: info@ei-ahma.org
WWW: http://www.ei-ahma.org

Program Data

Year certification began: 1969
Number certified: 15,000+
Organization members: 10,000
Additional certifications: Certified Engineering Operations Executive (CEOE®); Certified Food and Beverage Executive (CFBE®); Certified Hospitality Educator (CHE®); Certified Hospitality Housekeeping Executive (CHHE®); Certified Hospitality Sales Professional (CHSP®); Certified Hospitality Supervisor (CHS®); Certified Hospitality Technology Professional (CHTP®); Certified Hotel Administrator (CHA®); Certified Human Resources Executive (CHRE®); Certified Rooms Division Executive (CRDE®); Hospitality Skills Certification
Approximate certification costs: $350 (members), $425 (nonmembers)

Program Description

The Master Hotel Supplier (MHS®) designation recognizes experienced and knowledgeable supplier and sales professionals servicing the hospitality industry. This program acknowledges the role suppliers fill in anticipating, advising, and assisting the hospitality industry in meeting a wide range of needs.

Education/Experience

A candidate must be employed and have three years of experience as a supplier to the hospitality industry. Certification is based on passing an examination. AH&MA membership is not required.

Examinations

The examination covers the areas of a hospitality operation, such as the front office and food and beverage, and how each area is serviced.

Recertification

None.

CERTIFIED LEISURE PROFESSIONAL (CLP)
CERTIFIED LEISURE ASSOCIATE (CLA)

Sponsor

National Recreation and Park Association
  (NRPA)
2775 South Quincy St., Suite 300
Arlington, VA 22206
Phone: (703) 820-4940
E-mail: info@nrpa.org
WWW: http://www.als.uiuc.edu/nrpa/

Program Data

Certifying body: Association-sponsored
  independent board
Year certification began: 1973
Number certified: 7700
Organization members: 23,000+
Approximate certification costs: $100

Program Description

The Certified Leisure Professional (CLP) and Certified Leisure Associate (CLA) programs recognize professionals in the park, recreation, and leisure services industry. Membership in the NRPA is not required for certification. In most states, applications are made to the state organization. If candidates meet the minimum requirements for CLP, they may sit for the national examination. The CLA (formerly Certified Leisure Technician—CLT) has no examination. NRPA maintains an active ethics program.

Education/Experience

To sit for the CLP examination, a candidate must meet one of the following options.

- Bachelor's or higher degree from an NRPA/AALR accredited program

- Bachelor's degree with a major in recreation, park resources, or leisure services; current employment and two years of employment after graduation, in recreation, park resources, or leisure services

- Bachelor's degree, current employment, and five years of employment after graduation, in recreation, park resources, or leisure services

Professionals who fail to meet the employment requirement may be considered for the status of Provisional Professional.

The CLA, designed for professionals with less than a bachelor's degree, may be granted under any one of the three options:

- Associate's degree with a major in recreation, park resources, or leisure services, from a regionally accredited school

- Associate's degree in any other area; current employment and two years of employment after graduation in recreation, park resources, or leisure services

- High school diploma or equivalent; current employment and four years of employment after graduation in recreation, park resources, or leisure services

Examinations

The CLP certification examination was developed by a committee of professionals and educators in the field, with assistance from Applied Measurement Professionals, a professional testing company. The examination is based on an extensive job survey/analysis. The pass rate is 80%.

The exam assesses knowledge of job-related tasks considered standard for entry-level leisure professionals. The NRPA provides sample questions and a list of recommended study reading. The multiple-choice exam covers four major areas of the leisure profession: Leisure Services Management; Leisure/Recreation Program Delivery; Natural Resources and Facilities Management; and Therapeutic Recreation.

Recertification

Recertification is required every two years. Two CEUs or equivalent accredited college coursework in the industry must be completed for recertification.

CERTIFIED MEETING PROFESSIONAL® (CMP®)

Sponsor

Convention Liaison Council (CLC)
1575 Eye St. NW, Suite 1190
Washington, DC 20005
Phone: (202) 626-2764

Program Data

The CLC is made up of the 25 leading meeting, travel, and conference associations.

Certifying body: Independent board
Number certified: 1300
Approximate certification costs: $265

Program Description

The Certified Meeting Professional (CMP) designation recognizes experienced professionals in the corporate-meeting, conference, and convention fields. The meetings industry includes conventions, exhibitions, conferences, trade shows, and corporate meetings.

Education/Experience

Eligibility to sit for the CMP examination is based on a point system. Candidates must reach a minimum 75 out of 125 points to qualify for the examination:

- Management of meetings and people: 53 points maximum

- Experience in meeting management: 32 points maximum

- Professional contributions: 20 points maximum

- Education and continuing education: 15 points maximum

- Professional organization membership: 5 points maximum

Examinations

The exam is a 150-question, multiple-choice test. The pass rate is confidential. The test covers 25 meeting-management functions and 22 independent conditions influencing these functions. The parameters of the test were developed through surveying approximately 400 meeting managers. Areas tested include budgets and funding; facilities, set-up, and support services; legal and risk-management concerns; planning and site selection; promotion and publicity; speakers and entertainment booking; and travel and registration.

Recertification
Recertification is required every five years and is based on work and professional education in the field.

REGISTERED MEETING PLANNER (RMP)
CERTIFIED EVENT PLANNER (CEP)
CERTIFIED DESTINATION SPECIALIST (CDS)

Sponsor
International Society of Meeting Planners (IMPI)
8383 East Evans Road
Scottsdale, AZ 85260
Phone: (602) 483-0000
Fax: (602) 998-8022
E-mail: ismp@iami.org
WWW: http://www.iami.org/ismp.html

Program Data
Certifying body: Association
Approximate certification costs: $210

Program Description
The IMPI certifications recognize association members working in the travel/event field. The Registered Meeting Planner (RMP) designation applies to travel/event professionals planning business meetings, conferences, and trade shows. The Certified Event Planner (CEP) designation applies to travel/event professionals planning fairs, concerts, fund-raisers, and parties. The Certified Destination Specialist (CDS) designation applies to travel/event professionals with a particular expertise in a city, an area, or a tourist destination.

Education/Experience
Candidates must be currently employed in the travel/event field.

Examinations
Candidates must pass a take-home examination. CDS candidates must demonstrate expertise in their selected destination(s).

Recertification
None.

CERTIFIED PARK OPERATOR (CPO)

Sponsor
National Association of RV Parks and
   Campgrounds (ARVC)
8605 Westwood Center Drive, Suite 201
Vienna, VA 22182
Phone: (703) 734-3000

Program Data
Certifying body: Association
Number certified: 300+
Approximate certification costs: $75

Program Description
The Certified Park Operator (CPO) designation recognizes campground and RV park operators and staff. Certification is based on a point system; there is no examination component. Membership in ARVC is not required.

Education/Experience
A candidate must have one year of experience at an RV park or campground to be enrolled in the CPO program. Points are awarded for professional experience, professional education, and ARVC participation.

Recertification
The initial CPO certification must be renewed after three years. A CPO must earn 10 course credits. The recertification is valid "indefinitely." CPOs may continue to recertify and receive lifetime certification after five recertifications.

CERTIFIED ROOMS DIVISION EXECUTIVE (CRDE®)

Sponsor
Educational Institute of the American Hotel and
   Motel Association (EI/AH&MA)
1407 S. Harrison Road, Suite 300
East Lansing, MI 48823
Phone: (800) 752-5527
Fax: (517) 353-5527
E-mail: info@ei-ahma.org
WWW: http://www.ei-ahma.org

Program Data

Year certification began: 1969
Number certified: 15,000+
Organization members: 10,000
Additional certifications: Certified Engineering Operations Executive (CEOE®); Certified Food and Beverage Executive (CFBE®); Certified Hospitality Educator (CHE®); Certified Hospitality Housekeeping Executive (CHHE®); Certified Hospitality Sales Professional (CHSP®); Certified Hospitality Supervisor (CHS®); Certified Hospitality Technology Professional (CHTP®); Certified Hotel Administrator (CHA®); Certified Human Resources Executive (CHRE®); Hospitality Skills Certification; Master Hotel Supplier (MHS®)
Approximate certification costs: $275 (AH&MA-member properties), $325 (other properties)

Program Description

The Certified Rooms Division Executive (CRDE®) designation recognizes experienced managers of guest services and rooms division in the hospitality industry. Certification is based on passing an examination. AH&MA membership is not required.

Education/Experience

To sit for the CRDE examination, candidates must be currently employed as a rooms division, resident, front office, senior assistant, or executive assistant manager at a hospitality property or hospitality corporation and meet the one of the following requirements:

- An associate's or higher hospitality degree, or completion of the Educational Institute's five-course curriculum in rooms division management, and two years of experience in a rooms division management position

- Three years of experience in a rooms division management position

- Currently an instructor teaching hospitality management, with two years of experience in this capacity, and two years of experience in rooms division management

Examinations

The CRDE examination covers a wide range of areas needed by rooms division management, including front office, housekeeping, security, law, and supervision.

Recertification

CRDEs must renew their certification every five years. Certification is based on a point system; 50 points are needed to recertify. Points are earned through professional experience, continuing education, professional involvement, and educational service.

CERTIFIED TRAVEL COUNSELOR (CTC)

Sponsor

Institute of Certified Travel Agents (ICTA)
148 Linden St.
P.O. Box 56
Wellesley, MA 02181
Phone: (617) 237-0280
Fax: (617) 237-3860

Program Data

ACE PONSI recommends 12 undergraduate semester credits for the CTC program.

Certifying body: Nonprofit professional education organization
Year certification began: 1965
Number certified: 22,000+
Organization members: 7000+
Approximate certification costs: $1075

Program Description

The Certified Travel Counselor (CTC) designation recognizes travel agents and individuals who sell to, or work with, travel agents. Certification is based on completing CTC coursework. Most candidates complete the program in 18 months. The 200 hours of instruction include a writing project, oral presentation, and four essay examinations. Courses may be completed through independent study, group study, or licensed schools. Training materials include detailed study guides, audiotapes, reading materials, and exercises.

Education/Experience

To qualify for certification, candidates must have five years of industry experience. This requirement may be reduced to two years by gaining one year's credit each for any of the following:

- Graduates of certain travel programs
- Four years of nontravel work requiring contact with the public

- Bachelor's degree majoring in travel and tourism or business administration
- Master's degree

Curriculum

The CTC curriculum is constantly updated, and currently consists of the following:

- Communications for the Travel Professional
- The Travel Professional: Selling in a Competitive Service Environment
- Issues in Travel Agency Management
- Challenges in Leadership and Management
- The Travel Industry in the '90s and Beyond

Examinations

The essay examinations mirror the associated course. The pass rate is about 85%.

Recertification

CTCs who enrolled after January 1, 1993, must recertify every five years through continuing education. Recertification is based on a point system.

- Points required for recertification: 50
- Point examples:
  - 5–10 points per major industry training program/event
  - 1 point per contact hour industry training

Science and Engineering
Speciality

Certified Specialist in Analytical Technology (CSAT)

Sponsor
Instrument Society of America (ISA)
P.O. Box 12277
Research Triangle Park, NC 27709
Phone: (919) 990-9417
Fax: (919) 832-0237
E-mail: fgregory@isa.org,
WWW: http://www.isa.org/

Program Data
Certifying body: Association
Year certification began: 1992
Organization members: 49,000
Additional certifications: Certified Control
   Systems Technician (CCST)
Approximate certification costs: $160 (members),
   $210 (nonmembers)

Program Description
The Certified Specialist in Analytical Technology (CSAT) designation recognizes measurement and control practitioners. ISA's programs are designed to cross titles and job descriptions to all professionals involved in the field. Certification is based on an examination. Membership in ISA is not required.

Education/Experience
Candidates need eight years combined experience and education to qualify for the examination. In meeting this requirement, candidates show two years of education and three years of experience.

Examinations
Contact ISA for examination information.

Recertification
Certified specialists must recertify every three years. Recertification is based on a point system, with credit given for experience, education, professional service, and recognition.

Registered Biological Photographer (RBP)

Sponsor
Biological Photographic Association (BPA)
115 Stoneridge Drive
Chapel Hill, NC 27514
Phone: (919) 967-8247
WWW: http://138.5.50.40/RBP/RBP.html

Program Data
Certifying body: Association
Number certified: 400
Organization members: 1100
Approximate certification costs: $200

Program Description
The Registered Biological Photographer (RBP) designation recognizes professional photographers in dental, forensic, medical, natural science, ophthalmic, and veterinary photography. Certification is based on passing three examinations. Membership in BPA is not required.

Education/Experience
To begin the program, candidates must have two years of professional experience.

Examinations
The first examination is a 100-question, objective test covering photography materials, processes, optics, and chemistry; light and filters; photomicrography; photomacrography; video and motion film; ethics; and terminology.

The second examination is a practical portfolio. The candidate assembles a portfolio of 30 assignments, including clinical, reproduction, UV and IR photography; motion media; photomacrography; and technical writing. Examiners independently score the submitted portfolio.

The last examination is an oral presentation and a review of the portfolio. The candidate may also be asked questions by the examination panel.

Recertification
None.

BROADBAND COMMUNICATIONS ENGINEER (BCE)

BROADBAND COMMUNICATIONS TECHNICIAN (BCT)

Sponsor

Society of Cable Telecommunications Engineers (SCTE)
669 Exton Commons
Exton, PA 19341
Phone: (610) 363-6888
WWW: http://www.cable-online.com/sctehome.htm

Program Data

Certifying body: Association
Additional certifications: Broadband Installer

Program Description

The Broadband Communications Engineer (BCE) and Broadband Communications Technician (BCT) certifications recognize cable-television technical professionals. The BCE and BCT are separate programs that cover similar material; the engineer program requires a greater depth of knowledge and experience. Membership in SCTE is required.

Education/Experience

To sit for the BCE examinations, an engineer must have five years of professional experience and have completed formal electronics training (military, vo/tech, or college).

To sit for the BCT examinations, a technician must have two years of professional experience.

Examinations

Examinations are open-book, and all but one are multiple-choice. This is the full examination curriculum:

- Signal Processing Center Video and Audio Signals and Systems
- Transportation Systems
- Distribution Systems
- Data Networking and Architecture
- Terminal Devices
- Engineering Management and Professionalism (not multiple-choice)

Recertification

Both BCEs and BCTs must recertify every three years. Recertification may be through either passing a recertification examination, or accumulating the minimum number of recertification units (BCE=21, BCT=12) as follows:

- 4 per national speaker/paper presented
- 4 per article
- 2 per paper (local)
- 1 per year of SCTE membership
- 1 per year of local-chapter membership
- 1 per day of seminars and meetings
- 1 per CEU
- 1 per year officer/committee

CERTIFIED BROADCAST ENGINEER

CERTIFIED BROADCAST TECHNOLOGIST

Sponsor

Society of Broadcast Engineers, Inc. (SBE)
8445 Keystone Crossing, Suite 140
Indianapolis, IN 46240
Phone: (317) 253-1640
Fax: (317) 253-0418
E-mail: lgodby@sbe.org
WWW: http://www.sbe.org/

Program Data

Certifying body: Association
Year certification began: 1977

Program Description

The SBE certification program recognizes broadcast technologists and three levels of broadcast engineers. Membership in SBE is not required. An extensive preparation course is sold by SBE.

Education/Experience

For Technologist certification, a candidate must either pass an examination or have two years of experience and hold an FCC Life-time General Class, an Amateur Extra Class, or a foreign equivalent.

For engineers, the following levels of experience and education are required. There is no examination requirement for the professional level. For the Engineer and Senior Engineer experience requirements, the following education may substitute for the indicated experience:

- PE = four years
- Bachelor's degree = four years
- Associate's degree = two years
- Accredited education = one year for each

For the Engineer certification, candidates must have five years of experience or equivalent. For Senior Engineer certification, candidates must have 10 years of experience or equivalent.

For the Professional Broadcast Engineer (CPBE) certification, candidates must have 20 years of experience (or 16 with a P.E.). There is no exam component for the CPBE designation.

Examinations

The Broadcast Technologist (CBT) examination is a 50-question, multiple-choice examination on electronics, FCC rules, and safety. The candidate may choose to have questions concerning radio, television, or both.

The Broadcast Engineer Radio (CBRE)/Broadcast Engineer TV (CBTE) examination is a 50-question, multiple-choice examination for either the television or radio endorsement. The exam covers operating practices, broadcast theory, problems, and safety.

The Senior Broadcast Engineer Radio (CSRE)/ Senior Broadcast Engineer TV (CSTE) examination is a 50-question, multiple-choice examination with one essay question for either the television or radio endorsement. The exam covers operating practices, broadcast theory, problems, safety, and supervision and management.

Recertification

Technologists renew certification every five years by verifying continued service.

Engineers renew their certification every five years by accumulating professional credits through employment, continuing education, and association participation.

CERTIFIED PROFESSIONAL CHEMICAL ENGINEER (CCHE)

CERTIFIED PROFESSIONAL CHEMIST (CPC)

Sponsor

National Certification Commission in Chemistry and Chemical Engineering (NCCCCE)
American Institute of Chemists
501 Wythe St.
Alexandria, VA 22314

Phone: (703) 836-2090
Fax: (703) 836-2091
E-mail: 76744.2677@compuserve.com

Program Data

Certifying body: Association
Year certification began: 1977
Number certified: 275
Organization members: 3200
Approximate certification costs: $150 (members), $225 (nonmembers)

Program Description

The Certified Professional Chemical Engineer (CChE) and Certified Professional Chemist (CPC) designations recognize experienced chemical engineers and chemists. AIC membership is not required. Certification is based on a point system. There is no examination requirement.

Recertification

CChEs and CPCs must recertify every three years by earning an additional 300 points on the certification point system.

CERTIFIED COGENERATION PROFESSIONAL (CCP)

Sponsor

Association of Energy Engineers® (AEE)
4025 Pleasantdale Road, Suite 420
Atlanta, GA 30340
Phone: (770) 447-5083
Fax: (770) 446-3969
WWW: http://www.aeecenter.org

Program Data

Certifying body: Association
Number certified: 500+
Organization members: 8000
Additional programs: Certified Energy Manager (CEM); Certified Demand-Side Management Professional (CDSM); Certified Indoor Air Quality Professional (CIAQP); Certified Lighting Efficiency Professional (CLEP)

Program Description

The Certified Cogeneration Professional (CCP) designation recognizes experienced independent power generation/cogeneration professionals. Certification is based on passing an examination. Membership in AEE is not required.

Education/Experience
Candidates with degrees in business or engineering need three years of related experience. Other candidates may need additional experience.

Examinations
The four-hour, multiple-choice CCP examination is an open-book test in which the candidate partially selects sections based on proficiency and experience. A two-day preparation course is presented by AEE.

Recertification
None.

CORROSION SPECIALIST, TECHNOLOGIST, TECHNICIAN

Sponsor
NACE International
1440 South Creek Drive
Houston, TX 77084-4906
Phone: (713) 492-0535
Fax: (713) 492-8254
E-mail: member@mail.nace.org
WWW: http://www.nace.org/

Program Data
The NACE certification program is recognized by the Council of Engineering and Scientific Specialty Boards. The Environmental Protection Agency Office of Underground Storage Tanks also recognizes NACE certifications.

Certifying body: Association
Year certification began: 1971
Number certified: 4000+
Organization members: 15,000+
Approximate certification costs: $125–$250 (members), $325–$400 (nonmembers)

Program Description
The NACE International Professional Recognition Program provides professional recognition for individuals involved in corrosion science and technology to indicate to the general public, coworkers, employers, and others that an impartial organization has used a recognized and consistent method to assess the individual's experience, expertise, knowledge, and education.

All certification categories have requirements for (a) work experience in the field of corrosion, and (b) successful passing of required examinations.

Certification also requires signing a NACE International Attestation concerning professionalism. All examinations are open-book; a candidate may use any reference or aid wanted. The pass rate for all examinations is 90%.

The categories of certification are as follows:

Corrosion Specialist—Candidates must hold certification in a NACE Specialty Area and have eight years of corrosion work experience, with four being in a responsible charge position; or hold one of the following, along with four years of work experience in responsible charge: a P.E., P. Eng., or equivalent, an EIT Registration, a B.S. and Ph.D. in physical sciences or engineering. The examination is geared towards very experienced corrosion-control personnel, with broad and extensive expertise, in both the theory and practice of multiple areas of corrosion and corrosion control, and capable of performing work at a very advanced level.

Specialty Areas (includes Cathodic Protection Specialist; Protective Coatings Specialist; Chemical Treatment Specialist; Materials Selection/Design Specialist)—Candidates must meet the same experience requirements as for Corrosion Specialist (above). The specialty area examinations are geared towards very experienced and knowledgeable personnel with expertise in both the theory and practice of a particular area of corrosion and corrosion control, and who are capable of performing work at an advanced level in a particular field.

Senior Corrosion Technologist—Candidates must have either eight years of corrosion work experience, with four years in a responsible charge position; or hold a B.S. in physical sciences or engineering, along with four years of work experience in responsible charge. The examination is geared towards experienced personnel possessing primary practical knowledge over multiple areas of corrosion and its control, and capable of performing responsible work under the direction of Specialist-level personnel but requiring minimal supervision.

Corrosion Technologist—Candidates must have four years of corrosion work experience. The examination is geared towards moderately experienced personnel possessing basic knowledge of corrosion and corrosion control, and capable of performing some responsible work under the close direction of Specialist- or Senior Technologist-level personnel.

Corrosion Technician—Candidates must have two years of corrosion work experience. The examination is geared towards personnel with little experience but possessing some basic knowledge of corrosion and corrosion control, who are capable of performing routine but well-defined work under close direction of Specialist- or Senior Technologist-level personnel.

Recertification
NACE certifications must be renewed every three to five years through continued activity in the field of corrosion and professional development activities.

CERTIFIED COST CONSULTANT (CCC)
CERTIFIED COST ENGINEER (CCE)

Sponsor
AACE International (AACE)
P.O. Box 1557
Morgantown, WV 26507
Phone: (800) 858-COST
Fax: (304) 291-5728
E-mail: aace@vegas.com
WWW: http://www.vegas.com/pronet/aace/
aace.html

Program Data
Certifying body: Association
Number certified: 550
Organization members: 6000
Approximate certification costs: $175 (members), $250 (nonmembers)

Program Description
The Certified Cost Consultant (CCC) and Certified Cost Engineer (CCE) designations recognize engineers in the fields of cost estimation and control, project management, and planning and analysis. The program is based on an extensive skills and knowledge analysis. AACE membership is not required. The CCE designation is used by registered engineers and graduates of ABET-accredited engineering programs. The CCC designation is used by all other certified individuals. Certification is based on an examination and professional paper.

Education/Experience
Candidates must have either eight years of related experience or four years of experience and a related bachelor's degree or P.E. registration.

Examinations
The four-part, six-hour examination has both open-book and closed-book portions. Each part has two sections. To allow for the diverse background and fields of interest of cost engineers, candidates select half the questions in each section. Questions may be long-answer, short-answer, or multiple-choice. The test parts are Supporting Skills and Knowledge; Costs and Cost Estimating; Project Management; and Economic Analysis.

The paper is considered part of the examination. Candidates must write a 2500-word paper on a cost-engineering subject.

Recertification
Recertification is required every three years and is based on either passing an examination or accumulating experience, education, and professional association involvement.

PROFESSIONAL ENGINEER (P.E.)

Sponsor
National Council of Examiners for Engineering
    and Surveying (NCEES)
280 Seneca Creek Road
Clemson, SC 29633-1686
Phone: (800) 250-3196
Fax: (864) 654-6033
WWW: http://www.ncees.org

Program Description
The Professional Engineer (P.E.) designation is awarded only by state registration boards. The National Council of Examiners for Engineering and Surveying (NCEES) is made up of these state boards, and develops and scores the two basic examinations. Many state-based certifications and endorsements for P.E.s are available.

While actual requirements vary, most states require candidates to complete the following four requirements:

- Earn an approved four-year engineering degree
- Pass the NCEES Fundamentals of Engineering examination
- Complete an acceptable internship program
- Pass the NCEES Principles and Practice of Engineering examination

---

CERTIFIED ENGINEERING TECHNOLOGIST (CT)

Sponsor

National Institute for Certification in Engineering
 Technologies (NICET)
1420 King St.
Alexandria, VA 22314
Phone: (703) 684-2835

Program Data

NICET is sponsored by the National Society of Professional Engineers (NSPE).

Certifying body: Independent board
Number certified: 850+
Additional certifications: Certified Engineering
 Technician (CET)

Program Description

The Certified Engineering Technologist (CT) program recognizes engineering technology as a unique professional field. Certification is based on education and experience; an examination program is under development. Currently, only graduates of a program accredited by the Accreditation Board for Engineering and Technology (ABET) Technology Accreditation Commission are eligible for certification.

Education/Experience

Candidates are eligible for the grade of Associate Engineering Technologist (AT) upon graduation. After five years of verified work in the field, this can be upgraded to Certified Engineering Technologist (CT).

Recertification

None.

BOARD CERTIFIED ENTOMOLOGIST (BCE)

Sponsor

Entomological Society of America (ESA)
9301 Annapolis Road, Suite 300
Lanham, MD 20706
Phone: (301) 731-4535
Fax: (301) 731-4538
E-mail: bce@entsoc.org
WWW: http://www.entsoc.org/

Program Data

Certifying body: Association
Year certification began: 1972
Number certified: 620
Organization members: 8300

Board Certified Entomologists are listed in the ESA's membership directory, available from the above address.

Program Description

The Board Certified Entomologist (BCE) designation recognizes experienced professionals in insect-related specialties. BCEs will be found performing in many areas, including pest management; basic, applied, industrial, and product research; regulatory, medical, forensic, and veterinary entomology; and consulting. Certification is based on passing a general and a specialty examination. Membership in ESA is not required.

Education/Experience

To sit for the examinations, candidates must meet one of the following options:

- Three years of experience and a related bachelor's degree
- Two years of experience and a related master's degree
- One year of experience and a related doctoral degree

Examinations

Candidates must pass a both a general examination and a specialty examination. Candidates are tested on their knowledge and experience in the specialty or specialties in which they will be certified. Specialties are General Entomology; Medical/Veterinary Entomology; Pesticide Development Analysis and Toxicology; Plant-Related Entomology; Regulatory Entomology; and Urban and Industrial Entomology. The exams have a pass rate of 80%. BCEs may take specialty examinations in additional specialties.

Recertification

BCEs must recertify every three years. Recertification is through accumulating 120 continuing-education units. BCEs must earn at least 72 units through educational activities, such as conferences, workshops, licensing and credentialing, and writing. The remaining credits may be earned through professional association participation.

CERTIFIED PROFESSIONAL ERGONOMIST® (CPE®)

CERTIFIED HUMAN FACTORS PROFESSIONAL® (CHFP®)

Sponsor

Board of Certification in Professional
  Ergonomics® (BCPE®)
P.O. Box 2811
Bellingham, WA 98227
Phone: (360) 671-7601
Fax: (360) 671-7681
E-mail: BCPEHQ@aol.com

Program Data

The CPE/CHFP program is recognized by the Human Factors and Ergonomics Society (HFES) and the International Ergonomics Association (IEA).

Certifying body: Independent board
Year certification began: 1992
Number certified: 623
Approximate certification costs: $300

Program Description

The Certified Professional Ergonomist (CPE) and Certified Human Factors Professional (CHFP) designations recognize experienced ergonomics/ human factors practitioners. A practitioner of ergonomics is defined by the Board of Certification in Professional Ergonomics (BCPE) as a person having mastery of a body of ergonomics knowledge, a command of the methodologies used by ergonomists in applying that knowledge to a design of a product, system, job, or environment, and experience in applying this knowledge in the analysis, design, testing, and evaluation of products, systems, and environments. The Board regards ergonomics as synonymous with human factors and human factors engineering. Researchers and theoreticians in the ergonomics field are not considered practitioners. BCPE maintains an active ethics program.

Education/Experience

From June 1992 through December 1993, certification was based on education, an example of professional work, and seven years of practicing ergonomics. Beginning on January 1, 1994, candidates also had to pass a written examination. The applicant may choose either the CPE or CHFP designation. The minimum qualifications to sit for the examination are as follows:

- Master's degree in ergonomics/human factors. An educational equivalent within engineering, life, and natural sciences will be considered.

- Four years of professional experience in ergonomics, primarily in ergonomic design

- Presentation of an acceptable example of professional work on a technical product, process, or environment incorporating applied ergonomic data, methods, or principles

Examinations

The examination covers professional ergonomics practice by focusing on analysis, design, and evaluation techniques in ergonomic systems development. The exam content is based on task analysis results, expert panel review, and major texts in the field. The pass rate is 63%. Study guides and workshops are available.

The three-part examination covers the following areas:

- Ergonomics methods and techniques, including analytical tools involved in analysis, design, and evaluation

- Design of the human-machine interface, including workspace design and layout, job aids, and other design issues

- Humans as systems components, covering anthropometry, biomechanics, perception, and information processing

- Systems design and organization, including team performance, motivation, and related factors

- Professional practice, including ethics, working with diverse groups, and ergonomics resources such as standards and guidelines

Part 1 is 100 or more multiple-choice questions based on common human-factors/ergonomics texts. Parts 2 and 3 are scenario-based. Part 2 presents realistic work situations, during which the candidate selects and responds to a subset of presented scenarios. Answers are given as multiple-choice and fill-in. Part 3 presents scenarios and requires the candidate to respond in essay form.

Recertification

Criteria are currently being analyzed and evaluated for efficiency and fairness.

CERTIFIED FLUID POWER PROFESSIONAL

Sponsor

FPCB Secretariat
Fluid Power Society (FPS)
2433 N. Mayfair Road, Suite 111
Milwaukee, WI 53226
Phone: (414) 257-0910
Fax: (414) 257-4092

Program Data

The Fluid Power Certification Board is sponsored by the Fluid Power Society.

Certifying body: Association-sponsored independent board
Year certification began: 1970
Number certified: 3455
Organization members: 2500
Additional programs: Fluid Power Engineer
Approximate certification costs: $110 (members), $45 (student members), $160 (nonmembers)

Program Description

The Fluid Power Certification Program offers several levels of certification to technicians and engineers in the fields of hydraulics, pneumatics, vacuum, and electronic control. Certification is based solely on passing an examination. FPS membership is not required. Review seminars and a study course are available for each certification. The FPCB maintains an active ethics board with decertification powers.

Examinations

All examinations are based on task analyses and created by academia and consultants. The certification categories parallel the guidelines contained in the *Dictionary of Occupational Titles*, U.S. Department of Labor. The pass rate for all examinations is 60%.

The certifications and their examinations are as follows:

- Fluid Power Specialist—This certification is geared towards individuals involved in or managing hydraulic and pneumatic systems design, product selection, and installation. The open-book, multiple-choice, three-hour examination includes fluid power fundamentals, hydraulics and pneumatics, and electrical control.

- Fluid Power Technician—This certification is geared towards individuals responsible for developing project specifications, testing and modifying circuits and systems, and writing technical reports. Separate open-book, multiple-choice, three-hour examinations test Hydraulic Technicians and Pneumatic Technicians.

- Fluid Power Mechanic—This certification is for mechanics who install, maintain, and repair fluid power systems and components. Separate certification examinations test Industrial Hydraulic, Mobile Hydraulic, and Pneumatic Mechanics. The two-part examinations have an open-book, multiple-choice part and a job-performance part. Candidates must demonstrate their proficiency by completing six hands-on performance exercises.

Recertification

FPS certifications must be renewed every five years and are based on continued professional employment and education. The percent completing first recertification within the last five years is 18%.

CERTIFIED HYDROGRAPHER

Sponsor

American Congress on Surveying and Mapping (ACSM)
5410 Grosvenor Lane, Suite 100
Bethesda, MD 20814
Phone: (301) 493-0200
Fax: (301) 493-8245
WWW: http://www.techexpo.com:80/tech_soc/acsm.html

Program Data

The Certified Hydrographer designation is recognized by the U.S. Army Corps of Engineers.

Certifying body: Association-sponsored independent board
Year certification began: 1981
Number certified: 210
Organization members: Nonmembership
Additional certifications: Certified Survey Technician (CST)
Approximate certification costs: $200

Program Description

The ACSM Hydrographer certification program recognizes individuals who perform hydrographic surveys. Certification is based on passing an examination. ACSM membership is not required. Certification is in two separate areas, Inshore and Offshore.

Inshore Hydrographers are certified in using plane surveying techniques within 25 miles of the shore control for surveys of less than 100 square miles. Offshore Hydrographers are certified in using geodetic surveying techniques beyond 25 miles of the shore control or for surveying larger areas.

Education/Experience
Candidates must have five years of hydrographic surveying experience, with two years in technical supervision of surveys and two years performing field work. Written references from supervisors are required.

Examinations
The examination is an at-home essay examination on the candidate's requested certification area. A candidate is presented with a hypothetical survey. The candidate must complete an essay on planning, performing, and completing the survey, demonstrating thorough knowledge and techniques in methodology, standards, tools, and quality assurance. The pass rate was not disclosed.

Recertification
None indicated.

CERTIFIED LIGHTING EFFICIENCY PROFESSIONAL (CLEP)

Sponsor
Association of Energy Engineers® (AEE)
4025 Pleasantdale Road, Suite 420
Atlanta, GA 30340
Phone: (770) 447-5083
Fax: (770) 446-3969
WWW: http://www.aeecenter.org

Program Data
Certifying body: Association
Organization members: 8000
Additional programs: Certified Cogeneration Professional (CCP); Certified Demand-Side Management Professional (CDSM); Certified Energy Manager (CEM); Certified Indoor Air Quality Professional (CIAQP)

Program Description
The Certified Lighting Efficiency Professional (CLEP) designation recognizes experienced lighting management professionals, both in efficiency improvement and lighting design. Certification is based on passing an examination. Membership in AEE is not required.

Education/Experience
To take the CLEP examination, a candidate must be an engineering graduate or P.E. with three years of professional experience; have a business or related bachelor's or associate's degree with five to eight years of professional experience; or have 10 years of professional experience.

Examinations
The four-hour, multiple-choice CLEP examination is an open-book test covering lighting selection, maintenance, and techniques. A two-day preparation course is presented by AEE.

Recertification
None indicated.

CERTIFIED LIGHTING MANAGEMENT CONSULTANT (CLMC)

Sponsor
International Association of Lighting Management Companies (NALMCO)
34-C Washington Road
Princeton Junction, NJ 08550

Program Data
Certifying body: Association
Year certification began: 1989
Number certified: Not disclosed
Approximate certification costs: $500 (members), $1000 (nonmembers)

Program Description
The Certified Lighting Management Consultant (CLMC) designation recognizes individuals who manage the design, operation, modification, or maintenance of lighting systems. Membership in NALMCO is not required.

Education/Experience
Eligibility for certification is determined using a point system. The point-area minimum totals create these minimum requirements:

● Three professional education events
● Three years of lighting-related professional association membership
● Three years of professional experience

Examinations
The examination is an all-day test covering the scope of professional knowledge. It is designed to test experiential knowledge. Candidates use a

187

calculator, ruler, and lamp and ballast catalogs and price lists. The test includes these areas:

- Ballast
- Bidding and estimating
- Cleaning and relamping
- Energy management systems
- Equipment and safety procedures
- Lamps
- Lighting levels
- Lighting controls
- Power-reducing devices
- Utility rates

Recertification

A CLMC must recertify every three years. Recertification is based on a point system, in areas similar to initial certification; 240 credits are required to recertify.

CERTIFIED MANUFACTURING ENGINEER (CMFGE)

CERTIFIED MANUFACTURING TECHNOLOGIST (CMFGT)

Sponsor

Society for Manufacturing Engineers (SME)
One SME Drive
P.O. Box 930
Dearborn, MI 48121
Phone: (313) 271-1500
Fax: (313) 271-2861
E-mail: certification@sme.org
WWW: http://www.sme.org

Program Data

Certifying body: Association
Organization members: 70,000

Program Description

The SME's Manufacturing Engineering Certification Institute (MECI) recognizes skilled manufacturing professionals demonstrating competence through objective testing.

Education/Experience

CMfgT candidates must have four years of education and manufacturing-related experience.

CMfgE candidates must have 10 years of manufacturing-related work experience and education.

Examinations

The CMfgT multiple-choice, computer-based exam covers computer applications/automation; design; manufacturing economics; manufacturing management; manufacturing processes; materials; mathematics/applied science; and quality control. CMfgT candidates must also complete the SME Fundamentals of Manufacturing Exam.

CMfgE candidates must choose their area of concentration for the multiple-choice, computer-based exam:

- Integration and Control, including robotics; machine vision; common networks; computer systems; and computer-aided manufacturing.
- Processes, including electronics manufacturing; material removal; material forming; fabrication; assembly; finishing; and molding casting
- Support Operations, including maintenance; material handling; scheduling; planning; management; and design

CMfgE candidates who are not licensed PEs must also take the SME Fundamentals of Manufacturing exam.

Recertification

Certification must be maintained through continuing education.

CERTIFIED MAPPING SCIENTIST, REMOTE SENSING AND GIS/LIS

Sponsor

American Society for Photogrammetry and
  Remote Sensing (ASPRS)
5410 Grosvenor Lane, Suite 210
Bethesda, MD 20814
Phone: (301) 493-0290
Fax: (301) 334-6366
E-mail: certification@asprs.org
WWW: http://www.us.net/asprs/

Program Data

Certifying body: Professional association.
Year certification began: 1975
Number certified: 790 (all ASPRS certifications)
Organization members: 8000
Additional certifications: Certified
  Photogrammetrist

Program Description

The Certified Mapping Scientist program certifies professionals in two specialties: Remote Sensing and Geographic Information Systems/Land Information Systems (GIS/LIS). Membership in ASPRS is not required. Certification is based on experience and education. ASPRS maintains an active ethics board with decertification powers.

Education/Experience

For the Remote Sensing certification, candidates must have five years of responsibility-level photogrammetric experience and five years in remote sensing and data interpretation.

For the GIS/LIS certification, candidates must have four years of responsibility-level photogrammetric or mapping experience and five years of experience in geographic or land information systems.

Certain degree programs reduce the experience requirement.

Examinations

There are no mandatory examinations. An oral or written examination may be directed by the ASPRS certification program if deemed necessary.

Recertification

To keep certification active, Certified Photogrammetrists must recertify every five years. The recertification rate is 55%, with 92% completing their first recertification.

CERTIFIED CONSULTING METEOROLOGIST (CCM)

Sponsor

American Meteorological Society (AMS)
45 Beacon St.
Boston, MA 02108
Phone: (617) 227-2425
Fax: (617) 742-8718
E-mail: amsprof@ametsoc.org
WWW: http://atm.geo.nsf.gov/AMS/index.html

Program Data

Certifying body: Association-sponsored independent board
Year certification began: 1957
Number certified: 500+
Organization members: 11,000
Approximate certification costs: $275 (members), $600 (nonmembers)

Program Description

The Certified Consulting Meteorologist (CCM) designation recognizes experienced professional meteorologists who consult or provide meteorological services. While membership in the AMS is not required, candidates must meet the minimum requirements for AMS professional membership. AMS maintains an active ethics program.

Education/Experience

To qualify for AMS membership, a candidate must meet one of the following requirements:

- Bachelor's degree or higher in atmospheric or related oceanic or hydrological sciences

- Bachelor's or higher degree in science or engineering. Candidate must currently utilize the degree in employment in atmospheric or related oceanic or hydrological sciences

- Completion of 20 college semester hours in atmospheric or related oceanic or hydrological sciences, and work in the field for three of the last five years

Candidates for certification must also have a minimum of five years of professional meteorological practice. A master's degree may substitute for one year, and a doctorate for two years of practice.

Examinations

The chairperson of the Board of Certified Consulting Meteorologists assigns written examination questions that test both the candidate's depth of general knowledge and his or her specialized area. In addition, a candidate must submit a published paper or report representing his or her professional work. The examination answers and the report are evaluated and assigned scores by Board members.

After the written exam and report are satisfactorily completed, the candidate meets with a regional or Board member-only oral examination. The oral exam will include hypothetical problems that the candidate may face in a consulting situation.

Recertification

CCMs that become inactive in the field for more than three years must reapply for certification.

REGISTERED MICROBIOLOGIST (RM[ASM])
SPECIALIST MICROBIOLOGIST (SM[ASM])

Sponsor

American Society for Microbiology (ASM)
1325 Massachusetts Ave. NW
Washington, DC 20005
Phone: (202) 942-9226
Fax: (202) 942-9380
E-mail: certification@asmusa.org
WWW: http://www.asmusa.org/

Program Data

Certifying body: Association-sponsored
    independent board
Year certification began: 1960 (AMS)
Number certified: 4882
Organization members: 40,000
Additional programs: Diplomate—American
    Board of Medical Laboratory Immunology
    (ABMLI); Diplomate—American Board of
    Medical Microbiology (ABMM)

Program Description

The Registered and Specialist Microbiologist certification programs are administered by ASM's National Registry of Microbiologists. The registry identifies qualified microbiologists working in a variety of clinical and nonclinical settings. Certification is based on examination and level of experience.

Education/Experience

The Registered Microbiologist certification identifies entry-level qualified individuals. Candidates are certified in either Clinical and Public Health Microbiology, or Consumer Products and Quality Assurance Microbiology. To take the exam, candidates must have a bachelor's degree with acceptable coursework and one year of experience.

The Specialist Microbiologist certification identifies experienced individuals. Candidates are certified either in Consumer and Industrial Microbiology, or Public Health and Medical Laboratory Microbiology. Candidates must meet one of the following requirements:

- Master's or higher degree with four years of acceptable experience

- Medical degree and a residency in clinical microbiology

- Seven years of post-baccalaureate lab experience

Examinations

The 150-question, multiple-choice RM and SM examinations emphasize applied microbiology and include laboratory instruments and equipment; preparation; procedures; operations; and sample collection and handling.

Recertification

Recertification is voluntary, based on continuing education.

NARTE CERTIFIED ENGINEER (NCE)
NARTE CERTIFIED TECHNICIAN (NCT)

Sponsor

National Association of Radio and
    Telecommunications Engineers (NARTE)
P.O. Box 678
Medway, MA 02053
Phone: (508) 533-8333
Fax: (508) 533-3815

Program Data

NARTE is certified by the Federal Communications Commission (FCC) as a Commercial Operators License Examination Manager (COLE Manager), authorized to administer all examination elements for FCC licensure.

Certifying body: Association
Number certified: 11,000

Program Description

NARTE provides several levels of certification and endorsements for telecommunications and electromagnetic-comparability technicians and engineers. Membership in NARTE accompanies certification. Certification is based on experience, education, and either passing an examination or meeting other requirements. Approximately 50 endorsement subcategories are available.

Education/Experience

The telecommunications technician certification has four levels. Level IV requires supervisor recommendation and completion of a related course of study. Levels III, II, and I require completion of a related vocational training course. Level III requires two years of experience; Level II, four years of experience; Level I, six years of experience.

The EMC technician certification requires six years of experience and completion of a recognized technical education program.

The telecommunications engineer certification has three levels. For all levels, candidates must have either a technical bachelor's degree, P.E. registration, or four additional years of experience. Level III requires employer recommendation; Level II, four years of experience; Level I, eight years of experience.

The EMC engineer certification requires nine years of experience and a BSEE or equivalent.

Examinations
Technical examination study reference guides describe the testable areas for each level. For example, the Engineer Class III examination covers telecommunications principles; digital communication; data communications; opto-electronics; transmission lines; engineering economy; transmitters and receivers; and radio, microwave, and satellite links. Under certain circumstances, certification is possible without taking an examination. However, candidates must still meet all other requirements.

Recertification
None.

CERTIFIED PHOTOGRAMMETRIST

Sponsor
American Society for Photogrammetry and
   Remote Sensing (ASPRS)
5410 Grosvenor Lane, Suite 210
Bethesda, MD 20814
Phone: (301) 493-0290
Fax: (301) 334-6366
E-mail: certification@asprs.org
WWW: http://www.us.net/asprs/

Program Data
Certifying body: Professional association
Year certification began: 1975
Number certified: 790 (all ASPRS certifications)
Organization members: 8000
Additional certifications: Certified Mapping
   Scientist, Remote Sensing and GIS/LIS

Program Description
The Certified Photogrammetrist program recognizes professionals involved with photo and imaged-based surveys. Membership in ASPRS is not required. Certification is based on experience and education. Candidates must have nine years of

photogrammetry experience. A minimum of five years must have been in a position of professional responsibility rather than an operator/technician position. ASPRS maintains an active ethics board with decertification powers. Certain degrees reduce the experience requirement.

Examinations
There are no mandatory examinations. An oral or written examination may be directed by the ASPRS certification program if deemed necessary.

Recertification
To keep certification active, Certified Photogrammetrists must recertify every five years. The recertification rate is 55%, with 92% completing their first recertification.

CERTIFIED IN PLUMBING ENGINEERING® (CIPE®)

Sponsor
American Society of Plumbing Engineering
   (ASPE)
3617 Thousand Oaks Blvd., Suite 210
Westlake, CA 91362
Phone: (805) 495-7120

Program Data
Certifying body: Association
Number certified: 1300
Organization members: 6400+

Program Description
The Certified in Plumbing Engineering® (CIPE®) is a national certification program recognizing engineers in plumbing. The program is based on a job analysis performed by ASPE and the Educational Testing Service (ETS). ASPE membership is not required. Certification is based on passing an examination.

Examinations
The 100-question, multiple-choice examination covers evaluating the scope of work, system design, specifications, and construction services. The Educational Testing Service's Center for Occupational Assessment assisted in development and administers the test for ASPE.

Recertification
None.

CERTIFIED QUALITY ENGINEER (CQE)

Sponsor

American Society for Quality Control (ASQC)
611 E. Wisconsin Ave.
Milwaukee, WI 53201
Phone: (800) 248-1946
Fax: (414) 272-1734
WWW: http://www.asqc.org/educat/cert.html

Program Data

Certifying body: Association
Year certification began: 1966 (first program)
Number certified: 50,000 (all programs)
Organization members: 130,000
Additional programs: Certified Mechanical
  Inspector (CMI); Certified Quality Auditor
  (CQA); Certified Quality Manager (CQM);
  Certified Quality Technician (CQT); Certified
  Reliability Engineer (CRE)

Program Description

The Certified Quality Engineer (CQE) designation recognizes individuals knowledgeable and proficient in product- and service-quality evaluation and control. Certification is based on passing an examination. ASQC maintains an active ethics program. Candidates must demonstrate professionalism by either of the following:

- Holding Professional Engineer (P.E.)
  registration

- ASQC (or foreign affiliate society)
  membership

- Membership in a society belonging to
  the American Association of Engineering
  Societies or the Accreditation Board for
  Engineering and Technology

Education/Experience

Candidates must have eight years of combined education and experience in at least one area of the CQE body of knowledge. At least three years must be in a decision-making technical, professional, or management position. An associate's degree equals two years of experience; a bachelor's degree equals four years of experience; a master's degree equals five years of experience.

Examinations

The 160-question, multiple-choice examination is based on the CQE body of knowledge and covers general knowledge, conduct, and ethics; measurement systems; product, process, and materials control; quality practices and applications; safety and reliability; and statistical principals and applications.

CERTIFIED RELIABILITY ENGINEER (CRE)

Sponsor

American Society for Quality Control (ASQC)
611 E. Wisconsin Ave.
Milwaukee, WI 53201
Phone: (800) 248-1946
Fax: (414) 272-1734
WWW: http://www.asqc.org/educat/cert.html

Program Data

Certifying body: Association
Year certification began: 1966 (first program)
Number certified: 50,000 (all programs)
Organization members: 130,000
Additional programs: Certified Mechanical
  Inspector (CMI); Certified Quality Auditor
  (CQA); Certified Quality Engineer (CQE);
  Certified Quality Manager (CQM); Certified
  Quality Technician (CQT)

Program Description

The Certified Reliability Engineer (CRE) designation recognizes individuals knowledgeable and proficient in evaluating performance for product/systems safety, reliability, and maintainability improvement. Certification is based on passing an examination. ASQC maintains an active ethics program. Candidates must demonstrate professionalism by one of the following:

- Holding Professional Engineer (P.E.)
  registration

- ASQC (or foreign affiliate society)
  membership

- Membership in a society belonging to
  the American Association of Engineering
  Societies or the Accreditation Board for
  Engineering and Technology

Education/Experience

Candidates must have eight years of combined education and experience in at least one area of the CQA body of knowledge. At least three years must be in a decision-making technical, professional, or management position. An associate's degree equals two years of experience; a bachelor's degree equals four years of experience; a master's degree equals five years of experience.

Examinations

The multiple-choice examination is based on the CRE body of knowledge and covers reliability principles, concepts, and definitions; management control; prediction, estimation, and apportionment methods; failure mode, effect, and criticality analysis; part selection and derating; reliability design review; maintainability and availability; product safety; human factors in reliability; reliability testing and planning; data collection, analysis, and reporting; and mathematical models.

CERTIFIED SAFETY EXECUTIVE (WSO-CSE)

CERTIFIED SAFETY AND SECURITY DIRECTOR (WSO-CSSD)

CERTIFIED SAFETY MANAGER (WSO-CSM)

CERTIFIED SAFETY SPECIALIST (WSO-CSS)

CERTIFIED SAFETY TECHNICIAN (WSO-CST)

Sponsor

World Safety Organization (WSO)
WSO World Management Center
305 E. Market St.
P.O. Box 518
Warrensburg, MO 64093
Phone: (816) 747-3132

Program Data

WSO is in consultive status, Category II, with the United Nations Economic and Social Council.

Certifying body: Association
Additional certifications: Certified Hazardous Materials Executive (WSO-CHME); Certified Hazardous Materials Supervisor (WSO-CHMS); Certified Hazardous Materials Technician (WSO-CHMT)

Program Description

The Certified Safety Executive (WSO-CSE) designation recognizes corporate, government, and organizational executives responsible for setting safety, occupational-health, and security policies, programs, and methods.

The Certified Safety and Security Director (WSO-CSSD) designation recognizes security professionals concerned with the safety and security of people, property, resources, or environment.

The Certified Safety Manager (WSO-CSM) designation recognizes safety practitioners in mid-level management. Candidates are expected to supervise safety training, enforce safety requirements, and coordinate safety programs.

The Certified Safety Specialist (WSO-CSS) designation recognizes safety practitioners specializing in a specific area performing both technical and managerial functions.

The Certified Safety Technician (WSO-CST) designation is an entry-level certification for safety and safety-related professionals. There is no exam requirement for this certification.

Membership in WSO is required for all certifications.

Education/Experience

To qualify to sit for any examination but the WSO-CST exam, a candidate must have a bachelor's degree in safety or an acceptable related area, such as management, security, and engineering (two years of professional experience may substitute for each academic year required). Candidates must have either four years of professional experience, a master's degree and two years of professional experience, or a doctorate and one year of professional experience.

The WSO-CST examination requires current employment in the field and a bachelor's degree in safety or a safety-related major. Candidates need three years of related experience, current employment in the field, and an associate's degree in safety or a safety-related major.

Examinations

All exams include a 100-word essay on the candidate's professional expertise or contributions. All exams are three-hour, open-book, multiple-choice tests.

The exams cover the following:

- WSO-CSE—security, safety, and loss control; product safety, law, and regulations; risk management; professional liability; occupational health and safety; management; and ethics

- WSO-CSSD—security, safety, and loss control; law and regulations; risk management; professional liability; occupational health and safety; management; and ethics
- WSO-CSM—safety and loss control; law and regulations; risk management; occupational health and safety
- WSO-CSS—The first part of the two-part exam covers general safety, legal, and regulatory issues, and professional ethics. The second part covers the candidate's specialized area, such as industrial hygiene, fire safety, and hazardous materials management.
- WSO-CST—None. Certification is based on experience in the field and related education.

The WSO examinations average a first-attempt pass rate of 50%.

Recertification

WSO certifications must be renewed every three years. Renewal is based on accumulating 30 CEUs.

WSO-CSTs do not recertify; candidates may be assigned mentors who evaluate experience and training at the end of the five-year certification period. Technicians who wish to progress to other WSO certifications must complete five WSO-approved training courses.

CERTIFIED SAFETY PROFESSIONAL® (CSP®)

ASSOCIATE SAFETY PROFESSIONAL (ASP)

Sponsor

Board of Certified Safety Professionals (BCSP)
208 Burwash Ave.
Savoy, IL 61874
Phone: (217) 359-9263
Fax: (217) 359-0055

Program Data

The BCSP is a member of the Council of Engineering and Scientific Specialty Boards and accredited by the National Commission for Certifying Agencies (NCCA). The BCSP is sponsored by the American Society of Safety Engineers (ASSE); American Industrial Hygiene Association (AIHA); System Safety Society (SSS); Society of Fire Pro

tection Engineers (SFPE); National Safety Council (NSC); and the Institute of Industrial Engineers (IIE).

Certifying body: Independent board
Year certification began: 1969
Number certified: 8400 (CSP), 1705 (ASP)
Approximate certification costs: $455

Program Description

The Certified Safety Professional® (CSP®) designation recognizes professionals competent in and prepared for safety professional practice and the tasks associated with protecting workers, equipment, facilities, and the environment. Certification is through passing examinations in safety fundamentals and in comprehensive practice or a specialty area. There are no association membership requirements.

Education/Experience

All candidates must have at least four years of professional safety experience or credit. Experience must be as a full-time professional with safety making up at least half of the position's functions. Credit for one year of professional experience may be granted for ASSE or ABET accredited master's in safety, and for certification as an Occupational Health and Safety Technologist. Two years of experience credit will be given for a doctoral degree in safety.

Educational requirements are calculated on a point scale (Units of Credit). Candidates need a minimum point total of 48. Additional experience (1 per month) may be used to reach this total. Associate's degrees earn one-half the point totals of the bachelor's. Bachelor's degree examples: Safety accredited by ABET or ASSE equals 48 points; Engineering accredited by ABET equals 42 points; Physical/Natural Sciences equals 30 points; Business Administration equals 18 points.

Examinations

There are two exams for the CSP designation. The first is the Safety Fundamentals Examination, a seven-hour, multiple-choice exam of approximately 280 questions. Candidates holding Professional Engineer registration, certification from the American Board of Industrial Hygiene or Health Physics, or acceptable foreign certification are exempt from this examination. The exam includes:

- Basic and applied sciences, covering engineering; epidemiology; ergonomics; human behavior; biology; mathematics; chemistry; and physics

- Program management and evaluation, including safety program organization, communications, and legal and regulatory requirements
- Fire prevention and protection
- Equipment and facilities, including hazards identification and control, material handling, and design
- Environmental aspects: system safety and product safety, including legal considerations, analysis, reliability, and quality control

Candidates who pass this examination are designated Associate Safety Professional (ASP) to indicate progress towards the CSP.

All CSP candidates must take one of the seven-hour, multiple-choice specialty examinations. All specialty examinations cover engineering, management, applied science, and legal and profession affairs. Subject area weights vary depending on the specialty. These are the specialty examinations:

- Comprehensive Practice
- Engineering Aspects
- Management Aspects
- Product Safety Aspects
- System Safety Aspects

Recertification

CSPs must recertify every five years. Recertification is based on a point system that recognizes various approaches for keeping current in professional safety practice. CSPs may also recertify by passing any specialty examination, earning selected certifications, or by earning a degree beyond the one held when certified.

The ASP designation may be held up to eight years, but cannot be renewed.

CERTIFIED WELDING INSPECTOR (CWI)

CERTIFIED ASSOCIATE WELDING INSPECTOR (CAWI)

Sponsor

American Welding Society (AWS)
550 N.W. LeJeune Road
Miami, FL 33135
Phone: 800 (443-9353)
E-mail: info@amweld.org
WWW: http://www.aws.org/

Program Data

Certifying body: Association
Organization members: 46,000
Additional certifications: AWS Certified Welder; Certified Welding Educator (CWE)

Program Description

The Certified Welding Inspector (CWI) and Certified Associate Welding Inspector (CAWI) certifications recognize experienced individuals responsible for the following: verifying that welding materials, equipment, and procedures meet specifications; verifying job qualifications and inspecting welder's work; and maintaining welding records. CWIs work independently; CAWIs work under the direction of CWIs. Certification is based on passing a series of examinations. AWS membership is not required.

Education/Experience

Candidates must meet minimum near- and far-vision acuity standards and the following requirements:

CWI—High school diploma and five years of acceptable experience in welding design, production, construction, inspection, or repair. Up to two years of experience may be replaced with college, technical, or vocational experience. Candidates with schooling to eighth-grade level and 10 years of acceptable experience, or below eighth grade with 15 years of acceptable experience, will also be considered.

CAWI—One of the following four options:

- Two years of college, technical, or vocational courses in welding, engineering, engineering technology, or physical science, and six months of acceptable experience
- High school graduate with two years of acceptable experience
- Schooling to eighth grade and four years of acceptable experience. One or more years of welding vocational training may substitute for one year of experience.
- Less than eighth-grade schooling with six years of acceptable experience

Examinations

Candidates must pass three examinations for certification. The first test is an open-book, multiple-choice code/standard test. Candidates select one of the related industry code-books for the test; the primary purpose is to test the candidate's ability to use a code/standard. The second test is a closed-book, multiple-choice fundamentals test covering welding principles, methods, terminology, and processes. The third test is a practical application test given in two parts. The first part is a multiple-choice test covering job-related tasks and skills, including calculations, test interpretation, procedures, and tools. The second part is a hands-on inspection test.

Recertification

CWIs and CAWIs must recertify every three years. Recertification may be by either reexamination or verifying two years of continued work in the field. Recertification through continued work may only be done for two recertifications; the third recertification must be acquired through reexamination. As a minimum, CWIs and CAWIs recertify every nine years through examination. The examination is the practical test for the current certification. In addition, a current eye examination must be submitted.

SCIENCE AND ENGINEERING
Computers/Information Systems

ADOBE CERTIFIED INSTRUCTOR

Sponsor

Adobe Systems Incorporated
411 First Ave. South
Seattle, WA 98104-2871
Phone: (800) 833-6687
Fax: (206) 470-7127
E-mail: certification@adobe.com
WWW: http://www.adobe.com/supportservice/
learningres/aicp.html

Program Data

Certifying body: Corporation
Year certification began: 1995
Approximate certification costs: $395

Program Description

The Adobe Certified Instructor program ensures
that trainers and instructors of Adobe software products have the required technical expertise. Candidates must document their product and training
expertise. Certification is based on passing an examination.

Examinations

Candidates are certified in one or more Adobe
products: Adobe Photoshop, Adobe Acrobat, or
Adobe PageMaker. Tests are given through Sylvan
Prometrics.

Recertification

Adobe Certified Instructors are required to retest
after major product upgrades.

APPLE CERTIFIED SERVER ENGINEER (APPLE CSE)

Sponsor

Apple Computer, Inc.
1 Infinite Loop
Cupertino, CA 95014
Phone: (408) 862-3385
WWW: http://www.solutions.apple.com/

Program Data

Certifying body: Corporation
Year certification began: 1995

Program Description

The Apple Certified Server Engineer (Apple CSE)
recognizes information systems professionals with
Apple Server hardware and software expertise.
Certification is through passing a series of examinations. There are no education or experience
requirements.

Examinations

Candidates must pass three examinations:
AppleShare/Macintosh OS Servers; AppleTalk Network Design; and AppleTalk Network Management.

AUTOMATED EXAMINATION SPECIALIST (AES⁻)

Sponsor

Society of Financial Examiners® (SOFE®)
4101 Lake Boone Trail, Suite 201
Raleigh, NC 27607
Phone: (800) 787-SOFE

Program Data

SOFE has been designated the credentialing body
for the state-insurance-department classification
system by the National Association of Insurance
Commissioners (NAIC).

Certifying body: Association
Year certification began: 1981
Number certified: 1200
Organization members: 2000
Additional programs: Accredited Financial
Examiner (AFE®); Certified Financial Examiner
(CFE®)

Program Description

The Automated Examination Specialist (AES^SM)
designation recognizes experienced financial examiners specializing in information systems audits
and working in insurance, financial institution, and
credit union industries. SOFE membership is required. SOFE maintains an active ethics program.

Education/Experience

Besides SOFE membership, candidates must meet the following requirements:

- Hold Accredited Financial Examiner (AFE®) certification
- Pass the following four courses offered by the Insurance Data Management Association:
    - Data Administration
    - Insurance Accounting and Data Quality
    - Insurance Data Collection and Statistical Research
    - Systems Development and Project Management

Examinations

Candidates must pass the National Association of Insurance Commissioners proficiency test in audit software.

Recertification

AESs are required to maintain SOFE membership and to participate in the continuing education program.

ASSOCIATE IN AUTOMATION MANAGEMENT (AAM®)

Sponsor

Insurance Institute of America (IIA)
720 Providence Road
P.O. Box 3016
Malvern, PA 19355
Phone: (800) 644-2101
Fax: (610) 640-9576

Program Data

Program was developed with the National Association of Insurance Women (International) (NAIW). The IIA programs have been evaluated and recommended for college credit by the American Council on Education.

Certifying body: Independent education and certification organization

Additional programs: The IIA offers Associate designations in the following programs: Accredited Adviser in Insurance (AAI®); Insurance Services (AIS); Claims (AIC); Fidelity and Surety Bonding (AFSB); Insurance Accounting and Finance (AIAF); Loss Control Management (ALCM®); Management (AIM); Marine Insurance Management (AMIM®);

Premium Auditing (APA®); Reinsurance (Are); Research and Planning (ARP®); Risk Management (ARM); Underwriting (AU)

Program Description

The Associate in Automation Management (AAM®) designation recognizes professionals who have completed the three-course IIA insurance automation program. Each course is 12 weeks long. Weekly assignments are not graded or returned, but are designed to prepare the student to take the end-of-course examination. Courses can be either independent or group study. There are no education or experience requirements. Each course prepares candidates for an IIA examination; they are as follows:

- Essentials of Automation
- Automation in Insurance
- Managing Automated Activities

Recertification

There is no recertification requirement.

CISCO CERTIFIED INTERNETWORK EXPERT (CCIE)

Sponsor

Cisco Systems
170 West Tasman Drive
San Jose, CA 95134
Phone: (800) 553-6387
Fax: (408) 526-4100
E-mail: cs-rep@cisco.com
WWW: http://www.cisco.com

Program Data

Certifying body: Corporation

Program Description

The Cisco Certified Internetwork Expert (CCIE) designation recognizes information systems professionals with proficiency in supporting diverse internetworks using routing and bridging technologies. Two years of related experience is recommended. Certification is based on passing examinations and hands-on skill evaluations.

Examinations

Candidates must pass both the qualification test and an evaluation in a certification laboratory. The exam includes general internetworking theory and controls, corporate technologies (non-Cisco), and Cisco technology.

The hands-on evaluation requires the candidate to implement and troubleshoot an internetworking system in a high-level simulation environment.

COMPAQ ACCREDITED SYSTEMS ENGINEER (ASE)

Sponsor

Compaq Computer Corporation
P.O. Box 692000
Houston, TX 77269
Phone: (713) 518-1913
WWW: http://www.compaq.com

Program Data

Certifying body: Corporation

Program Description

The Compaq ASE certification is a multilevel program recognizing individuals knowledgeable in sales, support, planning, and optimization of Compaq computer platforms. Certification as a Compaq Associate ASE requires passing a series of Compaq examinations. Certification as a Compaq ASE requires passing Compaq and Compaq-approved operating system examinations. There is no education or experience requirement. Compaq provides extensive training and preparatory opportunities.

Examinations

For Associate ASE certification, candidates must pass three exams: the Compaq Systems Technologies Test; the Compaq Integration and Performance Test; and the Compaq Systems Management Test.

For ASE certification, candidates must meet all Associate requirements and earn certification in NetWare (Novell), UNIX, Microsoft Windows NT, or another recognized program.

Recertification

ASEs are provided continued product education; requirements depend on new and upgraded products.

CERTIFIED COMPUTING PROFESSIONAL (CCP®)

ASSOCIATE COMPUTING PROFESSIONAL (ACP®)

Sponsor

Institute for Certification of Computer
  Professionals (ICCP®)
2200 E. Devon Ave., Suite 268
Des Plaines, IL 60018
Phone: (708) 299-4227
Fax: (708) 299-4280
E-mail: 74040.3722@compuserve.com
WWW: http://poe.acc.virginia.edu/~afs/iccp.html

Program Data

The ICCP is a third-party independent certifying organization sponsored by the Association for Computing Machinery (ACM); Association for Systems Management (ASM); Association for Women in Computing (AWC); Black Data Processing Associates (BDPA); Business Technology Association (BTA); Canadian Information Processing Society (CIPS); Data Administration Management Association (DAMA); Data Processing Management Association (DPMA); Independent Computer Consultants Association (ICCA); Information Systems Consultants Association (ISCA); International Information Technology Company (IITC); International Society for Technology in Education (ISTE); Microcomputer Managers Association (MMA); National Systems Programmers Association (NaSPA); and the Network Professional Association (NPA).

Certifying body: Independent board
Year certification began: 1973
Number certified: 50,000+
Organization members: 500,000+ in sponsoring
  organizations
Approximate certification costs: $500

Program Description

The Certified Computing Professional (CCP) designation encompasses the three former ICCP designations: Certified Computer Programmer (CCP), Certified Data Processor (CDP), and Certified Systems Professional (CSP). The CCP designation recognizes skilled professionals working in all computer-related areas.

The Associate Computer Professional (ACP) credential is designed for entry-level computer professionals that are recent college and technical-school graduates or have limited work experience in the field. There are no association membership requirements. There are no prerequisites or qualifications to the ACP examination.

Education/Experience
There are no occupational or educational restrictions for pursuing ICCP certification. No association memberships are required. To qualify to sit for the CCP examination, a candidate must have four years of experience in the field. Up to two years may be substituted with a related degree or Associate Computer Professional (ACP) certification.

Examinations
CCP candidates must pass the ICCP core examination and either two specialty exams or one specialty and two language exams. ACP candidates must pass the core exam and one language exam.

The core examination covers human and organization framework; systems concepts; data and information; systems development; technology; financial management and analysis; management science; systems auditing; mathematics; and statistics.

The specialty exams are Business Information Systems; Communications; Data Resource Management; Management; Microcomputing and Networks; Office Information Systems; Procedural Programming; Software Engineering; Systems Development; Systems Programming; and Systems Security.

The language exams are: BASIC; C; C++; COBOL; Pascal; and RPG/400.

Recertification
CCP recertification is on a three-year cycle. CCPs may recertify through continuing education, passing ICCP specialty examinations, or reexamination.

CERTIFIED COMPUTER APPLICATIONS TRAINER (CCAT)

Sponsor
Association for Computer Applications Trainers (ACAT)
4938 Central Ave.
Charlotte, NC 28205
Phone: (800) 476-0881
E-mail: acat@sunbelt.net
WWW: http://webserve.hyper1.com/acat/

Program Data
Certifying body: Association
Year certification began: 1994
Organization members: 700

Program Description
The Certified Computer Applications Trainer (CCAT) designation recognizes skilled technical trainers who complete a three-day, comprehensive capstone course on training. The course emphasizes adult training theory and allows participants to be critiqued in an advanced setting. ACAT membership is required.

Education/Experience
While no defined experience is required, candidates must have in-class technology training experience to complete the CCAT capstone course.

Examinations
Candidates are critiqued and coached during the three-day session. Hands-on practice models are used throughout the course. New techniques for training computer systems are demonstrated and practiced. The session ends with a videotape and evaluation exercise.

Recertification
ACAT has a continuing education program. CCATs must maintain ACAT membership.

ELECTRONIC DOCUMENT AND PRINTING PROFESSIONAL (EDPP)

Sponsor
Xplor International
24238 Hawthorne Blvd.
Torrance, CA 90505
Phone: (800) ON-XPLOR
Fax: (310) 375-4240
E-mail: info@xplor.org
WWW: http://www.xplor.org/

Program Data
Certifying body: Association-sponsored independent board
Year certification began: 1990
Number certified: 100+
Organization members: 2000 corporate (7000 individuals)
Approximate certification costs: $35

Program Description

The Electronic Document and Printing Professional (EDPP) credential recognizes individuals responsible for using and managing electronic document and printing systems. Certification is based on a point system that includes the submission of work examples. Membership in Xplor International is not required. There is no examination. Xplor has an active ethics program.

Education/Experience

The candidate first submits a personal data form. Eligibility for the program is determined using this form for a point system. If the minimum point total is reached, the candidate then submits three work examples. Each work example must cover one identified area from the body of knowledge for Electronic Computer Application and Printing Systems Software Document Systems. These are the areas:

- Computer Hardware
- Document Design
- Document Distribution
- Management of the Electronic Document and Printing Function
- Printing and Imaging Technology

Statements describing the candidate's role, obstacles to completion, and equipment will accompany each work.

This is the point system:

- Total certification score: 1500, combined personal data form and work examples
- Point examples:
  - Personal Data Form, minimum of 670, maximum of 1150
  - Work examples, minimum of 350, maximum of 925
  - 100 points per year of professional experience
  - 75 points for a bachelor's degree
  - 10 points per Xplor meeting

Recertification

Certification must be renewed every five years and is based on a point system. Recertification requires 250 points. Lifetime certification is available to EDPPs at age 60 with 10 years of experience in electronic document systems.

IBM CERTIFICATION PROGRAM

Sponsor

IBM
The Professional Certification Program from IBM
11400 Burnet Road
Austin, TX 78758
Fax-on-demand: (800) IBM-4FAX
WWW: http://www.austin.ibm.com/pspinfo/
  profesnl.html

Program Data

Certifying body: Corporation

Program Description

IBM sponsors several product-related certifications. Certification is based on passing examinations. Preparatory courses and self-study materials are available. Certifications are offered in the following products/areas: AIX; CallPath; Client/Server; Database 2 Common Server; Local Area Network (LAN); VisualAge; OS/2 Warp; PC Servers; SystemView for AIX; and MQSeries.

Certified OS/2 Instructor and Certified LAN Server Instructor: Candidates must be certified as either an OS/2 or LAN Server engineer, show proof of instructor experience, and complete either a degree in education or an instructional skills course.

Examinations

All examinations are offered online by Sylvan Prometric.

Recertification

Recertification is required as product changes occur.

CERTIFIED DOCUMENT IMAGING ARCHITECT (CDIA)

Sponsor

Computing Technology Industry Association
  (CompTIA)
450 E. 22nd St., Suite 230
Lombard, IL 60148
Phone: (708) 268-1818
Fax: (708) 268-1384
WWW: http://www.comptia.org/

Program Data

The CDIA is supported by most major computer hardware vendors

Certifying body: Association
Year certification began: 1993
Number certified: 13,000
Organization members: 3000 companies
Additional programs: A+ Service Technician
  Certification (A+)
Approximate certification costs: $150 (members),
  $165 (nonmembers)

Program Description

The Certified Document Imaging Architect (CDIA) program certifies document-imaging/document-management technicians. This industry-wide certification is based on passing an examination; there are no experience or education requirements.

Examinations

The CDIA exam is based on extensive industry input. To become certified, candidates must pass a computer-based exam. The exam covers communications/networking; display; imaging business issues; input/capture; office computing; output; paper handling; pre-processing; records indexing; records management; records retrieval; and storage.

Recertification

None.

CERTIFIED IMAGING CONSULTANT (CIC)

CERTIFIED IMAGING MARKET SPECIALIST (CIMS)

CERTIFIED IMAGING SYSTEMS DEVELOPER (CISD)

CERTIFIED IMAGING SYSTEMS MANAGER (CISM)

Sponsor

Wang Laboratories, Inc.
M/S 01N-370
600 Technology Park Drive
Billerica, MA 01821-4130
Phone: (508) 967-1253
Fax: (508) 967-3993
E-mail: marty.cavanaugh@wang.com
WWW: http://www.wang.com

Program Data

Certifying body: Corporation
Year certification began: 1994
Approximate certification costs: $1000

Program Description

The Wang-sponsored certifications recognize imaging professionals completing coursework through the company's training program. Courses are taught world-wide by Wang instructors. There are no prerequisites.

Curriculum

The Certified Imaging Consultant (CIC) program is directed at systems integrators, value-added resellers, systems consultants, and programmers. Candidates must complete three core courses and complete one imaging project. Courses: a four-day imaging basics course, a four-day client/server imaging course, and a four-day image-enabling applications course.

The Certified Imaging Market Specialist (CIMS) program is directed at imaging sales, marketing, and configuration professionals. Candidates must complete two core seminars and complete one imaging proposal. Courses: a four-day imaging basics course and a one-day OPEN/image configuration course.

The Certified Imaging Systems Developer (CISD) program is designed for programmers and developers designing image-enabled applications. Candidates must complete three core courses, one elective course, and complete one imaging project. Core courses: a four-day imaging basics course, a four-day client/server imaging course, and a four-day image-enabling applications course.

The Certified Imaging Systems Manager (CISM) program is directed at imaging managers, project leaders, and lead designers responsible for implementing, designing, installing, and managing imaging systems. Candidates must complete three core courses, one elective course, and one imaging project. Core courses: a four-day imaging basics course, a four-day client/server imaging course, and a two-day imaging peripherals course.

Recertification

None.

CERTIFIED INFORMATION SYSTEMS AUDITOR (CISA®)

Sponsor

Information Systems Audit and Control
  Association (ISACA)
3701 Algonquin Road, Suite 1010
Rolling Meadows, IL 60008
Phone: (847) 253-1545
Fax: (847) 253-1443
E-mail: certification@isaca.org .
WWW: http://www.isaca.org/

Program Data

Certifying body: Association-sponsored
  independent board
Number certified: 12,000
Organization members: 13,500
Approximate certification costs: $250 (members),
  $325 (nonmembers)

Program Description

The Certified Information Systems Auditor (CISA)
designation recognizes professionals in information
systems auditing, security, and control. Certification
is based on passing an examination. ISACA membership is not required. ISACA maintains an active
ethics program.

Education/Experience

No experience is required to take the exam.
However, candidates need five years of professional experience prior to certification. One year of
experience will be credited for one year (maximum)
of information systems or auditing experience. Two
years of related university-instructor experience will
count as one year of experience. One year will be
credited for an associate's degree and two years
will be credited for a bachelor's degree.

Examinations

The CISA examination is based on job analyses
and is available in several languages. Sample
tests and an exam guide are available. The five-
hour, 250-question, multiple-choice test covers the
following:

- Information Systems Audit Standards and
  Practices and Information Systems Security
  and Control
- Practices
- Information Systems Organization and
  Management
- Information Systems Process

- Information Systems Integrity, Confidentiality,
  and Availability
- Information Systems Development,
  Acquisition, and Maintenance

Recertification

CISAs must recertify every three years by accumulating 120 hours of continuing education. At least
20 hours must be accumulated every year.

INTERNET/INTRANET CERTIFIED ENGINEER (I²CE)

Sponsor

Ascolta
2351 McGaw
Irvine, CA 92614
Phone: (714) 746-6109
Fax: (714) 852-8658
E-mail: training@ascolta.com
WWW: http://www.ascoltatraining.com/

Program Data

Ascolta is a subsidiary of Inacom Corporation.

Certifying body: Corporation
Year Certification began: 1996
Approximate certification costs: $3000

Program Description

The Internet/Intranet Certified Engineer (I²CE)
program has been developed to train and evaluate
information systems professionals managing internet and intranet systems. Certification is based on
completing coursework and passing an examination. There are no education or experience
requirements.

Curriculum

The Ascolta program is a two-phase course of
study. Phase one is a five-day, introductory course
covering basic internet engineering and design,
server operation, and current internet technology.

Phase two is a technical course covering one of
four specialities: Design, Security, Applications, or
Server. For certification, candidates must complete
one of the specialty courses.

Examinations

A certification exam is administered to candidates
completing phase two. The examination has two
parts: a written examination covering course content, and a hands-on lab requiring the candidate to
apply the course content to a real-world situation.

Recertification

None at this time. Candidates who successfully complete coursework and test in all four areas are awarded the Master I²CE designation.

LEARNING TREE PROFESSIONAL CERTIFICATION PROGRAMS

Sponsor

Learning Tree International
Reston Town Center
1805 Library St.
Reston, VA 22090
Phone: (800) 843-8733
WWW: http://www.learningtree.com

Program Data

The American Council on Education (ACE) recommends award of college credit for Learning Tree Certification Program courses.

Certifying body: Corporation
Approximate certification costs: Variable

Program Description

Learning Tree International offers product-independent, hands-on courses in many information systems-related fields. After taking a Learning Tree course, students may elect to take the associated examination at a designated testing center. There are no prerequisite, membership, or recertification requirements.

Contact Learning Tree International for individual certification requirements. The following certifications are available:

- C and C++ Programming Certified Professional
- Client/Server Systems Certified Professional
- Internet Certified Professional
- Internetworking Certified Professional
- Local Area Network Certified Professional
- NetWare Certified Professional
- Open Systems Certified Professional
- Oracle7 Application Development Certified Professional
- Oracle7 DBA Certified Professional
- PC Service and Support Certified Professional

- Software Development Certified Professional
- TCP/IP Certified Professional
- UNIX Programming Certified Professional
- UNIX Systems Certified Professional
- Wide Area Network Certified Professional
- Windows Application Development Certified Professional
- Windows NT Systems and Networks Certified Professional

CERTIFIED LOTUS PROFESSIONAL (CLP)

Sponsor

Lotus Development Corporation
400 Riverpark Drive
N. Reading, MA 01864
Phone: (617) 577-8500
E-mail: supportweb@lotus.com
WWW: http://www.lotus.com

Program Data

Lotus is a subsidiary of IBM Corporation.
Certifying body: Corporation

Program Description

The Certified Lotus Professional Program recognizes information systems professionals knowledgeable in Lotus product development, configuration, and maintenance. Certification is based on passing examinations. There are no education or experience requirements. Several training programs are available.

Candidates may be certified through examination in the following areas:

- Lotus Certified Notes Application Developer
- Lotus Certified Notes System Administrator
- Lotus Certified Notes Consultant
- Lotus Certified Notes Specialist
- Lotus Certified cc: Mail Specialist

Recertification

Recertification is required as products are upgraded.

MICROSOFT CERTIFIED PROFESSIONAL

Sponsor

Microsoft
One Microsoft Way
Redmond, WA 98052
Phone: (800) 688-0496
E-mail: moli_quest@msn.com.
WWW: http://www.microsoft.com

Program Data

Certifying body: Corporation

Program Description

The Microsoft Certified Professional program recognizes individuals with expertise in Microsoft products.

The Microsoft Certified Systems Engineer (MCSE) recognizes network professionals knowledgeable in planning, implementing, maintaining, and supporting multiple environments with the Microsoft Windows NT Server Microsoft BackOffice. Candidates must complete four operating exams and two elective exams.

The Microsoft Certified Solution Developer (MCSD) recognizes systems development professionals who create custom business solutions using Microsoft products. Candidates must complete two core technology exams and two elective exams.

The Microsoft Certified Product Specialist (MCPS) recognizes individuals demonstrating in-depth knowledge of one or more Microsoft products. Candidates must complete an operating system exam for certification. Additional exams are available to demonstrate specialized knowledge in specific applications with an emphasis on desktop support, systems engineering, or solution development.

The Microsoft Certified Trainer (MCT) recognizes instructional professionals qualified to deliver Microsoft Official Curriculum through Microsoft-authorized education sites. Candidates are certified on a class-by-class basis by examination.

NETSCAPE CERTIFIED INSTRUCTOR

Sponsor

Netscape Communications Corporation
501 E. Middlefield Road
Mountain View, CA 94043
Phone: (415) 937-3777
Fax: (415) 528-4124
E-mail: info@netscape.com
WWW: http://home.netscape.com

Program Data

Certifying body: Corporation
Year certification began: 1996
Approximate certification costs: $900 per course

Program Description

The Netscape Certified Instructor program prepares technical trainers to teach Netscape internet/intranet products. Certification is based on completing Netscape-sponsored courses. Candidates must be associated with Netscape Education Partners.

Education/Experience

Candidates must hold the Certified Technical Trainer (CTT) credential prior to completing Netscape coursework.

Curriculum

Instructors must complete the related course for authorization to teach a class. The Train-the-Trainer courses are in the following Netscape systems: Communications and Commerce Server (UNIX or Windows NT); Proxy Server; News Server; Mail Server (UNIX or Windows NT); IStore; Publishing System; Merchant System; and Community System.

Recertification

Recertification is required as products are upgraded.

CERTIFIED NETWORK EXPERT™ (CNX™)

Sponsor

Network General Corporation
4200 Bohannon Drive
Menlo Park, CA 94025
Phone: (800) CNX-EXAM
WWW: http://www.ngc.com/

Program Data

Certifying body: Corporation
Year certification began: 1995
Number certified: Not disclosed
Approximate certification costs: $250

Program Description

The Certified Network Expert™ (CNX™) program is a multi-protocol, multi-vendor certification for computer network maintenance technicians. Candidates may be tested in either Ethernet or token ring topologies.

Education/Experience

While there are no mandatory experience or education requirements, the CNX examination is geared towards network technicians with at least two years of troubleshooting experience using a network analyzer.

Examinations

The CNX examination is a computer-based, 60-question examination covering the following areas:

- Approximately 20 questions requiring interpretation of a network analyzer trace file printout. Questions may address IEEE 802 architecture; Open Systems Interconnect model; signal transmission; network technologies; and performance analysis.

- Approximately 40 questions on a specific topology (candidate-selected).

Recertification

None.

CERTIFIED NETWORK PROFESSIONAL™ (CNP)

Sponsor

Network Professional Association (NPA)
151 E. 1700 South
Provo, UT 84606
Phone: (800) 961-3926
E-mail: jmadsen@npa.org.
WWW: http://www.npa.org

Program Data

Certifying body: Association
Year certification began: 1995
Number certified: New program
Organization members: 12,000
Approximate certification costs: $200 (members), $300 (nonmembers)

Program Description

The Certified Network Professional (CNP) designation recognizes individuals highly skilled in the design, configuration, installation, management, and troubleshooting of computer networks. The CNP program is a multi-vendor certification independent of any particular vendor. The CNP maintains a strong and active ethics program.

Education/Experience

Candidates must earn two specialty certifications through at least two different vendors: CNX, Novell, Banyan, Lotus, Microsoft, Cicso, Compaq, or IBM. Candidates must have two years of professional network experience; up to one year may be substituted through formal education.

Examinations

The CNP examination covers networking core fundamentals: client operating systems; microcomputer hardware platforms; network operating system fundamentals; protocols; and topologies.

Recertification

CNPs must document at least four months of professional experience and earn 20 continuing-education and activity units annually.

NOVELL CERTIFICATION PROGRAMS

Sponsor

Novell, Inc.
122 East 1700 South
Provo, UT 84606
Phone: (800) 233-EDUC
WWW: http://education.novell.com/programs/crsprog.htm

Program Data

Novell education classes taken after January 2, 1995, are recommended for college credit by the American Council on Education (ACE). All Novell instructor-led courses are recognized by the International Association for Continuing Education and Training (IACET).

Certifying body: Corporation
Year certification began: 1989
Number certified: 60,000+

Program Description

The Novell certification programs ensure support technicians, engineers, and administrators are knowledgeable in the company's products. Certification is based on passing a series of examinations. Related courses are taught at Novell-authorized organizations. There are no prerequisites.

The Novell certifications are as follows:

Certified Novell Administrator (CNA)—A Certified Novell Administrator handles the day-to-day administration of an installed Novell networking product: NetWare® or GroupWare®. CNAs work in a variety of environments, including small businesses, work groups, and corporate information systems organizations. For certification, a candidate must pass one of the following exams: NetWare 2, 3, or 4 Administrator; GroupWise Administrator; InForms Administrator; or Soft-Solutions Administrator.

Certified Novell Engineer (CNE^SM)—CNEs specialize in Novell's networking products: NetWare® 3; NetWare® 4; or GroupWare®. CNEs may specialize in more than one area. For the CNE designation, a candidate must earn 19 credits through examination.

Enterprise Certified Novell Engineer (ECNE^SM)— The ECNE program stopped taking new applicants in 1995. ECNEs must earn an additional 19 credits and demonstrate proficiency in both 3.1x and 4.0. ECNE candidates must complete three or four (depending on track) advanced administration and system manager examinations and 10–12 credits of electives.

Master Certified Novell Engineer (Master CNE^SM)—The Master CNE is the highest certification awarded by Novell. Master CNEs specialize in at least one area: Network Management, Infrastructure and Advanced Access, or GroupWare Integration. Master CNEs must earn 10 credits through examination beyond their CNE.

Certified Novell Instructor (CNI^SM)—A CNI is authorized to teach Novell courses. CNIs specialize in one or more areas: Networking, Interoperability, or Development. Candidates must demonstrate in-depth technical knowledge through testing, have technical hands-on experience, and demonstrate strong presentation skills.

Recertification
Continuing education requirements depend on product enhancements, upgrades, and additions. All Novell-certified individuals must complete any company-directed requirements within six months to maintain certification.

CERTIFIED ORACLE7 DATABASE ADMINISTRATOR (DBA)

Sponsor
The Chauncey Group
P.O. Box 6541
Princeton, NJ 08541-6541
Phone: (800) 258-4914
Fax: (609) 951-6767
E-mail: dbatest@chauncey.com
WWW: http://www.chauncey.com/dbat001.htm

Program Data
Certifying body: Corporation
Approximate certification costs: $195

Program Description
The Oracle 7 Database Administrator certification program recognizes database professionals skilled in managing Oracle databases. Certification is based on passing an examination. There are no education/experience requirements.

Examinations
The 60-question, computer-delivered examination is based on an extensive job analysis. The examination was created with the assistance of Oracle Corporation and the International Oracle Users Group—Americas. The examination covers:

- Oracle architecture and options
- Security
- Data administration
- Backup and recovery
- Software maintenance and operation
- Resource management
- Tuning and troubleshooting

Recertification
Recertification is required as products are upgraded.

CERTIFIED POWERBUILDER DEVELOPER (CPD)

Sponsor
Powersoft
561 Virginia Road
Concord, MA 01742
Phone: (508) 287-1500
E-mail: education@powersoft.com
WWW: http://www.powersoft.com

Program Data

Powersoft is owned by Sybase, Inc.

Certifying body: Company
Number certified: 3000

Program Description

The Certified PowerBuilder Developer (CPD) program recognizes information systems professionals skilled in Powersoft's suite of tools for client/server applications development. Certification is based on passing examinations. Training courses are recommended. Candidates must have real-world PowerBuilder experience.

Examinations

CPD Associate certification is awarded upon passing the PowerBuilder Fundamentals and PowerBuilder Advanced Concepts examinations.

CPD certification is awarded to CPD Associates who pass the CPD Application exam. This exam is a hands-on test requiring candidates to apply PowerBuilder expertise by building a real-world application.

Recertification

Recertification is required as products are upgraded.

A+ SERVICE TECHNICIAN CERTIFICATION (A+)

Sponsor

Computing Technology Industry Association (CompTIA)
450 E. 22nd St., Suite 230
Lombard, IL 60148
Phone: (708) 268-1818
Fax: (708) 268-1384
WWW: http://www.comptia.org/

Program Data

The A+ program is supported by most major computer-hardware vendors.

Certifying body: Association
Year certification began: 1993
Number certified: 13,000
Organization members: 3000 companies
Additional programs: Certified Document Imaging Architect (CDIA)
Approximate certification costs: $150 (members), $165 (nonmembers)

Program Description

The A+ Service Technician Certification (A+) program certifies technicians in basic service skills. This industry-wide certification is based on passing an examination; there are no experience or education requirements.

Examinations

To become certified, candidates must pass two computer-delivered tests—one core exam and one specialty exam. The major vendors in the industry made extensive content contributions. Candidates certified between 1993 and 1995 were required only to pass the core examination. The computer-based exams include multiple-choice, situational, and identification questions.

The A+ Core Exam covers the following areas:

- Microcomputer configuration, including field-replaceable units; displays; printers; drives and other storage devices; operating systems; LANs; testing; and booting
- Installation and upgrades, including check-outs; peripherals; jumpers and switches; cables and connectors; system optimization; and upgrade procedures
- Diagnosis, including malfunctions, power supply, POST tests, environmental hazards, and troubleshooting
- Repair, including components, repair steps, replace or repair decisions, and repair completion
- Preventative maintenance, including cleaning, battery replacement, and common routines for printers
- Customer interaction, including customer service etiquette, service calls, warranties, and contracts
- Safety, including electrostatic discharge, common hazards, environmental concerns, and tools.

Microsoft™ Windows®/DOS® Specialty Exam tests candidate knowledge of configuring, installing, upgrading, diagnosing, and repairing personal computers running Windows and DOS.

Macintosh™ OS-based Computers Specialty Exam tests candidate knowledge of configuring, installing, upgrading, diagnosing, and repairing personal computers running the Apple Macintosh OS.

Recertification

None.

CERTIFIED SOFTWARE MANAGER (CSM)

Sponsor

Software Publishers Association (SPA)
P.O. Box 79237
Baltimore, MD 21279
Phone: (800) 388-7478
Fax: (202) 223-8756
E-mail: csminfo@spa.org
WWW: http://www.spa.org/

Program Data

Certifying body: Association
Year certification began: 1985
Number certified: 2400
Organization members: 1200 companies
Approximate certification costs: $100

Program Description

The Certified Software Manager (CSM) designation recognizes individuals with expertise in software compliance, software licensing, and software asset management. Certification is based on passing an examination. There are no education or experience requirements.

Examinations

The 100-question, multiple-choice examination is delivered by Sylvan Prometric. Candidates are encouraged to attend a one-day training course to prepare. The exam covers copyright law; disaster recovery; educating users about piracy and software management; freeware/public domain software; intellectual property; internet security; network security; self-audits; shareware; software licenses; software-piracy definition and liability; software management-plan development; software metering; spa anti-piracy actions; understanding license agreements; and viruses.

Recertification

None.

CERTIFIED SOLARIS ADMINISTRATOR (CSA)

Sponsor

Sun Microsystems, Inc.
2550 Garcia Ave.
Mountain View, CA 94043
WWW: http://www.sun.com

Program Data

Certifying body: Corporation

Program Description

The Certified Solaris Administrator (CSA) program recognizes information systems professionals skilled in managing client/server systems running Sun's Solaris (UNIX/AIX) operating system. Certification is based on passing exams. There are no education or experience requirements. Sun offers a wide range of training and preparatory options.

Examinations

Candidates must pass the two 90-minute CSA examinations covering Solaris fundamentals and Solaris administration.

Recertification

Recertification is required as products are upgraded.

SOLOMON PROFESSIONAL SKILLS CERTIFICATION

Sponsor

Solomon Software
200 E. Hardin St.
Findlay, OH 45840
Phone: (800) 879-2767
Fax: (419) 424-3400
E-mail: krisser@solomon.com
WWW: http://www.solomon.com

Program Data

Certifying body: Corporation

Program Description

The Solomon professional skills certification program recognizes accounting information systems professionals with expertise in Solomon software products. Certification is based on passing an examination for a particular skill set. There are no education or experience requirements. Training and preparatory classes are available. Candidates may be certified as any of the following:

- Solomon Certified Systems Engineer
- Solomon Certified Financial Specialist
- Solomon Certified Operations Specialist
- Solomon Certified Customization Developer
- Solomon Certified Application Developer

Recertification

Recertification is required as products are upgraded.

CERTIFIED SYBASE PROFESSIONAL®

Sponsor

Sybase, Inc.
6475 Christie Ave.
Emeryville, CA 94608
Phone: (800) 879-2273
WWW: http://www.sybase.com

Program Data

Certifying body: Corporation

Program Description

The Certified Sybase Professional program recognizes skilled information systems professionals with expertise in using Sybase database and open-client/open-server products. Certification is by examination. There are no education or experience requirements. Sybase offers a wide range of training and preparatory options. Individuals may be certified as any of the following:

- CSP Database Administrator
- CSP Performance and Tuning Specialist
- CSP Open Interfaces Developer

Recertification

Recertification is required as products are upgraded.

SCIENCE AND ENGINEERING
Environment

CERTIFIED PROFESSIONAL AGRONOMIST (CPAG)

CERTIFIED PROFESSIONAL CROP SCIENTIST/SPECIALIST (CPCS)

CERTIFIED PROFESSIONAL HORTICULTURALIST (CPH)

CERTIFIED PROFESSIONAL PLANT PATHOLOGIST (CPPP)

CERTIFIED PROFESSIONAL SOIL CLASSIFIER (CPSC)

CERTIFIED PROFESSIONAL SOIL SCIENTIST/SPECIALIST (CPSS)

CERTIFIED PROFESSIONAL IN WEED SCIENCE (CPWS)

Sponsor
ARCPACS
677 S. Segoe Road
Madison, WI 53711
Phone: (608) 273-8080
Fax: (608) 273-2021

Program Data
Certifying body: Association-sponsored independent board
Number certified: 6000
Additional programs: Certified Crop Advisor (CCA)

Program Description
ARCPACS certifies professionals in several different areas of agronomy, crops, and soils. Certification is based on education and experience. Candidates not meeting the experience requirements are awarded the appropriate Associate designation.

Education/Experience
Each designation requires candidates to have certain core and supportive college classes. Experience must be in an area related to the designation.

For all certifications but CPSC, candidates must meet one of the following options: bachelor's degree and five years of professional experience; master's degree and three years of professional experience; or a doctorate and one year of professional experience.

CPSC candidates must have a bachelor's degree or higher and five years of soil-surveying professional experience.

Recertification
Certification is renewed by earning six continuing-education units every three years.

CERTIFIED CROP ADVISOR (CCA)

Sponsor
ARCPACS
677 S. Segoe Road
Madison, WI 53711
Phone: (608) 273-8080
Fax: (608) 273-2021

Program Data
Certifying body: State association
Number certified: 800
Organization members: 12,500 (ASA)
Approximate certification costs: $75–$150

Program Description
The Certified Crop Advisor (CCA) designation recognizes individuals who advise farmers on crop management, and is administered by state organizations. Certification is based on passing a national and a state examination. ARCPACS acts as registrar and coordinator, and produces a national examination.

Education/Experience
Candidates must meet one of the following options: four years of professional experience; three years of professional experience and an associate's degree in agriculture; or two years of experience and a bachelor's degree in an agriculture-related field.

Examinations

The national examination is based on performance objectives prepared by Purdue University. The national examination covers soil fertility, soil and water management, pest management, and crop production.

Recertification

CCAs must recertify every two years by accumulating 60 hours of acceptable continuing education.

CERTIFIED ECOLOGIST

CERTIFIED SENIOR ECOLOGIST

CERTIFIED ASSOCIATE ECOLOGIST

Sponsor

Ecology Society of America (ESA)
2010 Massachusetts Ave. NW, Suite 400
Washington, DC 20036
Phone: (202) 833-8773
Fax: (202) 833-8775
E-mail: esahq@esa.org
WWW: http://www.sdsc.edu/1/SDSC/Research/
  Comp_Bio/ESA/ESA.htm

Program Data

Certifying body: Association-sponsored
  independent board
Year certification began: 1981
Number certified: 310
Organization members: 7000
Approximate certification costs: $95

Program Description

The Ecology Society of America's certification program recognizes experienced ecologists. Certification is based on a review of experience and education; there is no examination component. ESA membership is required. The ESA maintains an active ethics program.

Education/Experience

Ecologists are certified at one of three levels, depending on their experience and education. These are the certification levels and requirements:

- Certified Associate Ecologist—Bachelor's degree or higher, including 30 semester hours of biological science (including nine of

ecology) and 12 semester hours of physical and mathematical science. Candidates must have one year of post-degree experience that demonstrates technical competence.

- Certified Ecologist—Candidates must meet either of the following requirements: five years of experience demonstrating professional ecology work and a bachelor's degree or higher meeting the Associate educational requirements; or a master's degree in ecology and two years of experience.

- Certified Senior Ecologist—Candidate must meet one of the following requirements: 10 years of experience and the educational requirements for Ecologist certification; or a doctoral degree in ecology and five years of experience.

Examinations

None.

Recertification

All ESA certifications must be renewed every five years by demonstrating continued professional education.

DIPLOMATE ENVIRONMENTAL ENGINEER (DEE)

Sponsor

American Academy of Environmental Engineers
130 Holiday Court, Suite 100
Annapolis, MD 21401
Phone: (410) 266-3311
Fax: (410) 266-7653

Program Data

The Academy is a member of the Council of Engineering and Scientific Specialty Boards (CESB).

The Academy is sponsored by the Air and Waste Management Association (A&WMA); American Institute of Chemical Engineers (AICE); American Public Health Association (APHA); American Public Works Association (APWA); American Society for Engineering Education (ASEE); American Society of Civil Engineers (ASCE); American Society of Mechanical Engineers (ASME); American Water Works Association (AWWA); Association of Envi-

SCIENCE AND ENGINEERING
Environment

ronmental Engineering Professors (AEEP); National Society of Professional Engineers (NSPE); Solid Waste Association of North America (SWANA); and the Water Environment Federation (WEF).

Certifying body: Association-sponsored independent board
Year certification began: 1955
Number certified: 2512 (current)
Organization members: 500,000 (sponsoring organizations)

Program Description

The Diplomate Environmental Engineer (DEE) certification recognizes registered Professional Engineers (P.E.s) with specialized, in-depth knowledge and experience within environmental engineering. Certification is based on the candidate's experience, professional recommendations, and passing grade on the written and oral examinations in his or her specialty. The AAEE maintains an active ethics program.

Education/Experience

Diplomate candidates must have at least eight years of environmental engineering experience, with at least four years in responsible charge, controlling and supervising, or teaching within the field. Candidates must have a bachelor's degree and be registered to practice engineering. A master's degree may substitute for one year of experience, and a doctorate may substitute for three years of experience.

Examinations

The diplomate examinations have a written test and an oral examination/interview. Candidates with 15 years of experience, with 11 years in responsible charge, may be exempted from the written examination. A preparation guide is available from the Academy. Specialty certification exams are offered in Air Pollution Control; General Environmental Engineering; Hazardous Waste Management; Industrial Hygiene; Radiation Protection; Solid Waste Management; and Water Supply/Wastewater.

Recertification

DEEs must earn 40 hours of professional development hours every two years.

CERTIFIED ENVIRONMENTAL HEALTH TECHNICIAN (CEHT)

Sponsor

National Environmental Health Association (NEHA)
720 S. Colorado Blvd.
South Tower, 970
Denver, CO 90222
Phone: (303) 756-9090
Fax: (303) 691-9490

Program Data

Certifying body: Association
Year certification began: 1977
Organization members: 5700
Additional programs: Registered Environmental Health Specialist (REHS); Registered Hazardous Substance Professional (RHSP); Registered Hazardous Substance Specialist (RHSS); Registered Sanitarian (RS)
Approximate certification costs: $55 (members), $105 (nonmembers)

Program Description

The Certified Environmental Health Technician (CEHT) designation recognizes individuals who perform technical work under the direction of environmental scientists and other professionals such as health officers, sanitary engineers, and health physicians. Work in this field includes air pollution; community noise; food sanitation; housing hygiene; occupational health; radiation health; solid waste; vector control; and water and wastewater. Examination study materials are available.

Education/Experience

Candidates must meet one of the following criteria:

- Graduation from a recognized two-year environmental health program at a college, university, or community/technical college
- Graduation from a related, military technical school
- Two years of experience working in environmental health and a high school diploma. One year of related college or technical training may substitute for one year of experience.

Examinations

Candidates must pass a 100-question, multiple-choice test. The exam covers, at a two-year college level, the following areas:

- Air pollution
- Community noise
- Epidemiology
- Housing
- Milk and food
- Occupational health
- Radiation health
- Solid waste
- Vector control
- Water and wastewater

Recertification

Certificants must renew their certification every two years by accumulating 12 contact hours of continuing education.

REGISTERED ENVIRONMENTAL HEALTH SPECIALIST (REHS)

REGISTERED SANITARIAN (RS)

Sponsor

National Environmental Health Association (NEHA)
720 S. Colorado Blvd.
South Tower, 970
Denver, CO 90222
Phone: (303) 756-9090
Fax: (303) 691-9490

Program Data

Certifying body: Association
Organization members: 5700
Additional programs: Certified Environmental Health Technician (CEHT); Registered Hazardous Substance Professional (RHSP); Registered Hazardous Substance Specialist (RHSS)
Approximate certification costs: $100 (members), $160 (nonmembers)

Program Description

The Registered Environmental Health Specialist (REHS)/Registered Sanitarian (RS) (registrant's option) recognizes technically competent professionals in the public and environmental health fields. This program was recently redesigned on an extensive job/task analysis, nationwide sampling, and subject-matter-expert interface.

Education/Experience

Candidates need two years of experience with specific coursework. The experience requirement is waived for candidates holding a bachelor's degree in environmental health accredited by the National Environmental Health Science and Protection Accreditation Council (EHAC) or equivalent.

Examinations

The examination was created by the National Assessment Institute based on the job/task analyses and extensive field testing and validation. A comprehensive study guide is available. The multiple-choice exam covers the following areas:

- Air quality and noise
- Disaster sanitation
- Food protection
- Environmental health
- Hazardous materials
- Housing
- Institutions and licensed establishments
- Occupational safety and health
- Water and wastewater
- Radiation protection
- Solid and hazardous waste
- Statutes and regulations
- Swimming pools and recreational facilities
- Vectors, pests, and weeds
- Wastewater

Recertification

Registrants must renew their registration every two years by accumulating 24 contact hours of continuing education.

CERTIFIED ENVIRONMENTAL INSPECTOR (CEI)

Sponsor

Environmental Assessment Association (EAA)
8383 East Evans Road
Scottsdale, AZ 85260
Phone: (602) 483-8100
Fax: (602) 998-8022
E-mail: eaa@iami.org
WWW: http://www.iami.org/eaa.html

Program Data

Certifying body: Association
Year certification began: 1994
Approximate certification costs: $195

Program Description

The Certified Environmental Inspector (CEI) designation recognizes EAA members who have completed a one-day seminar on Phase I environmental inspections.

Education/Experience

Candidates must complete a one-day seminar on Phase I environmental inspections. There are no examination or experience requirements.

Recertification

None.

REGISTERED ENVIRONMENTAL MANAGER (REM)

Sponsor

National Registry of Environmental
   Professionals℠ (NREP℠)
P.O. Box 2068
Glenview, IL 60025
Phone: (708) 724-6631
Fax: (708) 724-4223

Government and industry professionals may locate professionals in the Official Registry of Environmental Professionals; contact NREP for more information.

Program Data

NREP credentials are endorsed by the Society of Environmental Management. The Resolution Trust Corporation, Department of Energy, U.S. Air Force, and U.S. Army recognize certain NREP certifications in bid proposals.

Certifying body: Independent board (professional
   registration)
Year registration began: 1988
Number certified: Not disclosed
Organization members: Nonmembership
Additional programs: Associate Environmental
   Professional (AEP); Associate Environmental
   Property Assessor (AEPA); Certified
   Environmental Auditor (CEA); Registered
   Environmental Laboratory Technologist
   (RECT); Registered Environmental Professional (REP); Registered Environmental
   Property Assessor (REPA); Registered
   Environmental Scientist (RES)
Approximate certification costs: $150

Program Description

The Registered Environmental Manager (REM) designation represents the highest registration level available through the National Registry of Environmental Professionals (NREP).

REP seeks to provide a consolidated, acknowledged recognition program for environmental practitioners. Three official advisory boards have responsibility for examination and career development, and are made up of representatives from leading universities, officials from U.S. government agencies, and major corporations. The NREP maintains documentation on all registrants, and will validate qualifications upon written request. NREP has an active ethics board with decertification powers.

Education/Experience

Candidates must meet the following requirements:

- Three years of professional experience in environmental engineering or environmentally related health, science, or management

- Bachelor's degree or higher in physical, biological, and health sciences; engineering; or other environmentally related discipline

Candidates without an appropriate degree or holding no degree may substitute three years of related experience for each year of an academic degree program.

Examinations

Examination questions are based on an academic review and written by academia and consultants. The NREP's Board of Environmental Educators, Board of Environmental Regulatory Officials, and Board of Industrial Environmental Managers provide guidance on test content. Refresher workshops are available through NREP-endorsed university programs and private training providers. NREP provides a list of recommended reading to applicants. Exams are open-book.

The four-hour, multiple-choice examination covers the following subjects:

- Project planning management
- Federal environmental regulations
- Treatment technologies for air, surface, process, and groundwater
- Noise and occupational health
- Emergency conditions—spills and injuries
- Public relations
- Hazardous materials chemistry and safety
- Global issues, ecosystems, and endangered species

Recertification

Registration must be renewed annually, and REMs must demonstrate continued professional education. NREP maintains records of CEUs and continuing professional training.

The recertification rate is 90%.

ASSOCIATE ENVIRONMENTAL PROFESSIONAL (AEP)

Sponsor

National Registry of Environmental
  Professionals℠ (NREP℠)
P.O. Box 2068
Glenview, IL 60025
Phone: (708) 724-6631
Fax: (708) 724-4223

Government and industry professionals may locate professionals in the Official Registry of Environmental Professionals; contact NREP for more information.

Program Data

NREP credentials are endorsed by the Society of Environmental Management. The Resolution Trust Corporation, Department of Energy, U.S. Air Force, and U.S. Army recognize certain NREP certifications in bid proposals.

Certifying body: Independent board (professional registration)
Year registration began: 1988
Number certified: Not disclosed
Organization members: Nonmembership
Additional programs: Associate Environmental Property Assessor (AEPA); Certified Environmental Auditor (CEA); Registered Environmental Laboratory Technologist (RECT); Registered Environmental Manager (REM); Registered Environmental Professional (REP); Registered Environmental Property Assessor (REPA); Registered Environmental Scientist (RES)
Approximate certification costs: $150

Program Description

The Associate Environmental Professional (AEP) designation is the entry-level registration program for the National Registry of Environmental Professionals (NREP). No experience is required if the educational requirement is met.

NREP seeks to provide a consolidated, acknowledged recognition program for environmental practitioners. Three official advisory boards have responsibility for examination and career development, and are made up of representatives from leading universities, officials from U.S. government agencies, and major corporations. The NREP maintains documentation on all registrants, and will validate qualifications upon written request. NREP has an active ethics board with decertification powers.

Education/Experience

Candidates must have completed at least two years of a bachelor's degree or higher in physical, biological, and health sciences; engineering; or other environmentally related discipline. Candidates without appropriate degree work may substitute three years of related experience for each year of an academic degree program.

Examinations

Examination questions are based on an academic review and written by academia and consultants. The NREP's Board of Environmental Educators, Board of Environmental Regulatory Officials, and Board of Industrial Environmental Managers provide guidance on test content. Refresher workshops are available through NREP-endorsed university programs and private training providers. NREP provides a list of recommended reading to applicants. Exams are open-book.

The four-hour, multiple-choice examination covers the following subjects:

- Project planning management
- Federal environmental regulations
- Treatment technologies for air, surface, process, and groundwater
- Noise and occupational health
- Emergency conditions—spills and injuries
- Public relations
- Hazardous materials chemistry and safety
- Global issues, ecosystems, and endangered species

Recertification

Registration must be renewed annually, and AEPs must demonstrate continued professional education or academic progress. NREP maintains records of CEUs and continuing professional training.

The recertification rate is 90%.

CERTIFIED ENVIRONMENTAL PROFESSIONAL (CEP)

Sponsor

National Association of Environmental
  Professionals (NAEP)
5165 MacArthur Blvd. NW
Washington, DC 20016
Phone: (202) 966-1500
Fax: (202) 966-1977
WWW: http://www.enfo.com/NAEP/

Program Data

Certifying body: Association-sponsored
  independent board
Number certified: 300+
Approximate certification costs: $200

Program Description

The Certified Environmental Professional (CEP) designation recognizes experienced environmental specialists. Administered by the Academy of Board Certified Environmental Professionals (ABCEP), certification is based on experience and passing an examination. NAEP membership is required. NAEP maintains an active ethics program.

Education/Experience

Candidates must have nine years of professional experience, with five years in responsible charge or responsible supervision. One year of professional experience will be credited for candidates holding a master's degree, and two years will be credited for doctoral degrees. In addition, candidates usually complete a personal interview.

Examinations

Candidates must answer two mandatory questions and three essay questions from their area of expertise. Candidates may be certified in environmental assessment; environmental documentation; environmental operations; environmental planning; or environmental research and education.

Recertification

None disclosed.

QUALIFIED ENVIRONMENTAL PROFESSIONAL (QEP)

Sponsor

Institute of Professional Environmental Practice
  (IPEP)
One Gateway Center, 3rd Floor
Phone: (412) 232-0901
Fax: (412) 232-0181
E-mail: swalsh@awma.org
WWW: http://www.awma.org/ipep.html

Program Data

The following associations are represented on the IPEP board of governors: Air and Waste Management Association (A&WMA); American Academy of Environmental Engineers (AAEE); National Association of Environmental Professionals (NAEP); Solid Waste Association of North America (SWANA); State and Territorial Air Pollution Program Administrators/Association of Local Air Pollution Control Officials (STAPPA/ALAPCO); and Water Environment Federation (WEF).

Certifying body: Independent board
Year certification began: 1993
Number certified: 400
Certification costs: $225

Program Description

The Qualified Environmental Professional (QEP) designation is a multi-disciplinary, international certification recognizing experienced environmental professionals. Certification is based on passing an examination. QEPs have demonstrated technical competence in environmental practice. IPEP maintains an active ethics program.

Education/Experience

Candidates must hold a bachelor's degree and have five to eight years of experience.

Examinations

The QEP examination is a six-hour, multiple-choice test. Candidates must pass both a general exam and a specialty exam. The general exam measures the candidate's scope of technical proficiency in general environmental science. The specialty exam measures technical proficiency in either air quality, water quality, waste management, or environmental science.

Through June 1996, senior environmental professionals could certify through a one-hour oral examination. Candidates for this option had to have either 20 years of experience or hold a technical bachelor's (or higher) degree and have 15 years of professional experience. The oral exam evaluated the candidate's experience and technical, policy, and ethical expertise.

Recertification

QEPs must recertify every five years through continuing education and professional activities.

REGISTERED ENVIRONMENTAL PROFESSIONAL (REP)

Sponsor

National Registry of Environmental Professionals^{SM} (NREP^{SM})
P.O. Box 2068
Glenview, IL 60025
Phone: (708) 724-6631
Fax: (708) 724-4223

Government and industry professionals may locate professionals in the Official Registry of Environmental Professionals; contact NREP for more information.

Program Data

NREP credentials are endorsed by the Society of Environmental Management. The Resolution Trust Corporation, Department of Energy, U.S. Air Force, and U.S. Army recognize certain NREP certifications in bid proposals.

Certifying body: Independent board (professional registration)
Year registration began: 1988
Number certified: Not disclosed
Organization members: Nonmembership
Additional programs: Associate Environmental Professional (AEP); Associate Environmental Property Assessor (AEPA); Certified Environmental Auditor (CEA); Registered Environmental Laboratory Technologist (RECT); Registered Environmental Manager (REM); Registered Environmental Property Assessor (REPA); Registered Environmental Scientist (RES)

Program Description

The Registered Environmental Professional (REP) designation is a special registration level recognizing experienced environmental practitioners with advanced education or other professional credentials. No examination is required.

The National Registry of Environmental Professionals (NREP) seeks to provide a consolidated, acknowledged recognition program for environmental practitioners. Three official advisory boards have responsibility for examination and career development, and are made up of representatives from leading universities, officials from U.S. government agencies, and major corporations. The NREP maintains documentation on all registrants, and will validate qualifications upon written request. NREP has an active ethics board with decertification powers.

Education/Experience

The REP designation is based on achieving professional recognition or advanced education. Candidates are eligible for the REP designation if one of the following criteria are met:

- Education
  - Graduate-level Environmental Specialty Certificate
  - Master's degree or doctorate from an accredited university in environmental health science or technology.
  - Law degree (J.D.) with environmental law specialization
- State Licensure
  - Professional Engineer (P.E.) with a specialty in Environmental Engineering
  - Licensed Environmental Manager
  - Registered Environmental Assessor
  - Register Professional Geologist/Hydrogeologist
- National Certification
  - American Academy of Environmental Engineers Diplomate
  - Certified Environmental Professional (CEP)
  - Certified Environmental Trainer (C.E.T.)
  - Certified Hazardous Materials Manager (CHMM)
  - Certified Health Physicist (CHP)
  - Certified Industrial Hygienist (CIH)
  - Certified Professional Geologist/Hydrogeologist
  - Certified Safety Professional (CSP)

Recertification

Registration must be renewed annually, and REPs must demonstrate continued professional education. NREP maintains records of CEUs and continuing professional training.

The recertification rate is 90%.

REGISTERED ENVIRONMENTAL SCIENTIST (RES)

Sponsor

National Registry of Environmental
  Professionals^{SM} (NREP^{SM})
P.O. Box 2068
Glenview, IL 60025
Phone: (708) 724-6631
Fax: (708) 724-4223

Government and industry professionals may locate professionals in the Official Registry of Environmental Professionals; contact NREP for more information.

Program Data

NREP credentials are endorsed by the Society of Environmental Management. The Resolution Trust Corporation, Department of Energy, U.S. Air Force, and U.S. Army recognize certain NREP certifications in bid proposals.

Certifying body: Independent board (professional registration)
Year registration began: 1988
Number certified: Not disclosed
Organization members: Nonmembership
Additional programs: Associate Environmental Professional (AEP); Associate Environmental Property Assessor (AEPA); Certified Environmental Auditor (CEA); Registered Environmental Laboratory Technologist (RECT); Registered Environmental Manager (REM); Registered Environmental Professional (REP); Registered Environmental Property Assessor (REPA)
Approximate certification costs: $90 (government employee: $50)

Program Description

The Registered Environmental Scientist (RES) designation recognizes professionals working in environmental sciences, including biology, chemistry, and health science.

The National Registry of Environmental Professionals (NREP) seeks to provide a consolidated, acknowledged recognition program for environmental practitioners. Three official advisory boards have responsibility for examination and career development, and are made up of representatives from leading universities, officials from U.S. government agencies, and major corporations. The NREP maintains documentation on all registrants, and will validate qualifications upon written request. NREP has an active ethics board with decertification powers.

Education/Experience

Candidates must meet the following requirements:

- Two years of professional experience working in a environmentally related scientist position

- Bachelor's degree or higher in environmental, physical, or biological and health sciences; or other environmentally related science discipline

Candidates without an appropriate degree or holding no degree may substitute three years of related experience for each year of an academic degree program.

Examinations

Examination questions are based on an academic review and written by academia and consultants. The NREP's Board of Environmental Educators, Board of Environmental Regulatory Officials, and Board of Industrial Environmental Managers provide guidance on test content. Refresher workshops are available through NREP-endorsed university programs and private training providers. NREP provides a list of recommended reading to applicants. Exams are open-book.

The four-hour, multiple-choice examination covers basic and environment-related knowledge of chemistry, physics, biology, zoology, earth sciences, and environmental health.

The pass rate for all NREP examinations is 70%.

Recertification

Registration must be renewed annually, and RESs must demonstrate continued professional education. NREP maintains records of CEUs and continuing professional training.

The recertification rate is 90%.

CERTIFIED ENVIRONMENTAL TRAINER® (CET)

ASSOCIATE ENVIRONMENTAL TRAINER (AET)

Sponsor

National Environmental Training Association (NETA)
2930 E. Camelback Road, Suite 185
Phoenix, AZ 85016
Phone: (602) 956-6099
Fax: (602) 956-6399
E-mail: netahqs@pipeline.com

Program Data

Certifying body: Association-sponsored independent board
Year certification began: 1986
Number certified: 850
Organization members: 1500
Approximate certification costs: $280 (members), $420 (nonmembers)

Program Description

The Certified Environmental Trainer® (CET) designation recognizes experienced trainers in environmental and health fields. The program is administered under contract to Arizona State University. Certification is based on meeting a strict application, recommendation, and examination process. The CET process measures the instructional competency and confirms the technical expertise of environmental safety and health training professionals. The CET board of examiners has decertification powers.

Education/Experience

Candidates must have a minimum of three years of technical experience and document providing 270 hours of training. Candidates must also provide professional references attesting to their instructional skills. Candidates with only one year of experience and 45 hours of training delivery may take the examinations and receive the Associate Environmental Trainer (AET) designation.

Examinations

Candidates must pass both a general exam and a specialty exam. All exams are based on task analysis and expert panel, with questions written by certificants. Study guides and workshops are available. The general examination in instructional technology measures the candidate's knowledge and application of adult education principles, including defining instructional objectives, performing needs assessments, sequencing instruction, selecting delivery methods and media, and evaluating training effectiveness.

Candidates, unless meeting the requirements for the technical examination waiver, must also take and pass at least one technical specialty examination:

- Air Quality
- Management and Transportation of Hazardous Materials and Waste
- Occupational Safety and Health
- Wastewater Treatment
- Water Treatment

Specialty examination waiver: Candidates holding acceptable state water or wastewater licensure/certification may request exemption from the corresponding CET specialty examination. Candidates holding the Certified Industrial Hygienist (CIH), Certified Safety Professional (CSP), or Occupational Safety and Health Technologist (OSHT) designation may request exemption from the Occupational Safety and Health specialty examination.

The pass rate is 75%.

Recertification

CETs must recertify every three years through experience and continuing education. CETs must receive six hours of instructional technology training and accumulate the 24 recertification points.

Point examples:

- 1 point per hour of training
- 1 point per six hours of training delivery (maximum of 12)
- 1 point per 10 accepted CET examination questions

The recertification rate is 70%.

CERTIFIED HAZARDOUS MATERIALS EXECUTIVE (WSO-CHME)

CERTIFIED HAZARDOUS MATERIALS SUPERVISOR (WSO-CHMS)

CERTIFIED HAZARDOUS MATERIALS TECHNICIAN (WSO-CHMT I/II)

Sponsor

World Safety Organization (WSO)
WSO World Management Center
305 E. Market St.
P.O. Box 518
Warrensburg, MO 64093
Phone: (816) 747-3132

Program Data

WSO is in consultive status, Category II, with the United Nations Economic and Social Council.

Certifying body: Association

Additional certifications: Certified Safety and Security Director (WSO-CSSD); Certified Safety Executive (WSO-CSE); Certified Safety Manager (WSO-CSM); Certified Safety Specialist (WSO-CSS); Certified Safety Technician (WSO-CST)

Program Description

The Certified Hazardous Materials Executive (WSO-CHME) designation recognizes senior professionals responsible for the design and implementation of hazardous materials programs and professionals in charge of emergency response programs.

The Certified Hazardous Materials Supervisor (WSO-CHMS) designation recognizes professionals responsible for hazardous materials storage and handling and supervisors of multiple emergency-response teams. Membership in WSO is required.

The Certified Hazardous Materials Technician Level I and Level II (WSO-CHMT I/II) designation recognizes hazardous materials workers and first responders.

Membership in WSO is required.

Education/Experience

CHME candidates must be WSO-CHMS or equivalent and complete one year in response or operations program management. Candidates must complete 100–150 hours of advanced training.

WSO-CHMS candidates must be WSO-CHMT II or equivalent and complete one year in a response or operations program. Candidates must complete 40–60 hours of advanced training.

WSO-CHMT candidates for Level I must complete 30–40 hours of training in basic hazardous materials recognition, identification, classification, and safety considerations, incident response, and control. Candidates must complete six months of field work. Candidates for Level II must have completed all Level I requirements, a six-month internship, and 140–150 hours of training in: chemistry; toxicology; operations and incident management procedures; control/containment and handling methods; containers; agricultural and pest control chemicals; protection and decontamination; and characteristics and detection of combustible, explosive, flammable, and toxic materials.

Examinations

All exams include a 100-word essay on the candidate's professional expertise or contributions. All exams are three-hour, open-book, multiple-choice tests. They cover the following areas:

- WSO-CHME—hazardous materials regulations; storage/handling and incidents requirements; procedures development; emergency response programs; safety programs; evaluating and purchasing protection equipment; cleanup planning and response; and local, state, national, and international emergency support services

- WSO-CHMS—hazardous materials regulations; operations supervision; program/procedure evaluation; purchasing; recording and documentation; safety department organization and personnel; safety management; and incident planning, command, resources, and reports

- WSO-CHMT I/II—Each level examination reflects the training requirements content.

The WSO examinations average a first-attempt pass rate of 50%.

Recertification

WSO certifications must be renewed every three years. Renewal is based on accumulating 30 CEUs.

REGISTERED HAZARDOUS SUBSTANCE PROFESSIONAL (RHSP)

Sponsor

National Environmental Health Association (NEHA)
720 S. Colorado Blvd.
South Tower, 970
Denver, CO 90222
Phone: (303) 756-9090
Fax: (303) 691-9490

Program Data

Certifying body: Association
Year certification began: 1987
Organization members: 5700
Additional programs: Certified Environmental Health Technician (CEHT); Registered Environmental Health Specialist (REHS); Registered Hazardous Substance Specialist (RHSS); Registered Sanitarian (RS)
Approximate certification costs: $135 (members), $210 (nonmembers)

Program Description

The Registered Hazardous Substance Professional (RHSS) designation recognizes technically qualified personnel working in hazardous-waste or toxic-substance control. Applicants with limited work history but who meet the educational requirements and pass the registration examination may receive an RHSP in Training (RHSP-I.T.) designation until they gain the required experience. Study materials for the examination are available.

Education/Experience

Candidates need two and one-half to five years of experience, depending on formal education.

Examinations

The 240-question, multiple-choice registration examination covers the following principles and practices of hazardous-waste and toxic-substance management:

- Federal regulations
- Public/Industry participation
- Risk assessment/Risk management
- Sampling/Monitoring
- Toxicology
- Treatment/Disposal

Recertification

Registrants must renew their registration every two years by accumulating 24 contact hours of continuing education.

REGISTERED HAZARDOUS SUBSTANCE SPECIALIST (RHSS)

Sponsor

National Environmental Health Association (NEHA)
720 S. Colorado Blvd.
South Tower, 970
Denver, CO 90222
Phone: (303) 756-9090
Fax: (303) 691-9490

Program Data

Certifying body: Association
Year certification began: 1995
Organization members: 5700
Additional programs: Certified Environmental Health Technician (CEHT); Registered Environmental Health Specialist (REHS); Registered Hazardous Substance Professional (RHSP); Registered Sanitarian (RS)
Approximate certification costs: $95 (members), $155 (nonmembers)

Program Description

The Registered Hazardous Substance Specialist (RHSS) designation recognizes individuals who perform technical work under the direction of environmental scientists and other professionals such as health officers, sanitary engineers, and health physicians. Study materials for the examination are available.

Education/Experience

Candidates must meet one of the following criteria:

- Graduation from a two-year program on hazardous materials or waste management

- Two years of experience in hazardous materials or waste management and a high school diploma

Examinations

The 200-question, multiple-choice examination covers:

- Disposal
- Federal laws and regulations
- Handling, transportation, and storage
- Hazardous waste
- Permitting and record-keeping
- Personal protection
- Sampling and analysis
- Waste reduction and recycling
- Waste treatment technology

Recertification

Registrants must renew their registration every two years by accumulating 24 contact hours of continuing education.

CERTIFIED PROFESSIONAL HYDROLOGIST

CERTIFIED PROFESSIONAL HYDROGEOLOGIST

Sponsor

American Institute of Hydrology (AIH)
3416 University Ave. SE
Minneapolis, MN 55414
Phone: (612) 379-1030
Fax: (612) 379-0169

Program Data

Certifying body: Association
Number certified: 1000+
Organization members: 1100+ individual and organizational members

Program Description

The Professional Hydrologist and Professional Hydrogeologist certifications are membership categories in AIH for professionals in design, water resources management, or land use planning. The certification may be as a Professional Hydrologist, Professional Hydrologist—Ground Water, or Professional Hydrogeologist. Certification is based on passing an examination.

Education/Experience

To sit for the examination, a candidate must have graduated with a major in hydrology, hydrogeology, engineering, or physical or natural sciences, and meet one of the following minimum requirements: eight years of experience and a bachelor's degree; six years of experience and a master's degree; or four years of experience and a doctorate. In addition, candidates must have professional publication credit in the field.

Examinations

The two-part certification examination is designed to test both basic knowledge and application. The first part is a 100-question, multiple-choice and short answer test covering hydrology and/or hydrogeology and the field's underlying basic science and engineering. The second part is an eight-hour open-book test. Professional Hydrologist candidates are tested on surface water. Hydrologist—Ground Water and Hydrogeologist candidates are tested on ground water. The second part asks the candidate to solve a hypothetical situation. The pass rate is approximately 85%.

Recertification

Continued work and professional involvement or continuing education is required to maintain certification.

CERTIFIED INDUSTRIAL HYGIENIST (CIH)
INDUSTRIAL HYGIENIST IN TRAINING (IHIT)

Sponsor

American Board of Industrial Hygiene® (ABIH)
4600 W. Saginaw, Suite 101
Lansing, MI 48917
Phone: (517) 321-2638

Program Data

The CIH/IHIT programs are endorsed by the American Industrial Hygiene Association (AIHA) and the American Conference of Governmental Industrial Hygienists (ACGIH).

Certifying body: Independent certification board
Year certification began: 1963
Organization members: Nonmembership. Diplomates are encouraged to join the American Academy of Industrial Hygiene (AAIH).
Approximate certification costs: $75

Program Description

The Certified Industrial Hygienist (CIH) designation recognizes skilled professionals involved in anticipating, recognizing, evaluating, and negating environmental factors and stresses affecting people in the workplace. The ABIH certifies industrial hygienists in two areas: Comprehensive Practice and Chemical Practice. The certification category depends on the candidate's experience and scope of practice. In addition, the ABIH has begun subspecialty examinations. The first offering, started in 1995, is in Indoor Environmental Quality.

Candidates with limited experience but meeting all other CIH requirements are eligible for the Industrial Hygienist in Training (IHIT) designation upon passing the CIH core examination.

Education/Experience

Candidates must meet the following requirements:

- Bachelor's degree in an applicable science field or supplementary coursework
- Five years of applicable experience/practice (one year for the core examination only and IHIT designation)
- Current full-time practice and two professional references

Examinations

The CIH designation requires passing two examinations: the CIH core examination and either the Comprehensive Practice or Chemical Practice examination. All exams are multiple-choice in format and take three and one-half hours to complete. Bibliographies and exam preparatory materials are available. Many local associations offer workshops and classes.

The Core and Comprehensive examinations cover health stress recognition; health stress evaluation; health stress control; program management; and ethics. The Chemical Practice examination concentrates on chemical stress factors.

Recertification

CIHs must recertify every six years and maintain practice in the field. IHIT designations may be held up to 10 years.

CERTIFIED IRRIGATION CONTRACTOR (CIC)
CERTIFIED IRRIGATION DESIGNER (CID)
CERTIFIED IRRIGATION MANAGER (CIM)
CERTIFIED LANDSCAPE IRRIGATION AUDITOR (CLIA)

Sponsor

The Irrigation Association (IA)
8260 Willow Oaks Corporate Drive, Suite 120
Fairfax, VA 22031
Phone: (703) 573-3551
Fax: (703) 573-1913
WWW: http://www.igin.com/ia.html

Program Data

Certifying body: Association

Program Description

The Irrigation Association offers several certifications within the irrigation field. Certifications are based on passing examinations. IA membership is not required.

The Certified Irrigation Contractor (CIC) designation recognizes irrigation professionals who install and maintain irrigation systems.

The Certified Irrigation Designer (CID) designation recognizes irrigation professionals who prepare designs, evaluate sites and requirements, select equipment, and verify installation and construction.

The Certified Irrigation Manager (CIM) designation recognizes irrigation professionals who manage and maintain irrigation systems.

The Certified Landscape Irrigation Auditor (CLIA) designation recognizes professionals trained to complete irrigation audits.

Education/Experience

Candidates must have three years of irrigation-related experience. Professional and academic courses may substitute for one year of experience.

Examinations

The CIC designation requires passing two exams. The first examination is the General Examination, which is a three-hour, 150-question, multiple-choice test that covers hydraulics; irrigation scheduling; pumps; electricity; terminology; and the relationships between plants, soils, and water. Once the General Examination is passed, the candidate must pass a Specialty Contractor examination.

The CID designation requires passing the general exam, the General Designer Examination, and a specialty examination.

The CIM designation requires passing the general exam and completing an assigned paper, a presentation at two seminars, or five audits.

The CLIA examination requires completing a training course and a multiple-choice exam covering audit terms, irrigation scheduling, data collection, and site inspection.

Recertification

None.

CERTIFIED LANDFILL MANAGER

CERTIFIED LANDFILL INSPECTOR

CERTIFIED COLLECTION MANAGER

CERTIFIED MUNICIPAL SOLID WASTE (MSW) MANAGER I

CERTIFIED RECYCLING MANAGER

CERTIFIED TRANSFER STATION MANAGER

Sponsor

Solid Waste Management Association (SWANA)
P.O. Box 7219
Silver Spring, MD 20907
Phone: (301) 585-2898
Fax: (301) 589-7086
WWW: http://www.swana.org

Program Data

Certifying body: Association
Number certified: 1800
Organization members: 6000
Approximate certification costs: Varies

Program Description

The SWANA certification programs acknowledge eligible professionals who have completed a SWANA training course and passed a certification examination.

Educational/Experience

Candidates must work in a comparable position.

Curriculum

The curriculum consists of the following:

- Certified Landfill Manager/Certified Landfill Inspector—The four-day Manager of Landfill Operations course, which covers the role of sanitary landfills in integrated municipal-solid-waste management; basics of site selection; complying with design requirements; waste acceptance and screening; leachate; landfill gas and settlement; control processes for gas and leachate; operational techniques; compliance and inspection; closure and long-term care; landfill economics; state/provincial regulations; landfill safety; and training on-site personnel. A field exercise is included.

- Certified Collection Manager—The three-day Collection Management course, which covers developing a collection strategy; planning; systems design and equipment; residential collections; organization and management; private service providers; health and safety; case studies; and routing.

- Certified Municipal Solid Waste (MSW) Manager I—The three-day Principles of Managing IMSWM Systems course, which covers legal issues and policies; planning; management reviews; management theory; organizational structure and planning; human resources; creativity and innovation; customer service and quality; ethics; the public sector; public consent and press relations; finance; and case method and analysis.

- Certified Recycling Manager—The three-day Solid Waste Recycling course, which includes municipal-solid-waste recycling; recycling as part of integrated municipal-solid-waste management; source reduction/waste prevention; planning for maximum recycling potential; marketing; collection alternatives; processing alternatives; public education; "buy recycled" programs; revenues; costs, financing, and ownership/operation options; recycling program evaluation; yard waste management; and commercial recycling reviews.

- Certified Transfer Station Manager—The two-day Transfer Station course, which covers system planning, station design, station operation, and station maintenance.

Examinations
The three-hour certification examinations cover the material presented in the training courses. Questions are multiple-choice and problem-solving. The pass rate is 83%.

Recertification
SWANA certification must be renewed every three years through demonstrating 30 hours of acceptable professional training.

CERTIFIED PROFESSIONAL IN SOIL EROSION AND SEDIMENT CONTROL (CPESC)

Sponsor
Soil and Water Conservation Society (SWCS)
CPESC Program—Administrative Office
7515 N.E. Ankeny Road
Ankeny, IA 50021
Phone: (800) THE-SOIL
Fax: (515) 289-1227
E-mail: SWCS@netins.net
WWW: http://www.netins.net/showcase/swcs/.index.html

Program Data
The CPESC program is sponsored by the Soil and Water Conservation Society (SWCS) and co-sponsored by the International Erosion Control Association (IECA).

Certifying body: Association
Year certification began: 1981
Number certified: 700+
Ethics board: Yes
Approximate certification costs: $75 (members), $100 (nonmembers)

Program Description
The Certified Professional in Soil Erosion and Sediment Control (CPESC) designation recognizes individuals in soil management with specific education, training, and expertise in erosion control. Certification is based on passing an examination and work experience. Membership in SWSC or IECA is not required. The SWCS maintains an active ethics board.

Education/Experience
To sit for the examination, candidates must meet one of the following requirements:

- Ten years of professional experience
- Six years of professional experience with a bachelor's degree in geology, soil science, natural resource management, or agricultural, civil, or environmental engineering
- Four years of professional experience with a master's degree in geology, soil science, natural resource management, or agricultural, civil, or environmental engineering
- Two years of professional experience with a doctorate in geology, soil science, natural resource management, or agricultural, civil, or environmental engineering

Examinations

The CPESC examination is based on task analysis, curriculum content, and expert input. The pass rate is 95%. Preparatory classes and workshops are available. The examination may have essay and objective components. The examination includes the principles, practices, and techniques of soil erosion and sediment control as well as laws and regulations.

Recertification

CPESCs must earn six continuing-education units every three years.

The recertification rate is 98%.

Science and Engineering
Technician/Technology

BROADBAND INSTALLER CERTIFICATION

Sponsor

Society of Cable Telecommunications Engineers
(SCTE)
669 Exton Commons
Exton, PA 19341
Phone: (610) 363-6888
WWW: http://www.cable-online.com/
sctehome.htm

Program Data

Certifying body: Association
Additional certifications: Broadband
Communications Engineer (BCE);
Broadband Communications Technician (BCT)

Program Description
The Broadband Installer Certification program
ensures entry-level competence for cable television
installers. Training and examinations take place at
the chapter or local-group level. Membership in
SCTE is required. Candidates complete classroom
and hands-on training in cable installation.

Examinations
The certification examination comprises a 50-question, closed-book examination and practical examinations in installation and signal-level meter
reading.

Recertification
Broadband installers must recertify every three
years.

CERTIFIED CONSTRUCTION HEALTH AND SAFETY TECHNICIAN (CHST)

Sponsor

ABIH/BCSP Joint Committee
208 Burwash Ave.
Savoy, IL 61874
Phone: (217) 359-2686
Fax: (217) 359-0055

Program Data

Cosponsored by the American Board of Industrial
Hygiene (ABIH) and the Board of Certified Safety
Professionals (BCSP).

Certifying body: Association-sponsored
independent board
Year certification began: 1994
Number certified: New program
Organization members: Nonmembership
Additional programs: Certified Occupational
Health and Safety Technologist (COHST);
Certified Safety Trained Supervisor—
Construction (STS-Construction)
Approximate certification costs: $165

Program Description
The Certified Construction Health and Safety Technician (CHST) designation recognizes specialists
managing safety in construction work. Developed
at the request of the construction-safety community, CHSTs conduct safety inspections; maintain
safety, accident, and injury records; plan and conduct safety training; and coordinate safety across
contractor organizations on sizeable construction-project sites. Certification is based on passing an
examination.

Education/Experience
Candidates must have three years of construction
experience, with at least two years as a first-line
supervisor or manager with at least 35% of job
duties in safety and health. Candidates must also
have a high school diploma and meet one of the
following educational requirements:

- Position as authorized Occupational Safety
  and Health Administration (OSHA) instructor
- Forty hours of training in construction safety
  and health
- Nine semester hours of college coursework
  in safety and health

Additional academic training may substitute for part
of the work experience requirements.

Examinations
The seven-hour, 200-question, multiple-choice examination covers eight job tasks: inspection; general safety training and safety orientation; safety
and health record-keeping; hazard communication

compliance; safety analysis and planning; accident investigations; program management and administration; and OSHA and other inspections.

Recertification
Recertification is currently being considered.

CERTIFIED CONTROL SYSTEMS TECHNICIAN (CCST)

Sponsor
Instrument Society of America (ISA)
P.O. Box 12277
Research Triangle Park, NC 27709
Phone: (919) 990-9417
Fax: (919) 832-0237
E-mail: fgregory@isa.org,
WWW: http://www.isa.org/

Program Data
Certifying body: Association
Year certification began: 1995
Organization members: 49,000
Additional certifications: Certified Specialist in Analytical Technology (CSAT)
Approximate certification costs: $160 (members), $210 (nonmembers)

Program Description
The Certified Control Systems Technician (CCST) designation recognizes individuals experienced in calibrating, loop checking, troubleshooting, and repairing/replacing pneumatic, mechanical, and electronic instrumentation. Certification is through a series of examinations. There are no membership requirements. ISA has an active ethics program.

Education/Experience
A CCST is tested and certified at three different levels. The combined education, training, and experience requirements are five years for Level I, seven years for Level II, and 13 years for Level III.

Examinations
The CCST exams are based on a comprehensive job analysis. The eight CCST performance domains are calibration; documentation; loop checking; maintenance/repair; project organization/administration; start-up; troubleshooting; and using microprocessor-based instruments and controllers.

Both the Level I and Level III exams are four-hour, 175-question, multiple-choice tests covering the eight performance domains. The Level II exam consists of eight simulated practical problems, one for each domain.

Recertification
Renewal is required every three years through work experience and continuing education.

CERTIFIED ELECTRON MICROSCOPY TECHNOLOGIST (CEMT)

Sponsor
Microscopy Society of America (MSA)
4 Barlows Landing Road, Suite 8
Pocasset, MA 02559
Phone: (800) 538-3672
Fax: 508-563-1211
E-mail: BusinessOffice@MSA.Microscopy.Com
WWW: http://www.msa.microscopy.com

Program Data
Certifying body: Professional society
Organization members: 5000+

Program Description
The MSA certification program recognizes skilled electron-microscope technologists in the biological sciences. MSA membership is required. Certification is based on a knowledge examination and a practical examination.

Education/Experience
Candidates must meet one of the following requirements:

- Two years of college with classes in transmission electron microscopy (TEM), chemistry, physics, biology, and mathematics
- One year of full-time biological TEM experience and one year of college with classes in chemistry and physics
- Two years of full-time biological TEM experience and a high school diploma
- Three years of full-time biological TEM experience

Examinations
The two certification examinations measure both the candidate's knowledge and practical skills. The three-hour, objective-question, written examination

includes instrumentation; tissue processing; sectioning and staining; procedures and techniques; chemistry and microbiology; math; and safety. The practical examination requires the candidate to prepare blocks, sections, and micrographs from three different tissues.

Recertification
Certified technologists must recertify every eight years by maintaining MSA membership and documenting continued work in the field.

CERTIFIED ELECTROPLATER-FINISHER (CEF)

ELECTRONICS SPECIALIST, CERTIFIED (ESC)

Sponsor
American Electroplaters and Surface Finishers Society (AESF)
12644 Research Parkway
Orlando, FL 32826
Phone: (407) 281-6441
Fax: (407) 281-6446
E-mail: 72420.2001@compuserve.com
WWW: http://www.finishing.com/AESF/index.html

Program Data
Certifying body: Association
Organization members: 7500+

Program Description
The Certified Elecroplater-Finisher (CEF) and Electronics Specialist, Certified (ESC) designations recognize individuals who pass voluntary certification examinations following AESF educational course completion.

Examinations
The CEF designation examination follows the training course in Electroplating and Surface Finishing, a four-day course in surface-finishing technology and processes.

The ESC designation examination follows the Electroplating and Surface Finishing for Electronic Applications, a four-day course focusing on surface finishing in electronic manufacturing.

Individuals who successfully pass both examinations are awarded the Certified Electroplater Finisher—Specialist in Electronics (CEF-SE) designation.

Recertification
None.

CERTIFIED ELECTRONICS TECHNICIAN (CET)

Sponsor
Electronics Technicians Association, International (ETA)
602 N. Jackson St.
Greencastle, IN 46135
Phone: (317) 653-8262

Program Data
Certifying body: Association
Year certification began: 1966
Number certified: 30,000 (all certifications)
Organization members: 1700
Additional programs: Certified Customer Service Specialist (CSS); Certified Satellite Installer (CSI)
Approximate certification costs: $30 (Associate), $40 (Journeyman), $65 (Senior), $90 (Master)

Program Description
The Certified Electronics Technician (CET) program recognizes experienced technicians at several experience and knowledge levels. There are no membership or education requirements. Certification is based on passing examinations. The CET program consists of four levels:

The Associate level (entry-level)—recognizes technicians with less than four years of experience and education. This level requires passing a basic electronics technology examination.

The Journeyman (CET) level—the first certification level, requiring four years of combined experience and education. If not registered at the Associate level, candidates first take the basic electronics examination. The journeyman examinations are in specialty areas; candidates select one or more areas. Currently, these are the specialties:
- Consumer electronics
- Video distribution
- Wireless communications
- Telecommunications
- Industrial
- Computer

- Biomedical
- Avionics
- Radar

The Senior (CETsr) level—recognizes technicians with eight years of combined education and experience. Certification at this level requires the candidate to score 85% (as opposed to 75%) on the CET specialty examination. If not taken previously, the Associate exam must also be passed.

The Master (CETma) level—recognizes technicians with eight years of experience who have passed at least six examinations.

Examinations

Examinations include questions regarding electrical safety and safe servicing procedures (for example, static damage). The current pass rate is 30%.

The CET Associate examination is an 87-question test on basic electronics, circuits and components, test equipment, and electrical theory.

The Journeyman option section comprises 35 questions within the selected specialty.

Recertification

Recertification is under development.

CERTIFIED ENGINEERING TECHNICIAN (CET)

Sponsor

National Institute for Certification in Engineering
 Technologies (NICET)
1420 King St.
Alexandria, VA 22314
Phone: (703) 684-2835

Program Data

NICET is sponsored by the National Society of Professional Engineers (NSPE).

Certifying body: Independent board
Additional certifications: Certified Engineering
 Technologist (CT)
Number certified: 81,000+

Program Description

The Certified Engineering Technician (CET) program is a comprehensive certification program recognizing several certification levels in many technical areas. Certification is based on passing examinations and verified work experience. There are currently two separate certification routes: general knowledge certification and job task competence.

General Knowledge Certification

The general knowledge programs offer broad-based certifications. Fields covered by these programs are being converted to the second certification route, job task competence. Certification is based on passing a two-part examination and work experience. While certification is divided into four levels, candidates take the same examination for all levels.

Level I—a passing grade on Part A of the examination

Levels II—a passing grade on both parts

Level III—a passing grade on both parts, and five years of experience

Level IV—a passing grade on both parts, and 15 years of experience

Certification is currently offered in these areas:

- Architectural/Building Construction
- Civil Engineering
- Electrical/Electronics Engineering
- Electrical Power Engineering
- Industrial Engineering
- Mechanical Engineering
- Telecommunications Engineering
- Electrical Testing Engineering (The exam for this area has a different Part A—tests electricity instead of physical science.)

Job Task Competence Certification

The primary certification route is through the program on job task competency. This program certifies technicians in specific fields and subfields. Each field has specific examinations in core work elements, specialized work elements, and technician-common elements. Within these fields, technician skill (measured by passing examinations) and experience (validated by the supervisor) are identified by levels, with Level IV the highest.

These are the certification levels and experience requirements:

Level I (Technician Trainee/TT)—Entry-level

Level II (Associate Engineering Technician/AET)—Two years of experience

Level III (Engineering Technician/ET)—Five years of experience

Level IV (Senior Engineering Technician)—10 years of experience

For certification, candidates must meet the examination requirements for the lower levels, even if they meet the experience requirements of a higher level.

The programs on job task competency are as follows:

- Building Construction
  - Code and Specification Compliance
  - Water and Wastewater Plants
- Computer Engineering Technology
- Construction Materials Testing
  - Asphalt
  - Concrete
  - Soils
- Electric Power Engineering Technology Substation
- Engineering Model Technology Piping
- Fire Protection Engineering Technology
  - Automatic Sprinkler System Layout
  - Fire Alarm Systems
  - Inspection of Fire Suppression Systems
  - Special Hazards Systems Layout
- Geosynthetic Materials Installation Inspection
  - CSPE Geomembranes
  - Geogrids
  - Geonets
  - Geosynthetic Appurtences
  - Geosynthetic Clay Liners
  - Geotextiles
  - HDPE Geomembranes
  - PVC Geomembranes
  - VLDPE Geomembranes
- Geotechnical Engineering Technology Construction
  - Laboratory
  - Exploration
  - Waste Containment
  - Generalist
- Hydro Projects
- Industrial Instrumentation
- Land Management and Water Control
  - Erosion and Sediment Control
- Mechanical Engineering Technology
  - HVAC
  - Industrial Plant Process Piping
- Site Development

- Telecommunications Engineering Technology
- Transportation
  - Bridge Safety Inspection
  - Highway Construction
  - Highway Design
  - Highway Bridge Layout
  - Highway Maintenance
  - Highway Materials
  - Roadway Layout
  - Highway Surveys
  - Highway Traffic Operations
- Underground Utilities Construction
  - Water and Sewer Lines

Examinations

General Knowledge Certification
Part A of the exam covers communications, mathematics, and physical science. Part B covers the certification area of interest.

Job Task Competence Certification
Each work-element test is an objective, one-half hour examination. Up to 34 examinations may be taken at one sitting. 20% of the candidates pass all of the needed tests at their first sitting for Level II. The number of work elements needed to pass varies with each field. In addition, the relevant work experience must meet content requirements based on supervision, involvement, and scope of responsibility. In order to take an element test, the candidate must have a supervisor verify actual performance of the related tasks on the job.

Recertification
None.

REGISTERED ENVIRONMENTAL LABORATORY TECHNOLOGIST (RELT)

Sponsor
National Registry of Environmental Professionals[SM] (NREP[SM])
P.O. Box 2068
Glenview, IL 60025
Phone: (708) 724-6631
Fax: (708) 724-4223

Government and industry professionals may locate professionals in the Official Registry of Environmental Professionals; contact NREP for more information.

Program Data

NREP credentials are endorsed by the Society of Environmental Management. The Resolution Trust Corporation, Department of Energy, U.S. Air Force, and U.S. Army recognize certain NREP certifications in bid proposals.

Certifying body: Independent board (professional registration)
Year registration began: 1988
Number certified: Not disclosed
Organization members: Nonmembership
Additional programs: Associate Environmental Professional (AEP); Associate Environmental Property Assessor (AEPA); Certified Environmental Auditor (CEA); Registered Environmental Manager (REM); Registered Environmental Professional (REP); Registered Environmental Property Assessor (REPA); Registered Environmental Scientist (RES)
Approximate certification costs: $75

Program Description

The Registered Environmental Laboratory Technologist (RELT) designation recognizes professionals in environmental laboratory analysis and management.

The National Registry of Environmental Professionals (NREP) seeks to provide a consolidated, acknowledged recognition program for environmental practitioners. Three official advisory boards have responsibility for examination and career development, and are made up of representatives from leading universities, officials from U.S. government agencies, and major corporations. The NREP maintains documentation on all registrants, and will validate qualifications upon written request. NREP has an active ethics board with decertification powers.

Education/Experience

Candidates must meet the following requirements:

- Two years of laboratory experience conducting research or performing analyses of environmental contaminants. Work experience must include the use of wet chemistry and laboratory analytical devices.

- Hold an Associate in Arts degree in a physical, a biological, or an environmental discipline. Four years of laboratory analysis work may be substituted.

Examinations

Examination questions are based on an academic review and written by academia and consultants. The NREP's Board of Environmental Educators, Board of Environmental Regulatory Officials, and Board of Industrial Environmental Managers provide guidance on test content. Refresher workshops are available through NREP-endorsed university programs and private training providers. NREP provides a list of recommended reading to applicants. Exams are open-book.

The four-hour, multiple-choice examination includes:

- Analytical techniques
- Basic environmental principals
- Evidence handling
- Proper laboratory practice working with environmental samples
- Quality control

The pass rate for all NREP examinations is 70%.

Recertification

Registration must be renewed annually, and RELTs must demonstrate continued professional education. NREP maintains records of CEUs and continuing professional training.

The recertification rate is 90%.

CERTIFIED MECHANICAL INSPECTOR (CMI)

Sponsor

American Society for Quality Control (ASQC)
611 E. Wisconsin Ave.
Milwaukee, WI 53201
Phone: (800) 248-1946
Fax: (414) 272-1734
WWW: http://www.asqc.org/educat/cert.html

Program Data

Certifying body: Association
Year certification began: 1966 (first program)
Number certified: 50,000 (all programs)
Organization members: 130,000
Additional programs: Certified Quality Auditor (CQA); Certified Quality Engineer (CQE); Certified Quality Manager (CQM); Certified Quality Technician (CQT); Certified Reliability Engineer (CRE)

Program Description

The Certified Mechanical Inspector (CMI) designation recognizes individuals knowledgeable and proficient in evaluating hardware documentation, performing laboratory procedures, inspecting products, and measuring performance. Certification is based on passing an examination. ASQC maintains an active ethics program. Candidates must demonstrate professionalism by either of the following:

- Holding Professional Engineer (P.E.) registration
- ASQC (or foreign affiliate society) membership
- Membership in a society belonging to the American Association of Engineering Societies or the Accreditation Board for Engineering and Technology

Education/Experience
Candidates need a high school diploma and two years of related experience.

Examinations
The 100-question, multiple-choice examination is based on the CMI body of knowledge and covers technical mathematics; blueprint reading; inspection tools and equipment; materials and processes; inspection planning; inspection; technology; statistics; sampling and sampling plans.

NABER CERTIFIED TECHNICIAN

Sponsor
National Association of Business and Educational Radio (NABER)
1501 Duke St.
Alexandria, VA 22314
Phone: (703) 739-0300

Program Data
Certifying body: Association
Organization members: 2000+ companies. The Association of Communications Technicians (ACT), a section of NABER, has 1500+ technician members.
Approximate certification costs: $125

Program Description
The NABER Technician Certification program recognizes professional mobile two-way radio technicians. Certification is based on passing an examination. Membership in ACT is not required. NABER sells a comprehensive study guide for the examination.

Examinations
The 150-question, multiple-choice examination is a computer-based test taken at independent PLATO testing centers. The examination covers FCC rules and regulations; two-way radio operations and technology; system troubleshooting; tools and instrumentation; and equipment installation.

Recertification
None.

CERTIFIED OCCUPATIONAL HEALTH AND SAFETY TECHNOLOGIST (COHST)

Sponsor
ABIH/BCSP Joint Committee
208 Burwash Ave.
Savoy, IL 61874
Phone: (217) 359-2686
Fax: (217) 359-0055

Program Data
The program is co-sponsored by the American Board of Industrial Hygiene (ABIH) and the Board of Certified Safety Professionals (BCSP). The OHST program is accredited by the Council of Engineering Specialty Boards (CESB).

Certifying body: Association-sponsored independent board
Year certification began: 1985
Number certified: 1250
Organization members: Nonmembership
Additional programs: Certified Construction Health and Safety Technician (CHST); Certified Safety Trained Supervisor—Construction (STS-Construction)
Approximate certification costs: $140

Program Description
The Certified Occupational Health and Safety Technologist (COHST) designation recognizes professionals who perform safety inspections, monitor industrial hygiene, maintain occupational accident and illness records, and provide health and safety training. Certification is based on passing an examination.

Education/Experience
Candidates must have a high school diploma and five years of professional experience. A bachelor's degree or an associate's degree in health and safety or a technical/scientific area may substitute for two years of experience.

Examinations

The seven-hour, multiple-choice examination covers the following areas:

- Basic and applied sciences
- Occupational health and safety laws, standards, certifications, and regulations
- Control concepts, including personal protective equipment
- Incident/Illness/Injury/Fire investigation
- Survey and inspection techniques
- Data computation and record-keeping
- Education, training, and instruction

Recertification

Recertification is currently under development.

CERTIFIED QUALITY TECHNICIAN (CQT)

Sponsor

American Society for Quality Control (ASQC)
611 E. Wisconsin Ave.
Milwaukee, WI 53201
Phone: (800) 248-1946
Fax: (414) 272-1734
WWW: http://www.asqc.org/educat/cert.html

Program Data

Certifying body: Association
Year certification began: 1966 (first program)
Number certified: 50,000 (all programs)
Organization members: 130,000
Additional programs: Certified Mechanical Inspector (CMI); Certified Quality Auditor (CQA); Certified Quality Engineer (CQE); Certified Quality Manager (CQM); Certified Reliability Engineer (CRE)

Program Description

The Certified Quality Technician (CQT) designation recognizes individuals knowledgeable and proficient in quality analysis and statistical process control. Certification is based on passing an examination. ASQC maintains an active ethics program. Candidates must demonstrate professionalism by one of the following:

- Holding Professional Engineer (P.E.) registration
- ASQC (or foreign affiliate society) membership
- Membership in a society belonging to the American Association of Engineering

Societies or the Accreditation Board for Engineering and Technology

Education/Experience

Candidates must have four years of combined education and experience in applying quality principles. An associate's degree equals two years of experience; a bachelor's degree equals three years of experience.

Examinations

The multiple-choice examination is based on the CQT body of knowledge and covers quality control concepts and techniques; fundamentals of practical statistical methods; application of sampling principles; reliability principles, applications, and simple calculations; metrology and calibration fundamentals; quality data, analysis, problem solving, and cost methodology; quality audit concepts and principles; and geometry, trigonometry, and metric conversion.

CERTIFIED SAFETY TRAINED SUPERVISOR—CONSTRUCTION (STS-CONSTRUCTION)

Sponsor

ABIH/BCSP Joint Committee
208 Burwash Ave.
Savoy, IL 61874
Phone: (217) 359-2686
Fax: (217) 359-0055

Program Data

The program is co-sponsored by the American Board of Industrial Hygiene (ABIH) and the Board of Certified Safety Professionals (BCSP).

Certifying body: Association-sponsored independent board
Year certification began: 1995
Number certified: New program
Organization members: Nonmembership
Additional programs: Certified Construction Health and Safety Technician (CHST); Certified Occupational Health and Safety Technologist (COHST)
Approximate certification costs: $120

Program Description

The Safety Trained Supervisor—Construction (STS-Construction) designation, developed at the request of the construction-safety community, recognizes supervisors in construction crafts who have responsibility for the job-site safety of work crews. The certification does not address safety within particular crafts, but rather those matters significant across a construction work site and among various crafts. Certification is based on passing an examination.

Education/Experience

Candidates must have the following:

- Two years of construction experience
- One year of experience as construction foreman, supervisor, or crew chief
- Thirty hours of safety training

Examinations

The two-hour, 75-question, multiple-choice examination covers the following eleven job tasks: conducting new employee safety orientation; performing basic hazard analysis; conducting basic hazard recognition and correction; issuing and monitoring the use of personal protective equipment; conducting safety meetings; performing hazard prevention analysis; inspecting tools and equipment; applying hazard communications standards; enforcing safety standards on job sites; participating in job-site safety inspections; and responding to accidents.

Recertification

Certified Safety Trained Supervisors must renew their certification every three years through reexamination.

CERTIFIED SATELLITE INSTALLER (CSI)

Sponsor

Electronics Technicians Association, International (ETA)
602 N. Jackson St.
Greencastle, IN 46135
Phone: (317) 653-8262

Program Data

The Certified Satellite Installer program is co-sponsored by the Satellite Dealers Association (SDA).

Certifying body: Association
Year certification began: 1966 (ETA certifications)
Number certified: 30,000 (all certifications)
Organization members: 1700
Additional programs: Certified Customer Service Specialist (CSS); Certified Electronics Technician (CET)
Approximate certification costs: $40

Program Description

The Certified Satellite Installer (CSI) program recognizes experienced satellite technicians and installers. There are no membership or education requirements. Certification is based on passing an examination.

Examinations

The CSI examination covers satellite systems installation, calibration, testing, and troubleshooting. The exam includes electrical safety and safe servicing procedures (for example, static damage).

Recertification

None.

CERTIFIED SURVEY TECHNICIAN (CST)

Sponsor

National Society of Professional Surveyors (NSPS) /American Congress on Surveying and Mapping (ACSM)
5410 Grosvenor Lane, Suite 100
Bethesda, MD 20814
Phone: (301) 493-0200
Fax: (301) 493-8245
WWW: http://www.techexpo.com:80/tech_soc/acsm.html

Certifications may be verified through the NSPS by phone.

Program Data

Certifying body: Association-sponsored independent board
Year certification began: 1981
Additional certifications: Certified Hydrographer
Approximate certification costs: $95, $30 each additional specialty

Program Description

The Certified Survey Technician (CST) designation recognizes survey technicians at various qualification levels and in different specialties. Certification is based on passing an examination and completing required experience hours. There are no membership requirements. Except at Level I, experience is credited within a survey specialty area. The levels, specialties, and requirements are as follows:

Level I—No specialty area, no minimum requirements

Level II—Experience requirements: one and a half years/3000 hours

- Specialty Areas: Construction Instrument Person; Boundary Instrument Person; Drafter; Computer Operator

Level III—Experience requirements: three and a half years/7000 hours (Level II plus two years/4000 hours)

- Specialty Areas: Party Chief—Boundary; Party Chief—Construction; Chief Computer Operator; Chief Draftsperson

Level IV—Experience requirements: five and a half years/11,000 hours (Level III plus two years/4000 hours)

- Specialty Areas: Chief of Parties; Office Manager

Examinations

Examinations are based on a task analysis and an academic review. Questions are written by certificants with assistance from consultants. Each level has a corresponding examination for each specialty area. CSTs may test in more than one specialty area on the same level after working in the area for one year. While the depth of coverage will change between levels, all examinations include computer operations, control points, equipment and instruments, ethics and standards, field notes, first aid/safety, mathematics and computation, plan reading, survey principles. Level III and IV examinations include supervision and management.

Recertification

None.

CERTIFIED TECHNOLOGY SPECIALIST (CTS)

Sponsor

International Communications Industries Association (ICIA)
11242 Waples Mill Road, Suite 200
Fairfax, VA 22030
Phone: (703) 273-7200
Fax: (703) 278-8082
E-mail: icia@icia.org
WWW: http://www.usa.net/icia/

Program Data

Certifying body: Association
Organization members: 1500

Program Description

The Certified Technology Specialist (CTS) designation recognizes expertise in communications products and systems sales, management, servicing, and manufacturing. Certification is based on experience and coursework.

Education/Experience

Candidates must be commercially involved and have two years of experience in the communications industry. End-user experience is excluded. Eligible experience includes work in video technologies, rental services, educational technologies, computer and multimedia technologies, and audio-video communications technologies.

Curriculum

All candidates must complete the ICIA's Institute for Professional Development and pass the course's final examination. Candidates must also accumulate an additional 60–180 hours of ICIA-sponsored programs, manufacturer/produced training, and professional education. Actual hours depend on training provider.

Recertification

CTSs must recertify every three years through completion of 50 hours of continuing education.

CERTIFIED WATER TREATMENT PROFESSIONAL (CWTP)

Sponsor

Association of Water Technologies, Inc. (AWT)
1735 N. Lynn St., Suite 950
Arlington, VA 22209
Phone: (703) 524-0905
Fax: (703) 524-2303
E-mail: meb@awt.org
WWW: http://www.awt.org/

Program Data

Certifying body: Association
Year certification began: 1994
Number certified: New program
Organization members: 400+ companies
Approximate certification costs: $400 (members), $1000 (nonmembers)

Program Description

The Certified Water Treatment Professional (CWTP) designation recognizes skilled individuals involved in boiler and cooling water systems associated with manufacturing facilities of HVAC operations. Membership in the Association of Water

Technologies, Inc. (AWT) is not required. The AWT is made up of over 300 small and medium-sized regional industrial-water-treatment companies and over 100 consultants, distributors, and manufacturers. The current program is a single level of certification in Water Treatment Technology (Level 1). The AWT plans to expand certification into several areas.

Education/Experience

Candidates must have the equivalent of five years of acceptable work experience. Experience may include technical consulting in industrial water treatment, direct sales and/or service of water treatment applications, or technical support of sales or service personnel. Experience credits are given as follows:

- 1 year credit per year of applicable work experience
- 1 year credit per bachelor's degree
- 1½ year credit per bachelor's degree in a technical discipline
- ¼ year credit per year of experience in a related field

Examinations

The Level 1 examination was developed by volunteers in the industry and is based primarily on the *AWT Technical Training Manual* and *AWT Raw Materials Specification Manual*. The examination covers the following areas:

- Basic water treatment chemistry and terminology
- Sodium zeolite softening
- Low-pressure boiler water treatment
- Cooling water treatment
- Closed system treatment
- Federal safety considerations
- Federal environmental and transportation affairs

Recertification

CWPTs must recertify every five years based on work experience and professional development.

MEDICAL
Management

CERTIFIED CASE MANAGER (CCM)

Sponsor

Commission of Certified Case Managers (CCCM)
1835 Rohlwing Road, Suite D
Rolling Meadows, IL 60008
Phone: (708) 818-1967

Program Data

CCCM is a sponsoring organization of the Foundation for Rehabilitation Certification, Education, and Research.

Certifying body: Independent board
Year certification began: 1993
Number certified: 15,591
Approximate certification costs: $275

Program Description

The Certified Case Manager (CCM) designation recognizes health and human services professionals with specialized knowledge and experience in identifying health and wellness service providers. Case managers work with individuals requiring health services and ensure timely and cost-effective use of resources for clients and reimbursement sources.

Education/Experience

Candidates must hold current RN licensure or acceptable licensure/certification in a health and human services profession. Candidates must demonstrate 24–36 months of acceptable clinical experience and 12–24 months of acceptable full-time case management employment.

Examinations

The 300-question, one-day, multiple-choice examination covers coordination and service delivery; physical and psychological factors; benefit systems and cost-benefit analysis; case management concepts; and community resources.

Recertification

CCMs must renew certification every five years by accumulating 80 clock hours of acceptable continuing education, or retake the CCM examination. They must also hold the underlying license or national certification that was the basis for their initial CCM certification.

CERTIFIED DIETARY MANAGER (CDM)

Sponsor

Certifying Board for Dietary Managers (CBDM)
One Pierce Place, Suite 1220W
Itasca, IL 60143
Phone: (708) 775-9200

Program Data

The CBDM is sponsored by the Dietary Managers Association (DMA).

Certifying body: Independent board
Number certified: 9000+
Approximate certification costs: $100 (members), $200 (nonmembers)

Program Description

The Certified Dietary Manager (CDM) designation recognizes managers and supervisors of institutional food service. CDMs work primarily in healthcare facilities. Membership in the Dietary Managers Association (DMA) is not required. Certification is based on passing an examination.

Education/Experience

To qualify to sit for the CDM examination, a candidate must meet one of four requirements:

- Active or associate membership in DMA
- Graduation from a dietary-management training program approved by the DMA or American Dietetic Association (ADA)
- Bachelor's degree in food management or related field, and completion of a dietetic-technician associate's degree program approved by the ADA

- High school diploma and five years of full-time experience in institutional food service management

Examinations

The 175-question, multiple-choice examination is based on competency areas identified in an in-depth study of dietary-manager role delineation. The examinations are administered by the American College Testing Program, Inc. (ACT), which also helps maintain the examination. The exam covers patient/client nutrition, service, and education; human resource management within food facilities; and food/kitchen operation, production, and management.

Recertification

CDMs must renew their certification every three years through continuing education. CDMs must earn 45 clock hours of approved continuing education during the three-year cycle.

{HEALTHCARE} FELLOW (FHFMA)

Sponsor

Healthcare Financial Management Association (HFMA)
Two Westbrook Corporate Center, Suite 700
Westchester, IL 60154
Phone: (708) 531-9600
WWW: http://www.hfma.org/

Program Data

Certifying body: Association
Number certified: 1500
Organization members: 34,000
Additional programs: Certified Managed Care Professional (CMCP); Certified Manager of Patient Accounts (CMPA)
Approximate certification costs: $200 plus membership

Program Description

The Fellow (FHFMA) designation recognizes senior healthcare-finance professionals, CFOs, treasurers, and administrators. Certification is based on passing an examination and earning certification points.

Education/Experience

Candidates must hold HFMA membership for two years to sit for the examination. Prior to certification, candidates must become advanced HFMA members, hold a bachelor's degree, attend an HFMA national seminar, and earn 100 points in Association activities.

Examinations

The four-part FHFMA examination has a pass rate of 60%. The exam covers accounting theory and practice, financial management, health services industry, and management process and information systems.

Recertification

To maintain certification, candidates must accumulate 100 hours of continuing education.

CERTIFIED HEALTHCARE EXECUTIVE (CHE)
FELLOW OF THE AMERICAN COLLEGE OF HEALTHCARE EXECUTIVES (FACHE)

Sponsor

American College of Healthcare Executives (ACHE)
One North Franklin St., Suite 1700
Chicago, IL 60606
Phone: (312) 424-2800
Fax: (312) 424-0023
E-mail: membership@ache.org
WWW: http://www.ache.org/index.html

Program Data

Certifying body: Association
Number certified: 10,000
Organization members: 32,000

Program Description

The Certified Healthcare Executive (CHE) and Fellow (FACHE) designations recognize ACHE members who demonstrate knowledge and proficiency within the healthcare management field. ACHE maintains an active ethics program.

Education/Experience

Applicants for membership must have a graduate degree and one year of experience, or a bachelor's degree and three years of experience.

CHE candidates must have 20 hours of related professional education within the previous two years.

Fellow candidates must have five years of CHE status, 50 hours of approved continuing education, and current employment in healthcare management. There are no examination requirements for Fellow status. Candidates must complete a professional project; either a related thesis, four case reports, or a mentorship project.

Examinations

The 275-question, multiple-choice, written CHE examination covers these ACHE areas: operation; education; ethics; financial and assets management; governance and organization; government regulations and law; healthcare-information-systems management; human resources; organizational arrangements and relationships; planning and marketing; plant and facility management; profession; quality assessment and improvement; and research.

The oral examination includes an introductory interview and a case study.

Recertification

Certificants must recertify through continuing education.

CERTIFIED PROFESSIONAL IN HEALTHCARE QUALITY (CPHQ)

Sponsor

Healthcare Quality Certification Board (HQCB)
P.O. Box 1880
San Gabriel, CA 91778
Phone: (800) 346-4722
Fax: (818) 286-9415

Program Data

HQCB is accredited by the National Commission for Certifying Agencies (NCCA) and sponsored by the National Association for Healthcare Quality (NAHQ).

Certifying body: Association-sponsored independent board
Year certification began: 1985
Number certified: 4765
Organization members: 6500+ (NAHQ)
Approximate certification costs: $285 (members), $350 (nonmembers)

Program Description

The Certified Professional in Healthcare Quality (CPHQ) designation recognizes healthcare professionals working in the areas of healthcare quality,

case utilization, and risk management. Certification is based on passing an examination.

Education/Experience

There are no membership requirements. Candidates must have two years of professional experience in the healthcare quality field and meet one of the following requirements:

- Associate's degree
- Registered or Licensed Practical Nurse
- Accreditation in medical-records technology

Examinations

The 125-question, multiple-choice examination was developed with the assistance of Applied Measurement Professions, Inc. (AMP). The examination is based on a job analysis. HQCB does not produce, sponsor, or endorse any review course or preparation text. The pass rate is about 80%. The exam covers the following areas:

- Management/Leadership activities, including strategic planning; organizational quality improvement; information management; performance measurement and improvement; accreditation and licensure survey process; education; training and communications

- Continuum of Care, including performance monitoring; utilization management; electronic data management; statistical process control; collaborative case management; risk management; quality program components; and accreditation and licensure requirements (Federal regulations, JCAHO, and National Commission for Quality Assurance)

Recertification

CPHQs must recertify within a two-year cycle by accumulating 30 continuing-education hours in quality, case utilization, and risk management.

ACSM HEALTH/FITNESS DIRECTOR℠

Sponsor

American College of Sports Medicine (ACSM)
P.O. Box 1440
401 W. Michigan St.
Indianapolis, IN 46202
Phone: (800) 486-5643
Fax: (317) 634-7817
E-mail: crtacsm@acsm.org
WWW: http://www.a1.com/sportsmed/index.htm

Program Data

Certifying body: Association
Year certification began: 1975
Number certified: 16,000 (all certifications)
Additional programs: ACSM certification for Exercise Leader, Exercise Specialist, Exercise Test Technologist, Health/Fitness Instructor, and Program Director

Program Description

The ACSM Health/Fitness Director℠ is the highest-level certification in the ACSM Health and Fitness Track. This certification recognizes professionals administering programs on health and preventative exercise. Certification is based on a written test and a practical examination. Current CPR certification is required.

Education/Experience

While not required for certification, ACSM recommends candidates have a bachelor's degree or equivalent training in health/fitness or a related field; one year of fitness program supervision; and three years of experience in health/fitness administrative management.

Examinations

ACSM certifications are based on behavioral objectives described in ACSM's *Guidelines for Exercise Testing and Prescription*. The written test is based on these objectives. The practical examination uses scenarios to assess candidates in business planning, situational management, and staff training.

Recertification

Certification must be renewed every four years and is based on continuing education. CPR certification must be maintained. Health/Fitness Directors must earn 120 continuing-education hours (or hour equivalents).

CERTIFIED MANAGED CARE EXECUTIVE (CMCE)

Sponsor

American Managed Care and Review Association (AMCRA)
1200 19th St. NW, Suite 200
Washington, DC 20036
Phone: (202) 728-0506

Program Data

Certifying body: Association
Year certification began: 1991
Number certified: 100
Organization members: 500 organizational members (HMOs, PPOs, etc.)
Approximate certification costs: $2500 (members), $5000 (nonmembers)

Program Description

The Certified Managed Care Executive (CMCE) designation recognizes MDs, DOs, managers, and directors in managed care who complete the AMCRA Executive Leadership Program for Medical Directors (ELP-MD) or the Executive Leadership Program (ELP). Participation for both programs is limited annually to 15 for the ELP-MD and 20 for the ELP. These one-year certification programs include academic and experiential components. To guide the experiential component, Fellows are provided a Primary Mentor, an experienced managed care executive. Secondary Mentors participate in different areas of the program. Mentors evaluate performance and must recommend certification.

Education/Experience

The requirements for the ELP-MD certification are as follows:

● Current employment within a managed care organization

● One year of full- or part-time position in managed care management

● License to practice medicine (MD or DO)

● Acceptable professional recommendation and performance

The requirements for the ELP certification are as follows:

● Current employment within a managed care organization

● Three years of experience in health-care management, with at least one year in a managed-care setting

● Bachelor's degree

● Acceptable professional recommendation and practice

Curriculum

The ELP-MD program covers both medical and administrative management, while the ELP program covers only administrative management. Medical management topics include quality assessment and utilization management; data collection and management systems; internal and external performance measures; physician-practice profiling; capitation; and the role of the medical director. Administrative management topics include managed-care systems; industry trends; health policy; negotiation skills and conflict management; organizational development; team building and leadership; and strategic planning and management.

Recertification

CMCEs must recertify every three years by completing 25 hours of AMCRA-sponsored education programs.

CERTIFIED MANAGED CARE PROFESSIONAL (CMCP)

Sponsor

Healthcare Financial Management Association (HFMA)
Two Westbrook Corporate Center, Suite 700
Westchester, IL 60154
Phone: (708) 531-9600
WWW: http://www.hfma.org/

Program Data

Certifying body: Association
Number certified: New program (1995)
Organization members: 34,000
Additional programs: Certified Manager of Patient Accounts (CMPA); Fellow (FHFMA)
Approximate certification costs: $150 plus membership

Program Description

The Certified Managed Care Professional (CMCP) recognizes individuals applying financial management principles and tools in a managed healthcare environment.

Education/Experience

Candidates must have two years of HFMA membership, two years of financial management or healthcare experience, and at least 60 college semester credits.

Examinations

The two-part CMCP exam covers the full range of managed-care skills. Part 1 covers managed-care models, legal risks and risk management, capitation, and current topics. Part 2 covers healthcare-related accounting, management, information systems, and industry issues.

Recertification

To maintain certification, candidates must accumulate 100 hours of continuing education.

DIPLOMATE, AMERICAN BOARD OF MEDICAL LABORATORY IMMUNOLOGY (ABMLI)

Sponsor

American Society for Microbiology (ASM)
1325 Massachusetts Ave. NW
Washington, DC 20005
Phone: (202) 942-9226
Fax: (202) 942-9380
E-mail: certification@asmusa.org
WWW: http://www.asmusa.org/

Program Data

Certifying body: Association-sponsored independent board
Year certification began: 1960 (ASM)
Number certified: 137
Organization members: 40,000
Additional programs: Diplomate—American Board of Medical Microbiology (ABMM); Registered Microbiologist (RM[ASM]); Specialist Microbiologist (SM[ASM])

Program Description

The ABMLI program recognizes microbiologists directing public health and clinical microbiology laboratories. Certification is based on an examination.

Education/Experience

Candidates must have a doctoral degree in biological sciences and three to six years post-doctoral work experience as a laboratory director or assistant director.

Examinations

The ABMLI has two examination components: written and oral. The written examination is a multiple-choice test covering basic immunological mechanisms, methodology, and immunodiagnosis and clinical laboratory correlation. The oral examination covers clinical implications, technical aspects, and laboratory practice.

Recertification

Diplomates must recertify every three years through continuing medical education.

DIPLOMATE, AMERICAN BOARD OF MEDICAL MICROBIOLOGY (ABMM)

Sponsor

American Society for Microbiology (ASM)
1325 Massachusetts Ave. NW
Washington, DC 20005
Phone: (202) 942-9226
Fax: (202) 942-9380
E-mail: certification@asmusa.org
WWW: http://www.asmusa.org/

Program Data

Certifying body: Association-sponsored
   independent board
Year certification began: 1960 (ASM)
Number certified: 876
Organization members: 40,000
Additional programs: Diplomate—American
   Board of Medical Laboratory Immunology
   (ABMLI); Registered Microbiologist (RM[ASM]);
   Specialist Microbiologist (SM[ASM])

Program Description

The ABMM program recognizes microbiologists directing public health and clinical microbiology laboratories. Certification is based on an examination. Candidates receive certification within one of the board's specialty areas: Medical and Public Health Microbiology, Mycology, Parasitology, or Virology.

Education/Experience

Candidates must have a doctoral degree in biological sciences and meet one of the following requirements:

- Six years of postdoctoral employment as a laboratory director or assistant director

- Two years of CPEP-approved training program and two years of experience

Examinations

The ABMM has both a written and an oral examination. Candidates are evaluated on their knowledge and related skills in directing a clinical microbiology lab in their specialty. The exams include managing diagnostic microbiology services supporting epidemiologic investigations, interpreting and communicating laboratory findings, and overseeing staff training and research projects.

Recertification

Diplomates must recertify every three years by either continuing medical or professional education.

CERTIFIED MEDICAL STAFF COORDINATOR (CMSC)

Sponsor

National Association Medical Staff Services
   (NAMSS)
P.O. Box 23350
Knoxville, TN 37933
Phone: (615) 531-3571
Fax: (615) 531-9939

Program Data

Certifying body: Association
Year certification began: 1981
Number certified: 2100
Organization members: 3100

Program Description

The Certified Medical Staff Coordinator (CMSC) designation recognizes professionals in medical staff services qualified to operate a medical staff department and to coordinate staff activities. A CMSC understands healthcare facility credentialing and regulatory requirements, participates in planning, provides support services to medical staff, and acts as a liaison between the medical staff and the facility administration. Certification is based on passing an examination. NAMSS membership is not required.

Education/Experience

Candidates must have three years of experience and 60 college semester credits.

Examinations

The CMSC examination is based on a job analysis and is administered by the Professional Testing Corporation for NAMSS. Questions are written by certificants. NAMSS offers study guides and preparatory classes.

The examination covers medical staff organization; physician accreditation knowledge; medical staff law; medical terminology; and administration and management.

Recertification
CMSCs must accumulate 30 hours of professional education every three years to maintain certification.

REGISTERED NURSE, CERTIFIED IN NURSING ADMINISTRATION (RN, CNA)

REGISTERED NURSE, CERTIFIED IN NURSING ADMINISTRATION, ADVANCED (RN, CNAA)

Sponsor
American Nurses Credentialing Center (ANCC)
American Nurses Association (ANA)
600 Maryland Ave. SW, Suite 100
Washington, DC 20024
Phone: (800) 274-4262

Program Data
Certifying body: Association-sponsored independent board
Year certification began: 1973
Additional programs: Registered Nurse, Certified (RN, C); Registered Nurse, Certified Specialist (RN, CS)
Approximate certification costs: $200 (members), $350 (nonmembers)

Program Description
The Registered Nurse, Certified in Nursing Administration (RN,CNA) designation recognizes RNs with management expertise. There are no membership requirements.

Education/Experience
All RN, CNA candidates must hold a current active RN license in the United States or its territories, and have a bachelor's degree, two years of management experience within the previous five years, and have 20 contact hours of continuing education

All RN, CNAA candidates must hold an active RN license in the United States or its territories, and have a master's or higher degree, two years of executive-level nursing experience within the past five years, and 30 contact hours of continuing education applicable to nursing administration.

Examinations
The half-day, multiple-choice exam covers practice, ethics, and knowledge related to a specific area.

Recertification
ANCC certification must be renewed every five years through continuing professional education.

CERTIFIED NURSING HOME ADMINISTRATOR (CNHA)

Sponsor
American College of Health Care Administrators (ACHCA)
325 South Patrick St.
Alexandria, VA 22314
Phone: (703) 739-7921
Fax: (703) 739-7901
E-mail: mich-a@spaceworks.com

Program Data
The CNHA designation is recognized by many state licensure boards, professional associations, the American Health Care Association, the American Association of Homes and Services of the Aging, and by the National Association of Board of Examiners for Nursing Home Administrators. Facilities may also receive additional rating points from state organizations for employing CNHAs.

Certifying body: Association-sponsored independent board.
Year certification began: 1979
Number certified: 431
Organization members: 6289
Position referral for employers: Michelle Anderson

Program Description
The Certified Nursing Home Administrator (CNHA) program recognizes experienced, licensed/qualified professionals in nursing home management. The exam-based certification not only examines candidate knowledge in several competency areas, but evaluates values and ethics related to nursing home administration. Study guides, self-study materials, workshops, and examination preparatory classes are offered. The ACHCA has an active ethics board with decertification powers.

The CNHA program was revised in 1993, with dual certification tracks in place through November, 1994. The former certification program included a certification workshop and a professional-development plan. The new program requires qualified candidates to pass a written examination.

Education/Experience

To qualify for the examination, the candidate must meet the following requirements:

- A current active Nursing Home Administrator license or federal qualifications held at least two years
- At least two years of experience as a nursing home administrator, excluding in-training time
- Twenty hours of continuing education for each of the last two years
- Bachelor's degree

Examinations

The examination, designed by the Corporate Psychology Center, Saville • Holdsworth, and the University of Minnesota, is a six-hour, two-part multiple-choice test. Part I covers the knowledge base of nursing home administration: marketing; personnel management; financial management; physical resource management; laws and regulations; and patient care. Part II tests numerical and verbal reasoning, and includes an occupational personality questionnaire and an ethics and values instrument.

Recertification

Recertification is required every five years. Twenty hours of approved continuing education is required for each of the previous five years. In addition, a CNHA must complete one of the following four options:

- Pass the certification examination
- Complete an Executive Portfolio application
- Attend an approved executive level program
- Complete a master's degree from a program accredited by the Accrediting Commission on Education for Health Services Administration

After three recertifications, CNHAs are considered Certified Masters and certified for life.

CERTIFIED MANAGER OF PATIENT ACCOUNTS (CMPA)

Sponsor

Healthcare Financial Management Association (HFMA)
Two Westbrook Corporate Center, Suite 700
Westchester, IL 60154
Phone: (708) 531-9600
WWW: http://www.hfma.org/

Program Data

Certifying body: Association
Number certified: 700
Organization members: 34,000
Additional programs: Certified Managed Care Professional (CMCP); Fellow (FHFMA)
Approximate certification costs: $150 plus membership

Program Description

The Certified Manager of Patient Accounts (CMPA) designation recognizes HFMA members who specialize in patient account management. Certification is based on passing an examination and earning certification points.

Education/Experience

Candidates must hold HFMA membership for one year to sit for the examination. Prior to certification, candidates must have two years of both healthcare finance experience and HFMA membership. Candidates must have 60 semester hours of college work or HFMA seminar equivalent. In addition, candidates must earn 50 points in association activities.

Examinations

The CMPA examination has a pass rate of about 70%. It is presented in a two-part format:

Part 1—Receivables Management, including planning; patient registration and admission; billing and collection; and legal considerations

Part 2—Accounting, Healthcare, Management, and Information Systems, including budgeting; accounting; cash management; healthcare delivery systems; legislation and regulation; management theory; human resources management; and information systems

Recertification

To maintain certification, candidates must accumulate 100 hours of continuing education.

PROGRAM DIRECTOR SPECIALIST (PDS)

Sponsor

Cooper Institute for Aerobics Research
12330 Preston Road
Dallas, TX 75230
Phone: (214) 701-6875

Program Data

Certifying body: Independent board
Approximate certification costs: $535

Program Description

The week-long Program Director Specialist (PDS) program provides advanced certification in exercise programming, supervision, and administration for program directors. A basic aerobics certification is required. After completing the workshop, the candidate must pass an examination.

Curriculum

The PDS coursework includes business and legal principles; health promotion, screening, and assessments; strength, aerobics, special needs, and flexibility programming; and weight control, stress, and supervision practicums.

Examinations

The PDS examination includes a multiple-choice test and an open-book series of questions.

Recertification

None.

REGULATORY AFFAIRS PROFESSIONAL CERTIFICATION

Sponsor

Regulatory Affairs Professionals Society (RAPS)
P.O. Box 14953
Lenexa, KS 66285
Phone: (913) 541-1427
WWW: http://www.medmarket.com/tenants/raps/ raps.html#lobby

Program Data

Certifying body: Association
Organization members: 6000
Approximate certification costs: $200

Program Description

The Regulatory Affairs Professionals Certification recognizes individuals who are responsible for monitoring compliance with pharmaceutical, medical device, biologic, and biotechnology regulations. Open to all professionals in healthcare regulatory affairs, membership is not required. Certification is based on passing an examination.

Education/Experience

Candidates must have either three years of experience in the field of regulatory affairs or a bachelor's degree.

Examinations

Based on a role-delineation study, the 100-question, multiple-choice certification exam concentrates on U.S. laws, regulations, policies, and guidelines. The exam includes questions concerning FDA-regulated products, and covers drugs, medical devices, biologics, and general regulatory issues.

Recertification

Continuing education in the field is required.

RETIREMENT HOUSING PROFESSIONAL (RHP)

RETIREMENT HOUSING PROFESSIONAL FELLOW (RHP FELLOW)

Sponsor

American Association of Homes and Services for the Aging (AAHSA)
901 E. St. NW, Suite 500
Washington, DC 20004
Phone: (202) 508-9435
Fax: (202) 783-2255

Program Data

Certifying body: Association
Approximate certification costs: $1245 (members), $1395 (nonmembers)

Program Description

The RHP program certifies professionals in the field of retirement housing and assisted living who complete the AAHSA certification programs curriculum.

Education/Experience

There are no requirements for the RHP certification.

RHP Fellow candidates must have three years of management experience in senior-housing facility.

Curriculum

Candidates must complete the following courses, either through the RHP Summer Institute, at AAHSA meetings, or through self-study. The three courses are as follows:

● Administering the Retirement Housing Community, including theories and principles of retirement-housing management; personnel development and administration; facility governance; supportive housing; marketing; and legal issues

- Management and the Aging Resident, which covers biomedical, psychological, and social aspects of aging, aging and the economic system, and long-term care delivery systems
- Managing the Financial and Physical Environments, including property management for retirement-housing professionals; current financing alternatives; financial-trends monitoring; automating management information systems; and environmental design

RHP Fellow candidates must complete an in-depth assessment and comprehensive management plan of their housing facility. This assessment is peer-reviewed and must be approved as part of the Fellow process.

Examinations
RHP candidates are given take-home exams to complete within four weeks of finishing the course.

Recertification
None.

CERTIFIED STERILE PROCESSING AND DISTRIBUTION MANAGER (CSPDM)

Sponsor
National Institute for the Certification of Healthcare Sterile Processing and Distribution Personnel (NICHSPDP)
P.O. Box 558
Annandale, NJ 08801
Phone: (201) 533-5586
Fax: (201) 533-8845

Program Data
The Institute is recognized by the American Society for Healthcare Central Service Personnel (ASHCSP) of the American Hospital Association. It is a member of the National Organization for Competency Assurance (NOCA), and approved by the Defense Activity for Non-Traditional Educational Support.

Certifying body: Independent certifying organization
Year certification began: 1995
Additional programs: Certified Sterile Processing and Distribution Supervisor (CSPDS); Certified Sterile Processing and Distribution Technician (CSPDT)
Approximate certification costs: $135

Program Description
The Certified Sterile Processing and Distribution Manager (CSPDM) program represents the top of a three-tier certification program in central service/sterile processing and distribution. The certification program is based on a national job analysis survey conducted in 1993 by Applied Measurement Services, Inc. NICHSPDP sells a comprehensive examination study guide.

Education/Experience
Candidates must have three years of experience as manager of a sterile processing and distribution department in healthcare central services. Previous certification as a Certified Sterile Processing and Distribution Technician (CSPDT) is not required.

Examination
The 175-question, multiple-choice examination is written by the NICHSPDP examination committee and administered by Applied Measurement Services, Inc. The question content is targeted at experienced managers in a healthcare facility. The examination covers the following areas:

- Fiscal management, including budget development and monitoring
- Personnel management, including job description development, providing education and training, performance appraisals, staffing and scheduling, and legal considerations
- Sterile processing and distribution standards and practices, including hazardous chemicals handling and supervision, biohazard handling, workplace safety, and OSHA regulations
- Responsibilities of sterile processing and distribution/central service, covering technical aspects of decontamination, sterile processing operations, equipment operation, and packaging and handling
- Anatomy, microbiology, and infection control
- Central service procedures, including policy development, emergency preparedness, and ethics
- Inventory and distribution, including supply-distribution-system development, logistics, and storage

Recertification
CSPDMs must recertify every five years. Recertification is based on an open point system, with no minimum requirements in any category.

CERTIFIED STERILE PROCESSING AND DISTRIBUTION SUPERVISOR (CSPDS)

Sponsor

National Institute for the Certification of Healthcare Sterile Processing and Distribution Personnel (NICHSPDP)
P.O. Box 558
Annandale, NJ 08801
Phone: (201) 533-5586
Fax: (201) 533-8845

Program Data

The Institute is recognized by the American Society for Healthcare Central Service Personnel (ASHCSP) of the American Hospital Association. It is a member of the National Organization for Competency Assurance (NOCA), and approved by the Defense Activity for Non-Traditional Educational Support.

Certifying body: Independent certifying organization
Year certification began: 1994
Additional programs: Certified Sterile Processing and Distribution Manager (CSPDM); Certified Sterile Processing and Distribution Technician (CSPDT)
Approximate certification costs: $135

Program Description

The Certified Sterile Processing and Distribution Supervisor (CSPDS) program represents the second of a three-tier certification program in central service/sterile processing and distribution. The certification program is based on a national job analysis survey conducted in 1993 by Applied Measurement Services, Inc. NICHSPDP sells a comprehensive examination study guide.

Education/Experience Requirements

Candidates must have three years of supervisory experience in a sterile processing and distribution department in healthcare central services. Previous certification as a Certified Sterile Processing and Distribution Technician (CSPDT) is not required.

Examination

The 175-question, multiple-choice examination is written by the NICHSPDP examination committee and administered by Applied Measurement Services, Inc. Question content is targeted at supervisory-level personnel responsible for day-to-day operations working with technicians, supervising small numbers of staff, and working under a department manager. The examination covers the following areas:

- Fiscal management, including budget development and monitoring
- Personnel management, including performance appraisals; job-description development; providing education and training; staffing and scheduling; and legal considerations
- Sterile processing and distribution standards and practices, including hazardous chemicals handling and supervision, biohazard handling, workplace safety, and OSHA regulations
- Responsibilities of sterile processing and distribution/central service, covering technical aspects of decontamination, sterile processing operations, equipment operation, and packaging and handling
- Anatomy, microbiology, and infection control
- Central service procedures, including policy development, emergency preparedness, and ethics
- Inventory and distribution, including supply distribution-system development, logistics, and storage

Recertification

CSPDSs must recertify every five years. Recertification is based on an open point system, with no minimum requirements in any category.

MEDICAL
Practitioners

ACTIVITY CONSULTANT CERTIFIED (ACC)
ACTIVITY DIRECTOR CERTIFIED (ADC)
ACTIVITY ASSISTANT CERTIFIED (AAC)

Sponsor

National Certification Council for Activity
   Professionals (NCCAP)
520 Stewart Ave.
Park Ridge, IL 60068
Phone: (708) 698-4263

Program Data

The NCCAP is an independent certification body
associated with the National Association of Activity
Professionals (NAAP).

Certifying body: Independent board
Year certification began: 1986
Number certified: 5750 (all certifications)
Approximate certification costs: $35 (AAC), $45
   (ADC), $55 (ACC) (NAAP members $5
   discount)

Program Description

The three certification levels for activity professionals recognize individuals involved in activity
leadership for the elderly. Membership in the National Association of Activity Professionals (NAAP)
is not required. There is no examination component.

Education/Experience

For all certifications, the required educational
components come from a list of 24 applicable
coursework areas. The NAAP and NCCAP offer a
basic education course and advance management
course which may be used towards the education
requirement. Experience must be related to an
activities program in association with an organization or a facility providing care to the elderly.
Mixed programs must serve a population of at least
50% elderly. Volunteer work may be used to meet
up to 20% of the experience requirement.

Continuing education must fall within one of 27 acceptable areas, including geriatrics; interpersonal
relations; regulatory requirements; care planning;
management; resources; and consulting.

The Activity Consultant Certified (ACC) designation
recognizes professionals providing consultation,
training, and advisory services in activities professions. Candidates must have 200 hours of activity-
consulting experience and 40 hours of continuing
education within the last three years, and meet one
of the following options: master's degree with
required coursework areas and 2000 hours of
experience, or a bachelor's degree with required
coursework areas and 4000 hours of experience.

The Activity Director Certified (ADC) designation
recognizes professionals responsible for coordinating, directing, or managing activities in
a geriatric setting. Provisional certification status
is available to those working towards meeting
the ADC requirements. Candidates must have
30 hours of continuing education and meet one of
the following options: bachelor's degree with
required coursework and 2000 hours of experience; 60 semester hours in acceptable areas and
6000 hours of experience; or 30 semester hours in
acceptable areas and 10,000 hours of experience.

The Activity Assistant Certified (AAC) designation
recognizes professionals who lead or assist
activities in a geriatric setting. Certification requires
20 hours of continuing education and either
30 semester hours of acceptable coursework and
2000 hours experience, or six semester hours (or
the NAAP/NCCAP Basic Education Course) and
4000 hours of experience.

Recertification

Certified activity professionals must renew their
certification every two years. ACCs need 40 hours
of continuing education, ADCs need 30 hours, and
AACs need 20 hours.

NATIONALLY CERTIFIED COUNSELOR (NCC)

Sponsor

National Board for Certified Counselors
   (NBCC®)
3 Terrace Way, Suite D
Greensboro, NC 27403
Phone: (910) 547-0607
Fax: (910) 547-0017
E-mail: nbcc@counselor.nbcc.org
WWW: http://www.nbcc.com/

Program Data

The NBCC program is accredited by the National Commission for Certifying Agencies (NCCA). Thirty-three states have adopted the NCE examination as part of their statutory credentialing process.

Certifying body: Independent board
Year certification began: 1982
Number certified: 27,000
Approximate certification costs: $200 (NCC exam)

Program Description

The Nationally Certified Counselor (NCC) designation recognizes skilled and knowledgeable counselors. Certification is based on passing an examination. The NBCC maintains an active ethics program. NBCC also offers specialty certification to NCCs completing additional requirements. Specialty certification is offered in career counseling, gerontological counseling, school counseling, clinical mental health counseling, and addictions counseling.

Education/Experience

In states using the NCE for licensure, NCC certification is granted after meeting the experience and education requirements.

All certification candidates must have a graduate degree with counseling as the major course of study (48 semester hours of graduate coursework in counseling or a related field). Candidates must have two academic terms of supervised counseling field experience, two professional references, and meet one of the following requirements:

- Graduation from a program approved by the Council for the Accreditation of Counseling and Related Educational programs (CACREP)

- Two years of post-master's degree experience, 3000 hours of client contact, and 100 hours of supervision

Examinations

The NCE was developed from an extensive task analysis with input from an expert board. The NCE covers appraisal; career and lifestyle development; group work; helping relationships; human growth and development; professional orientation and ethics; research and program evaluation; and social and cultural foundations. The NCE is based on counseling families, counseling for career development, counseling groups, fundamental counseling practices, and professional practice. The pass rate is 80%.

Recertification

NCC certification must be renewed after five years by accumulating 100 contact hours of professional education.

REGISTERED DIETETIC TECHNICIAN (RDT)
REGISTERED DIETITIAN (RD)

Sponsor

Commission on Dietetic Registration (CDR)
216 West Jackson Blvd., 8th Floor
Chicago, IL 60606-6995
Phone: (800) 877-1600
Fax: (312) 899-1772

Program Data

CDR is the official credentialing agency for the American Dietetic Association (ADA).

Certifying body: Independent board

Program Description

The Registered Dietitian (RD) designation is awarded to individuals who complete the required degree, practice, and examination requirements. RDs may also be board-certified in one of three specialties. The Registered Dietetic Technician (RDT) designation is awarded to individuals who complete the required education, practice, and examination requirements.

Education/Experience

RD candidates must have a bachelor's degree or higher meeting the ADA program requirements and have 900 hours of supervised practice.

RDT candidates must complete an ADA-approved dietetic technician program, including supervised field experience.

RDs may seek board certification in renal, pediatric, and metabolic nutrition. Candidates must have three years of registration status, currently work 16 hours per week within the specialty, and have 6000 hours of specialty practice.

Examination
Information was not disclosed.

DISABILITY ANALYST AND FELLOW

SENIOR DISABILITY ANALYST AND DIPLOMATE

Sponsor
American Board of Disability Analysts (ABDA)
345 24th Ave. N, Suite 200
Nashville, TN 37203
Phone: (615) 327-2984
Fax: (615) 327-9235

Program Data
Certifying body: Association
Year certification began: 1982
Number certified: 3700
Organization members: 3700
Approximate certification costs: $275

Program Description
The ABDA certification program recognizes professionals involved in the etiology, diagnosis, and rehabilitation of disabling conditions. Disability analysts come from many fields; medicine, occupational and physical therapy, psychology, social work, and allied fields. Disability analysts may also consult on Americans with Disabilities Act (ADA) issues. Certification is based on board review and passing an examination. The ABDA has an active ethics program.

Education/Experience
For the Disability Analyst and Fellow certification, candidates must have a graduate degree in an appropriate field and four years of professional experience.

For Senior Disability Analyst and Diplomate certification, candidates must have a graduate degree in an appropriate field and nine years of professional experience.

Examinations
For both certifications, exams may be written, oral, or both. Study guides, workshops, and self-study materials are available.

Recertification
Fellows and Diplomates must maintain ABDA membership and earn eight contact hours of professional education annually.

CERTIFIED DISABILITY SPECIALIST

{DISABILITY SPECIALIST} DIPLOMATE, ABPDC

Sponsor
American Board of Professional Disability
  Consultants (ABPDC)
1350 Beverly Road, Suite 115-327
McLean, VA 22101
Phone: (703) 790-8644

Program Data
Certifying body: Association
Year certification began: 1988
Number certified: 520
Approximate certification costs: $225

Program Description
The ABPDC certifications recognize experienced practitioners in the field of disability consulting. Certification is based on board review of experience. Specialists and diplomates evaluate, assess, treat, or represent disabled individuals. The ABPDC maintains an active ethics program.

Education/Experience
All candidates must be licensed to practice in their particular field: counseling; education; law; medicine; nursing; occupational therapy; osteopathy; physical therapy; podiatry; psychology; social work; or speech-language-hearing pathology.

Diplomate candidates must have a doctoral degree in their field and three years of post-degree experience.

Specialist candidates must have a master's degree in their field and five years of post-degree experience.

Recertification
Certificants must maintain current licensure and ABPDC membership.

CERTIFIED FAMILY LIFE EDUCATOR (CFLE)

Sponsor

National Council on Family Relations (NCFR)
3989 Central Ave. NE, Suite 550
Minneapolis, MN 55421
Phone: (612) 781-9331
Fax: (612) 781-9348

Program Data

Certifying body: Association
Year certification began: 1985
Number certified: 980
Organization members: 3800
Approximate certification costs: $175 (members),
$275 (nonmembers)

Program Description

The Certified Family Life Educator (CFLE) designation recognizes experienced individuals practicing in the field, including community education, counseling, curriculum and resource development, health care, and ministry. Certification is based on a review of experience and education. There are no examinations. NCFR membership is not required.

Education/Experience

Candidates must demonstrate appropriate academic preparation, professional development, and work experience in the 10 areas defined by NCFR. All candidates must have a bachelor's degree or higher. Candidates with a degree in family science, home economics, psychology, sociology, or a related field must have at least two years of full-time experience. All other candidates must have five years of experience. The 10 areas in which a CFLE must demonstrate adequate preparation, development, and experience are as follows: Ethics; Families in Society; Family Law and Public Policy; Family Life Education Methodology; Family Resource Management; Human Growth and Development over the Lifespan; Human Sexuality; Internal Dynamics of Families; Interpersonal Relationships; and Parent Education and Guidance.

Recertification

CFLEs must document continuing education every five years to maintain certification.

CERTIFIED REGISTERED NURSE INTRAVENOUS (CRNI)

Sponsor

Intravenous Nurses Certification Corporation (INCC)
Fresh Pond Square
10 Fawcett St.
Cambridge, MA 02178
Phone: (617) 441-2909
Fax: (617) 441-3009

Program Data

The INCC is an affiliated corporation of the Intravenous Nurses Society (INS).

Certifying body: Independent board
Year certification began: 1985
Number certified: 3200
Organization members: Nonmembership. INS—8000
Approximate certification costs: $225 (INS members), $380 (nonmembers)

Program Description

The Certified Registered Nurse Intravenous (CRNI) program assesses, validates, and documents the clinical eligibility and continued competency of nurses delivering intravenous therapy modalities in all practice settings. Certification is based on passing the CRNI examination.

Education/Experience

Candidates must be registered nurses with a minimum of 1600 hours in a clinical position related to the care and needs of I.V. therapy patients.

Examinations

The CRNI exam is a 200-question, multiple-choice test administered by Applied Measurement Professionals. Study guides and self-study materials are available. The exam covers the following areas:

- Antineoplastic therapy
- Fluid and electrolyte therapy
- Infection control
- Parenteral nutrition
- Pediatrics
- Pharmacology
- Quality assurance
- Technology and clinical application
- Transfusion therapy

Recertification

Recertification is required every three years. CRNIs must document 1000 hours of clinical experience during the previous three years and complete one of the following options:

- Retake the CRNI examination
- Earn 40 recertification points through INS education programs

---

NATIONALLY CERTIFIED IN THERAPEUTIC MASSAGE AND BODYWORK (NCTMB)

Sponsor

National Certification Board for Therapeutic Massage and Bodywork (NCBTMB)
1735 N. Lynn St., Suite 950
Arlington, VA 22209
Phone: (800) 296-0664
Fax: (703) 524-2303

Program Data

The NCTMB program is NCCA-accredited. The NCTMB examination is used for licensure by 12 states and six municipalities. The American Massage Therapy Association (AMTA) recognizes the NCTMB program as an avenue for membership.

Certifying body: Independent board
Year certification began: 1992
Number certified: 15,595
Approximate certification costs: $150

Program Description

The Nationally Certified in Therapeutic Massage and Bodywork (NCTMB) program is an entry-level certification for massage practitioners. The NCTMB program is open to message therapists and bodywork professionals working in all modalities. Candidates may work in clinical, resort, relaxation, rehabilitation, or eclectic areas. NCBTMB maintains an active ethics program.

Education/Experience

Eligibility to take the National Certification Examination is determined by a point system. In states using the national exam for licensure requirements, candidates must meet the state-licensure eligibility criteria to take the examination, but meet the NCBTMB eligibility requirements (if higher) before receiving national certification. Candidates not graduating from an accredited school of massage therapy or recognized educational program may be required to submit additional supporting material.

Fifty points are required to take the examination:

- 7.5 points per year of experience (maximum of 30)
- 10 points per 100 hours of approved massage instruction

Examinations

The National Certification Examination is based on an extensive task survey, and tests candidates in five knowledge areas common to the profession. The 150-question, multiple-choice examination covers these five specific areas:

- Human Anatomy, Physiology, and Kinesiology, including the major organs and organ systems; the musculo-skeletal, nervous, cardiovascular, lymphatic, and respiratory systems; relationships between anatomy and massage; and efficient and safe movement patterns

- Clinical Pathology and Recognition of Various Conditions, including the signs and symptoms of disease, medical terminology, hygiene, and injuries. Also covered are neurological, gastrointestinal, joint, and skeletal disorders; muscle/fascia, respiratory, and circulatory conditions; and emotional states.

- Massage/Bodywork Theory, Assessment, and Practice, including soft tissue techniques; observation and interview techniques; basic theory; physiological rationale; endangerment sites; and joint mobilization

- Adjunct Techniques, including hydrotherapy, stress management, and exercise methods

- Business Practices and Professionalism, including ethical standards, business practices, first aid, and scope of practice for disciplines outside of massage for purposes of referral

Recertification

The NCTMB certification must be renewed every four years by documenting a minimum of 200 hours of hands-on therapeutic massage and/or bodywork and 50 hours of continuing education. Retaking and passing the National Certification Examination may be used in lieu of the continuing education requirement.

INTERNATIONALLY CERTIFIED MASSAGE THERAPIST (ICMT®)

INTERNATIONALLY CERTIFIED BODYWORK THERAPIST (ICBT®)

INTERNATIONALLY CERTIFIED SOMATIC THERAPIST (ICST®)

Sponsor

Associated Bodywork and Massage
  Professionals (ABMT)
28677 Buffalo Park Road
Evergreen, CO 80439
Phone: (303) 674-8478
Fax: (303) 674-0859

Program Data

Certifying body: Association
Year certification began: 1995
Number certified: 1800
Organization members: 20,000
Approximate certification costs: $229

Program Description

The Internationally Certified Massage Therapist (ICMT®), Bodywork Therapist (ICBT®), and Somatic Therapist (ICST®) designations are titles available for use by certified-level members of Associated Bodywork and Massage Professionals (ABMT). There are two levels of certified membership: Certified Level 1 includes liability insurance (total cost $229 annually); Certified Level 2 does not (total cost $99 annually).

Currently ABMT is granting certified-level membership status under a grandfathering program. ABMT maintains an active ethics program.

Education/Experience

For certified-level membership status, candidates must meet one of the following requirements:

- 500 hours of massage education from an ABMT-approved program
- Current registered or certified-level membership in a recognized massage association
- Passing score on an ABMT-recognized examination
- Nursing or physical therapy degree and 50 hours of massage training

Recertification

None.

CERTIFIED MEDICAL ASSISTANT (CMA)

Sponsor

American Association of Medical Assistants
  (AAMA)
20 N. Wacker Drive, Suite 1575
Chicago, IL 60606
Phone: (312) 899-1500

Program Data

Certifying body: Association

Program Description

The Certified Medical Assistant (CMA) designation recognizes medical assistants who have demonstrated competence in both administrative and clinical duties. Medical assistants work under supervision of physicians. Certification is based on passing an examination. Membership in the AAMA is not required.

Education/Experience

To qualify to sit for the examination, a candidate must meet one of the following requirements:

- Student/Graduate of an AAMA Endowment-sponsored medical-assisting program
- One year of full-time or two years of part-time experience as a medical assistant, and graduation from a medical-assisting program accredited by the CAHEA. Medical-assisting instructors from accredited institutions also qualify.

Examinations

The CMA examination is based on an in-depth analysis on medical assistant competencies. The National Board of Medical Examiners (NBME) assists in the development and administration of the CMA examination. The 300-question, multiple-choice examination covers three areas: general medical, medical administration, and clinical.

Recertification

CMAs must recertify every five years. Recertification is based on continuing education or retaking the CMA examination.

REGISTERED NURSE CERTIFIED (RNC)

Sponsor

National Certification Corporation for the
Obstetric, Gynecological, and Neonatal
Nursing Specialties (NCC)
645 N. Michigan Ave., Suite 900
Chicago, IL 60611
Phone: (800) 367-5613

Program Data

Certifying body: Independent board
Year certification began: 1976
Number certified: 44,000

Program Description

The NCC Registered Nurse Certified (RNC) designation recognizes experienced nurses who have
passed one or more specialization examinations in
obstetrics, gynecology, or neonatal nursing. Exams
are offered in two general areas—nurse practitioner and nursing specialties.

Education/Experience

All candidates must hold current licensure as a
registered nurse for all NCC examinations.

Nurse-practitioner exams—Candidates must
have completed a formal nurse-practitioner program in a related field (either graduate degree or
advanced-nurse-practitioner certificate). Candidates must document two years of experience
and 2000 hours of practice time in a related field.

Nursing-specialty exams—Candidates must document two years of experience and 2000 hours
of practice time in a related field.

Examinations

Certification is based on passing an examination
within the candidate's field of practice. Experience
requirements must be met within the same area as
the examination. The average pass rate for all
examinations is 70%. Full sets of competency
statements for each specialty are available from
NCC. All exams include questions on professional
issues. Tests are available in these specialty areas:

- Women's Healthcare Nurse Practitioner
- Neonatal Nurse Practitioner
- Ambulatory Women's Healthcare Nursing
- High-Risk Obstetric Nursing
- Inpatient Obstetrics Nursing
- Low-Risk Neonatal Nursing
- Maternal Newborn Nursing
- Reproductive Endocrinology/Infertility Nursing

Recertification

RNCs must renew their certification every three
years, either by retaking the examination in their
specialty, or by earning 45 contact hours of acceptable continuing education.

REGISTERED NURSE, CERTIFIED (RN, C)
REGISTERED NURSE, CERTIFIED SPECIALIST (RN, CS)

Sponsor

American Nurses Credentialing Center (ANCC)
American Nurses Association (ANA)
600 Maryland Ave. SW, Suite 100
Washington, DC 20024
Phone: (800) 274-4262

Program Data

Certifying body: Association-sponsored
independent board
Year certification began: 1973
Additional programs: Registered Nurse, Certified
in Nursing Administration (RN,CNA);
Registered Nurse, Certified in Nursing
Administration, Advanced (RN, CNAA)
Approximate certification costs: $200 (members),
$350 (nonmembers)

Program Description

The Registered Nurse, Certified (RN,C) designation
recognizes RNs with expertise in a particular area
of practice. Certification is based on passing an
examination in a particular area. There are no
membership requirements.

Education/Experience

All candidates must currently hold an active RN
license in the United States or its territories. Practice and continuing education must be within the
specialty area. Most certifications require a bachelor's degree; most specialist certifications require
a master's degree. The specialties are as follows:

Registered Nurse, Certified (RN,C)—Medical-
Surgical Nurse; Gerontological Nurse; Psychi-
atric and Mental Health Nurse; Pediatric Nurse;
Perinatal Nurse; Community Health Nurse;
School Nurse; General Nursing Practice; College
Health Nurse; Nursing Continuing Education/
Staff Development; Home Health Nurse; Cardiac
Rehabilitation Nurse; and Informatics Nurse

Registered Nurse, Certified Specialist (RN,CS)—Clinical Specialist in Gerontological Nursing; Clinical Specialist in Medical-Surgical Nursing; Clinical Specialist in Community Health Nursing; Clinical Specialist in Adult Psychiatric and Mental Health Nursing; Clinical Specialist in Child and Adolescent Psychiatric and Mental Health Nursing; Clinical Specialist in Home Health Nursing; Gerontological Nurse Practitioner; Pediatric Nurse Practitioner; Adult Nurse Practitioner; Family Nurse Practitioner; School Nurse Practitioner; and Acute Care Nurse Practitioner

Examinations

The half-day, multiple-choice exam covers practice, ethics, and knowledge related to a specific area.

Recertification

ANCC certification must be renewed every five years through continuing professional education.

CERTIFIED NURSE-MIDWIFE (CNM)

CERTIFIED MIDWIFE (CM)

Sponsor

ACNM Certification Council, Inc.
8401 Corporate Drive, #630
Landover, MD 20785
Phone: (301) 459-1321
Fax: (301) 731-7825
E-mail: ACNMCertCN@aol.com.
WWW: http://www.acnm.org/

Program Data

The ACNM Certification Council is the official certifying body for the American College of Nurse-Midwives (ACNM).

Certifying body: Independent board
Year certification began: 1971
Number certified: 6225
Approximate certification costs: $385

Program Description

The ACNM certification process is an entry-level program testing safe and knowledgeable practice. Certification is based on passing an examination.

Education/Experience

The CNM candidate must be currently licensed as a Registered Nurse and complete a nurse-midwifery program accredited by the ACNM Division of Accreditation. Foreign prepared candidates must complete a precertification review and program.

The CM candidate who is not an RN must complete a basic midwifery program accredited by the ACNM Division of Accreditation.

Examinations

The ACNM examination is a three-part, short-answer and essay test. The exam covers antepartum; labor and delivery; postpartum; family planning; well-woman gynecology; newborn; and professional issues. Two-thirds of each area cover normal conditions, and one-third covers problems and abnormal conditions. The pass rate is 92%.

Recertification

CNMs and CMs certified after 1995 must renew their certification every eight years through continuing education.

OCCUPATIONAL THERAPIST, REGISTERED (OTR)

Sponsor

American Occupational Therapy Certification Board, Inc. (AOTCB)
4 Research Place, Suite 160
Rockville, MD 20850
Phone: (301) 990-7979
Fax: (301) 869-8492

Program Data

Forty-nine jurisdictional regulatory boards recognize AOTCB examinations for meeting regulatory requirements.

Certifying body: Independent board
Year certification began: 1930
Number certified: 90,000 (both certifications)
Additional programs: Certified Occupational Therapy Assistant (COTA)
Approximate certification costs: $250

Program Description

The Occupational Therapist, Registered (OTR) certification is a national certification program for entry-level occupational therapists. Most states have a separate licensure requirement for occupational therapists, many of which include the OTR examination. State licensure does not guarantee automatic AOTCB certification. AOTCB has an extensive and proactive disciplinary program.

Education/Experience

Candidates must hold a bachelor's degree or higher and graduate from an occupational therapy education program accredited by the Accreditation Council on Occupational Therapy Education (ACOTE). Accredited programs include therapist-level fieldwork. There is no other experience requirement.

Examinations

The OTR examination is based on an extensive job analysis that identified entry-level tasks and knowledge. The 200-question, multiple-choice examination is administered by the Professional Examination Service (475 Riverside Drive, New York, NY 10115-0089; phone 212-870-3161). The examination covers the following areas:

- Biological, physical and behavioral sciences
- Discharge plan development
- Documentation
- Human development
- Managing and organizing services
- Medical, clinical, and diagnostic functions
- Occupational performance assessment
- Occupational therapy theory and performance
- Professional practice
- Sensimotor, cognitive, and psychological components of OT
- Treatment plan development
- Treatment plan evaluation
- Treatment plan implementation

Recertification

Certification is automatically renewed every five years unless it has been suspended or revoked.

AMERICAN BOARD OF OPTICIANRY CERTIFIED (ABOC)

Sponsor

American Board of Opticianry (ABO)
10341 Democracy Lane
Fairfax, VA 22030
Phone: (703) 691-1061

Program Data

The ABO Board of Directors includes representatives from the National Academy of Opticianry, Opticians Association of America, National Federation of Opticianry Schools, and National Committee of State Opticianry Licensing Boards. Several states use the ABO examination as part of their licensing requirements.

Certifying body: Independent board
Number certified: 6930 (includes National Contact Lens Examiners certifications)

Program Description

The American Board of Opticianry Certified (ABOC) designation recognizes eyewear dispensers who meet the requirements defined in an extensive job analysis. Certification is based on passing an examination. There are no prerequisites to sitting for the ABO examination. However, candidates with broad-based experience, schooling, or company training have historically performed better on the examination.

Examinations

The Professional Examination Service administers the National Opticianry Competency Examination. The examination covers patient and customer interaction; prescriptions; fitting and dispensing eyewear; standards and regulations; and using standard equipment.

Recertification

Recertification is required every three years. Recertification is through accumulating 15 credits of approved continuing education.

ORTHOPAEDIC NURSE CERTIFIED (ONC)

Sponsor

Orthopaedic Nursing Certification Board (ONCB)
E. Holly Ave., Box 56
Pitman, NJ 08071
Phone: (609) 256-2311
Fax: (609) 256-2327

Program Data

The ONCB is the designated certifying agency for the National Association of Orthopaedic Nurses (NAON).

Certifying body: Association-sponsored
    independent board
Year certification began: 1988
Number certified: 3000
Organization members: 8500
Approximate certification costs: $180 (members),
    $225 (nonmembers)

Program Description

The Orthopaedic Nurse Certified (ONC) designation recognizes RNs involved in orthopaedic practice, including administration; adult care; education; critical care; medical-surgical; office practice; and pediatrics. Certification is based on passing an examination.

Education/Experience

Candidates must hold a current RN license, have two years of RN experience, and document a minimum of 1000 hours of orthopaedic work experience within the previous three years.

Examinations

The ONC exam, developed with the assistance of the Center for Nursing Education and Testing, is a four-hour comprehensive test. Study guides, workshops, and self-study materials are available. The exam covers degenerative diseases; inflammatory disorders; metabolic bone disease; neuromuscular/ pediatric/congenital; oncology; operative orthopaedics; sports injuries; and trauma.

Recertification

ONCs must renew their certification every five years, through earning 70 contact hours of orthopaedic and 30 contact hours of general nursing continuing education.

CERTIFIED PEDIATRIC NURSE (CPN)

CERTIFIED PEDIATRIC NURSE PRACTITIONER (CPNP)

Sponsor

National Certification Board of Pediatric Nurse
    Practitioners and Nurses (NCBPNP/N)
416 Hungerford Drive, Suite 222
Rockville, MD 20833
Phone: (301) 340-8213
Fax: (301) 340-8604

Program Data

Certifying body: Independent board
Year certification began: 1977
Number certified: 5875
Approximate certification costs: $195 (CPN),
    $300 (CPNP)

Program Description

The National Certification Board of PNP/N certifies both nurses and nurse practitioners in pediatrics. Certification is based on experience and passing an examination.

Education/Experience

For the CPN designation, candidates must be currently licensed as a Registered Nurse and meet one of the following requirements:

- BSN and two years/3500 hours of pediatric nursing experience within the past five years

- Three years/5250 hours of pediatric nursing experience. This option will not be available after 1996.

For the CPNP designation, candidates must hold a master's degree from an approved Pediatric Nurse Practitioner program and be currently licensed as a Registered Nurse.

Examinations

The CPN examination was created based on an extensive task analysis and input from a national task force on pediatric nursing. The multiple-choice examination covers these areas:

- Family dynamics
- Growth and development
- Health promotion of children and families
- Nursing process for common health problems
- Pediatric nursing in varied delivery systems
- Pediatric nursing principles and techniques
- Special needs

The CPNP examination was developed by an expert panel. The multiple-choice examination covers these areas:

- Common clinical problems
- Growth and development
- Healthcare delivery systems and methods
- Health maintenance

Recertification

CPNs must renew their certification every five years, either through reexamination or earning 10 contact hours of acceptable education annually.

CPNPs must renew their certification every seven years, either through reexamination or earning 10 contact hours of acceptable education annually.

BOARD CERTIFIED NUTRITION SUPPORT PHARMACIST (BCNSP)

BOARD CERTIFIED NUCLEAR PHARMACIST (BCNP)

BOARD CERTIFIED PHARMACOTHERAPY SPECIALIST (BCPS)

Sponsor

Board of Pharmaceutical Specialties (BPS)
American Pharmaceutical Association (APhA)
2215 Constitution Ave. NW
Washington, DC 20037
Phone: (202) 429-7591
Fax: (202) 783-2351

Program Data

The following organizations recognize one or more of the BPS programs: American College of Clinical Pharmacy (ACCP); American Association of Colleges of Pharmacy (AACP); American Society for Parenteral and Enteral Nutrition (A.S.P.E.N.); American Society of Consultant Pharmacists (ASCP); American Society of Health-System Pharmacists (ASHSP); American Society of Hospital Pharmacists (ASHP); Society of Infectious Diseases Pharmacists (SIDP); U.S. Department of Defense; U.S. Department of Veterans Affairs; U.S. Nuclear Regulatory Commission (BCNP only).

Certifying body: Association-sponsored independent board
Year certification began: BCNSP—1992, BCNP—1982, BCPS—1991
Number certified: BCNSP—377, BCNP—342, BCPS—932
Approximate certification costs: $500

Program Description

The licensing of medical pharmacists is a function of each state's government. Board certification within a specialty is not required for employment as a pharmacist. Preparatory materials are available. The BPS sponsors the following specialty certifications:

- Board Certified Nutrition Support Pharmacist (BCNSP)
- Board Certified Nuclear Pharmacist (BCNP)
- Board Certified Pharmacotherapy Specialist (BCPS)

Education/Experience

All candidates must hold a current license and an entry-level degree in pharmacy from a program accredited by the American Council on Pharmaceutical Education (ACPE). Experience requirements are met primarily in the area of specialty.

- BCNSP—Either three years of practice experience primarily in nutrition support, or a fellowship or residency with one year practice
- BCNP—4000 hours of nuclear-pharmaceutical practice experience
- BCPS—Completion of either a residency or fellowship program in pharmacotherapy or five years of practice

Examinations

The examinations are as follows:

BCNSP—A 200-question, multiple-choice exam covering provision of individualized nutrition support care, including assessment; therapeutic plan development, implementation, and monitoring/management; managing nutrition support; and practice advancement

BCNP—A 200-question, multiple-choice exam covering compounding; quality control; dispensing; distribution; radiation protection; consultation; and education

BCPS—Exam comprising 200 multiple-choice questions on collecting and interpreting data for patient-specific pharmacotherapy; interpreting, generating, and disseminating pharmacotherapy knowledge; and optimizing healthcare through system-specific policies and procedures

Recertification

All certificants must maintain state licensure and submit reports of practice.

BCNSP must recertify every six years through earning three contact hours of training and passing a 100-question, multiple-choice recertification exam.

BCNP must recertify every six years through continuing education, peer review, and a recertification exam.

BCPS must recertify every seven years either by passing a 100-question, multiple-choice test, or by completing an approved 120-hour professional development program.

PHYSICIAN ASSISTANT-CERTIFIED (PA-C)

Sponsor

National Commission on Certification of
    Physician Assistants (NCCPA)
2845 Henderson Mill Road, NE
Atlanta, GA 30341
Phone: (404) 493-9100

Program Data

Commission members include the American Academy of Physician Assistants (AAPA); American College of Surgeons (ACS); American Medical Association (AMA); Federation of State Medical Boards of the U.S.; U.S. Department of Defense; and other major medical organizations. Most states require initial NCCPA certification for Physician Assistants.

Certifying body: Independent board
Number certified: 30,000

Program Description

A Physician Assistant provides healthcare services under physician direction and performs many of the functions formerly done only by physicians. Candidates must have graduated from a physician-assisting program accredited by the Commission on Accreditation of Allied Health Education Programs. Candidates must pass a minimum of two examination components, and may elect to take extended core examinations in primary care or surgery.

Recertification

To maintain certification, PAs must complete 100 hours of continuing medical education every two years and take a recertification exam every six years.

PHYSICAL THERAPIST SPECIALIST CERTIFICATION

Sponsor

American Physical Therapy Association
1111 North Fairfax St.
Alexandria, VA 22314
Phone: (703) 684-2782
E-mail: spec-cert@apta.org
WWW: http://apta.edoc.com/

Program Data

Certifying body: Association-sponsored
    independent board
Year certification began: 1985
Number certified: 1345
Approximate certification costs: $1000
    (members), $1325 (nonmembers)

Program Description

The licensing of physical therapists is regulated by all 50 states. Board certification within a specialty is not required for a physical therapist to practice. The American Physical Therapy Association (APTA) sponsors the American Board of Physical Therapy Specialties (ABPTS) to provide clinical specialist certification. Board certification recognizes advanced clinical knowledge, experience, and skills within a specialty. Certification is based on passing an examination. ABPTS maintains an active ethics program.

Candidates may be certified in one or more of the following specialties:

- Cardiopulmonary Certified Specialist (CCS)
- Clinical Electrophysiologic Certified Specialist (CECS)
- Geriatrics Certified Specialist (GCS)
- Neurologic Certified Specialist (NCS)
- Orthopaedics Certified Specialist (OCS)
- Pediatric Certified Specialist (PCS)
- Sports Certified Specialist (SCS)

Education/Experience

All candidates must hold current state licensure as a physical therapist and have at least two years of experience in their specialty.

Cardiopulmonary—6240 clinical practice hours within the past 10 years, with at least 4160 in cardiopulmonary physical therapy; current Advanced Cardiac Life Support certification; participation in a research process

Clinical Electrophysiology—6240 clinical practice hours within the past 10 years, with at least 2080 in electrophysiologic testing; evidence of clinical educational experience in the specialty; review of candidate case reports

Geriatrics—8320 practice hours, with at least 6240 hours of clinical geriatric practice (4160 in direct patient care) within the last 10 years

Neurologic—4160 hours clinical practice in the specialty

Orthopaedics—10,400 practice hours, with 6240 hours of direct orthopaedic practice within the last six years

Pediatric—6240 clinical practice hours within the past 10 years, with at least 4160 in direct patient care

Sports—10,400 practice hours, with 6240 hours of direct sports-patient care within the last six years; current CPR certification; and completion of the Red Cross Emergency Responder Course or equivalent certification

Examinations

The exams for each specialty are based on a Description of Advanced Clinical Practice. Exams are offered electronically by Assessment Systems, Inc. (ASI). Each exam comprises approximately 200 questions, many in the form of case scenarios.

Recertification

Specialty certification is awarded for 10 years. Specialists must maintain licensure and clinical practice to renew certification.

CERTIFIED REHABILITATION COUNSELOR (CRC)

Sponsor

Commission on Rehabilitation Counselor Certification (CRCC)
1835 Rohlwing Road, Suite E
Rolling Meadows, IL 60008
Phone: (708) 818-1967

Program Data

CRCC is accredited by the National Commission for Certifying Agencies (NCCA) and is a sponsoring organization of the Foundation for Rehabilitation Certification, Education, and Research.

Appointing organizations for the commission are the American Deafness and Rehabilitation Association (ADARA); American Rehabilitation Counseling Association (ARCA); Canadian Association of Rehabilitation Personnel (CARP); Council on Rehabilitation Education (CORE); Council of State Administrators of Vocational Rehabilitation (CSVAR); National Association of Non-White Rehabilitation Workers (NANWRW); National Association of Rehabilitation Professionals in the Private Sector (NARPPS); National Council on Rehabilitation Education (NRCE); National Rehabilitation Counseling Association (NRCA).

Certifying body: Independent board
Year certification began: 1973
Number certified: 12,886
Approximate certification costs: $209

Program Description

The Certified Rehabilitation Counselor (CRC) recognizes counseling professionals who assist disabled individuals in independent living. CRCs may counsel and evaluate psychological, social, medical, and vocational needs and options. Certification is based on passing an examination and meeting minimum educational and work-experience standards. There are no membership requirements.

Education/Experience

To sit for the CRC examination, candidates must meet one of the following requirements:

- Master's degree in rehabilitation counseling or doctorate emphasizing rehabilitation and 600 clock hours of internship. If master's program is not accredited by CORE, candidates must have one year of experience.
- Master's degree outside rehabilitation counseling and between 36 and 60 months of experience, depending on the graduate courses taken
- Doctorate with 36 months employed in a rehabilitation-counseling education program

Experienced candidates without one year of work under the supervision of a CRC are granted provisional status (CRC/P) and must complete additional requirements.

Examinations

The 300-question, one-day, multiple-choice examination covers foundation of rehabilitation counseling; medical and psychological aspects of disability; individual and group counseling; family; gender; multicultural issues; assessment; institutional and employer consultation services; case management; workers' compensation; and program evaluation and research. The pass rate is 80%.

Recertification

CRCs must renew certification every five years by accumulating 100 clock hours of acceptable continuing education, or by retaking the CRC examination.

MEDICAL
Medical Technology/Allied Health

CERTIFIED ANESTHESIOLOGIST ASSISTANT

Sponsor

National Commission for Certification of
Anesthesiologist Assistants (NCCAA)
P.O. Box 15519
Atlanta, GA 30333

Program Data

The American Academy of Anesthesiologists
Assistants (AAAA) endorses the NCCAA examination.

Certifying body: Independent board
Year certification began: 1992
Number certified: 400
Approximate certification costs: $1075

Program Description

The NCCAA certification program recognizes
entry-level anesthesiologist assistants. Certification
is based on an examination. There are no membership requirements.

Education/Experience

Candidates must complete a formal education
program for anesthesiologist assistants accredited
by the Committee on Allied Health Education and
Accreditation (CAHEA) prior to taking the NCCAA
examination. Candidates must either currently
practice or be eligible to practice upon graduation.

Examinations

The one-day, 200-question examination is designed to measure entry-level cognitive and de-
ductive skills commensurate with recognized
standards. The exam was designed with the assistance of the National Board of Medical Examiners (NBME). The pass rate is 90%.

Recertification

None.

ASSISTIVE TECHNOLOGY PRACTITIONER (ATP)
ASSISTIVE TECHNOLOGY SUPPLIER (ATS)

Sponsor

Rehabilitation Engineering and Assistive
Technology Society of North America (RESNA)
1700 North Moore St., Suite 1540
Arlington, VA 22209-1903
Phone: (703) 524-6686
Fax: (703) 524-6630
TTY: (703) 524-6639
E-mail: nanderson@resna.org
http://www.resna.org/resna/reshome.htm

Program Data

Certifying body: Association
Year certification began: 1996
Number certified: New program
Approximate certification costs: $500

Program Description

The Assistive Technology Practitioner (ATP) and
Supplier (ATS) certifications recognize disability
professionals involved with assessing, training,
selling, and servicing assistive devices. Experience
and education in rehabilitation science (occupational therapy; physical therapy; speech-language-
gearing pathology; special education; rehabilitation
counseling; orthotics prosthetics), in nursing, or as
a medical doctor is required. Certification is based
on a two-part examination. There are no membership requirements.

Education/Experience

Candidates for the ATP or ATS designation must
meet one of the following requirements:

- Bachelor's degree in a rehabilitation science
  and two years of acceptable experience (at
  least one-fourth time in client services)
- Associate's degree in a rehabilitation science
  and two years of acceptable experience (at
  least one-half time in client services)

- Bachelor's degree (any) and four years of acceptable experience (at least one-half time in client services)
- Associate's degree (any) or high school diploma and four years of full-time experience in client services (two years for ATS)

Examinations
The ATP and ATS examinations are two-part tests; the first covering foundation information, and the second presenting case-based, designation-specific questions.

Recertification
Recertification is under review; this is a new program.

CERTIFIED BIOMEDICAL EQUIPMENT TECHNICIAN (CBET)

Sponsor
International Certification Commission (ICC)
3330 Washington Blvd., Suite 400
Arlington, VA 22201
Phone: (703) 525-4890

Program Data
The ICC has 10 membership organizations, including the Association for the Advancement of Medical Instrumentation (AAMI) and the Society of Biomedical Equipment Technicians (SBET).

Certifying body: Independent board
Number certified: 4100+
Additional programs: Certified Laboratory Equipment Specialist (CLES); Certified Radiology Equipment Specialist (CRES)
Approximate certification costs: $200

Program Description
The Certified Biomedical Equipment Technician (CBET) recognizes individuals who maintain, troubleshoot, and repair biomedical equipment. The CBET is a generalist certification based on an examination. There are no membership requirements. ICC does not sponsor or endorse any preparation materials; AAMI offers a one-day review session.

Education/Experience
Candidates must have either four years of experience; three years of experience and an associate's degree in electronics technology; or two years of experience and an associate's degree in biomedical equipment technology.

Examinations
The CBET examination is a 150-question, six-hour, multiple-choice test covering the following areas: anatomy and physiology; fundamentals of electricity and electronics; healthcare facility safety; medical equipment function and operation; and medical equipment troubleshooting.

Recertification
None.

REGISTERED DIAGNOSTIC CARDIAC SONOGRAPHER (RDCS)

Sponsor
American Registry of Diagnostic Medical
    Sonographers® (ARDMS®)
600 Jefferson Plaza, Suite 360
Rockville, MD 20852
Phone: (800) 541-9754
Fax: (301) 738-0312
WWW: http://www.ardms.org/

Program Data
ARDMS is recognized by the American College of Radiology (ACR); American Institute of Ultrasound in Medicine (AIUM); American Society of Echocardiography (ASE); International Society for Cardiovascular Surgery (ISCVS); Society of Diagnostic Medical Sonographers (SDMS); Society for Vascular Surgery (SVS); and the Society of Vascular Technology (SVT).

Certifying body: Independent board
Year certification began: 1975
Number certified: 27,000 (all programs)
Additional programs: Registered Diagnostic Medical Sonographer® (RDMS®); Registered Vascular Technologist® (RVT®)
Approximate certification costs: $200

Program Description
The Registered Diagnostic Cardiac Sonographer (RDCS) recognizes individuals skilled in either adult or pediatric echocardiography. Certification is based on passing a physics/principles exam and a specialty exam. There are no membership requirements. ARDMS neither sells nor endorses examination preparation materials.

Education/Experience

To sit for the certification examinations, candidates must meet one of the following requirements:

- Completion of an ultrasound/vascular technology education program approved by the Commission on Accreditation of Allied Health Education Programs (CAAHEP) or the Canadian Medical Association (CMA).

- One year of clinical ultrasound/vascular experience and either a bachelor's degree or completion of a two-year, patient care-related AMA or AMA-equivalent allied health education program

- Two years of clinical ultrasound/vascular experience and either two years of formal education beyond high school or two years of patient care-related experience

Examinations

RDCS requires the successful completion of a general principles examination and one of two specialty examinations. All candidates take the 120-question, two-hour, multiple-choice exam: Cardiovascular Principles and Instrumentation. This examination covers bioeffects and safety; cardiac hemodynamics principles; cardiac physiology and evaluation methods; congenital defects; doppler; embryology; features and artifacts; heart anatomy; pulse echo instrumentations and imaging principles; quality assurance; storage and display of images; and ultrasound transducers.

Candidates must pass one of two 180-question, three-hour specialty examinations. Some questions reference videotaped, two-dimensional cases. The specialty examinations are in Adult Echocardiography and Pediatric Echocardiography.

Recertification

Registrants must renew certification every three years through either continuing education or examination. RDCSs must earn 30 hours of related continuing education, pass the other specialty examination within their area, or earn the RDMS or RVT designation.

REGISTERED CENTRAL SERVICE TECHNICIAN (RCST)

CERTIFIED REGISTERED CENTRAL SERVICE TECHNICIAN (CRCST)

Sponsor

International Association of Healthcare Central Service Material Management (IAHCSMM)
213 W. Institute Place, Suite 307
Chicago, IL 60610
Phone: (312) 440-0078
Fax: (312) 440-9474

Program Data

The Center for Professional Correspondence Studies at Purdue University (Indiana) participates in this program.

Certifying body: Association
Year certification began: 1980
Number certified: 10,000
Organization members: 8000+

Program Description

The Registered Central Service Technician (RCST) designation recognizes technical and supervisory personnel in healthcare-facility central services. IAHCSMM membership is required. Registered status is awarded upon completing either an IAHCSMM-approved course or the Purdue University correspondence course on the principles of processing, handling, and distribution.

The Certified Registered Central Service Technician (CRCST) is granted to RCSTs upon their meeting the experience requirements and passing an examination.

Education/Experience

If an RCST did not have six months of experience prior to taking the IAHCSMM-approved course, 100 hours of specific experience must be documented.

Examinations

The CRCST examination is a multiple-choice test covering these areas:

- Basic microbiology
- Chemistry in central service
- Cleaning fundamentals
- Communications and human relations

- Disposables and reusables
- Equipment maintenance
- Infection control
- Instruments care and processing
- Inventory control
- Packaging
- Preparing procedure trays
- Preparing solutions
- Safety
- Sterilization
- Storage
- Supplies distribution
- Syringes and needles recognition and use

Recertification
Twelve recertification points are required annually.

REGISTERED DENTAL ASSISTANT (RDA[AMT])

Sponsor
American Medical Technologists (AMT)
710 Higgins Road
Park Ridge, IL 60068
Phone: (708) 823-5169

Program Data
AMT is a member of the National Organization for Competency Assurance (NOCA) and the National Committee for Clinical Laboratory Standards (NCCLS).

Certifying body: Association
Number certified: 370
Organization members: 21,000
Additional certifications: Medical Laboratory Technician (MLT); Medical Technologist (MT); Registered Medical Assistant (RMA); Registered Phlebotomy Technician (RPT)
Approximate certification costs: $59

Program Description
The Registered Dental Assistant (RDA) designation recognizes qualified dental assistants. Certification is based on passing an examination. Membership in AMT comes with certification.

Education/Experience
Candidates must hold current CPR certification. A candidate qualifies to sit for the RDA examination by meeting one of the following qualifications:

- Graduation from an accredited dental-assisting program that includes office assisting, dental sciences, clinical procedures, and radiology
- Graduation from a U.S. Armed Forces dental-assisting program that includes office assisting, dental sciences, clinical procedures, and radiology; and completion of one year of dental assisting

Examinations
The RDA examination is made up of approximately 200 multiple-choice questions. The questions are competency-based, and cover the following areas: office-assisting skills, dental sciences, clinical procedures, and radiology.

Recertification
None.

CERTIFIED DENTAL TECHNICIAN (CDT)

Sponsor
National Board for Certification in Dental Laboratory Technology (NBC)
3801 Mt. Vernon Ave.
Alexandria, VA 22305
Phone: (703) 683-5310

Program Data
The program is endorsed by the American Dental Association (ADA) and the National Association of Dental Laboratories (NADL).

Certifying body: Independent board
Number certified: 8800 plus (active)

Program Description
The Certified Dental Technician (CDT) designation recognizes dental technicians with both knowledge and practical ability. Certification is based on passing a specialty examination. There are no membership requirements.

Education/Experience

Candidates must meet one of the following requirements to take the certification examination:

- Completed a two-year, NBC-accredited dental technology program and either passed the NBC-administered Recognized Graduate examination or passed the comprehensive equivalency examination

- Completed five years of combined education and experience in dental technology and passed the comprehensive equivalency examination

Examinations

Candidates must have previously passed the Recognized Graduate (RG) examination or passed the comprehensive equivalency examination. Both examinations are 160-question, multiple-choice tests covering anatomy, materials, techniques, and fundamentals of complete dentures, partial dentures, crowns and bridges, ceramics, and orthodontics.

The CDT examination is a written and practical examination in a candidate's specialty: Complete Dentures, Partial Dentures, Crowns and Bridges, Ceramics, or Orthodontics. The practical examination takes five and one-quarter hours and requires the candidate to demonstrate an adequate range of competencies to complete work in a particular specialty. The written examination takes one and one-quarter hours; it is an 80-question, multiple-choice test covering terminology, health and safety, equipment, and technical considerations within the selected specialty.

Recertification

CDTs must renew their certification every two years by accumulating 10 continuing-education points annually. A minimum of four points (1 point per contact hour) must be earned in technical or scientific areas.

REGISTERED ELECTROENCEPHALOGRAPHIC TECHNOLOGIST (R. EEG T. ®)

Sponsor

American Board of Registration of Electroencephalographic and Evoked Potential Technologists (ABRET)
P.O. Box 916633
Longwood, FL 32791

Phone: (407) 788-6308
Fax: (407) 788-2084

Program Data

The ABRET registration programs are endorsed by the American Society of Electroneurodiagnostic Technology and the American EEG Society.

Certifying body: Independent board
Year certification began: 1964
Number certified: 2778
Additional programs: Registered Evoked Potential Technologist (R. EP T.)
Approximate certification costs: $150

Program Description

The Registered Electroencephalographic Technologist (R. EEG T. ®) designation recognizes skilled technicians passing both a written exam and an oral/practical exam in Electroencephalography. There are no membership requirements. Study guides are available.

Education/Experience

Candidates must document one year of continuous experience in the field. Candidates must also have completed either a formal education program in the field or a documented on-the-job training program.

Examinations

There are two parts to the R. EEG T. examination. Part 1 is a four-hour, 250-question, multiple-choice examination administered by the Professional Testing Corporation. Part 1 covers the following areas:

- Basic science
- Clinical conditions and EEG correlates
- EEG instrumentation, recording techniques, and pattern recognition
- Patient protection, safety, and environmental issues

Part 2 is an oral/practical examination administered by ABRET.

Recertification

Beginning in 1997, registration will need to be renewed every 10 years through education or testing.

REGISTERED EVOKED POTENTIAL TECHNOLOGIST (R. EP T.)

Sponsor

American Board of Registration of
Electroencephalographic and Evoked
Potential Technologists (ABRET)
P.O. Box 916633
Longwood, FL 32791
Phone: (407) 788-6308
Fax: (407) 788-2084

Program Data

The ABRET registration programs are endorsed by the American Society of Electroneurodiagnostic Technology and the American EEG Society.

Certifying body: Independent board
Year certification began: 1983
Number certified: 529
Additional programs: Registered
Electroencephalographic Technologist
(R. EEG T. ®)
Approximate certification costs: $150

Program Description

The Registered Evoked Potential Technologist (R. EP T.) designation recognizes skilled technicians passing both a written and an oral/practical examination in Electroencephalography. There are no membership requirements. Study guides are available.

Education/Experience

Candidates must document one year of continuous experience in the field. Candidates must also have completed either a formal education program in the field or a documented on-the-job training program.

Examinations

There are two parts to the R. EP T. examination. Part 1 is a four-hour, 250-question, multiple-choice examination administered by the Professional Testing Corporation. Part 1 covers the following areas:

- Anatomy and neurophysiology
- Clinical conditions
- Evoked potentials
- Technical sciences

Part 2 is an oral/practical examination administered by ABRET.

Recertification

Beginning in 1997, registration will need to be renewed every 10 years through education or testing.

ACSM EXERCISE LEADER℠

Sponsor

American College of Sports Medicine (ACSM)
P.O. Box 1440
401 W. Michigan St.
Indianapolis, IN 46202
Phone: (800) 486-5643
Fax: (317) 634-7817
E-mail: crtacsm@acsm.org
WWW: http://www.a1.com/sportsmed/index.htm

Program Data

Certifying body: Association
Year certification began: 1975
Number certified: 16,000 (all certifications)
Additional programs: ACSM certification for
Exercise Specialist, Exercise Test Technologist,
Health/Fitness Director, and Health/Fitness
Instructor, and Program Director

Program Description

The ACSM Exercise Leader℠ certification is the entry-level Health and Fitness Track certification. The certification recognizes trained leaders in health and fitness exercise. Certification is based on a written exam and a practical exam. Current CPR certification is required. An optional workshop is available.

Examinations

ACSM certifications are based on behavioral objectives described in the ACSM's *Guidelines for Exercise Testing and Prescription*. The multiple-choice written examination is based on these objectives.

The practical exercise consists of demonstrating skills at three practical stations:

- Heart rate/cycle ergometer, which includes measuring resting and exercise heartbeats, teaching clients to measure their own rates, and instructing beginners on exercise bicycles
- Exercise modifications, which measures candidate's ability to safely modify exercises for clients with musculoskeletal problems
- Group leadership, which measures exercise group leadership

Recertification
Certification must be renewed every four years and is based on continuing education. CPR certification must be maintained. Exercise leaders must earn 40 continuing-education hours (or hour equivalents).

ACSM EXERCISE SPECIALIST℠

Sponsor
American College of Sports Medicine (ACSM)
P.O. Box 1440
401 W. Michigan St.
Indianapolis, IN 46202
Phone: (800) 486-5643
Fax: (317) 634-7817
E-mail: crtacsm@acsm.org
WWW: http://www.a1.com/sportsmed/index.htm

Program Data
Certifying body: Association
Year certification began: 1975
Number certified: 16,000 (all certifications)
Additional programs: ACSM certification for Exercise Leader, Exercise Test Technologist, Health/Fitness Director, Health/Fitness Instructor, and Program Director

Program Description
The ACSM Exercise Specialist℠ is the second-level certification of the ACSM Clinical Track Certifications. This certification recognizes professionals trained in cardiovascular, pulmonary, or metabolic disease rehabilitation. Certification is based on passing a practical exam and a written exam. Current CPR certification is required.

Education/Experience
While not required for certification, ACSM recommends candidates have 600 hours of practical experience in a clinical program, a bachelor's degree in a related health field, and a demonstrated ability in clinical-exercise-program execution and patient education/counseling.

Examinations
ACSM certifications are based on behavioral objectives described in the ACSM's *Guidelines for Exercise Testing and Prescription*. The multiple-choice written examination is based on these objectives. The practical examination evaluates a candidate's performance of tasks such as patient assessment; exercise tests; recognizing arrhythmias; leading sessions; counseling; emergency scenarios; and implementing exercise prescriptions.

Recertification
Certification must be renewed every four years and is based on continuing education. CPR certification must be maintained. Exercise Specialists must earn 80 continuing-education hours (or hour equivalents).

ACSM EXERCISE TEST TECHNOLOGIST℠

Sponsor
American College of Sports Medicine (ACSM)
P.O. Box 1440
401 W. Michigan St.
Indianapolis, IN 46202
Phone: (800) 486-5643
Fax: (317) 634-7817
E-mail: crtacsm@acsm.org
WWW: http://www.a1.com/sportsmed/index.htm

Program Data
Certifying body: Association
Year certification began: 1975
Number certified: 16,000 (all certifications)
Additional programs: ACSM certification for Exercise Leader, Exercise Specialist, Health/Fitness Director, Health/Fitness Instructor, and Program Director

Program Description
The ACSM Exercise Test Technologist℠ is the first certification level of the ACSM Clinical Track Certifications. This certification recognizes professionals trained to conduct exercise-related tests. Certification is based on a two-day written and practical examination. Current CPR certification is required. Exercise test technologists can perform graded exercise tests, electrocardiograms, pulmonary function tests, and oxygen uptake. A voluntary workshop reviewing ETT behavioral objectives is available. There are no prerequisites.

Examinations
ACSM certifications are based on behavioral objectives described in the ACSM's *Guidelines for Exercise Testing and Prescription*. The multiple-choice written examination is based on these objectives. The practical examination covers patient

orientation, exercise ECG preparation, blood pressure monitoring, and recording and monitoring during the CGX.

Recertification

Certification must be renewed every four years and is based on continuing education. CPR certification must be maintained. ETTs must earn 40 continuing-education hours (or hour equivalents).

ACSM HEALTH/FITNESS INSTRUCTOR^{SM}

Sponsor

American College of Sports Medicine (ACSM)
P.O. Box 1440
401 W. Michigan St.
Indianapolis, IN 46202
Phone: (800) 486-5643
Fax: (317) 634-7817
E-mail: crtacsm@acsm.org
WWW: http://www.a1.com/sportsmed/index.htm

Program Data

Certifying body: Association
Year certification began: 1975
Number certified: 16,000 (all certifications)
Additional programs: ACSM certification for Exercise Leader, Exercise Specialist, Exercise Test Technologist, Health/Fitness Director, and Program Director

Program Description

The ACSM Health/Fitness Instructor^{SM} certification is the second level in the ACSM Health and Fitness Track. Health/Fitness Instructors lead exercise programs and evaluate health status and risk factors, and are skilled in client motivation, counseling, and education. Current CPR certification is required. Certification is based on a written exam and a practical exam.

Examinations

ACSM certifications are based on behavioral objectives described in the ACSM's *Guidelines for Exercise Testing and Prescription*. The written multiple-choice examination is based on these objectives, and includes kinesiology, anatomy, exercise physiology, and lifestyle modification. The practical examination consists of demonstrating skills at four practical stations: anthropometric/body

composition and flexibility assessment and exercise; muscular strength and muscular endurance assessment and exercise; physical work capacity preparation; and physical work capacity.

Recertification

Certification must be renewed every four years and is based on continuing education. CPR certification must be maintained. Health/Fitness Instructors must earn 80 continuing education hours (or hour equivalents).

BOARD CERTIFIED IN HEARING INSTRUMENT SCIENCES (BC-HIS)

Sponsor

National Board for Certification in Hearing Instrument Sciences (NBC-HIS)
20361 Middlebelt Road
Livonia, MI 48152
Phone: (810) 478-5712
Fax: (810) 478-9668

Program Data

The program is accredited by National Commission for Certifying Agencies (NCCA).

Certifying body: Independent board
Year certification began: 1981
Number certified: 2200
Approximate certification costs: $145

Program Description

The Board Certified in Hearing Instrument Sciences (BC-HIS) accreditation recognizes hearing aid specialists. NBC-HIS has an active ethics program.

Education/Experience

Candidates must demonstrate two years of experience.

Examinations

The examination is based on the NBC-HIS Role Competency Model, based on role-delineation studies. Printed self-study materials are available. The current pass rate is 60%. The 150-question, multiple-choice examination covers the following areas:

- Eliciting patient/client history and problem, including proper medical history, family hearing, the hearing problem, and hearing aid preferences
- Hearing assessment, including performing and interpreting audiometric tests and data

- Hearing aid fitting, including specifications, technology, analysis, and service
- Patient and family education
- Professional standards, including equipment maintenance, sanitation, marketing, and ethics

Recertification

Board certification must be renewed every three years either by accumulating 24 approved continuing-education hours, or by retaking the certification examination. The current recertification rate is 90%.

CERTIFIED LABORATORY EQUIPMENT SPECIALIST (CLES)

Sponsor

International Certification Commission (ICC)
3330 Washington Blvd., Suite 400
Arlington, VA 22201
Phone: (703) 525-4890

Program Data

The ICC has 10 membership organizations, including the Association for the Advancement of Medical Instrumentation (AAMI) and the Society of Biomedical Equipment Technicians (SBET).

Certifying body: Independent board
Number certified: 200+
Additional certifications: Certified Biomedical Equipment Technician (CBET); Certified Radiology Equipment Specialist (CRES)
Approximate certification costs: $200

Program Description

The Certified Laboratory Equipment Specialist (CLES) designation recognizes individuals who maintain, troubleshoot, and repair medical laboratory equipment. CLESs are responsible for understanding and troubleshooting equipment involved in chemistry and urinalysis, serology, hematology, histology, cytology, and bacteriology. Certification is based on an examination. There are no membership requirements. ICC does not sponsor or endorse any preparation materials; AAMI offers a one-day review session.

Education/Experience

Candidates must have either four years of experience; three years of experience and an associate's degree in electronics technology; or two years of experience and an associate's degree in biomedical equipment technology.

Examinations

The CLES examination is a 150-question, six-hour, multiple-choice test covering the following areas: healthcare facility safety; laboratory equipment troubleshooting; laboratory equipment function and operation; fundamentals of electricity and electronics; and anatomy and physiology.

Recertification

None.

REGISTERED LABORATORY TECHNICIAN (RLT)

Sponsor

International Society for Clinical Laboratory Technology (ISCLT)
818 Olive St., Suite 918
St. Louis, MO 63101
Phone: (314) 241-1445

Program Data

Certifying body: Association
Additional certifications: Physician Office Laboratory Technician (POLT); Registered Medical Technologist (RMT)

Program Description

A Registered Laboratory Technician (RLT) performs tests under supervision in a medical laboratory. Certification is based on passing an examination.

Education/Experience

Candidates must pass an examination and meet one of the following requirements:

- Completion of an accredited medical-laboratory-technician training program
- Associate's degree or 60 semester credit hours majoring in laboratory science
- Completion of a one-year course in military laboratory procedures

- Qualification as a medical technician under Chapter III of Title 20, Code of Federal Regulations
- Candidate is a Physician Office Laboratory Technician (POLT) with four years of experience and six CEUs (upgrade— no examination required)

Examination

Most candidates must pass an exam on general laboratory technology. Candidates also take one or more special discipline exams: Chemistry, Hematology, Immunohematology, Microbiology, or Serology.

Recertification

None required. ISCLT encourages certificants to participate in a voluntary continuing education program.

REGISTERED MEDICAL ASSISTANT (RMA[AMT])

Sponsor

American Medical Technologists (AMT)
710 Higgins Road
Park Ridge, IL 60068
Phone: (708) 823-5169

Program Data

The RMA is approved by the National Commission for Certifying Agencies (NCCA). AMT is a member of the National Organization for Competency Assurance (NOCA) and the National Committee for Clinical Laboratory Standards (NCCLS).

Certifying body: Association
Number certified: 13,821
Organization members: 26,000
Additional certifications: Medical Laboratory Technician (MLT); Medical Technologist (MT); Registered Dental Assistant (RDA); Registered Phlebotomy Technician (RPT)
Approximate certification costs: $95

Program Description

The Registered Medical Assistant (RMA) designation recognizes health professionals qualified to work in a medical office, an examining room, and a laboratory. Certification is based on passing an examination. Membership in AMT comes with certification.

Education/Experience

To qualify to sit for the RMA examination, a candidate must meet one of the four following requirements:

- Graduation from an Accrediting Bureau of Health Education Schools or regionally accredited medical-assisting program
- Graduation from a formal U.S. Armed Forces medical services training program
- Graduation from a COPA-recognized accredited program with one year of medical-assisting experience
- Five years of medical-assisting employment/experience

Examinations

The RMA examination is made up of approximately 200 multiple-choice questions. The questions are competency-based and cover the following areas:

- General medical assisting, including medical law; ethics; terminology, anatomy, and physiology; and patient education
- Administration, including insurance and bookkeeping
- Clinical medical assisting, including medical instruments, pharmacology, emergencies, examination room, and laboratory

Recertification

None.

MEDICAL LABORATORY TECHNICIAN (MLT®[AMT])

Sponsor

American Medical Technologists (AMT)
710 Higgins Road
Park Ridge, IL 60068
Phone: (708) 823-5169

Program Data

The MLT is approved by the National Commission for Certifying Agencies. AMT is a member of the National Organization for Competency Assurance (NOCA) and the National Committee for Clinical Laboratory Standards (NCCLS).

Certifying body: Association
Number certified: 1625
Organization members: 26,000
Additional certifications: Medical Technologist (MT); Registered Dental Assistant (RDA); Registered Medical Assistant (RMA); Registered Phlebotomy Technician (RPT)
Approximate certification costs: $95

Program Description

The Medical Laboratory Technician (MLT) designation recognizes technicians who perform clinical laboratory testing under close supervision. Certification is based on passing an examination or meeting the examination equivalency. Certification includes membership in AMT.

Education/Experience

Candidates who hold other certifications in medical laboratory technology may be considered for certification without taking the examination. Candidates must meet one of the following requirements:

- Associate's degree in medical technology from an accredited college

- Associate's degree in land science and two to three years of experience

Examinations

The MLT examination is made up of approximately 200 multiple-choice questions. The questions are competency-based and cover the following areas: chemistry, hematology, immunology/immuno-hematology, microbiology, urinalysis.

Recertification

None.

REGISTERED DIAGNOSTIC MEDICAL SONOGRAPHER (RDMS)

Sponsor

American Registry of Diagnostic Medical Sonographers® (ARDMS®)
600 Jefferson Plaza, Suite 360
Rockville, MD 20852
Phone: (800) 541-9754
Fax: (301) 738-0312
WWW: http://www.ardms.org/

Program Data

ARDMS is recognized by the American Institute of Ultrasound in Medicine (AIUM); American College of Radiology (ACR); American Society of Echocardiography (ASE); International Society for Cardiovascular Surgery (ISCVS); Society of Diagnostic Medical Sonographers (SDMS); Society for Vascular Surgery (SVS); and the Society of Vascular Technology (SVT).

Certifying body: Independent board
Year certification began: 1975
Number certified: 27,000 (all programs)
Additional programs: Registered Diagnostic Cardiac Sonographer® (RDCS®); Registered Vascular Technologist® (RVT®)
Approximate certification costs: $200

Program Description

The Registered Diagnostic Medical Sonographer (RDMS) designation recognizes individuals skilled in ultrasound and specializing in one of four areas. Certification is based on passing a physics/principles exam and a specialty exam. There are no membership requirements. ARDMS neither sells nor endorses examination preparation materials.

Education/Experience

To sit for the certification examinations, candidates must meet one of the following requirements:

- Completion of an ultrasound/vascular-technology education program approved by the Commission on Accreditation of Allied Health Education Programs (CAAHEP) or Canadian Medical Association (CMA)

- One year of clinical ultrasound/vascular experience and either a bachelor's degree or completion of a two-year, patient care-related AMA or AMA-equivalent allied health education program.

- Two years of clinical ultrasound/vascular experience and either two years of formal education beyond high school or two years of patient care-related experience in another area

Examinations

RDMS requires the successful completion of a general physics and principles examination, and one of four specialty examinations. All candidates take the 120-question, two-hour, multiple-choice Ultrasound Physics and Instrumentation exam. This examination covers bioeffects and safety; doppler; elementary principles; features and artifacts; images storage and display; pulse echo instruments and imaging principles; quality assurance; ultrasound propagation; and ultrasound transducers.

Candidates must pass one of four 180-question, three-hour specialty examinations. About half of the questions use sonograms for identification questions. The four specialty examinations are in Abdomen, Obstetrics and Gynecology, Neurosonology, and Ophthalmology.

Recertification

Registrants must renew certification every three years through either continuing education or examination. RDMSs must earn 30 hours of related continuing education, pass a different specialty examination within their area, or earn the RDCS or RVT designation.

MEDICAL TECHNOLOGIST (MT®(AMT))

Sponsor

American Medical Technologists (AMT)
710 Higgins Road
Park Ridge, IL 60068
Phone: (708) 823-5169

Program Data

The MT program is approved by the National Commission for Certifying Agencies. AMT is a member of the National Organization for Competency Assurance (NOCA) and the National Committee for Clinical Laboratory Standards (NCCLS).

Certifying body: Association
Organization members: 21,000
Additional certifications: Medical Laboratory Technician (MLT); Registered Dental Assistant (RDA); Registered Medical Assistant (RMA); Registered Phlebotomy Technician (RPT)
Approximate certification costs: $95

Program Description

The Medical Technologist (MT) designation recognizes technicians capable of performing clinical laboratory testing that requires independent judgment. Certification is based on passing an examination or meeting the examination equivalency.

Education/Experience

Candidates who meet one of the following may apply for certification without taking the AMT examinations:

- Passing score on the Health and Human Services CLT Proficiency examination and five years of acceptable experience

- Certification in medical technology from another source accepted by AMT

- Passing score on state licensure examination in medical technology approved by AMT

To sit for the MT examination candidates must have, as a minimum, a bachelor's degree in medical technology or a major in a biological or chemical science, and one year of approved experience.

Examinations

The MT examination is made up of approximately 200 multiple-choice questions. The questions are competency-based and cover the following areas: chemistry, hematology, immunology/immunohematology, microbiology, and urinalysis.

Recertification

None.

REGISTERED MEDICAL TECHNOLOGIST (RMT)

Sponsor

International Society for Clinical Laboratory Technology (ISCLT)
818 Olive St., Suite 918
St. Louis, MO 63101
Phone: (314) 241-1445

Program Data

Certifying body: Association
Additional certifications: Physician Office Laboratory Technician (POLT); Registered Laboratory Technician (RLT)

Program Description

A Registered Medical Technologist (RMT) performs laboratory tests with little supervision and may supervise technicians. Certification is based on passing an examination.

Education/Experience

Candidates must meet one of the following requirements:

- Bachelor's degree or 90 semester hours with a major in chemical, physical, or biological science

- Three years of experience and an associate's degree or 60 semester hours majoring in laboratory science

MEDICAL
Medical Technology/Allied Health

- Candidate is a Registered Laboratory Technician (RLT) with five years of experience and six CEUs (upgrade— no examination required)

Examination

Most candidates must pass an exam on general laboratory technology. Candidates also take one or more special discipline exams: Chemistry, Hematology, Immunohematology, Microbiology, or Serology.

Recertification

None required. ISCLT encourages certificants to participate in a voluntary continuing education program.

CERTIFIED NUCLEAR MEDICINE TECHNOLOGIST (CNMT)

Sponsor

Nuclear Medicine Technology Certification Board, Inc. (NMTCB)
2970 Clairmont Road, Suite 610
Atlanta, GA 30329
Phone: (404) 315-1739
Fax: (404) 315-6502

Program Data

Certifying body: Independent board
Year certification began: 1978
Approximate certification costs: $80

Program Description

The Nuclear Medicine Technology Certification Board was established in 1977 to certify technologists in both nuclear medicine equipment and procedures.

Education/Experience

Candidates must be graduates of a program on nuclear medicine technology that is recognized by the Joint Review Committee on Nuclear Medicine Technology (JRCNMT). These programs include both didactic and clinical requirements.

Prior to 1996, candidates could apply for alternative eligibility through documenting four years of clinical experience under certain Board-certified or authorized physicians.

Examination

The NMTCB examination is a task-oriented, 225-question, multiple-choice test. The exam materials are based on the NMTCB Task Analysis of Nuclear Medicine Technology, a standardized

equipment and procedures list, and task-related Components of Preparedness statements. The exam includes:

- Radiation safety
- Instrumentation
- Clinical procedures
- Radiopharmacy

Recertification

Certification is permanent unless revoked by the board. However, annual registration by fee is required to keep active status with the Board.

CERTIFIED OCCUPATIONAL HEARING CONSERVATIONIST

Sponsor

Council for Accreditation in Occupational Hearing Conservation (CAOHC)
611 E. Wells St.
Milwaukee, WI 53202
Phone: (414) 276-5338
Fax: (414) 276-3349
E-mail: caohc@globaldialog.com
WWW: http://www.globaldialog.com/~caohc/

Program Data

The program is recommended by the Occupational Safety and Health Administration (OSHA).

Certifying body: Association
Year certification began: 1973

Program Description

The CAOHC certification in occupational hearing conservation recognizes the completion of a 20-hour training course. The course is taught by a CAOHC-certified course director. The course includes OSHA regulations, audiometric testing, and hearing safety requirements.

Education/Experience

There are no prerequisites. Candidates must complete the 20-hour course and send all documentation to CAOHC.

Recertification

CAOHC certification must be renewed every five years by attending an eight-hour remediation course.

CERTIFIED OCCUPATIONAL THERAPY ASSISTANT (COTA)

Sponsor

American Occupational Therapy Certification
Board, Inc. (AOTCB)
4 Research Place, Suite 160
Rockville, MD 20850
Phone: (301) 990-7979
Fax: (301) 869-8492

Program Data

Forty-nine jurisdictional regulatory boards recognize AOTCB examinations for meeting regulatory requirements.

Certifying body: Independent board
Year certification began: 1970
Number certified: 90,000 (both certifications)
Additional programs: Occupational Therapist, Registered (OTR)
Approximate certification costs: $250

Program Description

The Certified Occupational Therapy Assistant (COTA) is an entry-level, national certification for occupational therapy paraprofessionals.

Education/Experience

Candidates must have graduated from an occupational-therapy-assisting education program accredited by the Accreditation Council on Occupational Therapy Education (ACOTE). Accredited programs include fieldwork. There is no other experience requirement.

Examinations

The COTA examination is based on an extensive job analysis that identified entry-level tasks and knowledge. The 200-question, multiple-choice examination is administered by the Professional Examination Service. The examination covers the following areas:

- Anatomy and behavior
- Discharge plan development
- Documentation
- Human development
- Occupational performance data collection
- Occupational therapy theory and performance areas
- Professional practice
- Sensorimotor, cognitive, and psychosocial components of OT
- Support service management
- Treatment plan development, evaluation, and implementation

Recertification

Certification is renewed every five years unless it has been suspended or revoked. AOTCB has an extensive and proactive disciplinary program.

PHYSICIAN OFFICE LABORATORY TECHNICIAN (POLT)

Sponsor

International Society for Clinical Laboratory
Technology (ISCLT)
818 Olive St., Suite 918
St. Louis, MO 63101
Phone: (314) 241-1445

Program Data

Certifying body: Association
Additional certifications: Registered Laboratory Technician (RLT); Registered Medical Technologist (RMT)

Program Description

The Physician Office Laboratory Technician (POLT) designation recognizes technicians who perform clinical laboratory procedures in offices and satellite laboratories. Candidates must either have one year of experience or complete an acceptable clinical training program with six months of experience. Certification is based on passing a medical office laboratory examination.

Recertification

None required. ISCLT encourages certificants to participate in a voluntary continuing education program.

BOARD CERTIFICATION IN PEDORTHICS (C.PED.)

Sponsor

Board for Certification in Pedorthics (BCP)
9861 Broken Land Parkway, Suite 255
Columbia, MD 21046
Phone: (410) 381-5729
Fax: (410) 381-1167

Program Data

BCP is approved by the National Commission for Certifying Agencies (NCCA), and recognized by the Pedorthic Footwear Association (PFA).

Certifying body: Independent board
Year certification began: 1974
Number certified: 1000+

Program Description

A pedorthist designs, manufactures, fits, and/or modifies footwear based on a physician's prescription. The Board Certification in Pedorthics (C.Ped.) program is based on an extensive role-delineation study for entry-level practitioners. Certification is based on passing an examination.

Education/Experience

Candidates must meet one of the following requirements to take the certification examination:

- Bachelor's degree or higher
- Associate's degree in a health- or science-related field
- Experience and education points equaling 300, based on 20 points per college credit hour, 1 point for each six and two-thirds hour of internship, and variable points for BCP-accredited courses

BCP is implementing an educational requirements program which combines pedorthic courses (both lecture and lab) with an internship.

Examinations

The C.Ped. examination is a multiple-choice test and takes three and one-half hours to complete. The examination is administered by Columbia Assessment Services, Inc. (CAS). To help candidates prepare for the test, BCP offers a study guide and list of recommended texts. The examination covers pedorthic assessment and techniques, patient management, practice management, and professional responsibility.

Recertification

Board certification must be renewed by earning 150 continuation points every three years.

NATIONALLY CERTIFIED PHARMACY TECHNICIAN (NCPT)

Sponsor

Pharmacy Technician Certification Board (PTCB)
2215 Constitution Ave. NW
Washington, DC 20037-2985
Phone: (202) 429-7576
Fax: (202) 429-7596
E-mail: melissa.murer@helix.stlcop.edu
WWW: http://www.mbnet.mb.ca/ptec/ptcb.html

Program Data

The PTCB was founded by the American Pharmaceutical Association (APhA), the American Society of Health-System Pharmacists (ASHP), the Illinois Council of Health-System Pharmacists (ICHP), and the Michigan Pharmacists Association (MPA).

Certifying body: Independent board
Year certification began: 1995

Program Description

The Pharmacy Technician Certification Board (PTCB) program recognizes pharmacy technicians passing an entry-level examination.

Education/Experience

A high school diploma is required. Completion of a pharmacy-technician education and training program accredited by the American Society of Health-System Pharmacists (ASHP) is recommended.

Examinations

The examination was developed with the assistance of the Professional Examination Service and is based on a job-content analysis. The examination includes the following: anatomy and physiology; compounding; ethics; medical terminology; over-the-counter medications; pharmacy law; pharmacy operations; and prescription medications.

Recertification

Recertification is under development.

REGISTERED PHLEBOTOMY TECHNICIAN (RPT[AMT])

Sponsor

American Medical Technologists (AMT)
710 Higgins Road
Park Ridge, IL 60068
Phone: (708) 823-5169

Program Data

AMT is a member of the National Organization for Competency Assurance (NOCA) and the National Committee for Clinical Laboratory Standards (NCCLS).

Certifying body: Association
Number certified: 600
Organization members: 26,000
Additional certifications: Medical Laboratory Technician (MLT); Medical Technologist (MT); Registered Dental Assistant (RDA); Registered Medical Assistant (RMA)
Approximate certification costs: $59

Program Description

The Registered Phlebotomy Technician (RPT) designation recognizes technicians responsible for collecting and transporting blood samples. Certification is based on passing an examination. Membership in AMT comes with certification. Candidates who hold other certifications in phlebotomy may be considered for certification without taking the examination. To qualify to sit for the RPT examination, candidates must meet one of the following requirements:

- Completion of a phlebotomy course at an Accrediting Bureau of Health Education Schools accredited program or school
- Completion of an acceptable phlebotomy program at an institution accredited by a recognized agency
- Completion of an acceptable program, including 120 hours each of didactic and clinical instruction
- A total of 1040 hours of experience within the last three years as a phlebotomy technician performing acceptable duties
- Passing score on a state phlebotomist licensure examination

Examinations

The RPT examination is made up of approximately 200 multiple-choice questions. The questions are competency-based and cover the following areas: blood samples; specimen collection; time manage-

ment; professional communications; clerical, safety, ethical, legal, and professional considerations; terminology; anatomy and physiology.

Recertification

None.

NATIONALLY CERTIFIED PSYCHIATRIC TECHNICIAN (NCPT)

Sponsor

American Association of Psychiatric Technicians, Inc. (AAPT)
P.O. Box 14014
Phoenix, AZ 85063
Phone: (602) 873-1890
Fax: (602) 873-4616
E-mail: aaptinc@aztec.asu.edu

Program Data

Certifying body: Association
Year certification began: 1993
Number certified: 1000
Organization members: 2500
Approximate certification costs: $75–$125, depending on level

Program Description

The Nationally Certified Psychiatric Technician (NCPT) program recognizes healthcare technicians caring for mentally ill, emotionally disturbed, or mentally retarded patients and participating in rehabilitation and treatment programs. There are four levels of certification, based on experience, education, and testing. AAPT membership is required.

Education/Experience

Designation level is based on education and experience. All college-level experience must be in a related field or part of a related degree program.

- NCPT1—High school diploma
- NCPT2—30 college semester hours and one year/2000 hours of experience
- NCPT3—Associate's degree and two years/4000 hours of experience
- NCPT4—Bachelor's degree and three years/6000 hours of experience

Examinations

All candidates take the Level 1 examination. Additional exams are taken for subsequent levels. Exams through 1995 were open-book, at-home tests; tests were closed-book from 1996 onward. The NCPT examinations are based on the *Outline of Knowledge for Psychiatric Technicians*, 600 learning objectives developed from a variety of licensure and professional sources. The exam includes the following areas: behavior; interventions; monitoring; observing and reporting; pharmacology; rehabilitation; security; specialization; supervisory tasks; and therapeutic environments.

Recertification
NCPTs must maintain AAPT membership and earn annual continuing-education units.

CERTIFIED PULMONARY FUNCTION TECHNOLOGIST (CPFT^{SM})

Sponsor
National Board for Respiratory Care (NBRC^{SM})
8310 Nieman Road
Lenexa, KS 66214
Phone: (913) 599-4200
Fax: (913) 541-0156
E-mail: nbrc-info@nbrc.org.
WWW: http://www.nbrc.org

Program Data
The NBRC is sponsored by the following: American Association for Respiratory Care (AARC); American College of Chest Physicians (ACCP); American Society of Anesthesiologists (ASA); American Thoracic Society (ATS); and National Society for Pulmonary Technology (NSPT). Some states use NBRC examinations for licensing/credentialing requirements.

Certifying body: Independent board
Year certification began: 1960
Number certified: 120,000 (all certifications)
Additional programs: Certified Respiratory Therapy Technician (CRTT^{SM}); Registered Pulmonary Function Technologist (RPFT^{SM}); Registered Respiratory Therapist (RRT^{SM})
Approximate certification costs: $110

Program Description
The Certified Pulmonary Function Technologist (CPFT^{SM}) designation is an entry-level certification. Certification is based on passing an examination.

Education/Experience
To qualify to sit for the CPFT examination, a candidate must meet one of the following conditions:

● Hold the CRTT or RRT designation

● Graduate from a respiratory therapy program either accredited by the AMA Committee on Allied Health Education and Accreditation, or supported by the Joint Review Committee for Respiratory Therapy Education

● Graduate from a program on pulmonary function technology that is approved by the National Society for Cardiovascular Technology/National Society for Pulmonary Technology

● Complete 62 semester hours of college, with coursework in biology, chemistry, and mathematics; and six months of clinical experience

● Be a high school graduate with two years of clinical experience

Examinations
The 100-question, multiple-choice examination covers data management, instrumentation, and diagnostic procedures.

Recertification
The NBRC annually verifies active employment status. A voluntary recredentialing program encourages retaking the credentialing examination every three to five years.

REGISTERED PULMONARY FUNCTION TECHNOLOGIST (RPFT^{SM})

Sponsor
National Board for Respiratory Care (NBRC^{SM})
8310 Nieman Road
Lenexa, KS 66214
Phone: (913) 599-4200
Fax: (913) 541-0156
E-mail: nbrc-info@nbrc.org.
WWW: http://www.nbrc.org

Program Data
The NBRC is sponsored by the following: American Association for Respiratory Care (AARC); American College of Chest Physicians (ACCP); American Society of Anesthesiologists (ASA); American

Thoracic Society (ATS); and National Society for Pulmonary Technology (NSPT). Some states use NBRC examinations for licensing/credentialing requirements.

Certifying body: Independent board
Year certification began: 1960
Number certified: 120,000 (all certifications)
Additional programs: Certified Pulmonary
  Function Technologist (CPFT^{SM}); Certified
  Respiratory Therapy Technician (CRTT^{SM});
  Registered Respiratory Therapist (RRT^{SM})
Approximate certification costs: $160

Program Description

The Registered Pulmonary Function Technologist (RPFT^{SM}) designation recognizes experienced pulmonary function practitioners, and is based on passing an examination. To qualify to sit for the examination, a candidate must hold the CPFT designation.

Examinations

The examination is a 100-question, multiple-choice test covering diagnostic procedures, instrumentation/equipment, and data management.

Recertification

The NBRC annually verifies active employment status. A voluntary recredentialing program encourages retaking the credentialing examination every three to five years.

CERTIFIED RADIOLOGY EQUIPMENT SPECIALIST (CRES)

Sponsor

International Certification Commission (ICC)
3330 Washington Blvd., Suite 400
Arlington, VA 22201
Phone: (703) 525-4890

Program Data

The ICC has 10 membership organizations, including the Association for the Advancement of Medical Instrumentation (AAMI) and the Society of Biomedical Equipment Technicians (SBET).

Certifying body: Independent board
Number certified: 200+
Additional programs: Certified Biomedical Equipment Technician (CBET); Certified Laboratory Equipment Specialist (CLES)
Approximate certification costs: $200

Program Description

The Certified Radiology Equipment Specialist (CRES) recognizes individuals who maintain, troubleshoot, and repair radiology equipment. Certification is based on an examination. There are no membership requirements. ICC does not sponsor or endorse any preparation materials; AAMI offers a one-day review session.

Education/Experience

Candidates must have either four years of experience; three years of experience and an associate's degree in electronics technology; or two years of experience and an associate's degree in biomedical equipment technology.

Examinations

The CRES examination is a 150-question, six-hour, multiple-choice test covering the following areas: anatomy and physiology; fundamentals of electricity and electronics; radiologic equipment function and operation; radiologic equipment troubleshooting; and radiology safety.

Recertification

None.

CERTIFIED RESPIRATORY THERAPY TECHNICIAN (CRTT^{SM})

Sponsor

National Board for Respiratory Care (NBRC^{SM})
8310 Nieman Road
Lenexa, KS 66214
Phone: (913) 599-4200
Fax: (913) 541-0156
E-mail: nbrc-info@nbrc.org.
WWW: http://www.nbrc.org

Program Data

The NBRC is sponsored by the following: American Association for Respiratory Care (AARC); American College of Chest Physicians (ACCP); American Society of Anesthesiologists (ASA); American Thoracic Society (ATS); and National Society for Pulmonary Technology (NSPT). Some states use NBRC examinations for licensing/credentialing requirements.

Certifying body: Independent board
Year certification began: 1960
Number certified: 120,000 (all certifications)
Additional programs: Certified Pulmonary
Function Technologist (CPFT^{SM}); Registered
Pulmonary Function Technologist (RPFT^{SM});
Registered Respiratory Therapist (RRT^{SM})
Approximate certification costs: $100

Program Description

The Certified Respiratory Therapy Technician
(CRTT^{SM}) designation is an entry-level certification
based on passing an examination.

Education/Experience

To qualify to sit for the CRTT examination, a
candidate must have graduated/completed a
respiratory therapy program accredited by the AMA
CAHEA or supported by the Joint Review Committee for Respiratory Therapy Education.

Examinations

The 140-question, multiple-choice examination
covers therapeutic procedures, equipment, and
clinical data.

Recertification

The NBRC annually verifies active employment
status. A voluntary recredentialing program encourages retaking the credentialing examination every
three to five years.

REGISTERED RESPIRATORY THERAPIST (RRT^{SM})

Sponsor

National Board for Respiratory Care (NBRC^{SM})
8310 Nieman Road
Lenexa, KS 66214
Phone: (913) 599-4200
Fax: (913) 541-0156
E-mail: nbrc-info@nbrc.org.
WWW: http://www.nbrc.org

Program Data

The NBRC is sponsored by the following: American
Association for Respiratory Care (AARC); American College of Chest Physicians (ACCP); American Society of Anesthesiologists (ASA); American

Thoracic Society (ATS); and National Society for
Pulmonary Technology (NSPT). Some states use
NBRC examinations for licensing/credentialing
requirements.

Certifying body: Independent board
Year certification began: 1960
Number certified: 120,000 (all certifications)
Additional programs: Certified Pulmonary
Function Technologist (CPFT^{SM}); Certified
Respiratory Therapy Technician (CRTT^{SM})
Registered Pulmonary Function Technologist
(RPFT^{SM})
Approximate certification costs: $210

Program Description

The Registered Respiratory Therapist (RRT^{SM})
designation recognizes experienced respiratory
therapy practitioners and is based on passing two
examinations.

Education/Experience

To qualify to sit for the RRT exams, a candidate
must be a CRTT and meet one of the following
requirements:

- Certificate of completion from accredited
  respiratory-therapist educational program
  and 62 semester hours of college credit

- Four years of clinical experience and
  62 semester hours of college credit,
  with courses in anatomy and physiology;
  chemistry; biology; microbiology; physics;
  and mathematics

- Two years of clinical experience and
  a bachelor's degree in any area, with
  courses in anatomy and physiology;
  chemistry; biology; microbiology;
  physics; and mathematics.

Examinations

The first examination is a 100-question, multiple-
choice test covering therapeutic procedures, equipment, and clinical data. The second examination is
a clinical simulation of 10 patient-management
problems.

Recertification

The NBRC annually verifies active employment
status. A voluntary recredentialing program encourages retaking the credentialing examination every
three to five years.

CERTIFIED STERILE PROCESSING AND DISTRIBUTION TECHNICIAN (CSPDT)

Sponsor

National Institute for the Certification of
   Healthcare Sterile Processing and Distribution
   Personnel (NICHSPDP)
P.O. Box 558
Annandale, NJ 08801
Phone: (201) 533-5586
Fax: (201) 533-8845

Program Data

The Institute is recognized by the American Society for Healthcare Central Service Personnel (ASHCSP) of the American Hospital Association. It is a member of the National Organization for Competency Assurance (NOCA), and is approved by the Defense Activity for Non-Traditional Educational Support.

Certifying body: Independent certifying
   organization
Year certification began: 1991
Number certified: 4300+
Additional programs: Certified Sterile Processing
   and Distribution Manager (CSPDM); Certified
   Sterile Processing and Distribution Supervisor
   (CSPDS)
Approximate certification costs: $95

Program Description

The Certified Sterile Processing and Distribution Technician (CSPDT) program is based on an extensive role analysis conducted by the Educational Testing Service (ETS). The role analysis evaluated the tasks and responsibilities of sterile processing and distribution technicians in a variety of settings. Certification is based on passing a single examination administered by Applied Measurement Services, Inc. NICHSPDP sells a comprehensive examination study guide.

Education/Experience

Candidates must meet one of the following requirements to sit for the examination:

- One year of full-time or equivalent part-time experience in sterile processing and distribution
- Six months of experience and completion of a related allied health program
- One year of experience in healthcare-product sales or service
- Passing grade in a Central Service/SPD training course

Examinations

The 125-question, multiple-choice examination covers the following areas:

- Roles and responsibilities, including quality assurance, inventory, and professional standards and ethics
- Life sciences
- Decontamination
- Sterilization
- Preparation and handling, including surgical instruments, packaging, and sterile storage of processed goods

Recertification

CSPDTs must recertify every five years. CSPDTs may recertify by either accumulating points for education and experience, or by taking a recertification examination.

CERTIFIED SURGICAL TECHNOLOGIST (CST®)

CST® CERTIFIED FIRST ASSISTANT (CST®/CFA®)

Sponsor

Liaison Council on Certification for the Surgical
   Technologist (LCC-ST®)
7108 S. Alton Way, Bldg. C
Englewood, CO 80112
Phone: (800) 637-7433
Fax: (303) 694-9169

Program Data

Both certifications are accredited by the National Commission for Certifying Agencies (NCCA). The LCC-ST is affiliated with the Association of Surgical Technologists, Inc. (AST).

Certifying body: Independent board
Year certification began: 1970
Number certified: 34,380 (CST), 800 (CST/CFA)
Approximate certification costs: CST—$120 (AST
   members), $225 (nonmembers);
   CST/CFA—$250

Program Description

The Certified Surgical Technologist (CST) designation recognizes members of the surgical team who act as scrub persons or circulators. As scrub persons, CSTs handle the instruments, supplies, and equipment for a surgical procedure; as circulators, they obtain additional instruments and materials during a surgical procedure. CSTs also watch for breaks in aseptic technique, care for specimens, prepare patients' rooms, and help transport patients.

The CST Certified First Assistant (CST/CFA) designation is an advanced specialization. CST/CFAs aid in exposure, hemostasis, and other technical functions under the direction of the surgeon during an operation.

Education/Experience

CST candidates must have completed a formal program on surgical technology (minimum one year, 450 hours of classroom time, 450 hours of clinical rotation) or a comparable program. Graduates of RN, LPN, and LVN programs with acceptable scrub experience are also eligible. AST sells a guide to help candidates prepare for the examination.

CST/CFA candidates must be current CSTs with two years of first-assistant experience within the past four years.

Examinations

The LCC-ST examinations are administered by The Psychological Corporation. The CST examination content and blueprint are based on a job analysis of practicing, entry-level surgical technologists. The CST pass rate is 72%. The 250-question, multiple-choice examination covers these areas:

- Infection control, such as aseptic technique, sterilization, and disinfection; packaging and dispensing of supplies; and the application of this knowledge to the surgical process carried out in the operating room

- Basic surgical procedures, including anatomy and physiology; setup of instruments, equipment, and other supplies; the sequence of procedures; maintenance of the sterile field; and the care, handling, and usage of the instruments, equipment, and other supplies during the procedure

- Patient care, including transportation; consents; positioning; records; observation and monitoring of vital signs; skin preparation; draping; counts; emergency measures; and medical, ethical, and legal responsibilities

The CST/CFA examination content and blueprint are based on practicing First Assistants with two years of experience. The CFA pass rate is 77%. The 150-question, multiple-choice examination covers these areas:

- Advanced surgical anatomy and physiology, with emphasis on surgical pathology, tissue assessment, and the principles of wound healing

- Tissue handling and hemostasis

- Techniques for aiding in exposure and wound closure

Recertification

LCC-ST certifications must be renewed every six years, either through retaking and passing the certifying examination or through surgical technology-related continuing education. CSTs must accumulate 80 continuing-education credits. CST/CFAs must accumulate 100 credits, with at least 30 directly related to first assisting. The recertification rate is 51%.

REGISTERED TECHNOLOGIST (R.T.[ARRT])

Sponsor

American Registry of Radiologic Technologists (ARRT®)
1255 Northland Drive
St. Paul, MN 55120
Phone: (612) 687-0048
Fax: (612) 687-0349

Program Data

The Registry is co-sponsored by the American Society of Radiologic Technologists (ASRT) and the American College of Radiology (ACR).

Certifying body: Independent board
Number certified: 210,000
Year certification began: 1922

Program Description

The Registered Technician (R.T.) designation recognizes healthcare professionals skilled in the application of ionizing radiation. The three disciplines—which may be indicated by an (R), an (N), or a (T) after the designation abbreviation—are radiography, nuclear medicine technology, and radiation therapy technology. Registration is based on passing an examination.

Education/Experience

To qualify to sit for the registration examination, candidates must complete a CAHEA-approved program (or gain special permission from the ARRT Board of Trustees) in their discipline.

Examinations

Each discipline has its own 200-question, multiple-choice examination. The exams are as follows:

- Radiography (pass rate of 85%)—Covers radiation protection; equipment; image production and evaluation; procedures; and patient care

- Nuclear Medicine Technology (pass rate of 80%)—Covers radiation protection; radiopharmaceutical preparation; quality control; procedures; and patient care

- Radiation Therapy Technology (pass rate 90%)—Covers radiation protection; quality assurance; planning; procedures; and patient care

Recertification

Currently, renewal of registration is done annually by payment of a renewal fee. In 1997, renewal will be required every two years, with R.T.s needing 24 credits of continuing education. Recertification will also be awarded for passing an examination in another discipline.

CERTIFIED THERAPEUTIC RECREATION SPECIALIST® (CTRS®)

Sponsor

National Council for Therapeutic Recreation
  Certification (NCTRC)
P.O. Box 479
Thiells, NY 10984
Phone: (914) 947-4346
Fax: (814) 947-1634

Program Data

NCTRC and the CTRS credential are accredited by the National Commission for Certifying Agencies (NCCA).

Certifying body: Independent board
Year certification began: 1981
Number certified: 14,000
Approximate certification costs: $200

Program Description

The Certified Therapeutic Recreation Specialist (CTRS) designation recognizes personnel practicing in the field of therapeutic recreation. There are no association membership requirements. Certification is based on passing an examination. NCTRC has a comprehensive disciplinary-review process.

Education/Experience

To qualify to sit for the CTRS examination, a candidate must meet the requirements of either the academic path or equivalency path. All candidates must hold a bachelor's degree or higher. Candidates qualify on the academic path if they majored in therapeutic recreation and complete a 360-hour field placement. All other candidates must use the equivalency path, with 24 hours of supportive coursework and five years of full-time experience.

Examinations

The examination is based on an extensive job analysis performed by the Educational Testing Service (ETS), whose Center for Occupational and Professional Assessment administers the examination for NCTRC. The examination covers these areas:

- Assessments
- Documentation
- Organizing and managing services
- Outreach and public relations
- Professional development
- Program/treatment evaluation
- Program/treatment planning
- Therapeutic-recreation program planning and implementation
- Treatment teams

Recertification

Certification must be renewed every five years. Renewal is based on a point system, with a minimum of 100 points required. Continuing education is worth 1 point per contact hour or 15 points per 1 semester credit; professional experience is worth 10 points per year; retaking the CTRS exam is worth 70 points.

CERTIFIED MEDICAL TRANSCRIPTIONIST (CMT)

Sponsor
American Association for Medical Transcription
(AAMT)
P.O. Box 576187
Modesto, CA 95357
Phone: (800) 982-2182
Fax: (209) 551-9317
E-mail: aamt@sna.com
WWW: http://www.sna.com/aamt/

Program Data
Certifying body: Association
Year certification began: 1979
Number certified: 3100
Organization members: 9300
Approximate certification costs: $300

Program Description
The Certified Medical Transcriptionist (CMT) designation recognizes entry-level medical language specialists competent across a broad range of specialty areas and work settings to interpret and transcribe routine patient-care documentation by physicians and other healthcare professionals. Membership in AAMT is not required. AAMT maintains an active ethics board with decertification powers.

Education/Experience
There are no educational or experiential requirements.

Examinations
The CMT certification exam has two parts: a written test and a practical test. Assessment Systems, Inc. (ASI) administers the written test and assists in test development. The written portion is available through electronic testing. The Medical Transcriptionist Certification Program (MTCP) of the AAMT administers the practical test. The exam is based on a task analysis and the work of a panel of experts; exam questions are written by certificants, consultants, and entry-level practitioners. AAMT offers self-study materials. The pass rate is 62%. The exam covers the following areas:

Part 1—The written examination includes medical terminology; English; anatomy and physiology; diseases; healthcare records; and professional development.

Part 2—The practical test is used to evaluate the candidate's ability to perform actual transcription. The two-hour test uses physician dictation to test accuracy and productivity. Candidates transcribe several different reports and notes.

Recertification
Recertification is required every three years, and is based on continuing education. CMTs must earn 30 continuing-education credits (CEC), with 20 credits coming from medical topics and 10 credits from related nonmedical topics.

REGISTERED VASCULAR TECHNOLOGIST® (RVT)®

Sponsor
American Registry of Diagnostic Medical
Sonographers® (ARDMS®)
600 Jefferson Plaza, Suite 360
Rockville, MD 20852
Phone: (800) 541-9754
Fax: (301) 738-0312
WWW: http://www.ardms.org/

Program Data
ARDMS is recognized by the American College of Radiology (ACR); American Institute of Ultrasound in Medicine (AIUM); American Society of Echocardiography (ASE); International Society for Cardiovascular Surgery (ISCVS); Society for Vascular Surgery (SVS); Society of Diagnostic Medical Sonographers (SDMS); and the Society of Vascular Technology (SVT).

Certifying body: Independent board
Year certification began: 1975
Number certified: 27,000 (all programs)
Additional programs: Registered Diagnostic Cardiac Sonographer® (RDCS®); Registered Diagnostic Medical Sonographer® (RDMS®)
Approximate certification costs: $200

Program Description
The Registered Vascular Technologist (RVT) designation recognizes individuals skilled in vascular ultrasound. Certification is based on passing a principles exam and a specialty exam. There are no membership requirements. ARDMS neither sells nor endorses examination preparation materials.

Education/Experience

To sit for the certification examinations, candidates must meet one of the following requirements:

- Completion of an ultrasound/vascular technology education program approved by the Commission on Accreditation of Allied Health Education Programs (CAAHEP) or the Canadian Medical Association (CMA)

- One year of clinical ultrasound/vascular experience and either a bachelor's degree or completion of a two-year, patient care-related AMA or AMA-equivalent allied health education program

- Two years of clinical ultrasound/vascular experience and either two years of formal education beyond high school or two years of patient-care related experience in another area

Examinations

RVT requires the successful completion of a general principles examination and a specialty examination. The 120-question, two-hour, multiple-choice exam, Vascular Principles and Instrumentation, covers physical principles; physiology and fluid dynamics; quality assurance and safety; and ultrasound physics and imaging.

Candidates must also pass the 180-question, three-hour, specialty examination on vascular technology. About half of the questions relate to images or diagrams.

Recertification

Registrants must renew certification every three years through either continuing education or examination. RVTs must earn 30 hours of related continuing education or earn the RDMS or RDCS designation.

TRADE/TECHNICAL

CERTIFIED APARTMENT MAINTENANCE TECHNICIAN (CAMT)

Sponsor

National Apartment Association (NAA)
201 North Union St., Suite 200
Alexandria, VA 22314
Phone: (703) 518-6141
E-mail: postmaster@naahq.Com

Program Data

Certifying body: Association
Organization members: 26,000
Additional certifications: Certified Apartment Manager (CAM); Certified Apartment Property Supervisor (CAPS)

Program Description
The Certified Apartment Maintenance Technician (CAMT) designation recognizes individuals prepared for apartment maintenance careers through NAA's comprehensive training program.

Education/Experience
Candidates must have one year of apartment maintenance experience for certification.

Curriculum
All candidates must complete the NAA CAMT 156-hour program. The courses include maintenance operations; safety; electronics; interior; exterior; preventative and pool maintenance; appliances; and plumbing.

Recertification
CAMTs must earn five continuing-education credits every year.

ASE CERTIFICATION PROGRAM

Sponsor

National Institute of Automotive Service
   Excellence (ASE)
13505 Dulles Technology Drive
Herndon, VA 22071
Phone: (703) 793-0100

Program Data

Certifying body: Independent board
Year certification began: 1972
Number certified: 375,000
Approximate certification costs: $15 per test; $20 registration fee per testing day

Program Description
The ASE certification recognizes automotive and truck service technicians. Certification is based on passing an examination.

Education/Experience
Candidates must have two years of full-time experience in the testing area. One year of experience may be substituted with either three years of high school training; two years of college, trade, or technical school; or an acceptable apprenticeship program.

Examinations
Candidates passing one examination in their field become ASE Certified. Candidates passing all of the required examinations in their field become ASE Certified Master. The multiple-choice examinations have between 40 and 80 questions. Examinations are administered and scored by the independent testing organization ACT. The certifications and required examinations are as follows:

- ASE Certified Automobile Technician
- ASE Certified Master Automobile Technician (eight exams)—Examinations in Engine Repair; Automobile Transmission/Transaxle; Manual Drive Train and Axles; Suspension and Steering; Brakes; Electrical Systems; Heating and Air Conditioning; and Engine Performance (diagnosis and repair)
- ASE Certified Medium/Heavy Truck Technician
- ASE Certified Master Medium/Heavy Truck Technician (either the Gasoline or Diesel Engines and the other four exams)—Examinations in Gasoline Engines; Diesel Engines; Drive Train; Brakes; Suspension and Steering; and Electrical Systems
- ASE Certified Technician

- ASE Certified Master Autobody/Paint Technician (four exams)—Examinations in Painting and Refinishing; Non-Structural Analysis and Damage Repair; Structural Analysis and Damage Repair; Mechanical and Electrical Components
- ASE Certified Engine Machinist (three exams)—Examinations in Cylinder Head Specialist; Cylinder Block Specialist; Assembly Specialist
- ASE Certified Technician, Alternative Fuels (one exam)—Examination in Light Vehicle Compressed Natural Gas
- ASE Certified School Bus Technician (eight exams)—Examinations in Body Systems and Special Equipment; Diesel Engines; Drive Train; Brakes; Suspension and Steering; Electrical/Electronic Systems; Heating and Air Conditioning; and Collision Repair

Recertification

ASE technicians and machinists must recertify every five years. Recertification is by passing a recertification test. The multiple-choice tests have between 20 and 40 questions.

AUTO GLASS TECHNICIAN

SENIOR AUTO GLASS TECHNICIAN

MASTER AUTO GLASS TECHNICIAN

Sponsor

National Glass Association (NGA)
8200 Greensboro Drive, 3rd Floor
McLean, VA 22102-3881
Phone: (703) 442-4890
Fax: (703) 442-0630
E-mail:76446.2330@compuserve.com
WWW: http://ourworld.compuserve.com/
    homepages/nga/

Program Data

Certifying body: Association
Year certification began: 1989
Number certified: 7000+
Additional programs: Certified Glazier
Approximate certification costs: $159

Program Description

The NGA's Auto Glass certification program recognizes auto glass installation technicians at three different levels. Certification is based on experience and passing an examination. Participants are encouraged (but not required) to attend the Auto Glass Technical Institute, a five-day, 40-hour training program.

Education/Experience

The requirements are as follows:

- Technician—Six months of validated experience
- Senior—Two years of validated experience and current Technician certification
- Master—Five years of validated experience and current Senior Technician certification

Examinations

The examination for each level is based on a task analysis and current industry standards as documented in the current *Auto Glass Certification Handbook.* All tests are 90-minute, multiple-choice exams administered by computer through Sylvan Prometric.

Recertification

Recertification is required every three years. Contact NGA for details.

CERTIFIED BATHROOM DESIGNER (CBD)

Sponsor

National Kitchen and Bath Association (NKBA)
687 Willow Grove St.
Hackettstown, NJ 07840
Phone: (800) 401-6522
Fax: (908) 852-1695

Program Data

Certifying body: Association
Additional certifications: Certified Kitchen
    Designer (CKD)
Approximate certification costs: $250

Program Description

The Certified Bathroom Designer (CBD) designation recognizes showroom sales, draftspersons, installers, and contractors involved in designing, planning, and supervising residential bathroom installations. Membership in the Society of Certified Bathroom Designers comes with certification.

Education/Experience

Candidates must have two years of experience and meet one of the following requirements:

- Two years of experience and a bachelor's degree
- Three years of experience and an associate's degree
- Four years of experience and completion of the NKBA Bathroom Designer correspondence course
- Six years of experience and completion of the Bathroom Design Preparatory Seminar
- Seven years of experience

Examinations

The CBD examination is a seven-hour test based on the industry's current technical manuals. The pass rate is 70%. The examinations were developed with the assistance of Virginia Polytechnic Institute.

Recertification

CBDs must recertify every three years by accumulating 10 professional-development points.

ACI {CONCRETE} CERTIFICATION

Sponsor

American Concrete Institute (ACI)
P.O. Box 19150
Detroit, MI 48219
Phone: (313) 532-2600
Fax: (313) 533-4747

Program Data

Certifying body: Association
Number certified: 40,000+
Organization members: 20,000

Program Description

The ACI Certification program certifies several categories of technicians and inspectors. ACI membership is not required. Certification is offered through local sponsoring groups and national groups. ACI sells videos and certification workbooks. Testing certifications are based on both ASTM tests and ACI practices. Certification categories are explained below.

Concrete Field Testing Technician—Grade I certification for technicians performing basic field tests on fresh concrete following seven ASTM Standard Test Methods. There are no prerequisites. The written examination is a closed book, 55-question, multiple-choice test on the ASTM Standard Methods. The performance examination requires the candidate to successfully perform and record six of these tests and to verbally describe a seventh. Recertification is required every five years by retaking and passing both examinations.

Concrete Laboratory Testing Technician—Grade I certification for technicians performing basic laboratory tests on aggregates and concrete following 11 ASTM Standard Test Methods. There are no prerequisites. The written examination is a closed-book, 100-question, multiple-choice test on the ASTM Standard Methods. The performance examination requires the candidate to successfully perform and record nine of these tests. Recertification is required every five years by retaking and passing the written examinations.

Concrete Laboratory Testing Technician—Grade II certification for technicians performing advanced laboratory tests on aggregates and concrete following 12 complex ASTM Standard Test Methods. Candidates must have one year of acceptable work experience and complete all certification requirements for Grade I. The written examination is a closed-book, 100-question, multiple-choice test on the ASTM Standard Methods. The performance examination requires the candidate to successfully perform and record these tests. Recertification is required every five years by retaking and passing the written examinations.

Concrete Construction Inspector—Level II certification for individuals who inspect concrete construction. Candidates must have two years of concrete testing and inspection and meet one of the following requirements:

- Two years of college or technical school
- High school diploma and one year of construction testing or inspection in any area
- Three years of construction testing or inspection in any area

Candidates must pass a four-hour, 100-question, open-book, multiple-choice examination. The examination covers a wide range of standards and practices for preplacement, placement, and post-placement inspection. Recertification is required every five years by retaking and passing the written examinations.

Concrete Construction Inspector-in-Training certification is given to individuals who pass the Concrete Construction Inspector—Level II examination but do not have sufficient work experience. Upgrade to Level II is given upon completion of work experience requirements.

Concrete Flatwork Finisher certification for experienced craftspersons in placing, finishing, and curing flatwork. Candidates must meet one of the following options:

- One year of flatwork-finishing experience, written/oral examination, and performance evaluation

- Three years of flatwork-finishing experience, written/oral examination, and an employer-signed affidavit certifying skills equivalent to the performance evaluation

The written/oral examination is a 50-question, multiple-choice test on technology, materials, and mixing, tests, tools, and techniques. The performance evaluation is an approximately eight-hour demonstration of placing through initial protection of a concrete slab. Recertification is required every five years by retaking and passing the written examinations.

Concrete Flatwork Technician certification is given to individuals who pass the Finisher written examination but do not have the required work experience. Upgrade to Concrete Flatwork Finisher is given upon completion of requirements for work experience and performance evaluation. Recertification is required every five years by retaking and passing the written examinations.

CERTIFIED DRAFTER

Sponsor

American Design Drafting Association (ADDA)
P.O. Box 799
Rockville, MD 20848
Phone: (301) 460-6875
Fax: (301) 460-8591
E-mail: racheladda@aol.com

Program Data

Certifying body: Association
Year certification began: 1993
Number certified: 714 (as of 12/94)
Approximate certification costs: $35

Program Description

The Drafter certification program is a professional-level certification from the American Design Drafting Association (ADDA). Certification is based on passing an examination. Membership in ADDA is not required. There are no qualifying criteria.

Examinations

The 90-minute certification examination tests a variety of drafting tasks at a general knowledge level. The test format is matching, true/false, and multiple-choice. The test does not cover computer-aided drafting (CAD).

The examination covers these areas:

- Object representation (orthographic and pictorial)

- Symbol/term knowledge, including dimensioning, sectioning, welding, and manufacturing processes; fits and tolerances; working drawings; and scales, lettering, and lines

- General drafting standards, including title blocks; face of drawing; drawing release procedures; record-keeping; reproduction; and typical drafting department procedures

- Basic geometric construction/analysis

Recertification

None.

GLAZIER

COMMERCIAL INTERIOR/RESIDENTIAL GLAZIER

STOREFRONT/CURTAINWALL GLAZIER

MASTER GLAZIER

Sponsor

National Glass Association (NGA)
8200 Greensboro Drive, 3rd Floor
McLean, VA 22102-3881
Phone: (703) 442-4890
Fax: (703) 442-0630
E-mail:76446.2330@compuserve.com
WWW: http://ourworld.compuserve.com/
   homepages/nga/

Program Data

Certifying body: Association
Year certification began: 1995
Additional programs: Auto Glass Technician
Approximate certification costs: $124

Program Description

The NGA Glazier certification program recognizes several levels of knowledge and experience for glazier technicians. Certification is based on experience and passing an examination.

Education/Experience

The requirements are as follows:

- Glazier (level 1)—One year of validated experience
- Commercial Interior/Residential Glazier (level 2)—Five years of validated experience, and current Level 1 Glazier Certification
- Storefront/Curtainwall Glazier (level 2)—Five years of validated experience, and current Level 1 Glazier certification
- Master Glazier (level 3)—Five years of experience, and current Level 2 Glazier certification

Examinations

The examination for each level is based on a task analysis and current industry standards as documented in the current *Basic Guide to Glass and Glazing Study Manual, Commercial Interior/ Residential Glazier Manual,* or *Storefront/Curtain- wall Glazier Manual.* All tests are 90-minute, multiple-choice exams administered by computer through Sylvan Prometric.

Recertification

Recertification is required every three years. Contact NGA for details.

CERTIFIED KITCHEN DESIGNER (CKD)

Sponsor

National Kitchen and Bath Association (NKBA)
687 Willow Grove St.
Hackettstown, NJ 07840
Phone: (800) 401-6522
Fax: (908) 852-1695

Program Data

Certifying body: Association
Additional certifications: Certified Bathroom De- signer (CBD)
Approximate certification costs: $250

Program Description

The Certified Kitchen Designer (CKD) designation recognizes showroom sales, draftspersons, in- stallers, and contractors involved in designing, planning, and supervising residential kitchen install- ations. Membership in the Society of Certified Kitchen Designers comes with certification.

Education/Experience

Candidates must have two years of experience and meet one of the following requirements:

- Two years of experience and a bachelor's degree
- Three years of experience and an associate's degree
- Four years of experience and completion of the NKBA Kitchen Designer correspondence course
- Six years of experience and completion of the Kitchen Design Preparatory Seminar
- Seven years of experience

Examinations

The CKD examination is a seven-hour test based on the industry's current technical manuals. The pass rate is 70%. The examinations were de- veloped with the assistance of Virginia Polytechnic Institute.

Recertification

CKDs must recertify every three years by accumu- lating 10 professional-development points.

CERTIFIED PHOTOGRAPHIC CONSULTANT™ (CPC)

Sponsor

Photo Marketing Association International (PMA)
3000 Picture Place
Jackson, MI 49201
Phone: (517) 788-8100
Fax: (517) 788-8371
WWW: http://www.pmai.org/

Program Data

Certifying body: Association
Organization members: 15,500 member firms
Approximate costs: $30

Program Description

The Certified Photographic Consultant (CPC) designation recognizes experienced professionals in photo-shop sales and service. Candidates are selected by PMA member firms. Certification is based on completing several courses and passing a final examination.

Curriculum

Candidates must complete the Photo Technology and the Retail Selling and Customer Relations self-study programs. Upon completion, candidates take the in-store Retail Selling and Customer Service course. Candidates then take a final exam covering the course materials.

Recertification

After two years of lapsed membership, CPCs must retake the examination.

CERTIFIED PICTURE FRAMER (CPF)

Sponsor

Professional Picture Framers Association (PPFA)
4305 Sarellen Road
Richmond, VA 23231
Phone: (804) 226-0430
Fax: (804) 222-2175
E-mail: ppfa-1@spaceworks.com

Program Data

Certifying body: Association
Year certification began: 1986
Number certified: 2800
Organization members: 6500
Approximate certification costs: $200 (members), $300 (nonmembers)

Program Description

The Certified Picture Framer (CPF) designation recognizes experienced picture framers who have passed PPFA's certification examination. CPFs may frame and be consulted on the presentation and preservation of a wide range of art work. PPFA provides candidates with a bibliography of suggested study references. Study guides are available.

Education/Experience

Membership in PPFA is not required. Candidates must have one year of experience as a professional picture framer.

Examinations

The examination, developed with the assistance of the Educational Testing Service (ETS), is based on an extensive job analysis and relevancy weights of picture-framer tasks. The current pass rate is 63%. The 150-question, multiple-choice examination covers these areas:

- Customer needs analysis
- Proper care and conservation

- Materials use and selection
- Materials preparation and framing techniques

Recertification

Under development.

CERTIFIED GRADUATE REMODELER™ (CGR)

Sponsor

National Association of Home Builders (NAHB)
  Remodelers Council
1201 Fifteenth St. NW
Washington, DC 20005
Phone: (800) 368-5242
Fax: (202) 822-0390
E-mail: info@nahb.org
WWW: http://www.nahb.com

Program Data

Certifying body: Association
Approximate certification costs: $300–$1200, depending on experience

Program Description

The Certified Graduate Remodeler™ (CGR) designation recognizes experienced residential home remodelers and emphasizes business management as the foundation of a successful remodeler operation. Membership in NAHB is not required.

Education/Experience

Certification is based on a combination of remodelling education, general education, and experience. The total amount of education required is based on completion of a professional profile.

Candidates must have at least five years of experience in remodeling business management prior to award of the CGR designation.

Candidates also must own, or hold a business management position, in a remodeling organization.

Curriculum

The CGR program is based on completing specific coursework. Depending on the experience and education documented on the CGR professional profile, candidates will take three, six, or nine courses. Courses are offered through the Graduate Builders Institute (GBI), sponsored by the NAHB's Home Builders Institute (HBI). HBI courses are sponsored by state and local home builder associations. At least one remodeling-specific and two other GBI courses are taken by all candidates. Each course is approximately six hours long.

There are five Remodeler courses:

- Building Technology for Remodelers
- Business Finance for Remodelers
- Design/Build for Remodelers
- Insurance Reconstruction
- Sales and Marketing for Remodelers

The general courses are as follows:

- Building Codes and Standards
- Business Management
- Computer Applications
- Construction Contracts and Law
- Customer Service
- Energy Efficient Construction
- Estimating
- Negotiation
- Project Management
- Quality Construction
- Scheduling

Recertification

CGRs must recertify every three years through professional education, including a Graduate Builder Institute or CGR course.

CERTIFIED REMODELER (CR)
CERTIFIED REMODELER ASSOCIATE (CRA)

Sponsor

National Association of the Remodeling Industry (NARI)
4301 N. Fairfax Drive, Suite 310
Arlington, VA 22203
Phone: (800) 966-7600
Fax: (703) 243-3465

Program Data

Certifying body: Association
Organization members: 5500
Approximate certification costs: $500 (members), $835 (nonmembers)

Program Description

The NARI certification program recognizes remodeling contractors demonstrating high standards of performance, in-depth industry knowledge, and a proven record of acceptable performance in remodeling. The NARI program also seeks to establish high standards of business ethics and practice in the remodeling industry. NARI maintains an active ethics program.

The Certified Remodeler (CR) designation recognizes skilled remodeling general contractors; the Certified Remodeler Associate (CRA) designation recognizes remodeling contractors specializing in a specific specialty.

Education/Experience

Candidates must have five years of continuous service (employee or owner) in the remodeling business. Candidates document their experience and background through a Qualification Matrix. After completing the matrix and agreeing to adhere to the NARI's standards of practice and code of ethics, candidates are eligible for the CR or CRA examination.

Examinations

The one-day, written CR and CRA examinations are prepared by the University of Illinois and cover construction and business practices. A comprehensive study guide and study groups are available. Both examinations cover business management, construction law, safety, and NARI's standards of practice and code of ethics. The CR examination covers general contracting related to major remodeling alterations. The CRA examinations are available in the following specialties:

- Ceramic Tile and Marble
- Concrete and Masonry
- Decks, Porches, and Patios
- Electrical
- Greenhouses and Sunrooms
- Gutters and Downspouts
- HVAC
- Insulation
- Painting and Paperhanging
- Plumbing
- Pools and Spas
- Roofing and Siding

- Windows, Doors, and Skylights
- Waterproofing

Recertification

Certificants must reregister annually.

CERTIFIED INSPECTION, CLEANING, AND RESTORATION TECHNICIAN

Sponsor

Institute for Inspection, Cleaning, and Restoration
  Certification (IICRC)
2715 E. Mill Plain Blvd.
Vancouver, WA 98661
Phone: (360) 693-5675
Fax: (360) 693-4858

Program Data

IICRC is sponsored by the following: Association of Cleaning Technicians; Association of Specialists in Cleaning and Restoration; Association of Wisconsin Cleaning Contractors; Carpet and FabriCare Institute; Carpet and Rug Cleaning Association of Illinois; Carpet Cleaners Institute of the Northwest; Floorcovering Institute of Ontario; Mid-South Professional Cleaners Association; Midwest Association of Professionals; New England Institute of Restorations and Cleaning; New York Rug Cleaners Institute; Ontario Professional Carpet Cleaners Association; Professional Carpet and Upholstery Cleaners Association; Society of Cleaning Technicians; Southwest Carpet Cleaners Association; and United Carpet Cleaner Institute.

Certifying body: Board created from a consortium
  of associations
Year certification began: 1972
Number certified: 10,115
Approximate certification costs: Varies

Program Description

The Certified Inspection, Cleaning, and Restoration Technician program is designed to recognize personnel having the knowledge and skills needed to properly care for fabrics. Leading association and industry experts ensure IICRC certification requirements meet up-to-date, safe standards. IICRC produces no training material nor sponsors training, but recognizes schools that meet IICRC requirements. Students enrolled in these programs have their examinations sent to the IICRC for processing. IICRC maintains an active ethics program. The certification levels, areas, and requirements are explained below.

Certified Technicians—These must complete 14 hours of instruction and successfully complete a two-hour examination. Technicians may be certified in the following areas:

- Carpet Cleaning Technician
- Carpet Repair and Reinstallation Technician
- Color Repair Technician
- Fire and Smoke Restoration Technician
- Odor Control Technician
- Upholstery and Fabric Cleaning Technician
- Water Damage Restoration Technician

Journeyman Cleaner—This status is granted when a technician has at least one year of certification and completes technician programs equal to five of 12 possible credits. Each two-day cleaning technician course is worth two credits, with all others worth one credit.

Certified Senior Carpet Inspector—This certification is recognized by major carpet manufacturer associations. The four major fiber producers recognize and use these inspectors when needing expert third-party opinion. Senior Carpet Inspectors complete 40–56 hours of classroom instruction, submit 10 inspection reports for peer review, and must pass a six-part comprehensive examination.

Master Cleaner Certification—This designation recognizes technicians with as least three years of experience and eight credits. Master Restoration Technicians must accumulate a total of 10 credits.

Examinations

Examinations follow the courses and cover course content. Technician certification examinations have a pass rate of approximately 75%.

Recertification

Recertification is based on continuing-education credits, with one credit equal to seven hours of instruction. Technicians must earn two credits in their field every four years. Inspectors must earn two credits in their field every two years. National conventions, supplier, association, and schools workshops are reviewed for credit. The recertification rate is 81%.

CERTIFIED RESTORER (CR)

Sponsor

Association of Specialists in Cleaning and
  Restoration (ASCR)
10830 Annapolis Junction Road, Suite 312
Annapolis Junction, MD 20701
Phone: (301) 604-4411
WWW: http://www.ascr.org/index.htm

Program Data

Certifying body: Educational division of a
  professional association
Approximate certification costs: $465 (members),
  $665 (nonmembers)

Program Description

The Certified Restorer (CR) designation recognizes
technicians who have completed the two-day,
National Institute of Disaster Restoration (NIDR)
certification program. Membership in ASCR is not
required. Candidates must have three years of
damage restoration experience, provide three
acceptable estimates completed for insurance
repair work, write a formal report on a restoration or
research project, and pass a personal interview.

The CR course includes hands-on training in the
basics of fire, water, and smoke damage. The
course covers identification and testing; damage
control; emergency treatments; techniques; inspection and evaluation; deodorization and decontamination; furniture, textiles, and computer/electronics;
building exteriors; and documentation.

Examinations

A written examination covering the course curriculum must be passed for certification.

Recertification

Information was not disclosed.

ADS® TECHCERT CERTIFIED TECHNICIAN
ADS® TECHCERT CERTIFIED MASTER
  TECHNICIAN

Sponsor

Association of Diesel Specialists (ADS®)
9140 Ward Parkway
Kansas City, MO 64114
Phone: (816) 444-3500
Fax: (816) 444-0330

Program Data

The ADS TechCert program was developed in
cooperation with the National Institute for Automotive Service Excellence (ASE).

Certifying body: Association
Year certification began: 1994
Approximate certification costs: $200 (members),
  $350 (nonmembers) for Technician level

Program Description

The TechCert certification program recognizes
knowledgeable diesel specialists and assures
manufacturers that an aftermarket technician network exists to service their products. Certification is
based on passing a series of exams.

Education/Experience

Technician candidates must have one year of
shop experience or have completed an accepted
technical-school diesel course before taking the
basic TC1 examination. Two years of shop experience is required for certification at the technician
level.

Master Technician candidates must have three
years of shop experience.

Examinations

Technician certification is based on passing the
basic TC1 examination and at least one other
examination. Master Technician certification requires passing all six examinations. All exams are
multiple-choice and measure knowledge of diagnostic and repair skills. Extensive study materials
are available. The exams are administered by
American College Testing (ACT). The exams are
as follows:

  TC1—Diesel Engine Theory and Operation

  TC2—Distributor Fuel Injection

  TC3—Inline Fuel Injection

  TC4—Rail Fuel Injection

  TC5—Turbochargers/Blowers

  TC6—Injectors/Unit Injectors

Recertification

Technician certification is good for five years.
Master Technician certification will be reviewed
after five years.

CERTIFIED TURFGRASS PROFESSIONAL (CTP)

Sponsor

Professional Lawn Care Association of America (PLCAA)
1000 Johnson Ferry Road NE, Suite C-135
Marietta, GA 30068
Phone: (800) 458-3466
Fax: (770) 578-6071
E-mail: plcaa@plcaa.org
WWW: http://www.plcaa.org/

Program Data

The program is offered through the University of Georgia Center for Continuing Education. Several companies within the industry support the CTP program, including Orkin Pest Control; Miles Specialty Products; O.M. Scott; Ciba Corporation; Lesco; ISK Biotech; PBI Gordon; and Dow Elanco.

Certifying body: Association
Approximate certification costs: $275

Program Description

The Certified Turfgrass Professional (CTP) designation recognizes lawn-care professionals who complete the 120-hour Principles of Turfgrass Management course. There are no education or experience requirements.

Curriculum

The Principles of Turfgrass Management home study course covers customer relations: establishment; fertilization; insects; irrigation; mowing; pesticides; soils; turfgrass and the environment; turfgrass characterization, identification, and adaptation; turfgrass diseases; turfgrass growth, development, and physiology; and weeds. Candidates must pass two proctored examinations on course materials for certification.

Recertification

CTPs must recertify every five years through retesting.

CERTIFIED IN UNDERGROUND STORAGE TANK INSTALLATION/DECOMMISSIONING (UST)

Sponsor

International Fire Code Institute (IFCI)
5360 Workman Mill Road
Whittier, CA 90601
Phone: (310) 699-0124

Program Data

The International Fire Code Institute is co-sponsored by the International Association of Fire Chiefs (IAFC), the International Conference of Building Officials (ICBO), and the Western Fire Chiefs Association (WFCA).

Certifying body: Association-sponsored independent board
Additional programs: Certified Uniform Fire Code Inspector

Program Description

The Certified in Underground Storage Tank Installation and Decommissioning certifications are based on passing the IFCI examination. The UST Installation/Retrofitting certification and the UST Decommissioning certification require separate examinations. There are no prerequisites or qualifications for either examination.

Examinations

Each UST certification examination is a closed-book examination. The pass rate for IFCI examinations is confidential. The exam questions reference several basic industry standards and specialized references. The UST Installation/Retrofitting examination includes:

- Contaminated soil handling
- Decommissioning and cleaning
- Excavation
- Materials
- Pre-installation
- Secondary containment
- System inspection, lining, and retrofitting
- Testing, monitoring, health, and safety
- Vapor recovery

The UST Decommissioning certification examination includes:

- Contaminated soil handling
- Health and safety
- Reporting requirements
- Site preparation
- Tank decommissioning and cleaning
- Tank storage and transportation

Recertification
Passing an examination on codes and standards every two years is required.

AWS Certified Welder

Sponsor
American Welding Society (AWS)
550 N.W. LeJeune Road
Miami, FL 33135
Phone: 800 (443-9353)
E-mail: info@amweld.org
WWW: http://www.aws.org/

Program Data
Certifying body: Association
Organization members: 46,000
Additional certifications: Certified Associate Welding Inspector (CAWI); Certified Welding Educator (CWE); Certified Welding Inspector (CWI)

Program Description
The AWS Certified Welder program certifies welders in several defined areas, such as structural steel, sheet metal, and military. Certification is based on passing a performance test in an area. Candidates must meet ASW minimum standards for visual acuity (corrected or uncorrected).

Examinations
Candidates perform test welds under observation of an AWS CWI.

Recertification
AWS welder certificants must renew certification annually. Renewal is based on reexamination or on employer certification of continued work performing welding in the defined area.

Certified Welding Educator (CWE)

Sponsor
American Welding Society (AWS)
550 N.W. LeJeune Road
Miami, FL 33135
Phone: 800 (443-9353)
E-mail: info@amweld.org
WWW: http://www.aws.org/

Program Data
Certifying body: Association
Organization members: 46,000
Additional certifications: Certified Associate Welding Inspector (CAWI); Certified Welding Inspector (CWI); AWS Certified Welder

Program Description
The Certified Welding Educator (CWE) designation recognizes classroom and hands-on welding instructors. Certification is based on meeting several experience and examination requirements. AWS membership is not required.

Education/Experience
Candidates must meet the following requirements:

- High school diploma and five years of welding experience in either production, construction, inspection, or repair
- Passing score on the CWI or CAWI practical examination or equivalent
- Passing score on the CWI or CAWI fundamentals examination or equivalent
- Passing score on an AWS Certified Welder test in the process to be taught
- Documentation of instructional experience and background meeting the requirements of the school or college where presently employed

Recertification
CWE certification must be renewed every four years. Renewal is by continued work in welding education.

CERTIFIED WELL DRILLER (CWD)
CERTIFIED PUMP INSTALLER (CPI)
MASTER GROUND WATER CONTRACTOR (MGWC)

Sponsor

National Ground Water Association (NGWA)
2600 Ground Water Way
Columbus, OH 43219
Phone: (800) 551-7379
Fax: (614) 337-8445
E-mail: h2o@h2o-ngwa.org
WWW: http://www.h2o-ngwa.org

Program Data

Certifying body: Association
Number certified: 1300
Organization members: 24,000

Program Description

The Well Construction and Pump Installation certification programs are designed to ensure quality work in well system installation and maintenance and to help protect the ground water supply. NGWA membership is not required. Certification is based on passing examinations.

Education/Experience

Candidates must have two years of operational or supervisory experience.

For the Master Ground Water Contractor (MGWC) designation, candidates must have five years of operational or supervisory experience.

Examinations

The certification examinations are multiple-choice tests on specialized equipment and geologic formations. All Certified Well Driller (CWD) and Certified Pump Installer (CPI) candidates take a general examination covering ground water and industry standards. Candidates also take a specialized examination in their area of expertise. These are the CWD specialized examinations:

- Air Rotary Drilling in Rock Material
- Air Rotary Drilling in Unconsolidated Material
- Boring and Augering in Unconsolidated Material
- Cable Tool Drilling in Unconsolidated Material
- Cable Tool Drilling in Rock Material
- Jetting and Driving Wells in Unconsolidated Material
- Monitoring Well Construction
- Mud Rotary Drilling in Rock Material
- Mud Rotary Drilling in Unconsolidated Material
- Reverse Rotary Drilling in Unconsolidated Material
- Well Servicing and Maintenance

The CPI pump installation tests are as follows:
- Domestic 1–3 hp
- Domestic 3–20 hp
- Industrial and Municipal, over 20 hp

For the Master Ground Water Contractor (MGWC) designation, all tests (except Monitoring Well Construction) must be passed.

Recertification

Recertification is done annually. All designations must maintain any state-required license and complete seven hours of acceptable continuing education.

APPENDIX A:
Certification by Designation Index

A+	A+ Service Technician Certification || Computing Technology Industry Association (CompTIA)
AAC	Activity Assistant Certified || National Certification Council for Activity Professionals (NCCAP)
AAI®	Accredited Adviser in Insurance || Insurance Institute of America (IIA)
AAM®	Associate in Automation Management || Insurance Institute of America (IIA)
AARE	Accredited Auctioneer Real Estate || Certified Auctioneers Institute (CAI)
ABC	Accredited Business Communicator || International Association of Business Communicators (IABC)
ABMLI	Diplomate, American Board of Medical Laboratory Immunology || American Society for Microbiology (ASM)
ABMM	Diplomate, American Board of Medical Microbiology || American Society for Microbiology (ASM)
ACC	Activity Consultant Certified || National Certification Council for Activity Professionals (NCCAP)
ACFRE	Advance Certified Fund Raising Executive || National Society of Fund Raising Executives (NSFRE)
ACM	Associate Certified Manager || Institute of Certified Professional Managers (ICPM)
ACP®	Associate Computing Professional || Institute for Certification of Computer Professionals (ICCP®)
ACR	Associate of Corporate Real Estate || International Association of Corporate Real Estate Executives (NACORE)
ACS®	Associate, Customer Service || Life Office Management Association (LOMA)
ACSR	Accredited Customer Service Representative || Independent Insurance Agents of America (IIAA)
ADC	Activity Director Certified || National Certification Council for Activity Professionals (NCCAP)
ADRP	Associate Disaster Recovery Planner || Disaster Recovery Institute (DRI)
AEP	Associate Environmental Professional || National Registry of Environmental Professionals[SM] (NREP[SM])
AEPA	Associate Environmental Property Assessor || National Registry of Environmental Professionals[SM] (NREP[SM])

AES℠   Automated Examination Specialist || Society of Financial Examiners® (SOFE®)

AET   Associate Environmental Trainer|| National Environmental Training Association (NETA)

AFC   Accredited Financial Counselor || Institute for Personal Finance (IFP)

AFE®   Accredited Financial Examiner || Society of Financial Examiners® (SOFE®)

AFM   Accredited Farm Manager || American Society of Farm Managers and Rural Appraisers (ASFMRA)

AFSB   Associate in Fidelity and Surety Bonding || Insurance Institute of America (IIA)

AHC   Accredited Housing Counselor || Association for Financial Counseling and Planning Education (AFCPE)

AIAA™   Associate, Insurance Agency Administration || Life Office Management Association (LOMA)

AIAF   Associate in Insurance Accounting and Finance || Life Office Management Association (LOMA)

AIC   Associate in Claims || Insurance Institute of America (IIA)

AICP   American Institute of Certified Planners || American Planning Association (APA)

AIE   Accredited Insurance Examiner || Insurance Regulatory Examiners Society (IRES)

AIM   Associate in Management || Insurance Institute of America (IIA)

AIS   Associate in Insurance Services || Insurance Institute of America (IIA)

ALCM®   Associate in Loss Control Management || Insurance Institute of America (IIA)

ALHC   Associate, Life and Health Claims || International Claims Association (ICA)

ALS   Accredited Legal Secretary || National Association of Legal Secretaries® (NALS)

AMEA   Accredited Machinery and Equipment Appraiser || Association of Machinery and Equipment Appraisers, Inc. (AMEA)

AMIM®   Associate in Marine Insurance Management || Insurance Institute of America (IIA)

AMS®   Association Management Specialist || Community Associations Institute (CAI)

APA®   Associate in Premium Auditing || Insurance Institute of America (IIA)

APM   Associate Professional Member {Pension Actuary} || American Society of Pension Actuaries (ASPA)

A.P.P.   Accredited Purchasing Practitioner || National Association of Purchasing Managers

Apple CSE   Apple Certified Server Engineer || Apple Computer, Inc.

APR   Accredited in Public Relations || Public Relations Society of America

ARA	Accredited Rural Appraiser ‖ American Society of Farm Managers and Rural Appraisers (ASFMRA)
ARe	Associate in Reinsurance ‖ Insurance Institute of America (IIA)
ARM®	Accredited Residential Manager ‖ Institute of Real Estate Management (IREM)
ARM	Associate in Risk Management ‖ Insurance Institute of America (IIA)
ARP	Associate in Research and Planning ‖ Life Office Management Association (LOMA)
ARU	Accredited Residential Underwriter ‖ Mortgage Bankers Association of America (MBA)
ASE	Associate Service Executive ‖ National Association of Service Managers (NASM)
ASP	Associate Safety Professional ‖ Board of Certified Safety Professionals (BCSP)
ATP	Assistive Technology Practitioner ‖ Rehabilitation Engineering and Assistive Technology Society of North America (RESNA)
ATS	Assistive Technology Supplier ‖ Rehabilitation Engineering and Assistive Technology Society of North America (RESNA)
AU	Associate in Underwriting ‖ Insurance Institute of America (IIA)
AVS	Associate Value Specialist ‖ Society of American Value Engineers (SAVE)
BCE	Board Certified Entomologist ‖ Entomological Society of America (ESA)
BCE	Broadband Communications Engineer ‖ Society of Cable Telecommunications Engineers (SCTE)
BC-HIS	Board Certified in Hearing Instrument Sciences ‖ National Board for Certification in Hearing Instrument Sciences (NBC-HIS)
BCNP	Board Certified Nuclear Pharmacist ‖ Board of Pharmaceutical Specialties (BPS)
BCNSP	Board Certified Nutrition Support Pharmacist ‖ Board of Pharmaceutical Specialties (BPS)
BCPS	Board Certified Pharmacotherapy Specialist ‖ Board of Pharmaceutical Specialties (BPS)
BCT	Broadband Communications Technician ‖ Society of Cable Telecommunications Engineers (SCTE)
C.A.	Chartered Accountant ‖ Association of Chartered Accountants in the United States (ACAUS)
C.A.	Certified Archivist ‖ Academy of Certified Archivists (ACA)
CAA	Certified Architectural Administrator ‖ Society of Architectural Administrators (SAA)
CACM	Certified Associate Contracts Manager ‖ National Contract Management Association (NCMA)

CAE	Certified Association Executive || American Society of Association Executives (ASAE)
CAFM	Certified Automotive Fleet Manager || National Association of Fleet Administrators, Inc. (NAFA)
CAI®	Certified, Auctioneer's Institute || Auction Marketing Institute (AMI)
C.A.M.	Certified Administrative Manager || Institute of Certified Professional Managers (ICPM)
CAM	Certified Apartment Manager || National Apartment Association (NAA)
CAMT	Certified Apartment Maintenance Technician || National Apartment Association (NAA)
CAPP	Certified Administrator of Public Parking || Institutional and Municipal Parking Congress (IMPC)
CAPS	Certified Apartment Property Supervisor || National Apartment Association (NAA)
CASS	Certified Administrator of Suggestion Systems || Employee Involvement Association (EIA)
CAWI	Certified Associate Welding Inspector || American Welding Society (AWS)
CBA™	Chartered Bank Auditor || Bank Administration Institute (BAI) Foundation
CBA	Certified Business Appraiser || Institute of Business Appraisers, Inc. (IBA)
CBC	Certified Business Communicator || Business Marketing Association
CBCO	Certified Bank Compliance Officer || Bank Administration Institute (BAI) Foundation
CBD	Certified Bathroom Designer || National Kitchen and Bath Association (NKBA)
CBET	Certified Biomedical Equipment Technician || International Certification Commission (ICC)
CBP	Certified Benefits Professional || American Compensation Association (ACA)
CBPE	Certified Business Planning Executive || National Association of Printers and Lithographers (NAPL)
CBRE	Broadcast Engineer Radio || Society of Broadcast Engineers, Inc. (SBE)
CBSE	Certified Building Service Executive || Building Service Contractors Association International (BSCAI)
CBT	Broadcast Technologist || Society of Broadcast Engineers, Inc. (SBE)
CBTE	Broadcast Engineer TV || Society of Broadcast Engineers, Inc. (SBE)
CC	Certified Cook || American Culinary Federation Education Institute (ACFEI)
CCA	Certified Crop Advisor || ARCPACS
CCAP	Certified Claims Assistance Professional || National Association of Claims Assistance Professionals, Inc (NACAP)

CCAT	Certified Computer Applications Trainer || Association for Computer Applications Trainers (ACAT)
CCC	Certified Cost Consultant || AACE International (AACE)
CCE	Certified Culinary Educator || American Culinary Federation Education Institute (ACFEI)
CCE	Certified Catering Executive || National Association of Catering Executives (NACE)
CCE	Certified Cost Engineer || AACE International (AACE)
CCEA	Certified Cost Estimator/Analyst || Society of Cost Estimating and Analysis (SCEA)
CChE	Certified Professional Chemical Engineer || National Certification Commission in Chemistry and Chemical Engineering
CCIE	Cisco Certified Internetwork Expert || Cisco Systems
CCM	Certified Case Manager || Commission of Certified Case Managers (CCCM)
CCM	Certified Club Manager || Club Managers Association of America
CCM	Certified Consulting Meteorologist || American Meteorological Society (AMS)
CCM	Certified Cash Manager || Treasury Management Association (TMA)
CCO	Certified Confidentiality Officer || Business Espionage Controls and Countermeasures Association (BECCA)
CCP	Certified Cogeneration Professional || Association of Energy Engineers® (AEE)
CCP	Certified Compensation Professional || American Compensation Association (ACA)
CCP®	Certified Computing Professional || Institute for Certification of Computer Professionals (ICCP®)
CCRA	Certified Commercial Real Estate Appraiser || National Association of Real Estate Appraisers (NAREA)
CCS	Cardiopulmonary Certified Specialist || American Physical Therapy Association
CCTE	Certified Corporate Travel Executive || National Business Travel Association (NBTA)
CCTS™	Certified Corporate Trust Specialist™ || Institute for Certified Bankers™ (ICB)
CCUE	Certified Credit Union Executive || Credit Union National Association, Inc (CUNA)
CDA	Child Development Associate || The Council for Early Childhood Professional Recognition (CECPR)
CDIA	Certified Document Imaging Architect || Computing Technology Industry Association (CompTIA)
CDM	Certified Dietary Manager || Certifying Board for Dietary Managers (CBDM)

CDME	Certified Destination Management Executive || International Association of Convention and Visitor Bureaus (IACVB)
CDRP	Certified Disaster Recovery Planner || Disaster Recovery Institute (DRI)
CDS	Certified Destination Specialist || International Society of Meeting Planners (IMPI)
CDSM	Certified Demand-Side Management Professional || Association of Energy Engineers® (AEE)
CDT	Certified Dental Technician || National Board for Certification in Dental Laboratory Technology (NBC)
CEA	Certified Environmental Auditor || National Registry of Environmental Professionals^{SM} (NREP^{SM})
CEAP®	Certified Employee Assistance Professional || Employee Assistance Certification Commission (EACC)
CEBS	Certified Employee Benefit Specialist || International Foundation of Employee Benefit Plans (IFEBP)
CEC	Certified Executive Chef || American Culinary Federation Education Institute (ACFEI)
CECP	Certified Electronic Claims Professional || National Association of Claims Assistance Professionals, Inc. (NACAP)
CECS	Clinical Electrophysiologic Certified Specialist || American Physical Therapy Association
CED®	Certified Economic Developer® || American Economic Development Council (AEDC)
CEF	Certified Electroplater-Finisher || American Electroplaters and Surface Finishers Society (AESF)
C.E.H.	Certified Executive Housekeeper || National Executive Housekeepers Association (N.E.H.A.)
CEHT	Certified Environmental Health Technician || National Environmental Health Association (NEHA)
CEI	Certified Electronic Imager || Professional Photographers of America (PPA)
CEI	Certified Environmental Inspector || Environmental Assessment Association (EAA)
CEM	Certified Emergency Manager || National Coordinating Council on Emergency Management (NCCEM)
CEM	Certified Energy Manager || Association of Energy Engineers® (AEE)
CEMT	Certified Electron Microscopy Technologist || Microscopy Society of America (MSA)
CEOE®	Certified Engineering Operations Executive || Educational Institute of the American Hotel and Motel Association (EI/AH&MA)

CEPC	Certified Executive Pastry Chef || American Culinary Federation Education Institute (ACFEI)
CEP	Certified Environmental Professional || National Association of Environmental Professionals (NAEP)
CEP	Certified Event Planner || International Society of Meeting Planners (IMPI)
CET	Certified Electronics Technician || Electronics Technicians Association, International (ETA)
CET	Certified Engineering Technician || National Institute for Certification in Engineering Technologies (NICET)
CET	Certified Environmental Trainer® || National Environmental Training Association (NETA)
CF	Consulting Fellow {Property} || National Property Manager Association, Inc. (NPMA)
CFA®	Chartered Financial Analyst || Association for Investment Management and Research (AIMR)
CFBE®	Certified Food and Beverage Executive || Educational Institute of the American Hotel and Motel Association (EI/AH&MA)
CFC	Certified Forms Consultant || Document Management Industries Association (DMIA)
CFE	Certified Festival Executive || International Festival and Events Association (IFEA)
CFE®	Certified Financial Examiner || Society of Financial Examiners® (SOFE®)
CFE	Certified Food Executive || International Food Service Executives Association (IFSEA)
CFE™	Certified Franchise Executive || International Franchise Association (IFA)
CFE	Certified Fraud Examiner || National Association of Certified Fraud Examiners (NACFE)
CFLE	Certified Family Life Educator || National Council on Family Relations (NCFR)
CFM	Certified Facilities Manager || International Facilities Management Association (IFMA)
CFM	Certified Food Manager || International Food Service Executives Association (IFSEA)
CFPIM™	Certified Fellow in Production and Inventory Management || American Production and Inventory Control Society (APICS™)
CFP®	Certified Financial Planner® || Certified Financial Planners Board of Standards
CFRE	Certified Fund Raising Executive || National Society of Fund Raising Executives (NSFRE)
CFS	Certified Fund Specialist || Institute of Certified Fund Specialists (ICFS)
CFSP	Certified Form Systems Professional || Business Forms Management Association (BFMA)

CFSSP™	Certified Financial Services Security Professional™		Institute for Certified Bankers™ (ICB)
CGAE	Certified Graphics Arts Executive		National Association of Printers and Lithographers (NAPL)
CGCM	Certified Graphics Communications Manager		International Publishing Management Association (IPMA)
CGM	Certified Grounds Manager		Professional Grounds Management Society (PGMS)
CGR	Certified Graduate Remodeler™		National Association of Home Builders (NAHB) Remodelers Council
CGWP	Certified Ground Water Professional		Association of Ground Water Scientists and Engineers (AGWSE)
CHAE	Certified Hospitality Accountant Executive		International Association of Hospitality Accountants (IAHA)
CHA®	Certified Hotel Administrator		Educational Institute of the American Hotel and Motel Association (EI/AH&MA)
CHC	Certified Housing Counselor		Association for Financial Counseling and Planning Education (AFCPE)
CHE	Certified Healthcare Executive		American College of Healthcare Executives (ACHE)
CHE	Certified Home Economist		American Home Economics Association (AHEA)
CHE®	Certified Hospitality Educator		Educational Institute of the American Hotel and Motel Association (EI/AH&MA)
ChFC	Chartered Financial Consultant		The American College (AC)
CHFP	Certified Human Factors Professional		Board of Certification in Professional Ergonomics (BCPE)
CHHE®	Certified Hospitality Housekeeping Executive		Educational Institute of the American Hotel and Motel Association (EI/AH&MA)
CHRE®	Certified Human Resources Executive		Educational Institute of the American Hotel and Motel Association (EI/AH&MA)
CHSE	Certified Hotel Sales Executive		Hospitality Sales and Marketing Association International (HSMAI)
CHSP®	Certified Hospitality Sales Professional		Educational Institute of the American Hotel and Motel Association (EI/AH&MA)
CHST	Certified Construction Health and Safety Technician		ABIH/BCSP Joint Committee
CHS®	Certified Hospitality Supervisor		Educational Institute of the American Hotel and Motel Association (EI/AH&MA)

CHTP®	Certified Hospitality Technology Professional		Educational Institute of the American Hotel and Motel Association (EI/AH&MA)
CIA	Certified Internal Auditor		Institute of Internal Auditors (IIA)
CIAQP	Certified Indoor Air Quality Professional		Association of Energy Engineers® (AEE)
CIC	Certified Imaging Consultant		Wang Laboratories, Inc.
CIC	Certified Insurance Counselor		Society of Certified Insurance Counselors (Society of CIC)
CIC	Certified Irrigation Contractor		The Irrigation Association (IA)
CID	Certified Irrigation Designer		The Irrigation Association (IA)
CIE	Certified Insurance Examiner		Insurance Regulatory Examiners Society (IRES)
CIF	Certified International Financiers		International Society of Financiers (ISF)
CIH	Certified Industrial Hygienist		American Board of Industrial Hygiene® (ABIH)
CIM	Certified Irrigation Manager		The Irrigation Association (IA)
CIMA	Certified Investment Management Analyst		Investment Management Consultants Association (IMCA)
CIMS	Certified Imaging Market Specialist		Wang Laboratories, Inc.
CIP	Certified Incentive Professional		The Association of Incentive Marketing (AIM)
CIPE®	Certified in Plumbing Engineering®		American Society of Plumbing Engineering (ASPE)
CIPPM®	Center for International Project and Program Management		Center for International Project and Program Management (CIPPM®)
CIPS	Certified International Property Specialist		National Association of REALTORS® (NAR)
CIRA	Certified Insolvency and Reorganization Accountant		Association of Insolvency Accountants (AIA)
CIRM™	Certified in Integrated Resource Management		American Production and Inventory Control Society (APICS™)
CIRS	Certified Insurance Rehabilitation Specialist		Certification of Insurance Rehabilitation Specialists Commission (CIRSC)
CISA®	Certified Information Systems Auditor		Information Systems Audit and Control Association (ISACA)
CISD	Certified Imaging Systems Developer		Wang Laboratories, Inc.
CISM	Certified Imaging Systems Manager		Wang Laboratories, Inc.

CISR	Certified Insurance Service Representative || Society of Certified Insurance Service Representatives (Society of CISR)
CKD	Certified Kitchen Designer || National Kitchen and Bath Association (NKBA)
CLA	Certified Legal Assistant || National Association of Legal Assistants (NALA)
CLA	Certified Leisure Associate || National Recreation and Park Association (NRPA)
CLA Specialist	Certified Legal Assistant Specialist || National Association of Legal Assistants (NALA)
CLEP	Certified Lighting Efficiency Professional || Association of Energy Engineers® (AEE)
CLES	Certified Laboratory Equipment Specialist || International Certification Commission (ICC)
CLI	Certified Legal Investigator® || National Association of Legal Investigators, Inc. (NALI)
CLIA	Certified Landscape Irrigation Auditor || The Irrigation Association (IA)
CLLM	Certified Laundry/Linen Manager || National Association of Institutional Linen Management (NAILM)
CLM	Certified Lake Manager || North American Lake Management Society (NALMS)
CLMC	Certified Lighting Management Consultant || International Association of Lighting Management Companies (NALMCO)
CLP	Certified Leisure Professional || National Recreation and Park Association (NRPA)
CLP	Certified Lotus Professional || Lotus Development Corporation
CLU	Chartered Life Underwriter || The American College (AC)
CLVS	Certified Legal Video Specialist || National Court Reporters Association (NCRA)
CM	Certified Manager || Institute of Certified Professional Managers (ICPM)
CM	Certified Midwife || ACNM Certification Council, Inc.
CMA	Certified Management Accountant || Institute of Certified Management Accountants (ICMA)
CMA	Certified Medical Assistant || American Association of Medical Assistants (AAMA)
CMB	Certified Mortgage Banker || Mortgage Bankers Association of America (MBA)
CMC	Certified Management Consultant || Institute of Management Consultants (IMC)
CMC	Certified Master Chef || American Culinary Federation Education Institute (ACFEI)
CMCE	Certified Managed Care Executive || American Managed Care and Review Association (AMCRA)
CMD	Certified Marketing Director || International Council of Shopping Centers

CMDRP	Certified Master Disaster Recovery Planner || Disaster Recovery Institute (DRI)
CMDSM	Certified Mail and Distribution Systems Manager || Mail Systems Management Association (MSMA)
CME	Certified Manager of Exhibits || International Exhibitors Association (IEA)
CME	Certified Marketing Executive || Sales and Marketing Executives International (SMEI)
CMEA	Certified Machinery and Equipment Appraiser || Association of Machinery and Equipment Appraisers, Inc. (AMEA)
CMFA	Certified Municipal Finance Administrator || Municipal Treasurers' Association of the United States and Canada (MTA US&C)
CMfgE	Certified Manufacturing Engineer || Society for Manufacturing Engineers (SME)
CMfgT	Certified Manufacturing Technologist || Society for Manufacturing Engineers (SME)
CMI	Certified Mechanical Inspector || American Society for Quality Control (ASQC)
CMM	Certified Mail Manager || International Publishing Management Association (IPMA)
C.M.M.	Certified Maintenance Manager || International Maintenance Institute (IMI)
C.M.P.	Certified Maintenance Professional || International Maintenance Institute (IMI)
CMP®	Certified Meeting Professional® || Convention Liaison Council (CLC)
CMPA	Certified Manager of Patient Accounts || Healthcare Financial Management Association (HFMA)
CMCP	Certified Managed Care Professional || Healthcare Financial Management Association (HFMA)
CMPC	Certified Master Pastry Chef || American Culinary Federation Education Institute (ACFEI)
CMRS	Certified Manager of Reporting Services || National Court Reporters Association (NCRA)
C.M.S.	Certified Maintenance Supplier || International Maintenance Institute (IMI)
CMSC	Certified Medical Staff Coordinator || National Association Medical Staff Services (NAMSS)
CMSS	Certified Manager of Suggestion Systems || Employee Involvement Association (EIA)
CMT	Chartered Market Technician || Market Technicians Association (MTA)
CMT	Certified Medical Transcriptionist || American Association for Medical Transcription (AAMT)
CNA	Certified Novell Administrator || Novell, Inc.
CNE^{SM}	Certified Novell Engineer || Novell, Inc.

CNHA	Certified Nursing Home Administrator		American College of Health Care Administrators (ACHCA)
CNI^{SM}	Certified Novell Instructor		Novell, Inc.
CNMT	Certified Nuclear Medicine Technologist		Nuclear Medicine Technology Certification Board, Inc. (NMTCB)
CNP	Certified Network Professional™		Network Professional Association (NPA)
CNX™	Certified Network Expert™		Network General Corporation
COTA	Certified Occupational Therapy Assistant		American Occupational Therapy Certification Board, Inc. (AOTB)
CP	Certified Planner		American Institute of Certified Planners (AICP)
CPA/PFS	Personal Financial Specialist		American Institute of Certified Public Accountants (AICPA)
CPAg	Certified Professional Agronomist		ARCPACS
CPBE	Professional Broadcast Engineer		Society of Broadcast Engineers, Inc. (SBE)
CPC	Certified Pastry Cook		American Culinary Federation Education Institute (ACFEI)
CPC	Certified Pension Consultant		American Society of Pension Actuaries (ASPA)
CPC	Certified Personnel Consultant		National Association of Personnel Services (NAPS)
CPC	Certified Photographic Consultant™		Photo Marketing Association International (PMA)
CPC	Certified Professional Chemist		National Certification Commission in Chemistry and Chemical Engineering
CPC	Certified Professional Consultant		The Consultants Institute (TCI)
CPCM	Certified Professional Contracts Manager		National Contract Management Association (NCMA)
CPCS	Certified Professional Crop Scientist/Specialist		ARCPACS
CPCU®	Chartered Property Casualty Underwriter		American Institute for Chartered Property Casualty Underwriters (AICPCU)
CPD	Certified PowerBuilder Developer		Powersoft
CPE	Certified Plant Engineer		Association for Facilities Engineering (AFE)
CPE	Certified Professional Ergonomist		Board of Certification in Professional Ergonomics (BCPE)
CPE	Certified Professional Estimator		American Society of Professional Estimators (ASPE)

CPE	Certified Program Evaluator || National Court Reporters Association (NCRA)
CPE	Certified Purchasing Executive || American Purchasing Society, Inc. (APS)
CPES	Certified Professional Employer Specialist || National Association of Professional Employer Organizations (NAPEO)
CPESC	Certified Professional in Soil Erosion and Sediment Control || Soil and Water Conservation Society (SWCS)
CPF	Certified Picture Framer || Professional Picture Framers Association (PPFA)
CPFB	Certified Professional Food Broker || Manufacturers' Representatives Educational Research Foundation (MRERF)
CPFM	Certified Professional Fleet Manager || National Private Truck Council (NPTC)
CPFM	Certified Parking Facility Manager || National Parking Association (NPA)
CPFT^{SM}	Certified Pulmonary Function Technologist || National Board for Respiratory Care (NBRC^{SM})
CPH	Certified Professional Horticulturalist || ARCPACS
CPHQ	Certified Professional in Healthcare Quality || Healthcare Quality Certification Board (HQCB)
CPI	Certified Pump Installer || National Ground Water Association (NGWA)
CPIM®	Certified in Production and Inventory Management || American Production and Inventory Control Society (APICS™)
CPIT	Certified Professional in Training {Packaging} || Institute of Packaging Professionals (IoPP)
CPL	Certified Professional Landman || American Association of Professional Landmen (AAPL)
C.P.L.	Certified Professional Logistician || Society of Logistics Engineers (SOLE)
CPM	Certified Professional Services Manager || Professional Services Management Association (PSMA)
C.P.M	Certified Purchasing Manager || National Association of Purchasing Managers
CPME	Certified Production Management Executive || National Association of Printers and Lithographers (NAPL)
CPMR	Certified Professional Manufacturers Representative || Manufacturers' Representatives Educational Research Foundation (MRERF)
CPN	Certified Pediatric Nurse || National Certification Board of Pediatric Nurse Practitioners and Nurses (NCBPNP/N)

CPNP	Certified Pediatric Nurse Practitioner || National Certification Board of Pediatric Nurse Practitioners and Nurses (NCBPNP/N)
CPO	Certified Park Operator || National Association of RV Parks and Campgrounds (ARVC)
CPO	Certified Protection Officer || International Foundation for Protection Officers (IFPO)
CPP	Certified Packaging Professional || Institute of Packaging Professionals (IoPP)
CPP	Certified Payroll Professional || American Payroll Association (APA)
CPP	Certified Professional Photographer || Professional Photographers of America (PPA)
CPP	Certified Protection Professional || American Society for Industrial Security (ASIS)
CPP	Certified Purchasing Professional || American Purchasing Society, Inc. (APS)
CPPA	Certified Professional Property Administrator || National Property Manager Association, Inc. (NPMA)
CPPB	Certified Professional Public Buyer || Universal Public Purchasing Certification Council
CPPM	Certified Professional Property Manager || National Property Manager Association, Inc. (NPMA)
CPPO	Certified Public Purchasing Officer || Universal Public Purchasing Certification Council
CPPP	Certified Professional Plant Pathologist || ARCPACS
CPPS	Certified Professional Property Specialist || National Property Manager Association, Inc. (NPMA)
CPRW	Certified Professional Résumé Writer || Professional Association of Résumé Writers (PARW)
CPSC	Certified Professional Soil Classifier || ARCPACS
CPSS	Certified Professional Soil Scientist/Specialist || ARCPACS
CPS®	Certified Professional Secretary® || Professional Secretaries International®
CPWS	Certified Professional in Weed Science || ARCPACS
CQA	Certified Quality Auditor || American Society for Quality Control (ASQC)
CQE	Certified Quality Engineer || American Society for Quality Control (ASQC)
CQM	Certified Quality Manager || American Society for Quality Control (ASQC)
CQT	Certified Quality Technician || American Society for Quality Control (ASQC)
CR	Certified Remodeler || National Association of the Remodeling Industry (NARI)
CR	Certified Restorer || Association of Specialists in Cleaning and Restoration (ASCR)

CRA	Certified Remodeler Associate || National Association of the Remodeling Industry (NARI)
CRA	Certified Review Appraiser || National Association of Review Appraisers & Mortgage Underwriters (NARA/MU)
CRB	Certified Real Estate Brokerage Manager || Real Estate Brokerage Managers
CRC	Certified Rehabilitation Counselor || Commission on Rehabilitation Counselor Certification (CRCC)
CRCM™	Certified Regulatory Compliance Manager™ || Institute for Certified Bankers™ (ICB)
CRCST	Certified Registered Central Service Technician || International Association of Healthcare Central Service Material Management (IAHCSMM)
CRDE®	Certified Rooms Division Executive || Educational Institute of the American Hotel and Motel Association (EI/AH&MA)
CRE	Certified Reliability Engineer || American Society for Quality Control (ASQC)
CREA	Certified Real Estate Appraiser || National Association of Real Estate Appraisers (NAREA)
CREC	Certified Rural Electric Communicator || Council of Rural Electric Communicators (CREC)
CRES	Certified Radiology Equipment Specialist || International Certification Commission (ICC)
CRI	Certified Reporting Instructor || National Court Reporters Association (NCRA)
CRM	Certified Records Manager || Institute of Certified Records Managers (ICRM)
CRNI	Certified Registered Nurse Intravenous || Intravenous Nurses Certification Corporation (INCC)
CRP™	Certified Relocation Professional || Employee Relocation Council (E-R-C)
CRR	Certified Realtime Reporter || National Court Reporters Association (NCRA)
CRS®	Certified Residential Specialist || Residential Sales Council (RS)
CRTT℠	Certified Respiratory Therapy Technician || National Board for Respiratory Care (NBRC℠)
CSA	Certified Solaris Administrator || Sun Microsystems, Inc.
CSAT	Certified Specialist in Analytical Technology || Instrument Society of America (ISA)
CSE	Certified Sales Executive || Sales and Marketing Executives International (SMEI)
CSE	Certified Service Executive || National Association of Service Managers (NASM)
CSI	Certified Satellite Installer || Electronics Technicians Association, International (ETA)

CSM	Certified Software Manager || Software Publishers Association (SPA)
CSM	Certified Shopping Center Manager || International Council of Shopping Centers (ICSC)
CSME	Certified Sales and Marketing Executive || National Association of Printers and Lithographers (NAPL)
CSP	Certified Speaking Professional || National Speakers Association (NSA)
C.S.P.	Certified Supplier Professional || International Maintenance Institute (IMI)
CSPDM	Certified Sterile Processing and Distribution Manager || National Institute for the Certification of Healthcare Sterile Processing and Distribution Personnel (NICHSPDP)
CSPDS	Certified Sterile Processing and Distribution Supervisor || National Institute for the Certification of Healthcare Sterile Processing and Distribution Personnel (NICHSPDP)
CSPDT	Certified Sterile Processing and Distribution Technician || National Institute for the Certification of Healthcare Sterile Processing and Distribution Personnel (NICHSPDP)
CSP®	Certified Safety Professional® || Board of Certified Safety Professionals (BCSP)
CSRE	Senior Broadcast Engineer Radio || Society of Broadcast Engineers, Inc. (SBE)
CSS	Certified Security Supervisor || International Foundation for Protection Officers (IFPO)
CSS	Certified Customer Service Specialist || Electronics Technicians Association, International (ETA)
C.S.T.	Certified Security Trainer || Academy of Security Educators and Trainers (ASET)
CST/CFA	CST Certified First Assistant || Liaison Council on Certification for the Surgical Technologist (LCC-ST)
CST	Certified Survey Technician || National Society of Professional Surveyors (NSPS)
CST	Certified Surgical Technologist || Liaison Council on Certification for the Surgical Technologist (LCC-ST)
CSTE	Senior Broadcast Engineer TV || Society of Broadcast Engineers, Inc. (SBE)
CT	Certified Engineering Technologist || National Institute for Certification in Engineering Technologies (NICET)
CTC	Certified Travel Counselor || Institute of Certified Travel Agents (ICTA)
CTFA™	Certified Trust and Financial Advisor™ || Institute for Certified Bankers™ (ICB)
CTL	Certified in Transportation and Logistics || American Society of Transportation and Logistics, Inc. (AST&L)
C.T.M.	Certified Maintenance Technician || International Maintenance Institute (IMI)
CTP	Certified Turfgrass Professional || Professional Lawn Care Association of America (PLCAA)

CTP	Certified Tax Preparer || Institute of Tax Consultants (ITC)
CTPM	Certified Tax Preparer Master || Institute of Tax Consultants (ITC)
CTPS	Certified Tax Preparer Specialist || Institute of Tax Consultants (ITC)
CTRS®	Certified Therapeutic Recreation Specialist® || National Council for Therapeutic Recreation Certification (NCTRC)
CTS	Certified Temporary-Staffing Specialist || National Association of Personnel Services (NAPS)
CTS	Certified Technology Specialist || International Communications Industries Association (ICIA)
CTT	Certified Technical Trainer || Educational Testing Service (ETS)
CVA	Certified in Volunteer Administration || Association for Volunteer Administration (AVA)
CVS	Certified Value Specialist || Society of American Value Engineers (SAVE)
CWC	Certified Working Chef || American Culinary Federation Education Institute (ACFEI)
CWD	Certified Well Driller || National Ground Water Association (NGWA)
CWE	Certified Welding Educator || American Welding Society (AWS)
CWI	Certified Welding Inspector || American Welding Society (AWS)
CWPC	Certified Working Pastry Chef || American Culinary Federation Education Institute (ACFEI)
DBA	Certified Oracle7 Database Administrator || The Chauncey Group
DEE	Diplomate Environmental Engineer || American Academy of Environmental Engineers
DREI	Distinguished Real Estate Instructor || Real Estate Educators Association (REEA)
EA	Enrolled Agent || Internal Revenue Service
ECNE^{SM}	Enterprise Certified Novell Engineer || Novell, Inc.
EDPP	Electronic Document and Printing Professional || Xplor International
ESC	Electronics Specialist, Certified || American Electroplaters and Surface Finishers Society (AESF)
ESS	Employment Services Specialist || International Association of Personnel in Employment Security (IAPES)
ETG	Employment and Training Generalist || International Association of Personnel in Employment Security (IAPES)
ETM	Employment and Training Master || International Association of Personnel in Employment Security (IAPES)

FACHE	Fellow of the American College of Healthcare Executives || American College of Healthcare Executives (ACHE)
FHFMA	Fellow {Healthcare} || Healthcare Financial Management Association (HFMA)
FLA	Forestland Appraiser || Association of Consulting Foresters of America, Inc. (ACF)
FLMI/M®	Master Fellow, Life Management Institute || Life Office Management Association (LOMA)
FLMI®	Fellow, Life Management Institute || Life Office Management Association (LOMA)
FMA	Facilities Management Administrator || Building Owners and Managers Association (BOMA) International
FMP	Fellow Marketing Professional || Society for Marketing Professional Services (SMPS)
FMP	Foodservice Management Professional || Educational Foundation of the National Restaurant Association
FSPA	Fellow, Society of Pension Actuaries || American Society of Pension Actuaries (ASPA)
GAA	General Accredited Appraiser || National Association of REALTORS® (NAR)
GCS	Geriatrics Certified Specialist || American Physical Therapy Association
GRI	Graduate, REALTOR® Institute || National Association of REALTORS® (NAR)
HIA	Health Insurance Associate || Health Insurance Association of America (HIAA)
ICBT®	Internationally Certified Bodywork Therapist || Associated Bodywork & Massage Professionals (ABMT)
ICMT®	Internationally Certified Massage Therapist || Associated Bodywork & Massage Professionals (ABMT)
ICST®	Internationally Certified Somatic Therapist || Associated Bodywork & Massage Professionals (ABMT)
IHIT	Industrial Hygienist in Training || American Board of Industrial Hygiene® (ABIH)
I²CE	Internet/Intranet Certified Engineer || Ascolta
JTS	Job Training Specialist || International Association of Personnel in Employment Security (IAPES)
LCSE	Lifetime Certified Service Executive || National Association of Service Managers (NASM)
LLIF	LIMRA® Leadership Institute Fellow || LIMRA® International
LMIS	Labor Market Information Specialist || International Association of Personnel in Employment Security (IAPES)
LTG	Leadership Training Graduate || Women's Council of REALTORS® (WCR)

LUTCF	Life Underwriter Training Council Fellow || Life Underwriter Training Council (LUTC)
MAI	General Appraiser, Appraisal Institute || Appraisal Institute (AI)
Master CNE^{SM}	Master Certified Novell Engineer || Novell, Inc.
MCM	Master Club Manager || Club Managers Association of America
MCR	Master of Corporate Real Estate || International Association of Corporate Real Estate Executives (NACORE)
MGWC	Master Ground Water Contractor || National Ground Water Association (NGWA)
MHP	Managed Healthcare Professional || Health Insurance Association of America (HIAA)
MHS®	Master Hotel Supplier || Educational Institute of the American Hotel and Motel Association (EI/AH&MA)
MLT® (AMT)	Medical Laboratory Technician || American Medical Technologists (AMT)
MP	Marketing Professional || Society for Marketing Professional Services (SMPS)
MPP	Military Packaging Professional || School of Military Packaging Technology (SMPT)
MSPA	Member, Society of Pension Actuaries || American Society of Pension Actuaries (ASPA)
MT®(AMT)	Medical Technologist || American Medical Technologists (AMT)
NCC	Nationally Certified Counselor || National Board for Certified Counselors (NBCC®)
NCE	NARTE Certified Engineer || National Association of Radio and Telecommunications Engineers (NARTE)
NCIDQ Certified	Certified Interior Designer || National Council for Interior Design Qualification (NCIDQ)
NCPT	Nationally Certified Pharmacy Technician || Pharmacy Technician Certification Board (PTCB)
NCPT	Nationally Certified Psychiatric Technician || American Association of Psychiatric Technicians, Inc. (AAPT)
NCS	Neurologic Certified Specialist || American Physical Therapy Association
NCT	NARTE Certified Technician || National Association of Radio and Telecommunications Engineers (NARTE)
OCS	Orthopaedics Certified Specialist || American Physical Therapy Association
OHST	Certified Occupational Health and Safety Technologist || ABIH/BCSP Joint Committee
ONC	Orthopaedic Nurse Certified || Orthopaedic Nursing Certification Board (ONCB)
OTR	Occupational Therapist, Registered || American Occupational Therapy Certification Board, Inc. (AOTB)

PA-C	Physician Assistant-Certified || National Commission on Certification of Physician Assistants (NCCPA)
PCAM®	Professional Community Association Manager || Community Associations Institute (CAI)
PCMH	Professional Certified in Materials Handling || Materials Handling and Management Society (MHMS)
PCMM	Professional Certified in Materials Management || Materials Handling and Management Society (MHMS)
PCS	Pediatric Certified Specialist || American Physical Therapy Association
PDS	Program Director Specialist || Cooper Institute for Aerobics Research
PHM	Certified Public Housing Manager || National Association of Housing and Redevelopment Officials (NAHRO)
PHR	Professional in Human Resources || Human Resource Certification Institute (HRCI)
PLS	Certified Professional Legal Secretary || National Association of Legal Secretaries® (NALS)
PMP	Project Management Professional || Project Management Institute(PMI)
POLT	Physician Office Laboratory Technician || International Society for Clinical Laboratory Technology (ISCLT)
PPS	Personal Protection Specialist || Executive Protection Institute
QEP	Qualified Environmental Professional || Institute of Professional Environmental Practice (IPEP)
QPA	Qualified Pension Administrator || American Society of Pension Actuaries (ASPA)
RAA	Residential Accredited Appraiser || National Association of REALTORS® (NAR)
RBP	Registered Biological Photographer || Biological Photographic Association (BPA)
RBSM	Registered Building Service Manager || Building Service Contractors Association International (BSCAI)
RCE	REALTOR® Association Certified Executive || National Association of REALTORS®
RCST	Registered Central Service Technician || International Association of Healthcare Central Service Material Management (IAHCSMM)
RD	Registered Dietitian || Commission on Dietetic Registration (CDR)
RDA (AMT)	Registered Dental Assistant || American Medical Technologists (AMT)
RDCS	Registered Diagnostic Cardiac Sonographer || American Registry of Diagnostic Medical Sonographers® (ARDMS®)

RDMS	Registered Diagnostic Medical Sonographer || American Registry of Diagnostic Medical Sonographers® (ARDMS®)
RDR	Registered Diplomate Reporter || National Court Reporters Association (NCRA)
RDT	Registered Dietetic Technician || Commission on Dietetic Registration (CDR)
REBC	Registered Employee Benefits Consultant || National Association of Health Underwriters (NAHU)
RECT	Registered Environmental Laboratory Technologist || National Registry of Environmental Professionals℠ (NREP℠)
R. EEG T. ®	Registered Electroencephalographic Technologist || American Board of Registration of Electroencephalographic and Evoked Potential Technologists (ABRET)
R.E.H.	Registered Executive Housekeeper || National Executive Housekeepers Association (N.E.H.A.)
REHS	Registered Environmental Health Specialist || National Environmental Health Association (NEHA)
REM	Registered Environmental Manager || National Registry of Environmental Professionals℠ (NREP℠)
REP	Registered Environmental Professional || National Registry of Environmental Professionals℠ (NREP℠)
REPA	Registered Environmental Property Assessor || National Registry of Environmental Professionals℠ (NREP℠)
R. EP T.	Registered Evoked Potential Technologist || American Board of Registration of Electroencephalographic and Evoked Potential Technologists (ABRET)
RES	Registered Environmental Scientist || National Registry of Environmental Professionals℠ (NREP℠)
RFC	Registered Financial Planner || International Association of Registered Financial Planners (IARFC)
RHP	Retirement Housing Professional || American Association of Homes and Services for the Aging (AAHSA)
RHP Fellow	Retirement Housing Professional Fellow || American Association of Homes and Services for the Aging (AAHSA)
RHSP	Registered Hazardous Substance Professional || National Environmental Health Association (NEHA)
RHSS	Registered Hazardous Substance Specialist || National Environmental Health Association (NEHA)
RHU	Registered Health Underwriter || National Association of Health Underwriters (NAHU)
RIA	Registered Investment Adviser || Securities and Exchange Commission (SEC)

R.L.L.D.   Registered Laundry/Linen Director || National Association of Institutional Linen Management (NAILM)

RLT   Registered Laboratory Technician || International Society for Clinical Laboratory Technology (ISCLT)

RM (ASM)   Registered Microbiologist || American Society for Microbiology (ASM)

RMA (AMT)   Registered Medical Assistant || American Medical Technologists (AMT)

RMP   Registered Meeting Planner || International Society of Meeting Planners (IMPI)

RMR   Registered Merit Reporter || National Court Reporters Association (NCRA)

RMT   Registered Medical Technologist || International Society for Clinical Laboratory Technology (ISCLT)

RMU   Registered Mortgage Underwriter || National Association of Review Appraisers and Mortgage Underwriters (NARA/MU)

RNC   Registered Nurse Certified || National Certification Corporation for the Obstetric, Gynecological, and Neonatal Nursing Specialties (NCC)

RN,C   Registered Nurse, Certified || American Nurses Credentialing Center (ANCC)

RN,CNA   Registered Nurse, Certified in Nursing Administration || American Nurses Credentialing Center (ANCC)

RN,CNAA   Registered Nurse, Certified in Nursing Administration, Advanced || American Nurses Credentialing Center (ANCC)

RN,CS   Registered Nurse, Certified Specialist || American Nurses Credentialing Center (ANCC)

RODC   Registered Organization Development Consultant || The Organization Development Institute

RODP   Registered Organization Development Professional || The Organization Development Institute

RPFT^{SM} Registered Pulmonary Function Technologist || National Board for Respiratory Care (NBRC^{SM})

RPM   Registered Professional Member || National Association of Real Estate Appraisers (NAREA)

RPR   Registered Professional Reporter || National Court Reporters Association (NCRA)

RPRA   Real Property Review Appraiser || American Society of Farm Managers and Rural Appraisers (ASFMRA)

RPT (AMT)   Registered Phlebotomy Technician || American Medical Technologists (AMT)

RRT^{SM} Registered Respiratory Therapist || National Board for Respiratory Care (NBRC^{SM})

RS   Registered Sanitarian || National Environmental Health Association (NEHA)

R.T.(ARRT)　　　Registered Technologist || American Registry of Radiologic Technologists (ARRT®)

RVT®　　　Registered Vascular Technologist® || American Registry of Diagnostic Medical Sonographers® (ARDMS®)

SCRP™　　　Senior Certified Relocation Professional || Employee Relocation Council (E-R-C)

SCS　　　Sports Certified Specialist || American Physical Therapy Association

SMA　　　Systems Maintenance Administrator || Building Owners and Managers Association (BOMA) International

SM (ASM)　　　Specialist Microbiologist || American Society for Microbiology (ASM)

SMP　　　Senior Marketing Professional || Society for Marketing Professional Services (SMPS)

SMT　　　Systems Maintenance Technician || Building Owners and Managers Association (BOMA) International

SPHR　　　Senior Professional in Human Resources || Human Resource Certification Institute (HRCI)

SRA　　　Residential Appraisal, Appraisal Institute || Appraisal Institute (AI)

UST　　　Certified in Underground Storage Tank Installation/Decommissioning || International Fire Code Institute (IFCI)

VMP　　　Value Methodology Practitioner || Society of American Value Engineers (SAVE)

WSO-CHME　　　Certified Hazardous Materials Executive || World Safety Organization (WSO)

WSO-CHMS　　　Certified Hazardous Materials Supervisor || World Safety Organization (WSO)

WSO-CHMT I/II　　　Certified Hazardous Materials Technician || World Safety Organization (WSO)

WSO-CSE　　　Certified Safety Executive || World Safety Organization (WSO)

WSO-CSM　　　Certified Safety Manager || World Safety Organization (WSO)

WSO-CSS　　　Certified Safety Specialist || World Safety Organization (WSO)

WSO-CSSD　　　Certified Safety and Security Director || World Safety Organization (WSO)

WSO-CST　　　Certified Safety Technician || World Safety Organization (WSO)

APPENDIX B:
Keyword Index

Accountancy 33
Activity 253
Administration 103
Adobe 197
Adviser 103
Agent 121
Agronomist 211
Analytical Technology 179
Anesthesiologist Assistant 267
Apartment 149
Apartment Maintenance 291
Apartment Property Supervisor 149
Apple 197
Architectural Administrator 79
Archivist 19
ASE 291
Assistive Technology 267
Association 79
Association Certified Executive 155
Association Management 150
Auctioneer Real Estate 155
Auctioneer's Institute (CAI®) 19
Auto Glass 292
Automated Examination 197
Automation Management 198
Automotive Fleet 80
Bank Auditor 43
Bank Compliance 43
Bathroom 292
Benefit 53, 54
Biological Photographer 179
Biomedical Equipment 268
Bodywork Therapist 258
Broadband 229
Broadband Communications 180
Broadcast 180
Building Service 139
Building Service Manager 139
Business 131
Cardiac Sonographer 268
Case Manager 241
Cash Manager 33
Catering 163
Central Service 269
Chartered Accountant 34
Chemical Engineer 181
Chemist 181
Child Development 20

Cisco 198
Claims 104–106
Club Manager 163
Cogeneration 181
Collection 225
Collection Sales 44
Collection Agency 44
Collector 45
Commercial Real Estate 131
Communicator 93, 94
Community Association 150
Compaq 199
Compensation Professional 54
Computer Applications 200
Computing 199
Concrete 293
Confidentiality 99
Construction Health and Safety 229
Consumer Credit 45
Contracts Manager 69
Control Systems 230
Corporate Real Estate 156
Corporate Travel 164
Corporate Trust 46
Corrosion 182
Cost Consultant 183
Cost Engineer 183
Counselor 254
Counselor, Real Estate 156
Court Reporters 65
Credit 47
Credit Bureau 47
Credit Executive 47
Credit Union 48
Crop Advisor 211
Crop Scientist 211
Culinary 165
Customer Service 20
Customer Service, Insurance 106, 107
Demand-Side Management 140
Dental Assistant 270
Dental Technician 270
Destination 176
Destination Management 165
Dietary Manager 241
Dietetic Technician 254
Dietitian 254
Disability Analyst 255
Disability Specialist 255
Disaster Recovery 21
Downtown Management 150
Drafter 294
Ecologist 212

Economic Developer 21
Electroencephalographic Technologist 271
Electron Microscopy 230
Electronic Document 200
Electronic Imager 22
Electronics 231
Electronics Technician 231
Electroplater-Finisher 231
Emergency 80
Employee Assistance 55
Employment and Training Master (ETM) 56
Energy 81
Engineer 183
Engineering Operations 166
Engineering Technician 232
Engineering Technologist 184
Entomologist 184
Environmental Engineer 212
Environmental Health 213, 214
Environmental Inspector 215
Environmental Manager 215
Environmental Professional 216–218
Environmental Property Assessor 157
Environmental Scientist 219
Environmental Trainer 220
Ergonomist 185
Estimator 23
Estimator/Analyst 23
Event 176
Evoked Potential 272
Exercise Leader 272
Exercise Specialist 273
Exercise Test Technologist 273
Exhibits 94
Facilities Manager 141
Facilities Management 140
Family Life 256
Farm 151
Festival 166
Fidelity and Surety 108
Financial 121, 122
Financial Analyst 122
Financial Consultant 123
Financial Counseling 49
Financial Counselor 124
Financial Examiner 49, 50
Financial Planner 124, 125
Financial Services Security 50
Financier 34
First Assistant 286
Fleet Manager 70
Fluid Power 186
Food and Beverage 167
Food Broker 26

Food Executive 168
Food Manager 168
Foodservice 168
Form Systems 24
Forms Consultant 24
Franchise 82
Fraud Examiner 35
Fund Raising 82
Fund Specialist 125
General 131
General Accredited Appraiser (GAA) 132
Glazier 294
Graduate, REALTOR 158
Graphics Arts 83
Graphics Communications 83
Ground Water 302
Hazardous Materials 221
Hazardous Substance 222, 223
Health Insurance 108
Health Underwriter 109
Health/Fitness Director 243
Health/Fitness Instructor 274
Healthcare 242
Healthcare Executives 242
Healthcare Fellow 168
Healthcare Quality 243
Hearing Instrument Sciences 274
Home Economist 25
Horticulturalist 211
Hospitality Accountant Executive 35
Hospitality Educator 169
Hospitality Housekeeping 169
Hospitality Sales 170
Hospitality Skills 171
Hospitality Supervisor 171
Hospitality Technology 172
Hotel Administrator 173
Hotel Sales 173
Hotel Supplier 174
Housekeeper 142
Housing Counselor 126
Human Factors 185
Human Resources 56, 57
Hydrogeologist 223
Hydrographer 186
Hydrologist 223
IBM 201
Imaging 201, 202
Indoor Air Quality 142
Industrial and Office 159
Industrial Hygienist 224
Information Systems Auditor 203
Insolvency and Reorganization Accountant 36
Inspector 143
Insurance Accounting 36
Insurance Counselor 109

Insurance Examiner 110
Insurance Rehabilitation 111
Insurance Service 112
Insurance Services 112
Integrated Resource Management 84
Interior Designer 25
Internal Auditor 37
International Property 158
Internet/Intranet 203
Intravenous 256
Investment Adviser 126
Investment Management 38
Irrigation 224
Kitchen 295
Laboratory Equipment 275
Laboratory Technician 275
Landfill 225
Landscape Irrigation 224
Laundry/Linen 84, 85
Leadership, Insurance 113
Leadership, Real Estate 160
Leadership Training Graduate 160
Learning Tree 204
Legal Assistant 66
Legal Assistant Specialist 66
Legal Investigator 66
Legal Secretary 67
Leisure 174
Life Management 113
Life Underwriter 114
Lighting Efficiency 187
Lighting Management 187
Logistician 71
Loss Control Management 115
Lotus 204
Machinery and Equipment 132
Mail and Distribution Systems 85
Mail Manager 86
Managed Care 244, 245
Managed Healthcare 116
Management 116
Management Accountant 39
Management Consultant 86
Manager 87
Manufacturers Representative 26
Manufacturing 188
Mapping Scientist 188
Marine Insurance 117
Market Technician 127
Marketing 95, 96
Massage 257
Massage Therapist 258
Materials Handling 71
Materials Management 71

Mechanical Inspector 234
Medical Assistant 258, 276
Medical Laboratory 276
Medical Laboratory Immunology 245
Medical Microbiology 246
Medical Sonographer 277
Medical Staff Coordinator 246
Medical Technologist 278
Meeting 175, 176
Meteorologist 189
Microbiologist 190
Microsoft 205
Midwife 260
Military Packaging Professional (MPP) 72
Mortgage Banker 51
Mortgage Underwriter 133
Municipal Finance 39
Municipal Solid Waste 225
NABER 235
NARTE 190
Netscape 205
Network 205, 206
Novell 206
Nuclear Medicine 279
Nurse, Certified 259
Nurse-Midwife 260
Nursing Administration 247
Nursing Home 247
Occupational Health and Safety 235
Occupational Hearing 279
Occupational Therapist 260
Occupational Therapy 280
Office Laboratory 280
Opticianry 261
Oracle7 207
Organization Development 58
Orthopaedic 262
Outplacement 58
Packaging 73
Park Operator 176
Parking Facility 144
Patient Accounts 248
Payroll 59
Pediatric Nurse 262
Pedorthics 280
Pension 59
Pension Actuaries 40
Pension Actuary 41
Pension Administrator 41
Personal Property 133
Personnel 60
Pharmacist 263
Pharmacy Technician 281

Phlebotomy 282
Photogrammetrist 191
Photographer 27
Photographic Consultant 295
Physical Therapist Specialist 264
Physician Assistant 264
Picture Framer 296
Planner 27
Plans Examiner 144
Plant Engineer 145
Plant Pathologist 211
Plumbing Engineering 191
PowerBuilder 207
Premium Auditing 42
Production and Inventory Management 73
Professional 134
Professional Consultant 87
Professional Employer 60
Professional Services 88
Program Director 248
Project and Program Management 89
Project Management 88
Property 151
Property Administrator 145
Property Casualty Underwriter 118
Protection 99–101
Psychiatric Technician 282
Public Accountant 42
Public Buyer 75
Public Housing 152
Public Parking 89
Public Purchasing 76
Public Relations 96
Pulmonary Function 283
Pump Installer 302
Purchasing 74, 76, 77
Quality Auditor 28
Quality Engineer 192
Quality Manager 61
Quality Technician 236
Radiology Equipment 284
Real Estate 134
Real Estate Brokerage 160
Real Estate Instructor 161
Real Property 135
Records 90
Recycling 225
Registered Environmental Laboratory Technologist (RELT) 233
Regulatory Affairs 249
Regulatory Compliance 51
Rehabilitation Counselor 265
Reinsurance 118
Reliability Engineer 192

Relocation 61
Remodeler 296, 297
Research and Planning 119
Residential 136
Residential Appraisal 132
Residential Property Manager 152
Residential Underwrite 52
Respiratory Therapist 285
Respiratory Therapy 284
Restoration 298
Restorer 299
Résumé Writer 62
Retirement Housing 249
Review 136
Risk Management 120
Rooms Division 176
Rural 136
Safety 193, 194
Safety Trained Supervisor 236
Sales 97
Sanitarian 214
Satellite Installer 237
Secretary 28
Security 101, 102
Service Executive 91
Service Technician 208
Shopping Center 91
Software Manager 209
Soil Classifier 211
Soil Erosion 226
Soil Scientist 211
Solaris 209
Solomon 209
Somatic Therapist 258
Speaking 29
Specialist 263
Steril Processing and Distribution 250, 251, 286
Suggestion Systems 62
Surgical Technologist 286
Survey Technician 237
Sybase 210
Systems Maintenance 146
Tax Advisor 127
Tax Preparer 128
TechCert 299
Technical Trainer 63
Technologist 287
Technology Specialist 238
Temporary-Staffing 63
Therapeutic Recreation 288
Transcriptionist 289
Transfer Station 225
Translator 30

Transportation and Logistics 78
Travel Counselor 177
Turfgrass 300
Underground Storage Tank 300
Underwriting 120
Uniform Fire Code 147
Value 30
Value Methodology 30
Vascular Technologist 289
Vocational 64
Water Treatment 238
Weed Science 211
Welder 301
Welding 195
Welding Educator 301
Welding Inspector 195
Well Driller 302